The Artillery At Anzac

Adaptation, Innovation And Education

Chris Roberts
Paul Stevens

16pt

Copyright Page from the Original Book

Copyright © Chris Roberts & Paul Stevens

First published 2021

This book is copyright. Apart from any fair dealing for the purposes of private study, research, criticism or review as permitted under the Copyright Act, no part may be reproduced, stored in a retrieval system or transmitted in any form or by any means, electronic, mechanical, photocopying, recording or otherwise, without written permission.

All inquiries should be made to the publishers.

Big Sky Publishing Pty Ltd

PO Box 303, Newport, NSW 2106, Australia

Phone: 1300 364 611

Fax: (61 2) 9918 2396

Email: info@bigskypublishing.com.au

Web: www.bigskypublishing.com.au

Cover design and typesetting: Think Productions

Printed in China

A catalogue record for this book is available from the National Library of Australia

Cover image caption: Observers scan the enemy line for targets on 30 April 1915 from a gun of the 7th AFA Battery, 3rd AFA Brigade, deployed close to the front line on Bolton's Ridge (AWM J06134).

TABLE OF CONTENTS

FOREWORD	vi
ACKNOWLEDGEMENTS	x
ABBREVIATIONS	xiv
INTRODUCTION	xvi
Chapter One: THE PRE-WAR ANTIPODEAN ARTILLERY AND ITS DOCTRINE	1
Chapter Two: TO WAR	30
Chapter Three: INTO ACTION	78
Chapter Four: ADAPTATION	106
Chapter Five: HOLDING THE LINE	164
Chapter Six: THE AUGUST OFFENSIVE: PREPARATIONS, LONE PINE AND THE NEK	192
Chapter Seven: THE AUGUST OFFENSIVE: THE ATTACKS ON SARI BAIR	254
Chapter Eight: HILL 60	343
Chapter Nine: EXPANSION AND CONSOLIDATION	370
Chapter Ten: EVACUATION	415
CONCLUSION AND LESSONS	437
APPENDIX 1: GUNS AND HOWITZERS USED AT ANZAC	454
APPENDIX 2: BREECH-LOADING AND QUICK-FIRING ARTILLERY	467
APPENDIX 3: BRITISH ARTILLERY AMMUNITION	470
APPENDIX 4: BRITISH ARTILLERY AT ANZAC	473
APPENDIX 5: THE ROYAL NAVY AT ANZAC	478
APPENDIX 6: ARTILLERY COMMANDERS' SERVICE AFTER ANZAC	501
APPENDIX 7: ARTILLERY ORDERS OF BATTLE	508
TABLE 1: LANDING OF GUNS AT ANZAC	517

TABLE 2: ALLOCATION OF GUNS IN IMMEDIATE AND ADDITIONAL SUPPORT OF THE 1ST AND 2ND AUSTRALIAN DIVISIONS, NOVEMBER 1915	521
TABLE 3: ALLOCATION OF GUNS IN IMMEDIATE AND ADDITIONAL SUPPORT OF THE NZ&A AND 54TH (EAST ANGLIAN) DIVISIONS, NOVEMBER 1915	522
TABLE 4: GUNS AVAILABLE FOR IMMEDIATE SUPPORT AT NIGHT IN EVENT OF ATTACK BY ENEMY, 1ST AND 2ND AUSTRALIAN DIVISIONS' SECTORS	525
TABLE 5: EVACUATION OF GUNS FROM 1ST AND 2ND AUSTRALIAN DIVISIONS' SECTORS	526
TABLE 6: EVACUATION OF GUNS FROM NZ&A DIVISION'S SECTOR	528
GLOSSARY OF TERMS	529
BIBLIOGRAPHY	533
ENDNOTES	558
BACK COVER MATERIAL	671
Index	673

List of Maps

1. General Hamilton's plan
2. The Sari Bair Range
3. Anzac: Hill 971 to Anzac Cove
4. The 1st Australian Division objectives, 25 April 1915
5. The Ottoman defensive dispositions in the Sari Bair-Gaba Tepe area, 24 April 1915
6. The situation at Anzac on the evening of 25 April 1915
7. Plan for the attack on Baby 700, 2 May 1915
8. Fire plan for the attack on Baby 700, 2 May 1915
9. Battery positions and defensive sections, 25 May 1915
10. Roads constructed within Anzac
11. Fire plan for the capture of Turkish Despair, 31 July 1915
12. Battery positions at the end of July 1915
13. Plan for the breakout and capture of the Sari Bair Range, night 6/7 August 1915
14. Corps fire plan for the August Offensive
15. Australian attacks at Lone Pine, German Officers' Trench, Quinn's Post, Pope's Hill and the Nek, 6/7 August 1915
16. Fire plan for the attack at Lone Pine

17.	Situation north of Anzac, early morning 7 August 1915
18.	Plan for the Light Horse attacks at Quinn's Post, Pope's Hill, and the Nek, 7 August 1915
19.	Preparatory fire plan for the Light Horse attacks, night 6/7 August 1915
20.	Supporting fire plan for the Light Horse attacks, 7 August 1915
21.	The terrain north of Anzac
22.	Fire plan and New Zealand attack on Chunuk Bair, 7 August 1915
23.	Fire plan and attacks on Sari Bair, 8 August 1915
24.	Fire plan and attacks on Hill Q and Chunuk Bair, 9 August 1915
25.	Enlarged Anzac area and defensive sections
26.	Plan for the attack at Hill 60, 21 August 1915
27.	Fire plan for the attack at Hill 60, 21 August 1915
28.	Fire plan for the attack at Hill 60, 27 August 1915
29.	Actual fire support provided for the attack at Hill 60, 27 August 1915
30.	NZ&A Divisional Artillery battery positions, September 1915

31.	Sketch map of Australian battery positions and arcs of fire, late August 1915
32.	1st Australian Divisional Artillery battery positions, September 1915
33.	Fire support for a putative attack at Hill 60 by the 54th (East Anglian) Division on 7 November

List of Organisation Charts

Organisation Chart 1: The 1st Australian Divisional Artillery, 1914

Organisation Chart 2: The New Zealand Field Artillery Brigade, March 1915

Organisation Chart 3: The 7th Indian Mountain Artillery Brigade

Organisation Chart 4: The 1st Australian Divisional Artillery, April to August 1915

Organisation Chart 5: NZ&A Divisional Artillery, prior to the August Offensive

Organisation Chart 6: British Divisional Artillery supporting ANZAC, 1 August 1915

Organisation Chart 7: British GHQ Artillery units supporting Anzac, October-November 1915

Organisation Chart 8: NZ&A Divisional Artillery, October-December 1915

Organisation Chart 9: The 1st Australian Divisional Artillery, October-December 1915

List of Diagrams

1. 8th AFA Battery gun emplacements at the Pimple, May 1915
2. Sketch map showing the guns ashore by 8 May 1915 and their locations
3. 9th AFA Battery gun positions and telephone system, June 1915
4. Artillery Communications Diagram, 26 April to 6 May 1915
5. Artillery Communications Diagram, 16 May to 3 June 1915
6. A gun pit with embrasure and the relative positions of the 4th AFA Battery's guns
7. Gun emplacement for No 2 Gun, 9th AFA Battery
8. Gun emplacement for No 4 Gun, 9th AFA Battery
9. Field of view, 9th AFA Battery observation station
10. Panoramic sketch from the war diary of the 4th AFA Battery observation post
11. Example registration card, 4th AFA Battery
12. Example ranging board, 9th AFA Battery
13. Hostile batteries, June, 1st Divisional Artillery War Diary
14. Artillery communications, 27 August 1915

FOREWORD

By Major General Steve Gower AO

This is a very valuable book, and the authors should be warmly congratulated for their detailed work and informed analysis.

There is no military campaign that resonates so much in Australia and New Zealand as the Gallipoli campaign. The acronym ANZAC, derived from the name of their combined corps, has come to represent a deep and tangible bond between the two nations, and has become a byword for courage, resilience and stoic endurance.

It may have taken a hundred years, but this book represents an important account of a hitherto neglected aspect of the campaign: fire support. Additional to that provided by the Australian and New Zealand artilleries, there were Royal Artillery general support units, along with Indian mountain artillery and ships of the Royal Navy.

Until now historians have invariable focused on the actions of the opposing infantry forces, in effect ignoring matters fundamental to the provision of effective fire support. I'm alluding to considerations such as higher command and control, the application of fire, the different characteristics of guns vis-à-vis howitzers, the selection of gun areas, calibration and registration and counter-battery fire, to mention a few.

The authors have been able to present some unique perspectives on their subject. Major General Paul Stevens brings unchallengeable eminence as a former Chief Instructor of the School of Artillery with a particular interest in the development and use of artillery in World War I. Brigadier Chris Roberts, a former Commanding Officer of the Special Air Service Regiment, has a detailed knowledge of the Gallipoli campaign. His book on the landing, particularly its discussion of Ottoman dispositions and movements, represents a seminal contribution.

The book commences by examining the standard of artillery training in Australia and New Zealand and the doctrine that guided what training took place prior to the outbreak of war. Only a basic capability existed before the forces embarked. Some had not even seen a gun fired!

Hard training took place in Egypt with some attempt to introduce lessons learnt from the Western Front. By March 1915, units were deemed to be coherent and efficient. However, the authors note that did not include a capacity for higher artillery command and control, nor did artillery commanders have any role in planning for operations.

Gallipoli presented challenges quite different to those encountered in the sands of Egypt. Only one 18-pounder was ashore and in action at the end of day one. Disorder marked the first few weeks, with batteries landing only to be sent off. With the Ottomans holding the high ground and having superior observation, suitable gun areas were at a premium, the difficulties exacerbated by the flat trajectory of the 18-pounder. Some positions had to be selected immediately to the rear of the infantry. A major manhandling effort was required to get guns into positions where they could fire effectively.

From an acknowledgement by a senior artillery commander that insufficient support had been available at the start, the authors establish how a satisfactory level of fire support came to be provided. This was acknowledged by Birdwood, who was said to be not impressed initially. Some deficiencies remained, particularly the lack of high-level command and control.

The book ends with the author's conclusions and assessments of lessons learnt. One paragraph resonated with me. It said '[Artillery] commanders at all levels [must] understand the capabilities and tactical employment of the available fire support ... and play a pivotal role in planning operations in integrated planning teams. They must keep abreast of emerging developments in fire support.' Timeless advice indeed, which should never be forgotten.

This book is a valuable addition to our knowledge of the Gallipoli campaign, and the authors deserve our thanks.

Major General Steve Gower AO (Retd)
Former Director, Australian War Memorial

ACKNOWLEDGEMENTS

This book has been written with the generous support of a good many people, beginning with Lieutenant Colonel Nick Floyd, who organised the Firepower series of seminars at which we first made short presentations on the artillery at Anzac. Dr Roger Lee, former Head of the Australian Army History Unit (AAHU), encouraged us to turn those presentations into an occasional paper and then, as our research unearthed further information, suggested a book for AAHU consideration. Happily, our application was successful, and we are grateful to the unit and its current Head, Colonel Tim Gellel (Retd), for the opportunity to publish this volume.

Dr Rhys Crawley generously provided digital copies of a host of documents in British repositories, material we could not have gathered in Australia, and we have quoted from his ground-breaking work *Climax at Gallipoli: The Failure of the August Offensive*. Dr Christopher Pugsley ONZM provided copies of New Zealand diaries, directed us to useful sources, and commented on the manuscript. His assistance allowed us to address a number of issues in greater depth than would otherwise have been possible, and both he and Richard Stowers generously provided photographs of New Zealand artillery at Anzac. Ian McGibbon and JoÚ Crawford, the New Zealand Defence Force historian, also read and commented on the New Zealand content in Chapter One.

Jeff Pickerd kindly provided his unpublished manuscript on the 8th Light Horse Regiment which contains a wealth of information on the tragic event that was the light horse attack at the Nek, including letters from survivors written soon after the disaster. Jeff also commented on the section of this volume that relates to the charge. The late Graham Wilson provided his manuscript for the chapter entitled 'The Silent Seven Minutes' and which was posthumously published in his book *Bully Beef and Balderdash* (Vol. II). Peter Burness, author of two books on the charge, offered comments on that section of our manuscript and provided additional material. The generous support of these historians allowed us to arrive at our conclusions concerning the supposed delay between the cessation of the artillery fire and the launching of the attack.

Charles Messenger and Richard Flory in the United Kingdom assisted us by providing details of the military career of Charles Cunliffe-Owen, the artillery adviser at the headquarters of the Australian and New Zealand Army Corps.

Commodore Peter Wykeham-Martin RN and Captain JoÚ Roberts RN were most helpful in describing the armaments of the Royal Navy's warships operating off Anzac. Ron Clifton, Alan Riley and Kevin Rowlinson of the United Kingdom and 'orokep' on the Great War Forum all supplied useful information on the British artillery units that served at Anzac. Dr Spencer Jones kindly read and provided comment on the first chapter.

Associate Professor Mesut Uyar offered suggestions on the Ottoman forces and actions during the August Offensive, and generously provided information on the Ottoman artillery at Anzac and excerpts from the manuscript of his forthcoming book, *The Ottoman Army in the First World War* should be in italics, to be published by Routledge. Richard Pelvin readily provided his article 'Sea Power at Suvla, August 1915: Naval Aspects of the Suvla Bay Landings and the genesis of Modern Amphibious Warfare' to assist our research into the naval support during the campaign.

Mike Cecil, a former Head of TecÚology and Heraldry at the Australian War Memorial, was instrumental in helping us develop the tecÚical data in the weapons and ammunition sidebars, and provided comment on the manuscript. Paul Evans of the British Army Museum Ogilby Trust kindly provided additional tecUical information on the guns.

Mrs Judy Mack translated shorthand excerpts from Charles Bean's diaries and notebooks, enabling us to delve into his accounts more deeply. Ms Kay Dancey of the Australian National University showed her patience and skill in the production of the excellent maps, while Mrs Cathy McCullagh edited the manuscript with her usual deft hand. Andrew Richardson and Nick Anderson, also of the AAHU, lent us their usual enthusiastic support and provided guidance and assistance with the publication of the book, as did our publisher, Denny Neave, and the talented team at Big Sky Publishing. Major General Steve Gower AO (Retd), a former gunner and former Director of the Australian War Memorial, kindly agreed to write the Foreword.

Our wives, Helen Stevens and Judy Roberts, endured long periods without us while we were ensconced in research and writing. As ever, we are grateful for their continuous support and understanding.

Canberra
23 October 2020

ABBREVIATIONS

ADC	Aide-de-camp
AFA	Australian Field Artillery
AIF	Australian Imperial Force
ANZAC	Australian and New Zealand Army Corps
Ammn	Ammunition
Bde	Brigade
BEF	British Expeditionary Force
BGRA	Brigadier General Royal Artillery
BL	Breech loading
BGGS	Brigadier General General Staff
BMRA	Brigade Major Royal Artillery
Bty	Battery
CB	Counter-battery
CEO	Corps Expeditionnaire D'Orient (French)
CF	Citizen Force (Australia)
CRA	Commander Royal Artillery
GOC	General Officer Commanding
Div	Division/Divisional
HE	High explosive
HMS	His Majesty's Ship
HQ	Headquarters
IMA	Indian Mountain Artillery
Lancs	Lancashire
LH	Light Horse

MEF	Mediterranean Expeditionary Force
NCO	Non-commissioned officer
NZ&A	New Zealand and Australian (Division)
NZEF	New Zealand Expeditionary Force
NZFA	New Zealand Field Artillery
NZMR	New Zealand Mounted Rifles
PF	Permanent Forces
QF	Quick firing
RA	Royal Artillery
RFA	Royal Field Artillery
RGA	Royal Garrison Artillery
RWF	Royal Welsh Fusiliers (renamed Royal Welch Fusiliers in 1922)
TF	Territorial Force (New Zealand)

INTRODUCTION

Throughout this book we have used the acronym ANZAC to denote the Australian and New Zealand Army Corps as a military formation, and the more generic 'Anzac' for the battlefield, the Australian and New Zealand troops who fought there, and other related matters.

While much has been written about Gallipoli, the part specifically played by the ANZAC artillery—its gunners—is somewhat limited. For the Australians, Charles Bean offers a chapter in Vol. II of his *Official History of Australia in the War of 1914-1918*, as does David Horner in *The Gunners: A History of the Australian Artillery*. For the New Zealanders, Alan Henderson and his co-authors include a chapter in their book, *The Gunners, A History Of The New Zealand Artillery*, and Lieutenant J.R. Byrne provides a narrative in his *New Zealand Artillery In The Field 1914-1918*.

We have set out to expand on these sources, to compile a detailed account of the part played by the artillery, and to examine whether the support provided was effective, believing such a work would appeal to Australian and New Zealand gunners and service personnel past and present, and to historians researching the campaign. Those with an interest in Gallipoli, or whose relatives served with the artillery on the peninsula, may also find it useful.

Our journey began with the centenary Firepower seminars arranged by the Royal Australian Artillery Historical Company and the Australian Defence Force Academy campus of the University of New South Wales to chart the contribution of the artillery to the Great War. We were asked to give short presentations on the command, control and employment of the ANZAC artillery, and were subsequently encouraged to combine these efforts into a more substantial study based on training manuals, wartime publications, war diaries, after-action reports, personal diaries and letters. We discovered as we evaluated this material that the varied perspectives that resulted from our differing regimental backgrounds—artillery and infantry—proved particularly advantageous.

The book begins with a review of the organisation of the Australian and New Zealand artilleries in 1914 and the doctrine that informed their training and employment. Some historians believe that the British artillery entered the Great War without any real doctrine. An examination of the pre-war manuals suggests otherwise, although the guidance that was available placed its emphasis on mobile warfare. This meant that aspects important in trench warfare, such as command and control at divisional and corps level, and countering hostile batteries, proved inadequate.

Our focus then shifts to the employment and experiences of the artillery in the Anzac beachhead, that of the Australians and New Zealanders, and that provided by the Royal Navy, the Royal Field Artillery, the Royal Garrison Artillery and Indian Mountain Artillery elements under ANZAC control. We do not cover the artillery at Cape Helles, even though five antipodean batteries served there between May and October 1915. The fighting in that sector was quite separate from that at Anzac. Nor do we cover the fighting at Suvla, which again was essentially quite separate, although we have documented the artillery coordination measures established at the boundary between the two operational sectors.

The ANZAC gunners had to contend with immense problems. Hurriedly trained, they were faced with static warfare in very unfavourable terrain, and had to adapt and innovate. There were difficulties in simply finding suitable firing positions, and in implementing the necessary command and control arrangements to have guns in one area effectively support the troops in another. On top of this, the gunners had to wage a constant battle with the Ottoman artillery, make early attempts to provide anti-aircraft fire, and endure the daily grind of trench warfare in providing support to the defenders along with harassing, interdiction and retaliatory fire. Overcoming these challenges proved a significant educational process.

While for the majority of the campaign ANZAC was on the defensive, in August the Corps launched attacks at Lone Pine, the Nek, the heights of the Sari Bair Range, and at Hill 60. We have examined the effectiveness of the fire support for these actions, as well as an earlier attack on Baby 700 in May, and a little-known plan to mount a final attack on Hill 60 in November. This analysis provides an understanding of the difficulties the gunners faced, and the extent to which they gained experience in supporting attacks against entrenched positions.

The campaign at Anzac is shrouded in myths and misconceptions, beginning with the popular view of the landing on 25 April. One of the most controversial artillery events concerns the ill-fated light horse charge at the Nek, where Bean records that the preparatory bombardment ceased seven minutes before the troops went over the top. Our research questions whether any such delay occurred, and suggests that the reasons for the failure of the attack lay elsewhere.

We then address the build-up of artillery assets in the enlarged Anzac beachhead following the August Offensive, the further development of command and control arrangements for the provision of immediate fire support from both the artillery and the navy, ongoing artillery support arrangements and activities and consider a plan to take the crest of Hill 60 in November. We conclude with the planning and execution of the evacuation of the guns in December 1915.

Campaigning at Anzac took place over a century ago, but in our minds the experience of those early gunners remains relevant to today's modern artillery. Adaptation and innovation are still crucial to providing effective support. Meeting the challenges of warfare is a continuing educational process. The environment in which campaigns are fought differ, as do the tecÚologies employed, but much can be learned from the past about the fundamentals of warfare.

Chapter One

THE PRE-WAR ANTIPODEAN ARTILLERY AND ITS DOCTRINE

Just over a week after landing at Anzac, Colonel Talbot Hobbs, the Commander Royal Artillery (CRA) of the 1st Australian Division, lamented that 'the artillery up to this time have not been able to give more assistance to the infantry.' He cited several reasons concerning the environment in which they were operating to explain why the fire support fell short of expectations.[1] While his assessment was accurate, there were other issues that had deeper origins, highlighting that an army's performance in the opening campaign of a war is rooted in its pre-war structure, doctrine and training. Thus any consideration of the artillery at Anzac begins with the foundations on which the Australian and New Zealand armies were built: organisation, the nature of battle at the time, and the prevailing doctrine and training regimes.

2

The Pre-War Artillery

Immediately prior to the Great War, rather than having a large standing army, both countries maintained small Permanent Forces (PF) comprising staff officers, instructors, and a few artillery units, largely coastal batteries. The PF were supplemented by larger, part-time forces established under compulsory military training schemes. In New Zealand this was the Territorial Force (TF), and in Australia the Citizen Forces (CF), both replacing the previous all-volunteer part-time Militia (paid) and Volunteer (unpaid) units that had been deemed to be ineffective in developing a capable defence force.[2] The intention was that New Zealand would raise a trained force of 30,000 men, and Australia a field force some 135,000 strong by 1919-1920,[3] each organised along British lines into infantry battalions and mounted rifle ('light horse' in Australia) regiments, together with field artillery brigades (the equivalent of modern artillery regiments), and engineer, transport and supply companies.[4]

E Battery of the New Zealand Territorial Force conducting a firing practice near Christchurch using 15-pounder BL field guns with the ammunition limbers beside each gun. This photograph shows the usual arrangement of a field battery in action with the guns side by side. The foliage to their front suggests they are practising in the indirect fire role from a semi-covered position (Alexander Turnbull Library 1/2-040861-G).

Over seven years the New Zealand force was to be organised as a field army of two mounted rifle brigades and two infantry divisions with the artillery component comprising four artillery brigades, each of two 4-gun batteries.[5] In Australia, by mid-1920, the army would comprise eight light horse brigades, six infantry divisions, and an additional infantry brigade, while Western Australia and Tasmania would each field a 'mixed force'. In each of the infantry divisions the artillery was to be limited to two field artillery brigades, each containing three 4-gun field batteries and one 4-gun howitzer battery. It was envisaged that the Australian Field Artillery (AFA) would consist of forty-two field batteries organised into fourteen artillery brigades, eight field batteries with the light horse brigades, and six howitzer batteries.[6]

The New Zealand TF replaced the Militia and Volunteer forces on 26 February 1910, its field artillery component initially comprising five 4-gun batteries, with a further three batteries to be raised. The 300-strong Royal New Zealand Artillery was reorganised to allow a third of its members to be posted to the field artillery to meet the envisaged expansion of that branch, with the remainder continuing to serve as instructors in the coastal batteries.[7] In Australia the CF came into being sixteen months later, on 1 July 1912, with the militiamen continuing their current engagements and 16,000 compulsory trainees called up.[8] Initially the artillery comprised one PF and fifteen CF batteries of the AFA, fourteen companies of Australian Garrison Artillery, and two field artillery brigade headquarters, one in Sydney, the other in Melbourne.[9] However, at this early stage the brigade headquarters largely performed administrative functions and supervised the training of their allotted sub-units. Four new field batteries were formed in 1912, with additional batteries and artillery brigade headquarters to be created proportionally each year as the force expanded.[10]

The CF and TF were designed for home defence, the main fear of the time, in Australia at least, being the possibility of Japanese invasion, despite the Anglo-Japanese Naval Agreement of 1902. Service required young men between the ages of eighteen and twenty-six to undertake annual training. In New Zealand the requirement was thirty drills (twenty out of doors), twelve half-day or six whole-day parades in the field, and a seven-day camp. The Australian commitment for artillerymen was twenty-five days, made up of seventeen days in camp and eight days, or their equivalent in half-day and night drills, in home training.[11] Each country was divided into military districts, four in New Zealand (two on each island) and six in Australia, the latter generally equating to the state boundaries. These were further broken down into regionally based area groups in New Zealand and battalion areas in Australia, which again were divided into training areas, with fifty-six training areas in New Zealand and 215 in Australia.

Sub-units were recruited locally within each training area.[12]

Although the new compulsory training schemes were a distinct improvement on the previous voluntary arrangements, the part-time nature of the forces, frequent absences from training, insufficient full-time instructors and the need to recruit locally, resulting in the dispersal of batteries, restricted what could be achieved. Furthermore, the nascent nature of the few artillery brigade headquarters and the lack of a divisional artillery organisation meant that much of the training was undertaken at battery level in the local drill hall or surrounding countryside. Only at the annual camps could they operate at unit level, and then only where they came under brigade direction. Consequently, for much of the year, the artillery training was largely devoted to tecÚical training, gun drills, manoeuvring the gun teams, and battery-level activities. There was little opportunity to operate as a brigade or complete combined-arms training. This, together with the annual increase in the number of batteries—often effected by splitting existing ones—limited what could be achieved in developing a proficient artillery force.[13]

In 1913 Major General Sir Alexander Godley, the British Regular Army officer seconded to command the New Zealand forces, noted that, although there had been a remarkable improvement in the field batteries' performance over the previous year, they were only in camp for seven days, adding that it was thus impossible to attain efficiency in manipulating modern field guns, and they had not yet had the opportunity of cooperating with the other arms. He urged that, for the New Zealand Field Artillery (NZFA) to attain real efficiency, the annual camp for batteries be increased from the current seven days to eleven.[14]

Cadets of the Royal Military College, Duntroon, conducting artillery practice with a 15-pounder BL field gun and ammunition limber west of Black Mountain, Canberra, in 1913. The cadet in the foreground is Walter Urquhart, a member of the first class to enter the college, which graduated early in August 1914 to enable its cadets to join the AIF. Urquhart served with the 7th AFA Battery on Gallipoli. Behind him are two cadets with semaphore flags to communicate with the observation station near Green Hill, 800 metres away (now part of the National Arboretum). This suggests they are practising firing in the indirect fire role. The gun position is in the open ground just north-west of the current Glenloch Interchange and the impact area was close to Coppin's Crossing (RMC Archives).

In Australia, with seventeen days in camp, more could be achieved, but with only two field artillery brigade headquarters, the opportunity to undertake unit-level training was restricted to New South Wales and Victoria, and this only if an annual brigade camp occurred. In Western Australia, South Australia, Tasmania and Queensland the independent batteries were on their own, with all training undertaken by the respective CF battery commanders supported by a PF instructor.[15] Although the 3rd Field Artillery Brigade headquarters was raised in Brisbane in mid-1914, it had little impact on training before war broke out. Nonetheless, in 1914 General Sir Ian Hamilton, the British Inspector General of Overseas Forces, noted of the Australian artillery that 'Some of the instruction ... is of the highest order, and the tecÚical training of the firing battery is in safe hands [including] successful firing at simple targets ... [although] some [batteries] showed very clearly the need for longer training and greater experience.' Above battery level, however, Hamilton considered the Australians not yet 'trained up to the level of the artillery of an army working in masses together in the field. They have not had time yet, or the opportunity, to practise that higher control and power of combination outside the battery, without which there can be no real fire co-operation.'[16] This latter point was to be an issue in the early months at Anzac.

Artillery Weapons

Following the South African War (1899-1902), reforms within the British Army saw the introduction of new field guns and howitzers to support the infantry. The weapons differed in that, generally speaking, guns had longer barrels, higher muzzle velocities, flatter trajectories, and longer ranges. Howitzers had shorter barrels, lower muzzle velocities and higher trajectories, and were designed to lob heavier projectiles onto targets that might be behind cover. Advances in gun design meant that, by the turn of the twentieth century, both types were loaded at the breech rather than the muzzle, and newer models were fitted with on-carriage elevation, traverse and recoil systems, allowing them to be laid more rapidly and to remain stationary while in action. Some also used smokeless propellants in cartridge cases mated to the projectile and were fitted with simple breech mechanisms to lock the cartridge case in place, along with sighting systems independent of the recoiling mass. These weapons could achieve high rates of fire, and were thus designated Quick Firing (QF). Weapons in which the breech was sealed by a partially threaded breech block that rotated on closing to engage threads on the breech, where obturation (sealing of the breech) was provided by the use of a compressible pad on the face of the breech block, and where the projectile and propelling charge were loaded separately, had a slower rate of fire and were designated Breech Loading (BL).

Refitting the Royal Artillery (RA) with newer weapons commenced with the introduction of the Mark I QF 18-pounder (3.3-inch/83.8mm) field gun in 1904, and the Mark II in 1906, both of which had an effective range of almost 6000 metres, which could be lengthened to 7100 metres with the trail dug in. Designed to support the infantry in an anti-personnel role, these guns fired shrapnel shells filled with 375 lead-antimony balls, and a fuse designed to burst the shell above the heads of the enemy, showering them with the high velocity balls along a beaten zone of approximately 20 metres wide and up to 275 metres deep depending on the height of the burst. This was the gun's only ammunition until late 1914, when the new 18-pounder high explosive (HE) round entered service. Both the Mark I and the Mark II versions were in service when war was declared, and they were the standard field gun of the British infantry division, each of which had three 18-pounder artillery brigades, each of three 6-gun batteries, giving a total of fifty-four 18-pounders.

Members of A Section, 31st Battery (Citizen Forces), posing with their two new QF 18-pounder field guns in 1914 during an annual camp at Seymour, Victoria. The 18-pounder began replacing the 15-pounder BL field gun issued to the Militia after the Citizen Forces came into being in July 1912. By August 1914 only thirty-six had been received, enough to equip nine batteries. These were taken by the AFA batteries of the 1st Australian Division Artillery when the AIF was raised (Wikipedia).

Entering service in 1910, the QF 4.5-inch (114mm) howitzer replaced the old BL 5-inch (127mm) field howitzer, with each infantry division allocated one howitzer brigade of three batteries, each containing six howitzers. The new howitzers fired both HE Lyddite (Picric Acid) and shrapnel shells with an effective range of 6000 metres. Rounding out the divisional artillery was the BL 60-pounder (5-inch/127mm) heavy field gun, which fired a 16-kilogram HE shell with an initial maximum range of 9400 metres. Developed in 1904, the 60-pounder entered service in 1905, with each infantry division allocated one 4-gun battery. Thus a standard regular British infantry division had a total of seventy-six modern artillery pieces, comprising fifty-four QF 18-pounders, eighteen QF 4.5-inch howitzers, and four BL 60-pounder heavy field guns.[17]

In accordance with imperial arrangements, the AFA and the NZFA both adopted the British QF 18-pounder field gun and, while the Australians retained the obsolete BL 5-inch howitzers, the NZFA acquired eight of the modern QF 4.5-inch howitzers—enough for two batteries.[18] However, supply of the new 18-pounders was slow, and by August 1914 there were only thirty-six of them in Australia, enough for nine batteries, the other batteries being equipped with obsolescent BL 15-pounders. The one howitzer battery trained on the equally obsolescent BL 5-inch howitzers, and the heavy battery in Queensland had four older QF 4.7-inch guns.[19]

Doctrine and Training

For training and for guidance on tactics the TF and CF relied on British manuals which were developed against the background of the largely mobile warfare of the late nineteenth and early twentieth centuries. Battles were normally decided on the day they were fought, orders were brief, and quick attacks were the norm. During the Franco-Prussian War (1870-71) at battles such as Wissembourg, Worth, Spicheren, Mars-le-Tour, Gravelotte and Sedan, the German armies went into action immediately on meeting the enemy with the outcome decided by nightfall. Similarly, in the South African War, the British mounted quick attacks at Elandslaagte, Stormberg, Magersfontein, Colenso and Diamond Hill, while other colonial conflicts reflected similar experience. During the Russo-Japanese War (1904-05), which featured large battles involving armies of between 125,000 and 200,000 men, the picture began to change, as exemplified by the siege of Port Arthur and the Battle of

Mukden. Even so, this was largely a war of manoeuvre in which many of the battles were quick attacks mounted at short notice against rudimentary defences.

In providing support during the manoeuvre battle, the horse-drawn 18-pounder was an extremely mobile piece. Going into action, the teams galloped up to the gun line, swung their pieces around and, in a matter of minutes, were ready to fire, the ammunition limber positioned alongside the gun. In the direct fire role, where the gunners could see the target, they could engage it and adjust fire quickly. In the indirect role, where the guns were hidden from the target, forward observers had to adjust the fire of the guns by sending corrections back to the crew, making it difficult to engage a moving target.

The crew and 15-pounder BL field gun of E Battery, New Zealand Territorial Force, firing in the direct fire role near Christchurch. After 1912 the 15-pounders were gradually replaced by the new 18-pounder QF field guns (Alexander Turnbull Library 1/2-040870-G).

While manoeuvre was regarded as key, conflicts such as the South African and Russo-Japanese wars brought home the realisation that advances in weaponry such as QF artillery, machine-guns, and magazine-fed breech-loading rifles meant the battlefield was becoming far more lethal at longer ranges than was previously the case. Opinion on the way forward was divided, and all armies struggled with the 'manifest increase in firepower for both defence and attack'.[20]

In Britain, the army's experience in the South African War led to considerable introspection, debate and reform.[21] The outcome was contained in a series of manuals, beginning with *Infantry Training 1902*, and *Field Service Regulations, Part I, Combined Training 1902*, followed by *Field Artillery Training 1904*, *Cavalry Training (Provisional) 1904*, and the *Manual of Military Engineering 1905*. All were revised as thinking evolved. Between 1902 and 1914 there were three revisions of *Infantry Training* (1905, 1911 and 1914), while *Combined Training* was updated in 1905 and then superseded by *Field Service Regulations, Part I, Operations, 1909*, and *Part II, Administration, 1909*, both reprinted with amendments in 1914. *Cavalry Training* was updated twice (1907 and 1912), as was *Field Artillery Training* (1912 and 1914).[22]

It has been suggested by some historians that the British Army entered the Great War without any real doctrine—that is, any central guidance permeating the army on the nature of the future battlefield and how future wars might best be fought.[23] In a sense Britain was handicapped in this regard because her small standing forces had to prepare for both colonial and potential continental commitments, while countries such as France and Germany could place emphasis on the latter alone. Thus it is understandable that in their work on the Edwardian army, Timothy Bowen and Mark Connolly point to the results of an examination of military manuals which revealed that the French and Germans had their own 'internally logical, but different, concepts of war which imbued their entire military culture', whereas Britain had nothing ostensibly similar. However, they also noted that neither France nor Germany 'had a notably greater grip on the nature of future operations and neither had made preparations for a long war.' Both also had 'equal problems defining the roles of cavalry and artillery, and infantry training was still based on the idea of mass assaults regardless of conditions.'[24]

British tradition tended towards the identification of general principles rather than tightly constricting rules. This left subordinates with a good deal of latitude and gave them much-needed flexibility in a small army with global responsibilities.[25] The central document was *Field Service Regulations 1909* which provided guidance based on consideration of the experiences of the South African and Russo-Japanese wars, although 'neither conflict taught simple, unambiguous lessons'.[26] All the other military publications were cross-referenced to it, all stressed the combined employment of the various arms, and all examined their respective employment in war within the divisional framework.[27] It could be argued that the material they contained approached the real purpose of doctrine which, based on experience and the uncertain nature of future war, is designed to provide guidance enabling a flexible approach and which can be adapted to the conditions confronting an army when conflict breaks out. As Brigadier General Lancelot Kiggell commented in 1913, 'the problems of war cannot be solved by rules, but by judgement based on a knowledge of general principles. To lay down rules would tend to cramp judgement, not to educate and strengthen it. For that reason, our manuals aim at giving principles but avoid laying down methods.'[28]

For the nascent Australian and New Zealand artilleries, the principal manual was *Field Artillery Training (Provisional) 1912*. An extensive publication (410 pages), the first six chapters were concerned with training—from equitation (horsemanship) through to gunnery—while the rest addressed the employment of artillery in conflict, along with tactics and associated matters across all phases of war. The 1914 edition, issued after the outbreak of war, repeated much of what was contained in its predecessor, with an additional chapter on ammunition supply, some material on the potential use of aircraft, and minor changes to the text and arrangements of paragraphs.

Horse-drawn gun teams of 15-pounder BL field guns from the Royal Military College, Duntroon, returning from firing practice in 1913. This image provides an indication of the road space required by a battery of four guns (RMC Archives).

Artillery historians Shelford Bidwell and Dominick Graham have highlighted the fact that the gunnery manuals 'did not define the form of war that [the field artillery] was confronting but tried to reflect the diversity of the imperial experience as well as guide the would-be continental warrior.' Whatever the conflict, the manuals were very clear that the primary function of the artillery was 'to assist the movement of its own infantry' and 'to prevent the movements of the enemy's infantry.' Subsidiary roles were to inflict losses and break down the enemy's morale, destroy his material, and reduce fortified localities.[29]

In mobile warfare the expectation was that artillery brigades would be paired with infantry brigades. One of the principal questions of the period was whether guns should continue to be pushed forward alongside the infantry in the direct-fire role or fire from concealed positions using indirect fire. The primary issue was survivability when deployed in the open on a longer range and more lethal battlefield. Behind it lay nascent questions. Could armies take advantage of the increased range of the guns, deploy them in some depth and, using indirect fire tecÚiques, concentrate the fire of multiple batteries, with all the difficulties that this posed for command and control, rapid communications and observation? Alternatively, should they continue to provide support using direct fire in close proximity to the infantry, which would limit the weight of fire available at that point, but alleviate problems associated with command and control, communications and observation?

British manuals reflected this debate. When discussing the defence, a relatively static period, *Field Service Regulations* stipulated 'Guns should usually be concealed as much as possible.' *Field*

Artillery Training devoted a section to 'concealment', advising 'concealment in action increases the difficulties of the hostile batteries, possibly even to the extent of conferring immunity from their fire, thus enabling the concealed artillery to devote their attention to the support and assistance of its own infantry.'[30] It went on to identify three types of positions the guns could occupy: open, semi-covered and covered. An open position was one 'in which the objective can be seen over the sights and in which direct laying is possible.' Semi-covered positions were out of view of the objective to the extent that indirect laying was required, but the degree of cover obtained was insufficient to conceal the flashes of the guns or the smoke and dust they raised after fire had been opened. Covered positions were those 'in which the guns and their flashes were completely covered from the enemy and in which it is necessary to use indirect laying.'[31]

The manual described the advantages and disadvantages of each type, highlighting that, while open positions were fully exposed to hostile fire, they allowed targets to be engaged quickly. However, while covered positions conferred immunity from fire, they increased the difficulty of control, engaging fresh targets, and dealing with moving targets. Bowen and Connolly note that in debates on this issue, senior British officers such as French and Haig favoured the guns closing with the enemy 'so as to give the infantry the best possible support, moral as well as material', whereas from 1904 onwards, gunners increasingly favoured indirect fire.[32] The manuals advised that 'the power of delivering effective fire from concealed positions is ... limited', and later 'concealment, both as regards position and manoeuvre must invariably be forgone for adequate reasons. To support infantry and enable it to effect its purpose the artillery must be willing to sacrifice itself.'[33] On a very practical level, battery commanders of the time were compelled to admit that their communications did not allow them to support the infantry effectively from concealed positions, especially in the attack.[34]

The guns of the Royal Field Artillery (RFA), the AFA and the NZFA were all capable of both direct and indirect fire, with howitzers generally operating in the indirect mode. In the RFA practice camps of 1912 and 1913, both types of positions were occupied.[35] The AFA and NZFA tended to favour the simplicity of direct fire, reflecting the limited training available to the part-time gunners. Although the New Zealand batteries undertook some firing from concealed positions, in his Inspection Report of 1914,

Hamilton, an advocate of concealed positions, noted '...care should be taken not to push the artillery into positions of undue exposure', indicating that the batteries he saw lacked experience or confidence in the more complex indirect-fire method. Similarly, in Australia in 1913, Major General Kirkpatrick recorded, 'where indirect laying was attempted, it was merely a demonstration of the method, and proved once more that [the officers lacked the experience] to get in [sic] action quickly enough by this method to render effective support to other arms.'[36]

Command of the artillery, and accordingly control of its fire, was another area of doctrinal debate. A divisional artillery commander, the CRA, was created in 1907, but uncertainty ensued over his responsibilities until they were outlined in Section 151 of *Field Artillery Training (Provisional) 1912*, which stipulated that the General Officer Commanding (GOC) a division was responsible for the tactical employment of the artillery, and the CRA for executing his orders as they related to the guns. Broadly, it was envisaged that in circumstances in which the division was operating as an entity, the artillery would be commanded by the CRA, who would deploy it and control its fire by allotting 'tasks to each field artillery brigade or zones in which he thought their fire could be employed effectively.' In situations in which tactical operations were dispersed and infantry brigades or units were operating independently, the manuals advised that the artillery and infantry 'should be formed temporarily into groups under one commander', normally the infantryman. In such cases the CRA would delegate command of artillery units, and thus control of their fire, to the group commander, and their employment would rest with him.[37]

Although the CRA's duties had been stipulated, there appears to have been a lack of consistency in their application. According to Bidwell and Graham, 'Some divisional commanders allocated their field artillery brigades to infantry brigadiers and ignored the CRA ... Others tended to deploy and control the artillery as they deployed infantry brigades, using the CRA as a channel of command like a brigade commander ... Yet others kept their artillery as a reserve under the CRA until the battle developed, confusing fire reserves with gun reserves.'[38] After the Great War Lieutenant Colonel Alan Brooke noted with regard to the CRA that 'our pre-war conception of this appointment seems to have visualised primarily the role of an artillery adviser to the General Officer Commanding the division, and to have considered the occasions on which he would exercise direct command of the artillery as exceptional.'[39] He concluded that British tactical doctrine favoured mobility over firepower, consequently decentralisation was expected to be the rule, and there was a lack of artillery organisations that could exercise effective centralised control.[40] Potentially this led, as *Field Artillery Training* reflected, to the reduction of the 'fighting capacity of the division as a whole'.[41]

Some effort was made to address the problem in *Training and Manoeuvre Regulations 1913*, which stipulated that 'during training of divisional artillery schemes must be perfected to illustrate the higher command of artillery in battles.'[42] Yet it is doubtful that much was achieved, with war breaking out the next year. Consequently, it appears that the functions of the CRA, and the control of fire support provided by the divisional artillery, had not been settled by the time war was declared.

In whatever role he was to be used, it should be noted that the CRA had only a limited staff and primitive communications with which to control his brigades. His headquarters consisted of a Brigade Major Royal Artillery (BMRA), a staff captain, and an aide-de-camp (ADC), who later became a Reconnaissance Officer.[43] Its means of communication ranged from visual devices (semaphore, heliograph or lamps), which were dependent on line of sight and weather conditions, to mounted orderlies or staff officers who could be killed or incapacitated relaying information, and telephone cable which, while useful in static positions, was susceptible to being cut by shellfire and traffic, and was not practical during mobile operations.

An additional problem for British armies was that doctrine peaked at divisional level and did not address issues at corps level or higher. While the corps had been a standard formation in some continental armies for many years, in the British Army no standing corps headquarters *per se* existed prior to the Great War, reflecting the army's priority of policing the Empire and engaging in colonial conflicts. The 1901 army estimates allowed for six army corps based on regional commands, but these arrangements remained theoretical until 1907 when the Haldane reforms established a six-division British Expeditionary Force (BEF), in which Aldershot Command with its two infantry divisions and the requisite additional troops was nominated to form I Corps should the need arise.[44] The other two corps headquarters would be raised if the BEF was committed to operations.

The lack of corps doctrine indicated that the British Army had paid insufficient heed to implications arising from conflicts such as the Russo-Japanese War in which heavy artillery had played a significant part in supporting field operations, or of the organisation of the German Army that included heavy artillery resources at corps level, or of the French Army, which had reinforcing regiments of field artillery organic to each corps. The RA had no weapons above divisional level save for the 6-inch BL howitzers of the Royal Garrison Artillery (RGA), and these were earmarked for siege use as required, rather than deployment with the field force.

Brooke and others also identified that the artillery was regarded as an accessory. The CRA and his subordinates were generally not involved in the planning of an operation, and it was a matter of the artillery supporting the infantry plan to the best of its ability.[45] Brooke further observed that the doctrine relating to dealing with hostile batteries was deficient. In both attack and defence, *Field Artillery Training* charged the artillery with locating the enemy's batteries and subduing their fire.[46] Brooke considered this a throwback to the Franco-Prussian War when both sides deployed artillery in the open, and the infantry attack was preceded by an artillery duel. While the requirement to subdue hostile batteries remained, when British forces were attacking the enemy batteries were now likely to be in concealed positions. The doctrine, with its emphasis on mobility, made no allowance for the time or staff required to locate and engage these concealed batteries.[47]

The uncertainty of neutralising the enemy artillery had adverse implications for support for the infantry during the attack. *Field Artillery Training* stated that 'during the progress of the fight it will usually become necessary for the artillery to move forward to positions from which it will have a clearer view of the infantry fight and thus be able to afford the infantry more effective support.'[48] It also advised that 'to support an attack with success a battery commander must be able to see the ground over which the infantry is advancing and also be able to control the fire of his battery rapidly and effectively, but the more cover that can be obtained *compatible with control by voice* [emphasis added] the better.'[49] For Brooke it was clear that attack doctrine required the close support of actual guns, but that support could only be sustained if the fire of hostile batteries had been thoroughly subdued, a result that was improbable.[50]

Senior Australian and New Zealand artillerymen would have been well aware of these debates. All had a keen interest in military matters, all had reasonably lengthy permanent or part-time service, some had undertaken attachments to British units, while others were members of the RA on secondment to the New Zealand or Australian armies. However, their opportunity to test the prevailing doctrine or explore alternatives would have been limited, as the compulsory service schemes in both nations had not matured to the point that a division had been formed. The highest formations in existence were infantry and mounted rifle brigades and, while termed as such, the artillery brigade was in reality a unit equivalent to an infantry battalion or mounted rifle regiment. As Jean Bou notes, these brigades 'were, perhaps, still more theoretical than real.'[51] They were primarily administrative entities, supervising the training of their subordinate units and sub-units, which themselves were dispersed regionally across local drill halls. For much of the year the artillery worked at battery or lower level with perhaps some work at brigade level at an annual camp in Victoria and New South Wales.[52] Consequently, most of the artillery training was undertaken at sub-unit level, which limited training in higher deployment and command and control issues. There is also little evidence from annual reports that meaningful combined-arms training took place at all.

Chapter Two

TO WAR

Mobilisation

When war broke out in August 1914, the Defence Acts of both Australia and New Zealand precluded the mobilisation of the CF and TF for overseas service, leaving the two governments no option but to call for volunteers to man the forces they offered to Britain. From the initial rush Australia formed the Australian Imperial Force (AIF), initially comprising the 1st Australian Division, an extra infantry brigade (the 4th), three light horse brigades, and some ancillary units. The New Zealand Expeditionary Force (NZEF) consisted at first of an infantry brigade, a mounted rifles brigade, and a field artillery brigade.

Experienced PF, CF and TF officers filled the artillery command positions in the AIF and NZEF, while at lower levels members of the CF and TF forces also stepped forward, although perhaps not in the numbers envisaged. While Charles Bean claimed that some of the Australian CF batteries enlisted almost to a man, the 1st AFA Brigade, hoping to recruit 50% of its men from the CF, recorded that its members were not volunteering as expected, although one of its batteries, the 1st AFA, was primarily manned by volunteers from the permanent artillery. Another, the 2nd AFA, with a battery establishment strength of 145 all ranks, enlisted forty-four CF artillery trainees and another sixty-five with previous artillery training, either in the Militia or the RA. The 8th AFA Battery, part of the 3rd AFA Brigade, took fifty-eight CF trainees on strength, along with men with previous training in various branches of the service.[1] Across the Tasman, it has been estimated that more than two-thirds of the NZEF had previous military training, with more than half drawn from the TF, although the historian of the Otago Regiment writes that probably three-fifths of that unit had no previous military training. The numbers in the New Zealand artillery batteries with previous training are not recorded.[2]

In the two and a half months between their raising and embarkation in October, Australian batteries and brigades spent much of their time administering, organising and outfitting the influx of recruits, drawing equipment, acquiring horses and undertaking some recruit training. War diaries show that limited gunnery instruction was attempted, with only the 8th AFA Battery recording a live-firing range practice, and that on just one day. However, no time was wasted on the long journey to Egypt, when gun drills and individual training in tecÚical skills were undertaken.[3]

Arriving in Egypt in December, the combat formations of the AIF and NZEF were incorporated into the Australian and New Zealand Army Corps (ANZAC) under the command of Lieutenant General Sir William Birdwood. ANZAC's two subordinate formations were the 1st Australian Division, led by the Australian Major General William Throsby Bridges, formerly an artilleryman, and the newly created New Zealand and Australian (NZ&A) Division, under Godley, the British regular commanding the NZEF. The 1st Australian Division was an infantry formation based around the 1st, 2nd and 3rd Infantry brigades, while the NZ&A Division was a composite formation containing the New Zealand Infantry and 4th Australian Infantry brigades, the New Zealand Mounted Rifles (NZMR) Brigade, and the 1st Australian Light Horse (LH) Brigade.

The 1st Australian Divisional Artillery consisted of the Headquarters (HQ) Divisional Artillery, the Divisional Ammunition Column, and the 1st, 2nd and 3rd AFA brigades and their brigade ammunition columns. Each field artillery brigade comprised three batteries: the 1st, 2nd and 3rd AFA batteries in the 1st AFA Brigade, the 4th, 5th and 6th in the 2nd, and the 7th, 8th and 9th in the 3rd. All batteries were equipped with four QF 18-pounder field guns, with each battery capable of being divided into two sections of two guns, which in turn comprised two sub-sections each of one gun. Thus the division had thirty-six 18-pounders compared with the fifty-four in a British infantry division, but it lacked both the howitzer brigade and the 60-pounder battery that were organic to a British division.

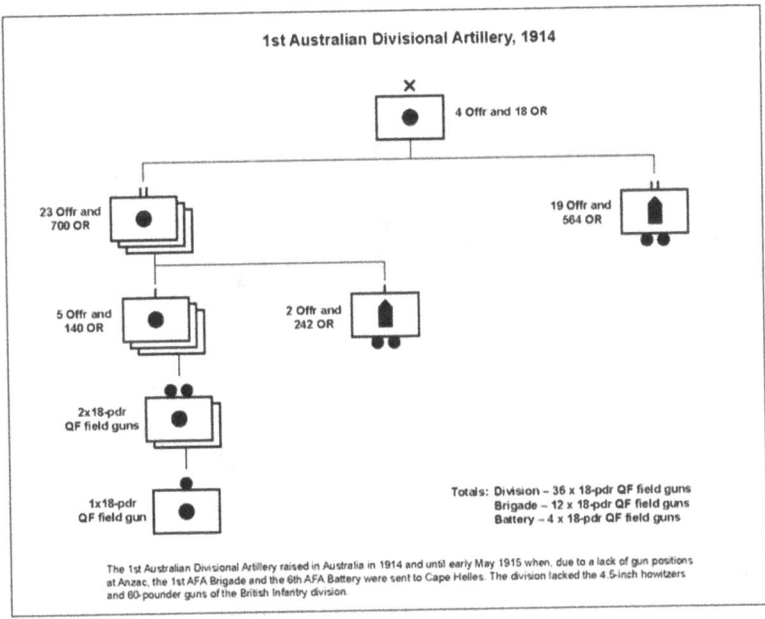

Organisation Chart 1: The 1st Australian Divisional Artillery, 1914

The NZ&A Division had only the NZFA Brigade, which comprised the 1st, 2nd and 3rd

NZFA batteries, the Brigade Ammunition Column and, from February 1915 onwards, the 4th NZFA (Howitzer) Battery and its ammunition column. The 1st, 2nd and 3rd batteries were equipped with four 18-pounders, and the 4th Battery with four QF 4.5-inch howitzers. A section of a British divisional ammunition column was temporarily attached and, on the division's formation, a cable was sent to New Zealand requesting the despatch of the second 4.5-inch howitzer battery and a howitzer brigade ammunition column.[4]

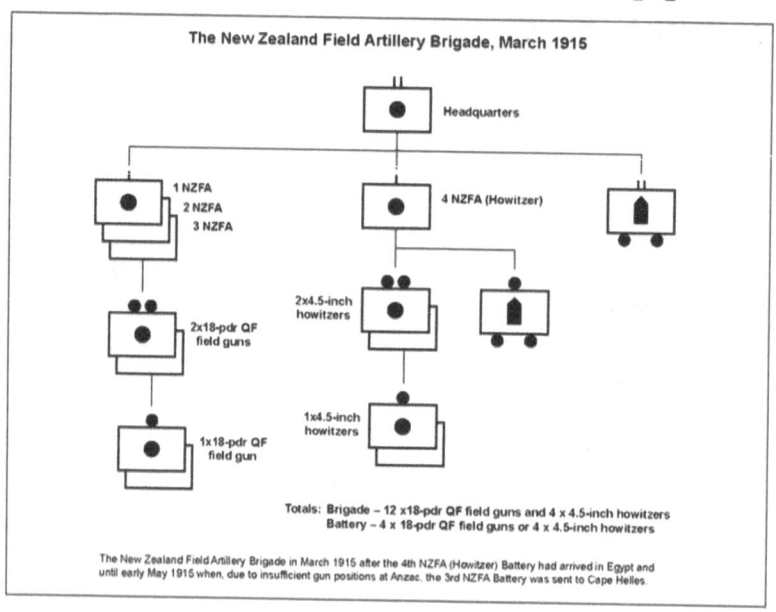

Organisation Chart 2: The New Zealand Field Artillery Brigade, March 1915

Compared to a two-division British corps, ANZAC's artillery complement was very light. It was short sixty 18-pounders, thirty-two

4.5-inchers, and eight 60-pounders. The lack of howitzers and 60-pounders would be sorely felt during the first three months on Gallipoli, although the deficiency in field guns would prove less problematic due to the terrain and lack of sufficient gun positions within the Anzac beachhead.

The artillery commanders of the ANZAC divisions came from quite different backgrounds. A British regular, Canadian-born Lieutenant Colonel Napier JoÚston, assumed the role for the NZ&A Division. After graduating from the Royal Military College of Canada, he accepted a commission in the RGA, and later served as an artillery instructor in India. He had a long association with New Zealand, posted as Artillery Staff Officer from 1904 to 1907 with the task of reorganising the field artillery, and returning to that country in 1911 as Director of Artillery and Chief Instructor.[5] With the raising of the NZEF he was promoted lieutenant colonel and appointed to command the NZFA Brigade, retaining this command after becoming CRA of the NZ&A Division in January 1915, thereby filling both appointments.

George Napier JoUston, who held the appointments of Commanding Officer of the New Zealand Field Artillery Brigade (August 1914-July 1915) and Commander, Royal Artillery of the New Zealand and Australian Division (January-December 1915). This is a later photograph, taken after he had been promoted brigadier general (Wikipedia).

JoÚ Joseph Talbot Hobbs, commander of the 1st Australian Divisional Artillery at Anzac. This is a later photograph, taken when he was commanding the 5th Australian Division in France (AWM E05007).

Colonel Talbot Hobbs, an architect and CF officer, held the Australian position. Born in England, he entered the British volunteer system (1st Cinque Ports Artillery Volunteers) in 1883 before emigrating to Australia, where he joined the Volunteer Field Artillery in Perth, and in 1903 commanded the 1st (Western Australian) Field Battery. Taking his part-time soldiering seriously, Hobbs twice attended gunnery courses in England and also completed a course run by the Department of Military Science of the University of Sydney. In 1913 he was appointed to command the newly formed CF 22nd Infantry Brigade.[6] Volunteering for the AIF in 1914, he was appointed CRA, 1st Australian Division.

Lieutenant Colonel George JoÚston, Commanding Officer of the 2nd Australian Field Artillery Brigade at Anzac. This is a pre-war photograph of him taken during his time in the Citizen Forces (Wikipedia).

Hobbs' three field artillery brigade commanders were also experienced gunners. Lieutenant Colonel Sydney Christian, commanding the 1st AFA Brigade, was an Australian-born PF gunner who had seen active service during the South African War with A Battery, New South Wales Permanent Artillery.[7] In 1907 he spent twelve months on exchange with the RA, and was later Chief Instructor for the Militia artillery in New South Wales and Queensland. At the outbreak of the war he was commanding the 1st AFA Battery, a PF sub-unit. The other two brigade commanders were Australian-born CF officers. Melbourne businessman Lieutenant Colonel George JoÚston enlisted in the Victorian Militia Artillery in 1887 and saw active service in South Africa attached to the 62nd Battery, RFA.[8] He assumed command of the Victorian Field Artillery Brigade in 1909 and, on enlisting in the AIF, was appointed to command the 2nd AFA Brigade. His counterpart in the 3rd AFA Brigade was Melbourne architect Lieutenant Colonel Charles Rosenthal, who had enlisted in the Geelong Battery of the Victorian Militia Artillery in 1892, and in 1908 was promoted major to command a howitzer battery. In 1914 he assumed command of the 2nd Field Artillery Brigade CF before his enlistment in the AIF.[9]

Lieutenant Colonel Charles Rosenthal, Commanding Officer of the 3rd Australian Field Artillery Brigade at Anzac (Wikipedia).

Training in Egypt

Training of the ANZAC artillery commenced in earnest as soon as the AIF and NZEF arrived in Egypt. In accordance with *Field Artillery Training,* the men initially continued to receive individual instruction—duties in action, laying, gun drill, fuse setting, signalling, musketry, gun maintenance, reconnaissance and range finding—and, once the horses had recovered from their long voyage, equitation and driving. Battery manoeuvres—advancing, retiring, deploying, route marching, ammunition resupply, fire discipline, and dry firing—followed, with Lieutenant Byrne of the NZFA noting that 'the country was not eminently suited for artillery training, and the heavy sand made hard going for the horses, and heavy work for the gunners.'[10]

On 12 January the 1st Australian Division recorded that thirty rounds per 18-pounder would be available for training and, eight days later, live firing commenced with an elementary firing practice for the AFA brigades. The records indicate that this practice consisted of each battery occupying an open position and firing a total of twenty-four rounds (six rounds per gun) at three different targets represented by screens. The 1st AFA Battery began the firings and Bridges recorded its efforts as 'bad'. Subsequent batteries fared somewhat better, with gunners from the 4th AFA Battery very pleased to have bested their mostly PF counterparts. Artillery brigade training—route marching, selection and occupation of positions, application of fire and cooperation with other arms—followed in late January and continued through February.[11]

Brigadier General Charles Cunliffe-Owen, Birdwood's artillery adviser at HQ ANZAC (Wikipedia).

In early February, Brigadier General Charles Cunliffe-Owen, a British officer, arrived to become the Brigadier General Royal Artillery (BGRA) at HQ ANZAC. A graduate of the Royal Military Academy, Woolwich, he had been commissioned into the RA in 1883, and subsequently saw service in India and the South African War. He was the British Military Attaché in Greece during the Balkan Wars and in Constantinople from 1913 until August 1914, during which time he completed a survey of the Dardanelles defences. In the first months of the war he had commanded a field artillery brigade during the 'Great Retreat' and the Battle of the Aisne, and temporarily commanded an infantry brigade at the First Battle of Ypres.

As the senior gunner in the Corps, Cunliffe-Owen would be the artillery adviser to Birdwood, having neither staff nor any command function over the divisional artilleries. Both he and Birdwood noted the lack of experience in the divisional artilleries. Commenting on the capabilities of the AIF and NZEF in December 1914, Birdwood had remarked, 'Their artillery too is very indifferent', and on 2 February 1915 wrote, 'I find that 80 per cent of my Australian and 50 per cent of the NZ artillery have never yet seen a gun fired.' This is perhaps an exaggeration given the percentage of enlistees with previous training and the live firings that had occurred in January, but reflective of a nascent artillery capability.[12]

Cunliffe-Owen recollected after the war that when he arrived the artillery 'was practically untrained. No one had ever worked with a bigger unit than a battery ... and cooperation between units was unknown ... Very few officers had ever shot a battery.'[13] Rosenthal took exception to these remarks, asserting that 'The First Australian

Divisional Artillery was composed of at least 80% of well trained officers and men' and that 'All officers in Australia in pre-war days had ample opportunity every year to shoot their batteries, ammunition allowance being very liberal.'[14] Nonetheless, when Birdwood and Cunliffe-Owen first saw them, all the Australian and New Zealand batteries and artillery headquarters were recently raised, there had been little time to reach a level of tecÚical proficiency let alone undertake collective training, many of the commanders were in positions at a higher level than they had occupied in peacetime, and few would have exercised batteries or artillery brigades tactically.

Cunliffe-Owen's experience meant that he was well placed to guide the artillery training. He gave lectures on modern warfare in France and Belgium to all the artillery officers and non-commissioned officers (NCOs) and personally participated in battery training, covering aspects such as adjusting the fall of shot from a flank, taking advantage of ground when deploying, arranging combined shoots with the infantry brigades, and ammunition resupply.[15] Even so, before his arrival Hobbs and Napier JoÚston had already moved to align training with lessons from the war based on reports available from officers in France and 'Notes On Artillery In The Present

War' issued by the headquarters of the BEF. The tenor of the advice was that the modern battlefield was largely empty, direct fire was impractical, concealment was paramount, indirect laying was the norm, observers were displaced from the battery, and communications were proving difficult.[16]

Hobbs gave lectures on these notes in late December 1914, with Sergeant Ellsworth of the 4th AFA Battery writing home that 'all our drill has been altered', explaining that occupying a position would be done 'in the dead of night & as soon as we get there we have to dig the guns and wagons into the ground & entirely concealed from the enemy. The ground', he wrote, 'is banked up 4 feet high all around the guns & trenches for the gunners are dug 6 feet deep on each side', somewhat similar to the field works shown in *Field Artillery Training*.[17] During subsequent training, the Australian batteries often reported occupying positions in accordance with these precepts. They also conducted indirect firings from concealed and prepared positions, with the 4th AFA Battery conducting a shoot as if with aircraft observation and, separately, the 3rd AFA Brigade drawing praise from Birdwood and Cunliffe-Owen during practices in mid-February.[18]

Byrne records that the New Zealand batteries undertook similar deployments, and Henderson's history of the New Zealand artillery contains a quote from the diary of a New Zealand gunner referring to an indirect firing practice on 29 January that Napier Jo(ston apparently characterised as the 'best shooting I have ever seen in all my experience of artillery'.[19]

Late February and early March saw the Australian batteries conducting section shooting to allow officers other than the battery commander to practise ranging (the adjustment of fire onto a target), a task inherent to indirect fire.[20] Observation of fire was primarily the responsibility of the battery commander, and the training of the other officers was designed to equip them to step in should he become a casualty.[21]

A New Zealand field artillery battery returning to camp at Maadi, south of Cairo, after training in the local area. Sand and dust often made movement of the guns and ammunition wagons difficult (AWM H18499).

For the remainder of March the ANZAC gunners continued battery and brigade training, undertook tactical manoeuvres with the infantry brigades, and participated in divisional artillery, divisional signals, and ammunition resupply exercises. No further live firings were recorded in the available war diaries. On 5 March Birdwood advised the divisional commanders that ANZAC was earmarked for operations at Gallipoli, early advice suggesting that the 1st Australian Division would land on the south of the peninsula while the NZ&A Division would land on the Asian shore. As a sign of impending action all the artillery brigades were involved in camouflage painting of guns and wagons. Some batteries practised the passage of obstacles, including the negotiation of steep slopes with guns and wagons, the rafting of guns, and the swimming of horses.[22]

As a further sign of forthcoming commitment to battle, in late March the ANZAC artillery was strengthened with the allocation of the 7th Indian Mountain Artillery (IMA) Brigade as Corps Troops artillery. The Brigade consisted of two batteries, the 21st (Kohat) and 26th (Jacob's), each with six BL 10-pounder (2.75-inch, 70mm) mountain guns capable of firing explosive (gunpowder), shrapnel and star ammunition. These were older pattern weapons, without on-carriage recoil and traverse mechanisms.[23]

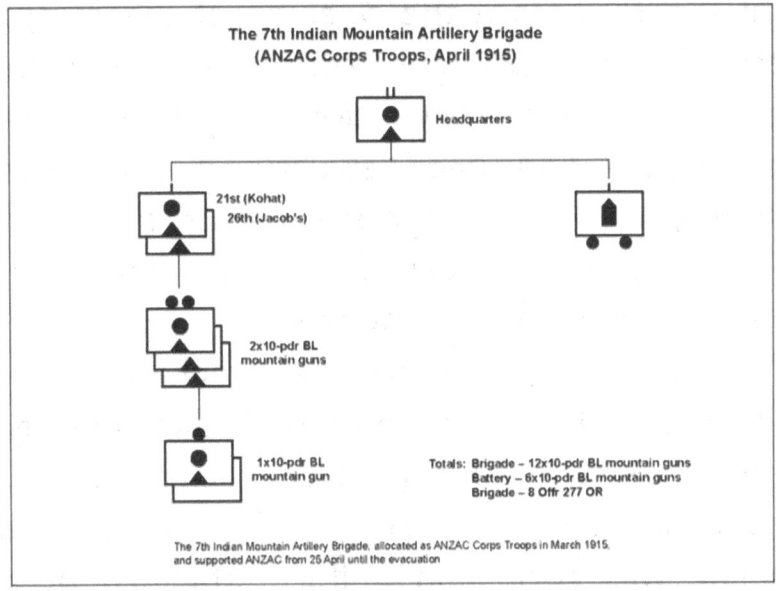

Organisation Chart 3. The 7th Indian Mountain Artillery Brigade

The ANZAC artillery entrained for Alexandria at the beginning of April. There it was loaded on the transports bound for Mudros Harbour on the island of Lemnos, and then Gallipoli. In the three and a half months of training that had been available, the gunners had attempted to blend the pre-war training regimes of *Field Artillery Training* with the emerging realities of the war. The time granted to them had been short, and the development of shooting prowess limited by ammunition shortages. The latter particularly affected the New Zealand howitzer battery. It did not fire before going into action on the peninsula as the only rounds available until shortly before the opening of the campaign were the 800 brought from home, and these were reserved for operations.[24] Nevertheless, the training had been structured and orderly, following a logical progression from fundamental to more complex skills. Credit for this must go to Hobbs and Napier JoÚston.

Summarising what had been achieved by the end of March, Hobbs recorded that, during its time in Egypt, each Australian battery fired 120 rounds, including two series of night firing, that training was good and uniform throughout and, by 25 March, he adjudged the divisional artillery was ready for war. Byrne wrote of the New Zealanders, 'Long days—and nights—of training had brought ample reward ... Units had become a coherent, disciplined, and perfectly efficient force ... Individually the men were in perfect physical condition, and were full of eager anticipation'. Whether the training of both artilleries was sufficient was about to be tested. It continued in Mudros Harbour with practice landings of the guns and the slinging of horses, and it was there on 11 April that ANZAC learnt of its role in the forthcoming campaign, and orders for the landing were drafted and promulgated.[25]

The Anzac Battlefield

ANZAC's commitment to Gallipoli had its genesis in the failure of the Anglo-French fleet to force the Dardanelles on 18 March 1915, and the subsequent acceptance in London of the recommendation of General Sir Ian Hamilton, GOC Mediterranean Expeditionary Force (MEF), and his naval counterpart, that military forces should be committed. Hamilton's plan was to capture the southern portion of the Gallipoli peninsula, thus removing the Ottoman batteries firing from the western shore of the Straits.

The main assault (see Map 1) would be made by the British 29th Division. Landing at Cape Helles, on the toe of the peninsula, it would advance up the nine-kilometre-long, glacis-like slope and secure the Achi Baba Ridge. From there, reinforced by the divisional-sized French Corps Expeditionnaire D'Orient (CEO), it would then strike north and take the Kilid Bahr Plateau. Rising to an average elevation of 170 metres, the plateau sits like a great bastion astride the peninsula, overlooking the narrowest part of the Dardanelles, where its fortifications masked the heavy artillery batteries that covered both the Narrows and the approaches to it. To the north, it dominates the broad valley, some three to six kilometres wide, running west-east from the promontory at Gaba Tepe on the Aegean coast to Maidos (modern-day Eceabat) on the Dardanelles. Horse-drawn artillery can move easily along the full length of the valley. Overlooking the valley further north is the Sari Bair Range. Undertaking a subsidiary operation, ANZAC would seize the heights of Sari Bair, and then advance east to cut the Ottoman road communications, with the intention of stopping reinforcements from the north reaching Kilid Bahr.

With its feet lying on the Aegean, and running north-east, the Sari Bair Range (see Map 2) thrusts inland for six kilometres, rising to a height of almost 300 metres at Hill 971, four kilometres from the coast. From there it extends another two kilometres to a broad bluff 150 metres high overlooking a low saddle, through which the Maidos-Boghali-Biyuk Anafarta road ran. The range is a commanding feature. Its tactical importance lies in its extensive fields of observation over the surrounding country, and its dominance over the roads north of Maidos, which itself was a major ferry point across the Dardanelles. With artillery observation posts on the heights, field guns on its southern flanks could command the whole of the Maidos-Gaba Tepe valley, providing an interlocking field of fire with guns on the northern side of the Kilid Bahr

Plateau. Ottoman forces occupying the range would pose a direct threat to the flank of any force attempting to push across the valley from Gaba Tepe. Thus an Allied force seeking to isolate or attack the Kilid Bahr Plateau from the west, north-west and north had to secure Sari Bair.

From the coast to the broad bluff, numerous ridges and spurs shoot out from Sari Bair. On the northern side they drop sharply, intermingled with cliffs and a mass of tangled, steep-sided gullies and valleys, many of which are so broken as to make egress from the beach to the crest of the range extremely difficult. They are difficult to ascend, and provide excellent delaying positions to the high ground. These would feature during the August Offensive.

On the southern side of the range only three significant ridges exist. These are broader than those to the north and descend gently, like long fingers, to the Gaba Tepe-Maidos valley. Movement along the crests is easy and they provide suitable approaches to the spine of the range. Tactically, the most significant of them, and ANZAC's ultimate objective, slips off the range 500 metres east of Hill 971 running almost due south for four and a half kilometres to Mal Tepe, a 160-metre-high hill two and a half kilometres from the Dardanelles. This ridge dominated the road junctions in the area and the 1915 north-south land communications down the peninsula; the current coastal road skirting the shore of the Dardanelles did not exist at that time. Holding Mal Tepe and the ridge to the crest of Sari Bair would interdict these routes and cut off the forces on the Kilid Bahr Plateau from those in the north of the peninsula. Mal Tepe also provides observation over the kink in the Dardanelles and its narrowest section, enabling the accurate adjustment of naval and artillery gunfire over this portion of the waterway and the main ferry points between the peninsula and the Asiatic shore.

From Hill 971 (see Map 3), the spine of the range runs south-west towards the Aegean coast through Hill Q, a two-humped feature, to the slightly lower height of Chunuk Bair, where the range bifurcates and the next prominent ridge on the southern side of the range, Third or Gun Ridge, branches off to the south to end at Gaba Tepe on the coast. These three heights were the vital ground. Whoever held them controlled the Sari Bair Range. Hill 971 covers the upper reaches of the Mal Tepe Ridge, and Chunuk Bair covers those of Third Ridge—any force holding them can sweep down and take an enemy line along the two ridges from the flank. The heights also provide observation over both the

Maidos-Gaba Tepe valley to the south and the Anafarta Valley in the north, covering the main road junctions, and enabling accurate adjustment of artillery and naval gunfire to interdict them.

Curving around to the west from Chunuk Bair, Third Ridge descends gently for six kilometres to its low-lying foot at Gaba Tepe. Numerous long spurs run off either side, giving its seaward slopes a corrugated landscape. Any defender holding it sits directly on the flank of an invasion force moving along the Maidos-Gaba Tepe valley, and has observation over the low ground extending to the Mal Tepe Ridge. For the Allies, the ridge offered an avenue of approach to the vital ground and a good position for a flank guard or covering force against any Ottoman forces approaching from Maidos. It also offered good field gun positions with long fields of fire over the valley to the east, while howitzers could hug the folds on its seaward side.

Continuing south-west from Chunuk Bair, the main range descends through another two broad, rounded crests—Battleship Hill and the slightly lower Baby 700—where the range bifurcates again, with the main range continuing as First Ridge—or as it later became known, Russell's Top—and Second Ridge descending to the south-west. Dominating the upper reaches of both First and Second ridges, Baby 700 is the ground of tactical importance for any force occupying either ridge.

Second Ridge, with its steep, almost precipitous seaward slopes, runs south-south-west from Baby 700 for 1000 metres before broadening out into a two-lobed upland known as the 400 Plateau; the northern lobe became known as JoUston's Jolly and the southern, Lone Pine. From there the ridge divides, like the fingers of a hand, into several smaller ridges and spurs. Two go west: the Razorback which drops into Shrapnel Gully, and McCay's Hill, which juts over the northern end of the ribbon of sand that became known as Brighton Beach. Neither offers access for horse-drawn artillery.

Next, Bolton's Ridge slips off the corner of the 400 Plateau, running south-west for a kilometre before turning south and looming over Brighton Beach for another 1300 metres. Inland of Bolton's are six roughly parallel spurs. Branching off Bolton's Ridge, the significant Holly Ridge closely parallels it for 800 metres. Then three short features, Silt Spur, Sniper's Ridge and Weir Ridge, run south off the southern lobe of the plateau forming a series of narrow gullies in between them, making movement inland difficult even for infantry. Finally, Pine Ridge slides off the south-eastern corner of the plateau and cuts south-west for 1000 metres roughly paralleling Bolton's Ridge. Overlooked by the upper reaches of Third Ridge, Battleship Hill and Baby 700, Second Ridge was of little tactical value apart from its extension, Bolton's Ridge, which dominates the northern half of Brighton Beach and provides a steep ascent for any invader coming ashore there; horse-drawn guns could not be hauled up its slopes and the only suitable egress from the beach for them was the mouth of Legge Valley. Once atop Bolton's, however, it provides an avenue of approach for infantry to the vital ground via the 400 Plateau, along Second Ridge to Baby 700 and thence up the main range through Battleship Hill.

Separating Third and Second ridges is the extensive and grass-covered Legge Valley, widening as it descends to reach the coast just north of Gaba Tepe. Horse-drawn artillery could move easily up the length of the valley to the foot of Mortar Ridge, which runs off the southern edge of Baby 700 and provides access for guns taking post on Third Ridge, Pine Ridge and, from it, the 400 Plateau.

From the bifurcation at Baby 700, the spine of the range continues across the Nek, a narrowing of the crest to about 55 metres across before broadening to about 100 metres, and heads south-west for one kilometre as the steep-sided Russell's Top, or First Ridge. It then drops to the aptly named Razor Edge, an exceptionally narrow, sharp-sided 250-metre-long feature, along which a man can walk only with difficulty, before rising again to the small, flat-topped Plugge's Plateau which overlooks Anzac Cove. From Plugge's the ground drops sharply to Ari Burnu, the northern headland of Anzac Cove, while to the south it descends as a long spur—MacLagan's Ridge—enclosing the cove to Hell Spit, a small, rounded headland, which offered relatively flat ground that was suitable for a gun position.

The northern side of First Ridge drops sharply in tangled gullies and cliffs, the most prominent being The Sphinx, which thrusts out from Russell's Top presenting a perpendicular face to the coast. The only suitable access to Russell's Top from North Beach is up Walker's Ridge. With its foot 650 metres north of Anzac Cove and 100 metres from the sea, this narrow spur ascends steeply to join Russell's Top 300 metres short of the Nek. On the southern side of Russell's Top, the narrow, steep-sided Monash Valley separates First and Second ridges. Running from the Nek into Shrapnel Gully, the valley emerges on the coast at the northern end of Brighton Beach between Hell Spit and McCay's Hill, and movement by horse-drawn artillery up its length is extremely difficult. In April 1915 most of the battlefield was covered in knee to waist-high scrub, except for the aptly named Pine Ridge which was clothed in pine trees. Only JoÚston's Jolly—the northern lobe of the 400 Plateau—the flat-bottomed Legge Valley, and the broad Maidos-Gaba Tepe plain were grassed.

The ANZAC Plans

To achieve his objective, Birdwood decided on a two-phase operation. In phase one, Bridges' 1st Australian Division would seize a covering position extending in a wide arc from the Fisherman's Hut on the coast some 1600 metres north of Anzac Cove, to Chunuk Bair and down along Third Ridge to Gaba Tepe. Behind this screen, which was designed to delay and disrupt any Ottoman reinforcements, the remainder of the Corps would land, ostensibly unmolested. In the second phase, the Corps would advance east to capture the Mal Tepe Ridge, presumably supported by artillery deployed along Third Ridge and/or moving with the infantry.[26]

Given the tortuous nature of the country inland from the Fisherman's Hut and on the northern side of the main range, Bridges decided to limit the size of the covering position to a line from Chunuk Bair along Third Ridge to Gaba

Tepe and extend his mission to include Hill Q and Hill 971, thereby securing the vital ground in the first phase (see Map 4). The 3rd Australian Infantry Brigade would provide the covering force, landing on the northern half of Brighton Beach with its left flank immediately adjacent to Anzac Cove, and seize a position extending from Chunuk Bair along Third Ridge to Gaba Tepe, thus providing a screen to cover the landing of the main body. Following behind, the 2nd Australian Infantry Brigade, echeloned slightly north to include Anzac Cove, would move along First and Second ridges to Baby 700, then up the main range, passing through the left-hand corner of the covering force, and seize the highest features of the range—Hill Q and Hill 971.[27] Naval support would be provided by the 2nd Naval Squadron under Rear Admiral Thursby, whose force consisted of five battleships, a cruiser, eight destroyers, a seaplane carrier, a balloon ship, a submarine depot ship, and four trawlers.[28]

The Ottoman Defence

The defence of the peninsula was entrusted to the Ottoman *Fifth Army* under the German General Otto Liman von Sanders. Responsible for the southern portion was the *9th Infantry*

Division, which had two regiments deployed south of the Kilid Bahr Plateau and one, *the 27th Infantry Regiment,* responsible for the Semerly Tepe-Gaba Tepe-Sari Bair area (see Map 5). Here a light screen of one battalion, the *2nd (2/27th Infantry),* was deployed in isolated platoon posts covering twelve kilometres of coastline from the Fisherman's Hut to Semerly Tepe. The remainder of the regiment, the *1st* and *3rd battalions (1/27th Infantry* and *3/27th Infantry)* and the machine-gun company *(27th MG Company),* were in reserve seven kilometres inland from Gaba Tepe at Maidos on the Dardanelles shore. The *Fifth Army* reserve, the *19th Infantry Division,* was encamped five kilometres due east of Anzac Cove, and could only be deployed with Liman von Sanders' approval.

The *2/27th Infantry's* immediate artillery support comprised the *7th Mountain Battery* of the *3rd Battalion, 9th Field Artillery Regiment (3/9th Artillery).* Its four 75mm (3-inch) mountain guns were located on the 400 Plateau, 900 metres inland from Anzac Cove. Other artillery deployed in the area consisted of two obsolescent 87mm (3.5-inch) 'Mantelli' field guns, one of which was inoperable, at Gaba Tepe three kilometres south of Anzac Cove, and further south still was a six-gun coastal battery of short 150mm (5.9-inch) howitzers, with two pieces at Cam Tepe out of range of Anzac Cove, and four at Palamutluk Sirti (the Olive Grove). These latter weapons were within range of the landing, but the siting of their firing positions and the lack of forward observation prevented them effectively engaging land targets in the first instance.[29]

Should operations develop in the *2/27th Infantry's* area, commanders could call on the mountain guns of the *8th Battery, 3/9th Artillery,* which were in reserve south of Maidos. In addition, the *19th Division's 39th Field Artillery Regiment,* comprising the four field batteries of the *1st* and *2nd battalions (1/39th Artillery* and *2/39th Artillery)* with eight obsolescent 87mm Mantelli guns and eight 75mm guns) and the *3rd Battalion's (3/39th Artillery) 6th Mountain Battery* (four 75mm mountain guns) located at Boghali could be released with *Fifth Army* agreement. The *3/39th Artillery's* other battery had not yet received its guns; they would arrive on 28 April.[30]

Within reach of ANZAC's proposed landing site the Ottomans thus had twelve 75mm mountain guns, eight 75mm field guns, nine 87mm field guns, and four 150mm howitzers, a mixture of modern and older types. The 75mm field guns (Krupp 75mm *Feldkanone* L30/03) and most of the mountain guns (Krupp 75mm *Gebirgskanone* L14/05) were modern QF types firing shrapnel and HE (Picric acid) shells. The howitzers were either the Krupp 150mm *schwere Feldhaubitze* L14/05, a modern QF type firing similar types of ammunition to the field and mountain guns, or possibly the Krupp 150mm *schwere Feldhaubitze* 1893. These and the 'Mantelli' field guns (Krupp 87mm *Feldkanone* L24/85) were obsolescent breech-loaders without on-carriage recoil and traverse, whose explosive rounds were filled with gunpowder rather than HE, and thus less effective. If ANZAC could get its guns ashore relatively quickly it would have superior field gun strength and a rough parity in howitzer and mountain gun strength, although the Ottoman mountain gun was the more modern weapon.[31]

Fire Support Plans

For the covering force action, Birdwood decided against a preliminary naval bombardment in favour of a surprise pre-dawn landing. Once the troops were ashore, the naval covering force, the battleships HMS *Triumph* and *Majestic* and the cruiser HMS *Bacchante*, would provide the initial fire support. The Indian mountain batteries would be the first artillery into action, and it was expected that fire from the battleships HMS *Queen*, *London* and *Prince of Wales*, and perhaps the fire of the destroyers would become available once they had completed their role in ferrying the troops. There was no immediate role for the field artillery.

Cunliffe-Owen issued two instructions concerning naval gunfire and the functions and requirements of the related observation officers. He also chaired a conference on board the transport *Minnewaska* on 21 April in which the naval gunfire support arrangements were discussed in detail with all concerned, including captains of ships, signals, aircraft and gunnery officers, and army unit commanders. A further conference was held in which he discussed the questions of fire support and observation with the gunnery and signals officers concerned. By this stage Hobbs had already allotted zones to the three artillery officers seconded to duty as naval gunfire observers. Dividing the landing zone in half, he allotted the southern sector to two observers working with HMS *Triumph,* and the northern sector to the other observer and HMS *Majestic.*[32]

The pre-dreadnought battleship HMS Majestic. Launched in 1895, Majestic carried four 12-inch guns, twelve 6-inch guns and sixteen 12-pounder (3-inch) guns. She took part in the bombardment of the Dardanelles forts and the attempt to force the Straits on 18 March, and on 25 April supported the ANZAC landing as one of the covering battleships, engaging Ottoman troops threatening to attack the left flank of the beachhead in the afternoon. She continued to provide fire support in the following weeks before being torpedoed and sunk off Cape Helles on 27 May (Wikipedia).

Naval orders noted that the primary target for the ships was the Ottoman artillery, best engaged with shrapnel unless destruction was warranted. The secondary objective was Ottoman troops. For these purposes, the ammunition allocation was twenty rounds per gun of main armament, and eighty to 100 rounds per gun of secondary armament.[33] To provide observation, the seaplane carrier HMS *Ark Royal* was to send an aircraft aloft, even though it was limited in its ability to communicate with the ships, while the balloon ship HMS *Manica* would provide a tethered observation balloon linked to the ship by telephone. Ashore, two flank radio stations were to be established to pass fire tasks from the forward brigades to the ships, with the naval gunfire observers linked to these stations by telephone line. Until these shore resources could be emplaced, and as a means of identifying the forward troops, the infantry were to carry red and yellow flags to mark their positions. These flags could be waved if fire was required and held steady when it was effective, illustrating the limitations of communications at the time.[34] The instructions issued by Cunliffe-Owen, the conferences he chaired, and the considerable number of instructions contained in the various war diaries show that the preparations for the provision of naval gunfire support, and indeed for the landings of the infantry and other supporting units, were more comprehensive than is sometimes suggested.

The balloon ship HMS Manica. Acquired in March 1915, Manica was a converted cargo steamship whose forward hold was rebuilt to allow a kite balloon to be stowed and launched. Arriving in Lemnos on 14 April, Manica supported the ANZAC landing on 25 April, sending up a kite balloon at 5.00am with two observers to spot for naval gunfire support and report on activities ashore. Thereafter she supported ANZAC and later IX Corps at Suvla for the remainder of the campaign (Wikipedia).

The only artillery tasking was the attachment of the 7th IMA Brigade to the covering force. The Brigade was directed to take position on the 400 Plateau on Second Ridge and support the troops on the main range and in the centre of Third Ridge. While Hobbs circulated detailed instructions for the disembarkation of the guns, it appears that neither he nor Napier Jouston issued tactical orders relating to the tasks for the field guns once they were ashore, other than assigning the 3rd AFA Battery to the 3rd AFA Brigade until its parent headquarters had landed.[35]

25 April 1915

At 4.30am on Sunday 25 April 1915, the 3rd Australian Infantry Brigade landed and swept aside the Ottoman rifle platoon above Anzac Cove. Ahead of it, Third Ridge lay undefended as the men moved quickly inland. However, apart from three small parties of Australians, the brigade failed to reach its objective. Almost immediately after landing, the brigade commander, Colonel Ewan Sinclair-MacLagan, put the brakes on the advance, ordering the covering force to halt and dig in along the seaward edge of Second Ridge, 900 metres from Anzac Cove, and roughly 1500 metres short of his brigade's objective. Returning to the beach, he then diverted the 2nd Australian Infantry Brigade away from the main range to the right flank on McCay's Hill and Bolton's Ridge, the lower slopes of Second Ridge. These two hasty decisions turned the landing from an offensive operation to a defensive one, handing the initiative to the enemy. Once ashore, the divisional commander, Bridges, did nothing to revitalise the advance while there was still the opportunity. Consequently, the Australians lay unmolested on Second Ridge until the Ottoman counter-attacks began around midday.[36]

Initially the Ottoman artillery played little part in opposing the landing. The lone operable 87mm field gun at Gaba Tepe opened fire at 4.45am, engaging the boats bringing in successive waves but, with a slow rate of fire, had little effect. Captain Sadik, commanding the *7th Mountain Battery* at Lone Pine, refused calls to fire on Anzac Cove, insisting that the orders to do so had to come from the Commanding Officer of the *2/27th Infantry*. Before these arrived, however, the fleeing Ottoman infantry reported that the enemy were close on their heels. Sadik ordered the guns to be dismantled and packed onto mules so as to join the retreat, but the battery was overrun, with only one gun escaping.

Men of the 2nd Australian Infantry Brigade landing at around 5.00am on 25 April. The Cressy class cruiser HMS Bacchante is offshore in the middle distance engaging the Ottoman 87mm field gun at Gaba Tepe to little effect, as the gun continued a slow shelling of boats coming ashore throughout the morning (AWM P10140.004).

The first Ottoman reinforcements, the *1/27th Infantry, 3/27th Infantry* and the *27th MG Company*, began arriving at the southern end of Third Ridge at 7.40am, soon to be joined by the lone gun of the *7th Mountain Battery, 3/9th Artillery*, that had evaded capture and, at 10.30am, by the four guns of the *8th Mountain Battery, 3/9th Artillery*. A little later, an Ottoman warship off Maidos in the Dardanelles began shelling the transports, forcing them to retire temporarily. In the north of the landing area the leading elements of the *57th Infantry Regiment*

(19th Division) reached Chunuk Bair-Hill 971 at around 10.00am, followed later by the *6th Mountain Battery, 3/39th Artillery*. However, it was midday before that regiment was in a position to launch its counter-attack down the main range, supported by the *1/27th Infantry* attacking Lone Pine, and the nine guns of the *6th, 7th* and *8th Mountain batteries* firing from superior positions on Chunuk Bair and Third Ridge.[37]

At this point, a few companies of Australian infantry held Baby 700 on the Sari Bair Range, the ground of tactical importance for the ANZAC line along Second Ridge, and around 180 men of the 11th Battalion held Battleship Hill, the next feature inland. Reinforcements were sent to support them, but many were diverted to join the bulk of the two brigades holding the lower portions of Second Ridge and the area south of Lone Pine. The only artillery support available comprised the mountain guns of the 26th (Jacob's) Battery, which had come ashore around 10.00am, and by midday were in action on the 400 Plateau. Naval gunfire was available, but the communications were as yet incomplete.[38]

A battery of Ottoman 75mm mountain guns. Four of these guns of the 3/9th Artillery were on the 400 Plateau on the morning of 25 April, but did not fire. Three were captured by the Australians at around 6.00am, but were recaptured by the 1/27th Infantry that afternoon. Nine of them (five from the 3/9th Artillery and a battery of the 39th Artillery Regiment), firing from superior positions on Third Ridge, forced the 26th (Jacob's) Battery on the 400 Plateau out of action at 2.30pm on 25 April (Ed Erickson image).

The counter-attack launched by the three battalions of the *57th Infantry Regiment* swept down the main range, pushed back the small force on Battleship Hill and, after a gruelling firefight, at 4.30pm drove the mix of Australian and New Zealanders off Baby 700 and back along Russell's Top. The attacks won for the Ottomans possession of a portion of Russell's Top around the Nek, Baby 700, and the upper end of Second Ridge, which gave them observation and fields of fire along the ANZAC line as far as Lone Pine, and of the upper reaches of Monash Valley, the principal supply route to the ANZAC front line. Further south the *1/27th Infantry* pushed the Australians back across Lone Pine and recaptured the three mountain guns lost in the morning.[39]

Indian mountain gunners and two of their 10-pounder mountain guns on the beach at Anzac Cove at around 10.30am, 25 April. Australian engineers are standing in the foreground. From here the battery went into action on the 400 Plateau at midday, providing the only artillery support to the infantry on 25 April, but were driven out of action at 2.30pm by fire from the Ottoman mountain guns on Third Ridge (Alexander Turnbull Library PAColl-7581-84).

The ANZAC infantry fought the day largely without artillery assistance as hostile batteries had forced the 26th Battery out of action by 2.30pm. Naval gunfire support was limited because the terrain in the centre generally masked Ottoman movement, and the closeness of the fighting made it difficult for those seeking to call for fire to accurately locate the enemy and their own troops. On top of this, the observers were not yet linked to the flank radio stations by telephone.[40] Therefore, the ships could only become involved when they could see an obvious target. HMS *Bacchante* took on the single 87mm field gun at Gaba Tepe, apparently with little effect as the gun continued firing throughout the day, and in the afternoon HMS *Majestic* successfully engaged Ottoman troops on the northern flank threatening to mount an attack. In depth, the ships performed more valuable service. The Ottoman warship that shelled the transports in the early morning was driven off by fire from HMS *Triumph*.[41]

Anzac Cove at around 10.30am on 25 April showing the mast of the left flank wireless station established at the northern end of the cove to provide communications for naval gunfire support between the Forward Observation Officers and the battleships and cruisers lying offshore. The Cressy class cruiser HMS Bacchante is offshore. In the event, telephone communications between the Forward Observation Officers and the wireless stations was not established until 26 April (AWM G00905 copy held by AAHU).

By nightfall on 25 April, Birdwood's force found itself confined to a narrow, shallow, cramped beachhead of roughly 161 hectares (see Map 6). Charles Bean likened it to a Greek amphitheatre in which ANZAC occupied the stage, and the Ottomans the tiers of seating. In outline from north to south, the ANZAC line ran from the foot of Walker's Ridge (on the coast around 650 metres north of Anzac Cove) up the steep ridge to Russell's Top, where it swung north-west along the Top to a point 130 metres short of the Nek and 1300 metres from Anzac Cove. To the right was a gap where the head of the left fork of Monash Valley separated the Top from Pope's Hill, a short spur dropping from the flank of Baby 700, of which the Anzacs held the lower portion. Another larger gap existed between Pope's where Waterfall Gully and the Bloody Angle, the heads of the right fork of Monash Valley, and Dead Man's Ridge cut through the Anzac line. Recommencing at Quinn's Post, the line followed the seaward edge of Second Ridge to the 400 Plateau—JoÚston's Jolly and Lone Pine—before swinging back towards the coast and down Bolton's Ridge to a point 1300 metres south of Anzac Cove.[42]

This small beachhead would prove a difficult prospect for the ANZAC gunners. The shallowness of the area between the beach and the front line and the preponderance of steep ridges and narrow valleys offered very few positions suitable for the 18-pounders with their relatively flat trajectory. There was little room to manoeuvre, the area provided no depth and it restricted the number of guns that could be landed. Furthermore, the Ottomans held the high ground overlooking the ANZAC position, giving them superior observation and direct-fire positions. The terrain behind Third Ridge also enabled them to site most of their guns and howitzers in defilade, out of sight of the Anzac observers, and gave them space to change battery positions should they be engaged by counter-battery fire, a luxury the ANZAC gunners would be denied.

Chapter Three

INTO ACTION

Disembarkation

As previously indicated, the 1st Australian Division's orders for the landing made no mention of the artillery's tasks apart from the attachment of the 7th IMA Brigade to the covering force and the 3rd AFA Battery to the 3rd AFA Brigade.[1] While waiting at Mudros, Hobbs circulated instructions for the disembarkation of the guns which stated that, once landed, batteries were to move to rendezvous points in the beachhead from which they would be directed to tactical positions.[2]

Once the mountain gunners had landed from the transports *Hessen* (26th Battery) and *Pera* (21st Battery), Covering Force orders directed them to take position on the 400 Plateau on Second Ridge and support the troops on the main range and in the centre of Third Ridge.[3] The two batteries should have landed at around 8.30am, but it was 10.00am before the first—the 26th (Jacob's)—arrived, and around noon before it came into action between Lone Pine and JoÚston's Jolly. The 21st (Kohat) Battery, for which the lighters arrived at 3.00pm and the tugs at 5.30pm, landed at 6.00pm.[4]

The field artillery was to go ashore once the infantry of the 1st Australian Division had been landed. According to naval arrangements, the sequence in which the artillery transports were to discharge was not specified, the principle being that they would either 'berth in the anchorages or remain under way some distance out as the military situation requires, and continue disembarkation according to the List of Tows with Military Transport officers.' However, in his operation order, General Bridges of the 1st Australian Division directed that batteries on two transports, *Karoo* and *Cardiganshire,* 'will disembark first'. This was subsequently reflected in an indicative order of arrival for the ships issued by the navy, which also showed the Australian artillery transports generally preceding their New Zealand counterparts, mirroring the order of landing of the divisions.[5]

The apparent reason Bridges wanted *Karoo* and *Cardiganshire* to discharge as a priority was that they carried the principal elements of the two artillery brigades supporting the two leading infantry brigades. *Karoo* carried the 2nd AFA Brigade headquarters along with the 4th, 5th and 8th AFA batteries; *Cardiganshire* carried the headquarters of the 3rd AFA Brigade, its ammunition column and the 7th and 3rd AFA batteries. It is puzzling that the 3rd and 8th batteries were loaded on ships with an artillery brigade headquarters other than their own. Prima facie, to maintain normal affiliations the 6th Battery should have travelled on *Karoo* instead of the 8th, and the 8th Battery on *Cardiganshire* in place of the 3rd, which was a 1st AFA Brigade battery. These anomalies may have stemmed from the relatively rushed loading of the division in Alexandria. Whatever the cause, the presence of the 3rd Battery on *Cardiganshire* explains the statement in divisional orders that the 3rd AFA Battery would be attached to the 3rd AFA Brigade until the 1st AFA Brigade landed. No such allotment was necessary for the 8th Battery because it could join its parent brigade immediately on landing.[6]

The remainder of the Australian divisional artillery was spread across four transports: *Indian* with the headquarters of the 1st AFA brigade, its ammunition column, and the 2nd AFA Battery; *Atlantian* carrying the 1st and 9th AFA batteries; *Itria,* with the 6th AFA Battery; and *Armadale* with the 2nd AFA Brigade ammunition column. The NZ&A Division's artillery was carried on *Katuna,* which embarked the 1st NZFA Battery; *Australind* with some NZFA Brigade personnel as well as the 4th NZFA (Howitzer) Battery and its ammunition column; *Californian,* the 3rd NZFA Battery and part of the brigade ammunition column; and *Surada,* the 2nd NZFA Battery and the remainder of the brigade ammunition column.[7]

In terms of ammunition, the field batteries were to carry 176 rounds per gun, and the corps would establish an ammunition point at the beach to provide a temporary additional supply. This would consist of 3000 rounds of 18-pounder ammunition and 150 rounds of 10-pounder for the Australian division, and 1300 rounds of 18-pounder for the New Zealanders.[8]

25 April—A Day of Frustration

Arriving on the beach mid-morning, Hobbs and Napier JoÚston discovered that the front line was static and there was little room to deploy their guns. Constrained by steep hills and gullies, and realising that there was almost no possibility of employing guns on the left and centre of the position, at 11.30am Hobbs headed to the right, initially selecting a position for two guns on the southern end of MacLagan's Ridge above Anzac Cove, some 740 metres behind the infantry clinging to the western edge of Second Ridge.[9] New Zealand troops were generally directed to the left of the ANZAC position, limiting the area in which Napier JoÚston might search.

Colonel Hobbs and members of the 1st Australian Divisional Artillery coming ashore on Ari Burnu Point at 10.30am on 25 April. Hobbs is centre foreground in the pith helmet and to his left is his Brigade Major Royal Artillery, Major Stuart Anderson (AWM G00904, copy held by AAHU).

At 1.00pm Rosenthal of the 3rd AFA Brigade was rowed ashore by members of his ammunition column in advance of any of his guns. Reporting to Hobbs at around 1.30pm, he was told that General Bridges had decided no guns were to be landed.[10] After the war the divisional Chief of Staff at the time, Colonel Cyril Brudenell White, gave four reasons for Bridges' unusual decision: the ground was impractical for 18-pounders; with the position of his leading troops uncertain, artillery could not usefully support them; given the tactical situation at the time the guns on shore might be vulnerable to capture; and Bridges may have been considering evacuation quite early in the day.[11]

Offshore, the disembarkation of the guns was disrupted by the shelling of the anchorages. Despite this several reached the beach, only to be turned back in accordance with Bridges' injunction. However, one from Major Owen Phillips' 4th AFA Battery—along with the 2nd AFA Brigade commander, George JoÚston, and a portion of his headquarters—came ashore at 3.30pm. It was hauled up onto the southern end of MacLagan's Ridge at Hell Spit where it went into action at 6.00pm, firing 62 rounds at the Ottoman field gun at Gaba Tepe.[12] Perversely, the 2nd and 3rd brigade ammunition columns had more success in getting men ashore on the first day, landing forty-eight and twenty-one men respectively.[13]

That evening Rosenthal reconnoitred the right flank behind the infantry firing line and reported that he could effectively position a battery on Bolton's Ridge and another on what later became known as Shell Green. Bridges initially agreed, but then restricted him to two guns, perhaps because the overall situation was grave. Later that evening Bridges urged Birdwood to evacuate the whole force, a recommendation Birdwood forwarded to Hamilton, who overruled it around midnight, ordering ANZAC to dig in.[14] By way of contrast, the British 29th Division at Helles, landing with heavy casualties against much stronger opposition and gaining only a very precarious foothold several hundred metres deep, was preparing to force its way inland the next morning. Despite the shallowness of the toehold around W and X beaches, and demonstrating a willingness to sacrifice guns if necessary to support the infantry, the British gunners had six field guns, four mountain guns and a section of 4.5-inch howitzers ashore by the evening of the 25th, albeit assisted by the fact that the terrain was more suitable for artillery than that of Anzac.[15]

An 18-pounder gun of the 4th AFA Battery is hauled up a track cut by Australian engineers at the southern end of MacLagan's Ridge at around 5.00pm on 25 April. This was the only field gun landed on 25 April. Coming ashore at 3.30pm it went into action on Hell Spit, the southern headland of Anzac Cove, at 6.00pm, firing sixty-two rounds of shrapnel at the Ottoman 87mm field gun at Gaba Tepe (AWM G00918, copy held by AAHU).

26 to 30 April—The Guns Come Ashore

With the decision that ANZAC would stay, its field guns and howitzers began disembarking. In the NZ&A Division the first section of Major Norris Falla's 4th NZFA (Howitzer) Battery landed at 6.30am on 26 April and, from positions in Anzac Cove and with an observation station on Plugge's Plateau, was in action shortly afterwards. The second section landed around noon and took post on North Beach below Walker's Ridge, where it would remain for the duration of the campaign. Its first target was the Fisherman's Hut.[16]

In the 1st Australian Division, a further party from the 2nd AFA Brigade Ammunition Column arrived, while the men of the 3rd Brigade column were being used to assist the 26th (Jacob's) Battery fight its mountain guns. By this stage, the 21st (Kohat) Battery had come into action in the lower reaches of Monash Valley, with arcs of fire up to the head of the valley and Baby 700.[17]

The landing of the field guns was beset with confusion, with control over their disembarkation lost. Guns were apparently despatched by naval and military transport officers as floats and lighters became available, rather than being called forward by Hobbs or his two brigade commanders ashore, or in accordance with Bridges' instruction that the batteries on *Karoo* and *Cardiganshire* were to be discharged first. Thus, some of the guns that came ashore belonged to the 1st AFA Brigade, whose headquarters was still afloat, rather than the 2nd or 3rd AFA brigades, whose commanders were ashore. Landing at 3.00am, one gun of Major Henry Sweetland's 1st AFA Battery (1st AFA Brigade) was sent to the right flank under Rosenthal's control, going into action on Shell Green before being re-embarked that evening.[18] During the morning the remaining guns of Phillips' 4th AFA Battery (2nd AFA Brigade) arrived, two joining their companion on MacLagan's Ridge, another being sent to Rosenthal, who then controlled two guns from brigades other than his own. A section of Major Gifford King's 3rd AFA Battery (1st AFA Brigade) reached the cove at 12.30pm, and was promptly sent back to its transport by Hobbs, as were one section of Major Reginald Rabett's 2nd AFA Battery (1st AFA Brigade) and two guns of Major Hector

Caddy's 5th AFA Battery (2nd AFA Brigade). The remaining two guns of Caddy's battery had better luck and managed to stay ashore. One joined the 4th Battery on MacLagan's Ridge, while the other was moved into Shrapnel Gully.[19]

Later in the day, one of Rosenthal's 3rd AFA Brigade's batteries, Major Francis Hughes' 7th, landed and was pushed into the infantry firing line on Bolton's Ridge. The three guns in position by nightfall replaced the two guns from the 1st and 4th AFA batteries, which were returned to their parent sub-units. That evening an Ottoman attack was launched against the Australian line at the Wheatfield near the northern end of Bolton's Ridge and Hughes' battery, firing point blank, wreaked havoc among the attackers.

An 18-pounder gun and crew of the 7th AFA Battery in a direct fire position on Bolton's Ridge in late April/early May. This battery landed on 26 April and helped repulse the series of Ottoman attacks that occurred throughout 27

April. Above the slouch hat of the left-hand man is a range-finder leaning against the sandbag wall, while some of the ammunition is stacked beside the gunner lying against the wall (AWM P00117.053).

Observers scan the enemy line for targets on 30 April 1915 from a gun of the 7th AFA Battery, 3rd AFA Brigade, deployed close to the front line on Bolton's Ridge. The Battery Commander, Major Hughes, is at the range-finder in the centre of the photograph, while the Brigade Commander, Lieutenant Colonel Rosenthal, observes through binoculars to his left. Camouflage is rudimentary, and the gun wheel is partially covered to prevent its iron tyre glinting in the sun (AWM J06134).

The final guns to arrive were from Major Alfred Bessell-Browne's 8th AFA Battery, also of the 3rd AFA Brigade. The battery brought a section ashore at 2.30pm and both guns were dragged up to a rendezvous on the right flank where, at 6.30pm, despite Rosenthal's preparations to receive them, they were ordered to re-embark, together with another gun of the battery that had landed later in the afternoon.[20] The reasons for the re-embarkation of this battery are hard to fathom; it was part of Rosenthal's command, positions for two of its guns were being prepared and, together with the 7th AFA Battery, its arrival gave Rosenthal control of two of his three batteries in an area where suitable battery positions existed.

The disorder of the day, which saw ten of the nineteen Australian guns returned to their transports, probably resulted from factors such as Hobbs' preoccupation with finding suitable positions to the detriment of coordination, the lack of experience of his small staff, difficulty in communication between shore and ship and at the anchorages, and the fact that, other than those carried on *Karoo* and *Cardiganshire*, there was no prescribed order of landing for the remainder of the artillery. In relation to the latter, the Royal Navy historian recorded that, during the day, the landing of the artillery was disrupted from time to time when Ottoman warships in the Dardanelles fired on the transports. Return fire from the navy controlled by balloon observers scattered these ships each time, but 'the interference was serious'.[21]

Nonetheless, the disruption caused by Ottoman ships does not adequately explain the landing of guns from the 1st AFA Brigade when the priority lay with those from the 2nd and 3rd AFA brigades. Nor does it explain why guns of the 2nd and 3rd brigades were returned to their transports. At the root of the problem was a lack of control over the disembarkation of the guns.

By nightfall on 26 April, ANZAC had four howitzers, ten field and twelve mountain guns ashore, comprising the 4th NZFA (Howitzer) Battery, the 4th and 7th AFA batteries, a section of Caddy's 5th AFA Battery, and the 7th IMA Brigade. Facing them, the Ottomans had a total of thirty-seven guns from the *39th Artillery Regiment* (four mountain and sixteen field guns), the *3/9th Artillery's* two mountain batteries (including the three guns recovered at Lone Pine during the counter-attack on 25 April), the 150mm howitzer position at Palamutluk Sirti, the 87mm Mantelli located at Gaba Tepe, and a mountain battery of the *7th Artillery Regiment* (*7th Infantry Division*) that had arrived after a forced march from the north. This gave the Ottomans a numerical supremacy they were to maintain throughout the campaign, although offset to some degree by ANZAC's naval support. The ability to use that support improved on 26 April when telephone communication between the observers and the naval flank radio stations was established.[22]

In the early hours of 27 April, Major Francis Sykes' 2nd NZFA Battery disembarked, but it was not in action when the Ottomans launched a series of major counter-attacks on the ANZAC line from Russell's Top to Bolton's Ridge throughout the day. The guns already ashore, together with the navy, materially assisted in repelling these attacks although, somewhat strangely, the 21st (Kohat) Battery recorded no firing. On this occasion the ships could see the target and, when the Ottoman *64th Infantry Regiment* poured over the crest of Baby 700, the 12 and 15-inch guns of the battleships *Queen* and *Queen Elizabeth* respectively hammered them, throwing the attack into utter confusion. No Australian guns were landed during the day, perhaps because of the heavy fighting, perhaps because shelling of the beach and tows by Ottoman warships above the Narrows hampered disembarkation. The 6th AFA Battery (2nd AFA Brigade) appeared in the cove at midnight, but it was promptly ordered back to its ship.[23]

Birdwood now set about reorganising his defensive line to correct the mixing of units that had occurred in the early stages of the fighting. He allocated responsibility on the left to the

NZ&A Division, which was to place the New Zealand Infantry Brigade on Walker's Ridge and Russell's Top, and the 4th Australian Infantry Brigade along the upper end of Second Ridge, including what would become Quinn's and Courtney's posts. Extending south from the latter location, the 1st Australian Division was to hold the centre of the line down to the 400 Plateau just south of Lone Pine with the 1st Infantry Brigade, while the 2nd Infantry Brigade would hold the right of the line along Bolton's Ridge to the sea north of Gaba Tepe.[24]

A 4.5-inch howitzer of the 4th NZFA Battery in action in May 1915. This gun landed at dawn on 25 April and took post on North Beach where it remained for the rest of the campaign (Alexander Turnbull Library PA1-0-308-22, copy held by AAHU).

On 28 April, a section of the 2nd NZFA Battery came into action on the spur above Ari Burnu, and the two guns of the 5th AFA Battery that had been sent back to the transports on 26 April returned. No positions for the latter were immediately available, so they were held in reserve.[25] As part of Birdwood's reorganisation, support from the 7th IMA Brigade was split, with the headquarters and the 21st Battery operating with the 1st Australian Division, and the 26th Battery with the NZ&A Division.[26] Control of naval gunfire support was also rearranged with seven artillery officers tasked as observers, each to work through one of the two naval radio stations on shore to send targets and spotting observations via HMS *Queen* to one of six firing ships covering a nominated area of the front. Hobbs acknowledged the intent, but recorded that these officers were still experiencing great difficulty in observing the results of the fire owing to the nature of the ground.[27]

Two guns of the 2nd NZFA Battery on the Ari Burnu spur (the northern headland of Anzac Cove) photographed between 28 April and 9 May. The battery landed in the early hours of 27 April, and one section came into action on this position on 28 April. The rudimentary nature of the position indicates that this photograph was taken very soon after it was occupied. North Beach is in the background with Walker's Ridge running up to Russell's Top on the right background. This section joined the other section of the battery on Plugge's Plateau on 9 May (Stower Collection WF-007559-421).

A horse-drawn gun from Major Frank Symon's 1st NZFA Battery moving along North Beach in the first week of May. Ari Burnu, the southern headland of Anzac Cove, is in the background leading up to Plugge's Plateau on the left of the photograph. The battery landed three guns on 30 April, and the fourth on 1 May. Initially it was positioned on North Beach at the foot of Walker's Ridge but, owing to the restricted fields of fire, was soon withdrawn into reserve. It finally took post on Russell's Top on 17 May (AWM P00196.012).

No guns were landed on 29 April. That night the second section of the 2nd NZFA Battery was hauled up a hastily prepared track to a position on Plugge's Plateau, which also hosted a section from the 26th (Jacob's) Battery.[28] The following day three guns from Major Frank Symon's 1st NZFA Battery came ashore, to be joined by the remaining gun a day later. Napier Jo/Uston initially deployed this battery to the north of Anzac Cove on the narrow beach at the foot of Walker's Ridge. With only a restricted field of fire, it would be withdrawn shortly into reserve, but not before taking the opportunity to support an impending attack.[29]

The Attack on Baby 700, 30 April-3 May 1915

With his line reorganised and the Ottomans beginning to press on his left, Birdwood sought to improve his own position. On 30 April he issued ANZAC Order Number 5, ambitiously calling for the capture the next day of Baby 700, Mortar Ridge, and the western edge of the gully running behind the 400 Plateau and Pine Ridge to its south.[30] Godley of the NZ&A Division sought a deferral to allow more time for planning, and during this period, following a protest by Brigadier General Harold 'Hooky' Walker—Birdwood's Chief of Staff and now commanding the 1st Australian Infantry Brigade following the death of Colonel Henry MacLaurin on 27 April—it was agreed that the 1st Australian Division would hold its line, leaving the NZ&A Division to capture the upper reaches of Second Ridge and Baby 700 on the evening of 2 May.[31]

Godley's outline plan (see Map 7) was for the Otago Battalion from the New Zealand Infantry Brigade to exit the northern fork at the head of Monash Valley at Pope's Hill and advance to seize Baby 700. At the same time, the 13th and 16th battalions of the 4th Australian Infantry Brigade would exit the head of the valley from the southern fork and capture the crest of the ridge between the New Zealanders' objective and Quinn's Post, an area that became known as the Chessboard. Zero Hour was set for 7.15pm.[32]

The fire plan supporting this operation stemmed from notes scrawled by Godley on the back of a copy of the ANZAC operation order. As promulgated in the orders of the NZ&A Division and the New Zealand Infantry Brigade (see Map 8), it specified the preliminary bombardment of a line 384 metres in length running north-south across Baby 700 and onto Mortar Ridge, as well as in a 'parallelogram to its east', from 7.00 until 7.15pm. No depth for the parallelogram was specified in the orders, but a memorandum from Godley to HQ ANZAC for transmission to the navy asked for fire to be applied as far back as Battleship Hill, a depth of some 790 metres. At 7.15pm, to prevent any Ottoman reinforcement or counter-attack on Baby 700, the fire was then to lift further up the main range and cover the 1100 metres of ground running from Battleship Hill to the seaward slopes of Chunuk Bair. In the orders issued by the commander of the New Zealand Infantry Brigade, the coverage is specified differently, but this is almost certainly due to typographical errors in the grid references.[33]

The majority of the fire support was to be drawn from the eight battleships and cruisers off Anzac, mustering a possible ten 12-inch, two 10-inch, two 9.5-inch, seven 7.5-inch, and twenty-nine 6-inch guns. In his memorandum Godley asked for the fire of 'one or more ships'. Unfortunately, the records are silent on the resources allocated, although Bean suggests that all eight were involved.[34] From its artillery resources the NZ&A Division allocated two howitzers, five 18-pounders and four mountain guns to the New Zealand Infantry Brigade, and two howitzers, two 18-pounders and two mountain guns to the 4th Australian Brigade, with communications between the guns and each brigade headquarters to be arranged by Napier Johnston.[35] The original intention may have been for the infantry brigade commanders to nominate separate artillery targets to be engaged, but any ability to do so was removed by an order issued on 2 May for all guns to fire in accordance with the divisional operation order. Copies of the order were also sent to the 1st Australian Division, with a request that its artillery add weight to the fire plan if practical.[36]

There are no records to hand confirming the targeting of the naval gunfire or the New Zealand guns. The IMA war diaries show that both batteries straddled Baby 700 between 7.00 and 7.15pm, and afterwards lifted their fire to the designated area between Battleship Hill and Chunuk Bair. The staff officer's diary at HQ 1st Australian Divisional Artillery indicates that a gun from the 8th AFA Battery supported the attack on Baby 700, and the 2nd AFA Brigade covered the area of the lift. The 2nd AFA Brigade's war diary provides no relevant confirmation, and nor does that of the 5th AFA Battery. However, the 4th AFA Battery recorded that it fired 142 rounds into the area around Battleship Hill after 7.30pm 'previous to an Infantry attack', which reflects a misunderstanding as to the time of Zero Hour (7.15pm), but accords with the report in the staff officer's war diary and the desired location of supporting fire at that time. The 8th Battery diary contains no reference to firing that night, and thus it is doubtful that it provided the support for the attack on Baby 700 as the staff officer believed.[37]

A New Zealand 18-pounder gun and crew from either the 1st NZFA Battery on Russell's Top or the 2nd NZFA Battery on Plugge's Plateau. It occupies an open pit in a direct fire role and is heavily camouflaged with vegetation. However, the dust raised by the firing of rounds may have given the position away to Ottoman observers (AWM P01155.003).

Although the number of ships and guns that fired is uncertain, the 16th Battalion historian considered the fire that fell at 7.00pm 'impressive', while the New Zealand Infantry Brigade recorded that 'the bombardment by the guns had a great effect and the whole ridge was covered with Lyddite'.[38] However, when the fire lifted at 7.15pm and the 16th climbed out of Monash Valley onto the ridge, it was met by intense fire from the crest and in enfilade. After a short advance it went to ground and began digging in.

Following on behind and to the left of the 16th, the men of the 13th Battalion hauled themselves up to the Chessboard where their attack stalled because of heavy Ottoman fire, and because the Otago Battalion had not come up on their left. Delayed moving up to their start line at Pope's, the Otagos attacked ninety minutes after the preliminary bombardment ceased, managing to secure a foothold on the lower slope of Baby 700, but failing to gain the rest of the feature.[39] Despite Godley committing extra battalions during the night and seeking additional naval fire on and around Baby 700, the Ottoman defences held firm.[40]

The next morning the attackers came under accurate enfilade fire, with the 16th also being accidentally shelled from the rear, causing some troops to fall back into Monash Valley. One historian of the campaign attributed this shelling to the destroyers, while the NZ&A Division thought it came from 'our 18-pounders' and Monash accused the Australian batteries. An investigation showed that this accusation was unjustified.[41] Whoever was at fault, the shelling was just part of the difficulties faced by the attackers on the morning of 3 May. Suffering increasing losses, they gradually retired.

In his after-action report, Godley expressed the view that the plan might have succeeded had the Australian and New Zealand battalions attacked simultaneously. Certainly this would have prevented the defenders concentrating on the 16th and 13th battalions, although the Otagos would still have been vulnerable to enfilade fire from Ottoman trenches on Russell's Top and the Nek and the slopes leading from it to Baby 700, which were not subject to suppressing fire. In addition, the time taken for them to cover the distance between their start line and the objective would probably have afforded the Ottoman defenders on Baby 700 the opportunity to recover from the bombardment and man their trenches, as demonstrated by how quickly they targeted the 16th Battalion with enfilade fire.

Overall, this action was poorly managed. Final orders were issued as late as 2.30pm on the day itself, and the long march of the Otago Battalion to its starting position led to delays. The fire plan also had its limitations. First, the commanders had to rely primarily on naval gunfire spread over a large target area containing entrenchments that, although rudimentary at that stage of the campaign, would have provided some degree of protection to the defenders, essentially limiting the effect of the fire to suppression while the rounds were falling. Second, no plans were made to neutralise the Ottoman positions on the left flank of the assault, perhaps because of the proximity of the opposing lines on Russell's Top. Third, despite the statement in the NZ&A Division report on the operation that 'the Razor Ridge (Dead Man's Hill) and the ground to its north were well shelled', the target area specified in orders did not encompass the 16th Battalion's objectives on the upper end of Second Ridge.

The First Week

The unsuccessful attack on Baby 700 brought the first week at Anzac to an end. On 1 May, two 18-pounders of the 1st NZFA Battery, together with Bessell-Browne's 8th AFA Battery, and a gun of the 3rd AFA Battery landed. Why that single gun was disembarked when the rest of its battery and parent brigade remained afloat and neither the 2nd nor 3rd AFA brigades were complete on the ground, is unclear. However it remained ashore, ultimately to join Major William Burgess' 9th AFA Battery, which sent one of its guns to the 3rd Battery as a replacement.[42]

At this stage the artillery on hand totalled four howitzers, twenty-five field guns, not all of which were in action, and twelve mountain guns. In the 1st Australian Division, JoÚston's 2nd and Rosenthal's 3rd AFA brigade headquarters had deployed, along with the sixteen field guns in Phillips' 4th, Caddy's 5th, Hughes' 7th, and

Bessell-Browne's 8th batteries, and the lone gun from the 3rd AFA Battery. The 2nd and 3rd brigade ammunition columns were also ashore, less their wagons and drivers, which were soon to be returned to Alexandria as the rugged terrain in the Anzac area meant that ammunition resupply had to be carried out either by hand or by mule. The NZ&A Division had the eight field guns and four howitzers of Symon's 1st, Sykes' 2nd and Falla's 4th (Howitzer) batteries.[43]

The week had been exacting for the gunners, largely because the limited depth of the beachhead and the broken terrain made finding field gun positions difficult, and this, along with disruptions at the anchorages, had affected the orderly landing of the Australian batteries. Challenges for the gunners increased on 1 May when Hamilton instructed ANZAC that, pending further orders, it was not to initiate a general advance. It was to complete its disembarkation and then only undertake local operations designed to facilitate an advance at some future time, such as the NZ&A Division attack on Baby 700 then being planned, or to prevent the movement of Ottoman forces to Cape Helles. In essence, ANZAC was placed on the defensive. A few days later arrangements were made to transfer Christian's 1st AFA Brigade (1st, 2nd and 3rd

AFA batteries), together with Major JoÚ Mills' 6th AFA and Major Ivan Standish's 3rd NZFA batteries, to the British 29th Division at Helles.[44] ANZAC's gunners, having anticipated a war of manoeuvre, now had to adapt to fighting on a confined, static front, on unfavourable ground.

Ammunition numbers on a gun from the 7th AFA Battery deployed in the direct fire role close to the front line on Bolton's Ridge on 30 April 1915. The gunners are setting time-fuses on shrapnel rounds for engaging the enemy at point-blank range (AWM J06132).

Chapter Four

ADAPTATION

Initial Difficulties

May 1915 was a period of adaptation for ANZAC's gunners. Reporting on 3 May on initial difficulties, Hobbs wrote, 'It is regretted that the artillery up to this time have not been able to give more assistance to the infantry...' He then listed as reasons the unsuitability of the terrain of the beachhead for the employment of field guns; the enormous difficulty in observing the results of fire; constant damage to the telephone lines between the observers and the guns; difficulty in distinguishing between the ANZAC and enemy trenches because of their close proximity; the flat trajectory of the field gun at the short ranges involved, which made it impossible to reach into gullies; and the intensity of fire from the enemy's batteries, rifle fire and snipers concealed all around the ANZAC position.[1]

The gunners also had to contend with the fact that the only maps available were 1:40,000 scale and not of the accuracy required for artillery work. This series remained in use until it was replaced on 1 August by a more accurate 1:20,000 series with 1:10,000 derivatives. In the meantime, and because there were also no means as yet on any war front of calibrating the guns or determining corrections to account for meteorological conditions to ensure effective fire, the guns had to confirm the line, range and fuse setting necessary to engage a target by firing on it, a process known as registration. This alerted the Ottomans and exposed the ANZAC guns to counter-battery fire. The only compensation was that the Ottoman artillery experienced the same disadvantage.[2]

In addition, the ANZAC artillery commanders faced two issues related to ammunition. The first lay in shell effectiveness. The 18-pounders only had shrapnel, which was useful against exposed troops or for driving men under cover, but not against defences or materiel. The newly developed HE shells for the gun did not become available in any quantity until August, and thereafter constituted less than 10% of the 18-pounder ammunition fired.[3] Both types of ammunition were also sometimes defective, with instances of shrapnel manufactured in 1915 functioning while in the bore, and HE degraded by premature explosions, ultimately identified as a fuse issue.[4]

The mountain guns also had problems with shell effectiveness. In mid-May the commander of the 7th IMA Brigade reported that his explosive projectiles—common shells filled with gunpowder—had only a weak terminal effect, and the bullets from his shrapnel shells tended to clump rather than spread properly. Further, his guns, which on top of their previous wear had each fired 616 rounds since the landing, were so worn that the driving bands on the projectiles were not engaging the rifling properly, leading to inaccuracy. His request for his weapons to be replaced by mountain howitzers or the new 12-pounder mountain gun was denied, but he was issued with some less worn 10-pounders in June.[5]

The second ammunition issue related to supply. In the first eight days of the campaign, expenditure records for the 1st Division show that nearly 7000 rounds were fired, and the records for the NZ&A Division, although incomplete, indicate the expenditure of nearly seven hundred 4.5-inch howitzer rounds in the first five days.[6] These were unsustainable rates for a subsidiary campaign at the end of long supply routes, and at a time when British factories were having difficulty supplying enough shells to meet the requirements in France and Belgium. Consequently, it is no surprise that on 13 May HQ MEF issued an order requiring the husbanding of rounds, noting that expenditure until then had been considerable.[7]

The strictures of this order were set aside during the major Ottoman attack on 19 May, but a day later another order from HQ MEF limited the 18-pounders and the howitzers to two rounds per gun per day for the maintenance of the line, stating that even when this restriction was lifted while supporting or repulsing future attacks, the gunners were expected to exercise economy.[8] Part of the reason for the high expenditure, as Cunliffe-Owen pointed out on 25 May, was that inexperienced infantry units were using the artillery to deal with targets they should have handled themselves. The NZ&A Division issued a special order on this day reinforcing this point, advising the restrictions on artillery ammunition expenditure, and enjoining its forces to only use the artillery on substantial targets.[9]

A mountain gun of the 21st (Kohat) Battery on the south-western edge of the 400 Plateau in early May with McCay's Hill in the background. The detachment is in the process of pulling through the barrel to clean out residue left from propellants after firing (AWM C02192).

Expenditure records show that, in the course of the campaign, the artillery averaged six to eight rounds per gun per day, with higher totals, naturally, in periods of intense activity. The gunners chafed under such constrained allocations. Hobbs complained in his diary on 3 July of the continuing shortage of ammunition, and Byrne, the New Zealand historian, recorded that, throughout June and July, the 'guns of the Army Corps only fired with any freedom on those few crucial occasions of attack or counter attack.' His chapter on this period is entitled 'How The Guns Were Starved'.[10]

Defensive Tasks

With ANZAC on the defensive, the tasks of the artillery in accordance with *Field Artillery Training* were four-fold: to force the enemy to deploy at a distance and then delay his subsequent advance; to prevent the Ottoman artillery gaining mastery of the battlefield and thus facilitating the attacks of the Ottoman infantry; to assist with the close defence of the ANZAC positions; and to support ANZAC counter-attacks and offensive forays.[11] Achieving the first of these tasks would be difficult given the proximity of the front trenches and the Ottoman possession of the high ground which, in the centre and on the left in particular, obscured the field of view from the ANZAC positions. Close defence and countering the Ottoman artillery thus became the priorities, the achievement of which required the completion of the deployment of the guns, the institution of a command and control system governing their fire, the revision of naval gunfire support arrangements, and the construction of protective field works.

Completing the Artillery Deployment

While positions for the howitzers with their curved trajectories were readily found, the siting of the field guns proved more difficult. The only flat areas were immediately behind the front line on the 400 Plateau opposite JoUston's Jolly and Lone Pine, at Shell Green—a concealed position behind Bolton's Ridge—and at Plugge's Plateau and Hell Spit on the coast. Elsewhere, the valleys were too narrow and the hills too steep to accommodate the 18-pounders' flat trajectories. The only other option was to place the guns on the crests of the principal spurs running from Second Ridge to the coast. In examining the proximity of the opposing trench lines, Anderson, Hobbs' BMRA, recorded that the lack of depth in the Corps position precluded the gunners from getting 'back far enough to make proper use of our guns—therefore we have to go right forward and build a series of "cockshies", this is the only way to engage these close targets.' Hobbs and Napier JoUston spent days scouring the area for 18-pounder positions on the heights that offered useful, if limited, arcs of fire along with a degree of protection from enemy observation and fire.[12]

On the left of Anzac, the two sections of the 2nd NZFA Battery joined to occupy a battery position on Plugge's Plateau on 9 May with a primary field of fire over the northern end of Second Ridge. A mountain gun section (Rossiter's) was also there, with a field of fire from Baby 700 around to Scrubby Knoll on Third Ridge. The howitzers of the 4th NZFA Battery were in section positions near the beach north and south of Ari Burnu. That left Symon's 1st NZFA Battery which, after being withdrawn from its exposed position at the foot of Walker's Ridge, attempted to site a gun in the firing line near Courtney's Post on 11 May. This proved unsuccessful and the attempt was abandoned. A position was finally found for the battery on Russell's Top, where its four guns were dragged into position on 17 May after engineering work to build a track up Walker's Ridge. Here it joined two sections of mountain guns that had moved onto the Top in previous days. One of these sections (Kirby's) faced north. The other (Whitting's) and some guns of the field battery enfiladed the Ottoman trenches on the 400 Plateau.[13]

In the centre of Anzac, where the 4th, 5th and 8th AFA batteries were deployed, the location of positions involved a good deal of trial and error. As noted, to engage the enemy trenches and other close targets the guns had to be deployed forward and this initially led to some being positioned close behind the firing line. Bridges dismayed Hobbs by directing Bessell-Browne's 8th AFA Battery to prepare such emplacements on the 400 Plateau.[14] On 2 May a section was taken to a position just west of the plateau, which necessitated hauling the guns up slopes of around 60 degrees to a height of 128 metres above sea level. Gun platforms were prepared during the night, and thirty rounds fired at hostile battery locations. On the night of 3/4 May, two guns were dragged further forward, but daybreak revealed them to be exposed. They were camouflaged and, after dark, run back into Brown's Dip. At 6.00pm on 5 May the two guns were again dragged up to the fire trench, where they fired fourteen rounds at an Ottoman trench at a range of 411 metres while under shrapnel and rifle fire, and then run back. The process was repeated at 4.00pm on 6 May, when twenty rounds were fired. Bridges requested another twenty rounds to be fired three hours later, but by then the Ottomans had registered the range, and casualties were incurred as the guns were being withdrawn.[15]

During the night of 6/7 May, the 8th Battery's guns began to move around 140 metres eastwards to a battery position behind the salient known as 'the Pimple'. Constructed with the assistance of working parties from the ammunition columns, it ultimately comprised a sunken road, together with five gun emplacements from which the gun barrels protruded at ground level, and four cover pits in which the guns were kept when not in action. This position was initially so close to the firing line that, for firing at close targets, sandbags had to be removed from the infantry parapet. Two of the guns were positioned to fire to the north-east, the other two to the east and south. The fifth platform enabled another gun to be repositioned firing northwards if required.[16]

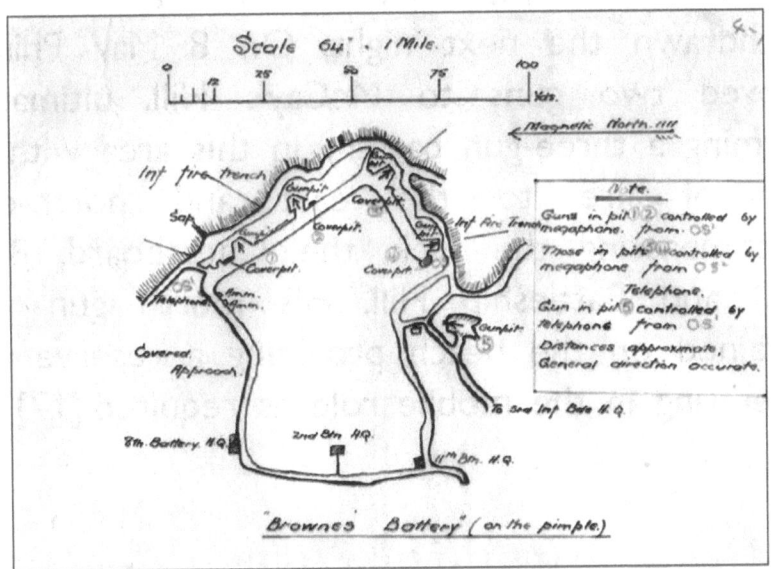

Diagram 1: 8th AFA Battery gun emplacements at the Pimple, May 1915. The 8th AFA Battery position at 'the Pimple' immediately behind the front line at Lone Pine. Two guns face north-east along the front of the Australian and

New Zealand line on Second Ridge and up to the main range, one south-east towards Pine Ridge, and one south across the front of the Australian line along Bolton's Ridge. A fifth position for use if required, also faces north-east. Each gun position has a cover pit into which the guns can be run if under Ottoman artillery fire.

Phillips' 4th AFA Battery began its redeployments on the night of 4 May when a gun from MacLagan's Ridge and another from the beach were moved forward to the upper reaches of the Razorback around 250 yards behind the firing line. By the night of 6/7 May a third gun had moved forward, initially taking post behind the Pimple, where it was hit and withdrawn the next night. On 8 May Phillips moved two guns to McCay's Hill, ultimately forming a three-gun battery in this area with an arc of fire to the east and north-east encompassing the Nek, the Chessboard, Baby 700 and Battleship Hill. His fourth gun was retained on the beach providing a reserve and operating in the mobile role as required.[17]

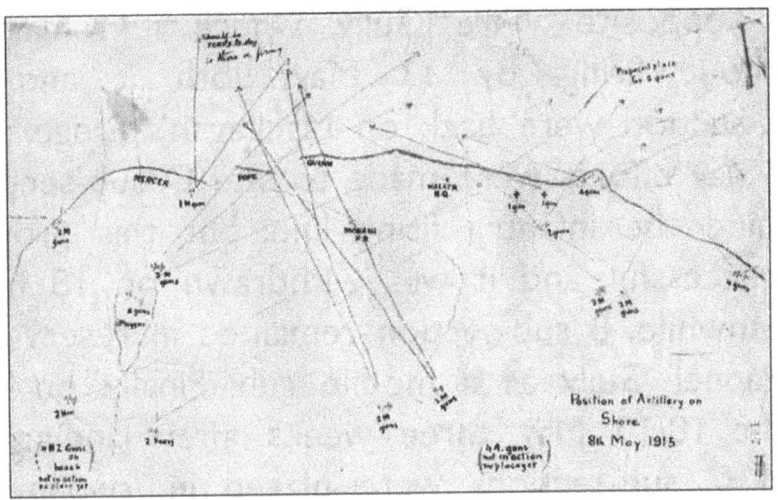

Diagram 2: Sketch map showing the guns ashore by 8 May 1915 and their locations. A sketch map from the 1st Divisional Artillery war diary indicating the location of the guns ashore on 8 May 1915 and their arcs of fire.

Caddy's 5th AFA Battery had a longer struggle to find positions, illustrating the difficulty the gunners experienced in finding suitable locations for their 18-pounders. A and C sub-sections landed on 26 April and were positioned on MacLagan's Ridge close to Phillips' 4th AFA Battery guns, while the remaining two pieces came ashore on 28 April and were parked near the beach. On the night of 6/7 May, A sub-section was moved, hauled into place immediately west of the Pimple. Daylight found it too exposed, and so it was withdrawn the next evening. The following night (8/9 May) C sub-section was taken to the rear of the firing line opposite Wire Gully, where it remained without firing. By 13 May both it and A sub-section were back on MacLagan's Ridge. On 16 May efforts were made to site D sub-section behind the infantry firing line, but this proved unsuccessful, and it was withdrawn on 18 May. Meanwhile, B sub-section remained in reserve in Shrapnel Gully as a mobile gun. Finally, on the night 18/19 May, three weeks after landing, A and C sub-sections were placed in 'two good positions' on the Razorback and, two days later, D sub-section took post on MacLagan's Ridge. This ended the search for suitable positions and, from this point on, Caddy commanded a three-gun battery that was split over the two locations, covering arcs to the east and north-east. As with Phillips' battery, his fourth gun was retained near the beach operating as a mobile battery.[18]

No.4 Gun, 7th AFA Battery, firing over a section of no man's land known as 'the Wheatfield' on 4 May 1915. During attacks in this area, shrapnel shells were sometimes set to burst at the muzzle, and enemy were killed at twenty-five yards' range (AWM G00937).

On the right of Anzac, Hughes' 7th AFA Battery remained immediately behind the infantry front line on Bolton's Ridge, although alternative positions for two guns were found. The four guns were fought independently, Nos 1 and 2 with arcs to the south and south-east from Gaba Tepe around to Pine Ridge, and Nos 3 and 4 with arcs to the east and north-east towards Pine Ridge and the 400 Plateau.[19]

The other battery in this area, Burgess' 9th AFA Battery, had a more unsettled introduction. On 30 April its gun detachments were sent ashore and employed, relieving the gunners of the 7th and 8th batteries. All the battery's guns were ashore by 7 May, but it was not until 14 May that one was emplaced at the base of McCay's Hill on Brighton Beach, in what became known as the Brighton Battery. On 16 May two guns were formed into a mobile section, although the tracks and roads in the beachhead were rudimentary at this stage. Burgess came ashore on 17 May and assumed command. Four days later, a position for two more of his guns was found and, by 23 May, according to the unit's war diary, the battery was in three locations: two guns on McCay's Hill (Burgess' Battery), one in the Brighton Battery and one under Lieutenant Arthur Jopp (Jopp's Battery) on the Razorback, all linked by telephone. On 7 June, the 9th AFA Battery coalesced into two locations, with the Brighton Battery joining Jopp's. The arcs for these batteries covered the south of the ANZAC position.[20]

Some confusion surrounds the 9th Battery deployments in that maps issued by the 1st Australian Division and the Divisional Artillery in this period do not show the guns in the positions given in the battery war diary. They have Burgess' Battery sited on the ridge immediately south of McCay's Hill, Brighton Battery at the foot of McCay's, and Jopp's Battery on McCay's Hill. It seems probable that the discrepancy resulted from a misunderstanding by Burgess of the names of the features on which his guns were deployed. This misunderstanding is evident from the sketch map of the locations of the battery's guns in the unit's war diary for June 1915.[21]

Map 9 shows the location of ANZAC's guns at the end of May. Positions for the mountain guns of the 21st (Jacob's) Battery that had been settled since the middle of the month saw two sections located just south of the 8th Battery at the top of Victoria Gully—one (Thom's) with arcs to the north and the other (Rawson's) to the south—while the third (Trenchard's) was located at the foot of the Razorback Ridge, with arcs to the north-east.

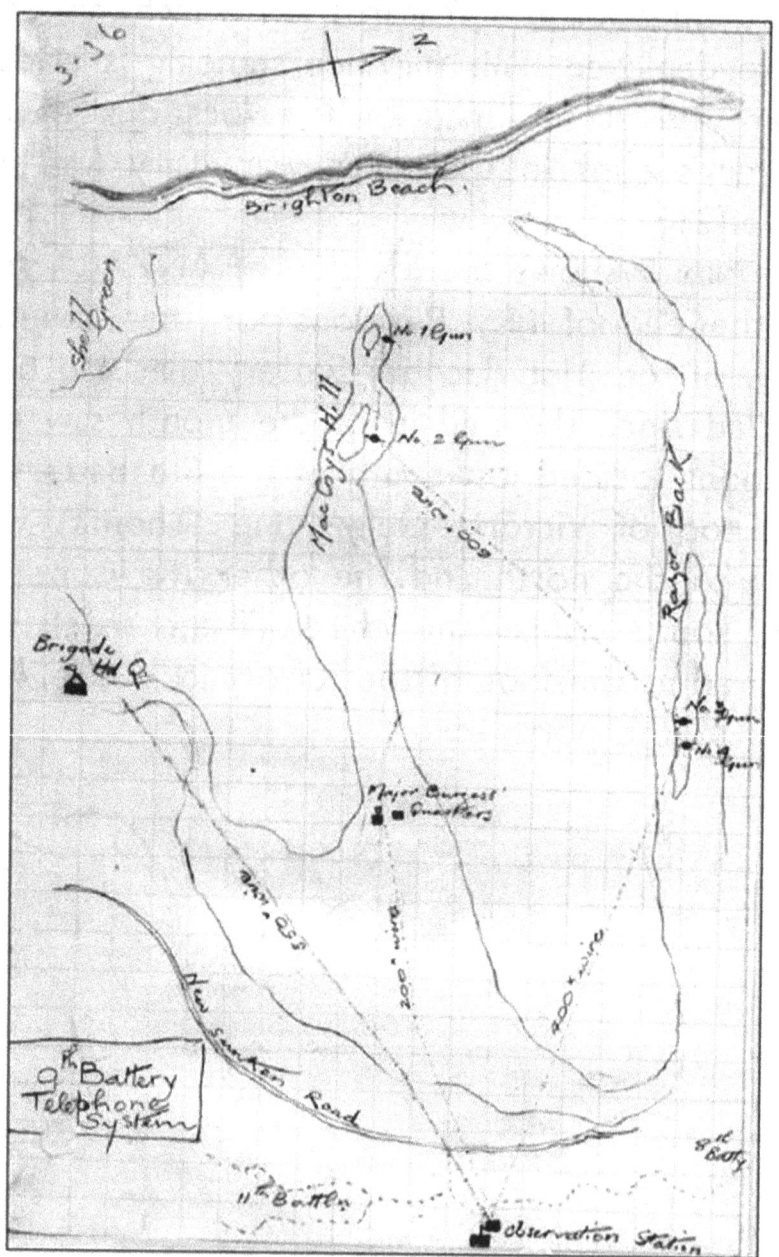

Diagram 3: 9th AFA Battery gun positions and telephone system, June 1915. Sketch of the 9th AFA battery position split over two locations, and the telephone links between the guns and the battery observation station south of Lone

Pine. Artillery Road (the New Sunken Road) is shown running behind Bolton's Ridge. The designations 'Razorback' and 'McCay's Hill' in this sketch are incorrect. 'Razorback' is actually a portion of McCay's Hill, and 'McCay's Hill' the unnamed ridge between Victoria Gully and Clarke Valley

As an indication of the ammunition supply arrangements prevailing at the end of May, the 1st Australian Division specified that, for the 18-pounders, 176 rounds per gun were to be held on the gun position, seventy-six in the brigade ammunition column, and 276 in a depot on the beach. Because of the restricted space in the beachhead, the divisional ammunition columns were not deployed.[22] With regard to the ammunition supply system, the sketchy records available suggest that divisional ammunition parks were established on shore, from which the brigade ammunition columns drew their supplies. The men of the brigade ammunition columns constructed revetments for their ammunition holdings and carried out daily resupply of each battery depending on the number of rounds expended. In addition, they found themselves in demand for a variety of tasks, such as providing replacements for casualties in the batteries, forming working parties to assist batteries dig in or to assist the divisions to build roads or improve the water supply.

Command and Control

As they grappled with the problem of finding suitable field gun positions, the gunner commanders were also trying to develop a system of command of the guns and control of their fire that would provide the infantry in the front line with responsive support from the guns best placed to engage the target. In such a small area it was obvious that command of the guns would be exercised by the divisional commander though the CRA. But in terms of their fire, it was not a simple matter of delegating control over the fire of guns to the infantry in whose area the guns were deployed. The range and wider arcs of fire of the howitzers and some of the field and mountain guns enabled them to support a number of units without moving, not just those to their immediate front. Furthermore, with the limited arcs of fire available from most of the field gun positions and with the advantage of firing in enfilade when the front lines were as close as they were, it was often a gun or battery in the other division, or in another infantry brigade area in the same division, that could best support a particular infantry unit. The 1st NZFA Battery's coverage of the 400 Plateau from Russell's Top, and that of the 4th and 5th AFA batteries of the New Zealand defences at the head of Monash Valley, are cases in point.[23]

In these circumstances, *Field Artillery Training* supported centralised command and control, suggesting that 'the bulk of the artillery should occupy positions under the orders of the Divisional Artillery Commander, who will allot to each Field Artillery Brigade commander tasks or zones in which he thinks their fire can be employed most effectively.'[24] However, at Anzac there were two divisions occupying a confined space, and a system was required for the allotment of tasks and zones across divisions as well as within them.

If at all practical, command and control should have been exercised at Corps level. The logical officer to take a leading role here was Cunliffe-Owen, and in his history of the Royal Australian Artillery, Horner records criticism of him for his lack of coordination of the artillery at this time. Napier JoÚston expressed similar views when he appeared before the Dardanelles Commission after the campaign.[25] However, Cunliffe-Owen was only an adviser and did not have the authority, staff or communications to command the Corps artillery. The evidence suggests he conferred with Hobbs and Napier JoÚston, and that on 30 April Hobbs provided him an officer to augment his staff, along with a map of the then gun positions in both divisions. On another occasion the three senior gunners met to coordinate a joint firing by the two divisions. Some criticism may be warranted in that, while he had no command capability, Cunliffe-Owen could issue coordinating instructions on fire support matters as he had done with naval gunfire, and it was not until 25 May that he did so for the provision of artillery support.[26] Even so, it has to be remembered that this was a new situation for all the commanders, all were feeling their way, and Cunliffe-Owen was engaged at the same time with the coordination of naval gunfire and the monitoring of ammunition supply.

With command and control thus exercised by the two divisional headquarters problems arose. Lamenting the situation, Anderson noted on 3 May, 'The necessity of [the] Artillery of [the] whole line of defence being under one control or at least all HQ being close together is very apparent and has been [the] cause of difficulty all through—there is no one person who knows what all guns are doing or can do—The Terrain must be divided almost [in]to areas for single guns—Better communications between [the] batteries and [the infantry is] most necessary to prevent delay[s] caused by request[s] for fire coming through Aust Div and NZ and

A Div also [unreadable] to Div Art[illery]—There are too many sieves.' He believed that the allotment of guns to defensive sections would improve matters as the guns of one defensive section would not be able to fire onto the front of another without permission.[27]

Here Anderson was referring to the four defensive sections that had evolved following Birdwood's reorganisation of the ANZAC line. The 1st Australian Division occupied the southern two: Section 1 (Gaba Tepe to just south of Lone Pine) and Section 2 (just south of Lone Pine to just south of Courtney's Post). The NZ&A Division manned the northern pair: Section 3 (Courtney's Post to Pope's Hill) and Section 4 (Russell's Top and Walker's Ridge). An infantry brigade was assigned to each section, with the infantry brigade commander acting as the defensive section commander. Rosenthal's 3rd AFA Brigade, consisting of Hughes' 7th and Burgess' 9th batteries, was in Section 1. With Rosenthal's 8th AFA Battery occupying the Pimple in Section 2, it was transferred to JoÚston's 2nd AFA Brigade, which had already lost the 6th AFA Battery to the British at Cape Helles. Hence JoÚston now controlled his own 4th and 5th batteries along with Rosenthal's 8th in Section 2, while Rosenthal controlled his remaining two batteries—the 7th and 9th. In the NZ&A Division area the artillery support was divided so that three mountain guns, a section of 4.5-inch howitzers and the 2nd NZFA Battery supported Section 3, and three mountain guns, the 1st NZFA Battery, a section of 4.5-inch howitzers supported Section 4.[28]

On 5 May, HQ 1st Australian Division issued an arrangement for the direction of artillery fire which precluded the Australian guns firing north of Section 2 onto the New Zealand front without being directed to do so by the officer commanding Section 2 or divisional headquarters. It also stated that the fire of the guns of the 3rd AFA Brigade on the right would be directed by the officer commanding Section 1, and the fire of the remainder of the guns by the officer commanding Section 2.[29] This arrangement might have been useful in preventing guns in one defensive section arbitrarily firing on the front of another without accurate knowledge of the defences or activities in that area. However, it was deficient in that delegating control of artillery fire to the defensive section commanders potentially led, as *Field Artillery Training* put it, to the reduction of the 'fighting capacity of the division as a whole' and, in this context, restricted the capacity of the Corps artillery.[30]

This early arrangement was apparently communicated to the NZ&A Division in terms that Australian guns would not fire into Section 3 without a staff officer of that section being present in the Australian headquarters. On 7 May Godley requested the 1st Division to rescind this restriction. In his view the Australian guns had by then a good knowledge of the locations of the defenders and had registered most of the hostile targets in front of the New Zealand line and, in addition, his sections could not spare a staff officer. The next day, Hobbs agreed to cover the New Zealand defensive sections on request.[31]

On 9 May Hobbs issued instructions that the infantry commanders were to pass their requirements direct to the artillery brigade commanders who were to provide the necessary assistance, so far as it was within their power to do so.[32] These instructions indicate that overall control of the fire had reverted to the divisional artillery rather than the infantry defensive section commander.

Two days later, HQ MEF Force Order Number 8 was issued, giving further impetus to artillery coordination, although some of its strictures were more suited to the gentler terrain of Helles than the ridges of Anzac, where the field guns had limited arcs. It stated that the hostile area in front of friendly trenches was to be divided into sub-areas, and batteries were to be detailed for the purpose of providing assistance to the infantry defending each of these subareas in case of attack. Artillery observation officers were to be in the trenches day and night, and the guns carefully registered on likely targets. When an Ottoman attack occurred in a particular area, guns not directly involved were to make a wall of fire 200 to 500 yards in advance of the defenders with a view to interdicting enemy support. This order also called for as many guns as possible to engage any one portion of the front, and for artillery telephone lines to be run in duplicate or triplicate.[33]

In the Anzac area, in the absence of a single artillery commander, the artillery command and control problem could only be solved by increased cooperation between the divisional artilleries. Initially this was attempted through meetings between the two CRAs and Cunliffe-Owen as evidenced in a conference on 11 May to coordinate a joint bombardment the next day. Likewise, records of Australian guns firing in support of Section 3 on 14 May and the New Zealand howitzers engaging targets around Lone Pine between 14 and 16 May also demonstrate increased cooperation.[34] At the same time, Hobbs was writing to his subordinates to clarify their responsibilities in relation to controlling the fire in each defensive section, enjoining them to fire if practical on all targets requested by the infantry after obtaining permission from the section commander or divisional artillery headquarters, excepting in the case of a fleeting opportunity, when they should fire on their own initiative. Batteries were to register targets in their zones, control ammunition expenditure, and leave the guns laid on important targets when not firing. If active hostile batteries could not be located, Hobbs ordered his subordinates to fire on targets in their zones to try to draw Ottoman fire away from the infantry. Finally, he wanted the detachments withdrawn to safety if a hostile battery was firing accurately at their gun.[35]

A further conference leading to improved coordination took place on 15 May. Brigadier General Walker, who had temporarily assumed command of the 1st Australian Division when Bridges was wounded, met with Hobbs, stressing the need for the artillery to adapt to what was essentially 'fortress warfare'. He called for plans showing the arcs of fire of all ANZAC's guns, and the adoption of new gun positions if necessary to ensure coverage of the entire front. Over the next few days Anderson set about compiling the material, recording the problems in adequately covering the 400 Plateau from within Australian resources, problems that were potentially eased around 17 May with the deployment of two sections of the 26th (Jacob's) Battery and the 1st NZFA Battery on Russell's Top, and a promise from Napier JoÚston that the latter battery would provide assistance in covering JoÚston's Jolly.[36]

In the major Ottoman attack on 19 May, Anderson recorded, 'there is still a lack of coordination between [the] NZ Art[illery] and our own [,] try as we will we cannot get them to cover our centre from their position on [the] left.'[37] Hobbs saw the difficulties more as a matter of targeting than a lack of cooperation, noting that he 'had a great deal of worry and trouble trying to get the NZ Arty on the targets within their zones.'[38] This is consistent with New Zealand records which show that, on 19 May, the New Zealand howitzers provided support on the 400 Plateau, and at 9.35am Symon's 1st NZFA Battery reported that it had altered its emplacement and could now engage JoÚston's Jolly.[39] Although Napier JoÚston reported that the field battery was engaging the Jolly, and the howitzer battery the enemy reserves, Symon was not sure he was engaging the right target. Hobbs sent an officer from the 2nd AFA Brigade to confirm the target, but the battery was still unable to bring fire onto it. At a second attempt it was finally registered. From the NZ&A Division's perspective, Australian support for the defence of Courtney's and Quinn's posts was much improved, with General Godley stating in his after-action report that the 5th AFA Battery had rendered valuable assistance.[40]

On 20 May Hobbs recorded that the New Zealand field guns 'appeared to be dropping shells into our own trenches', noting that 'it would be much better if the Bgdr Gen CRA [Cunliffe-Owen] allotted zones & tasks to the NZ & Aust Arty & we should know definitely then where ours began and ended.'[41] New Zealand investigations showed that their guns were not at fault.[42] However, Cunliffe-Owen had recognised the need for better cooperation and begun to issue headquarters with maps of the gun positions and the zones they covered. This stopped short of allotting zones and tasks, but facilitated the identification of the best guns to engage a target for both the infantry and the artillery. In issuing this material, Cunliffe-Owen emphasised that guns from one flank were often best positioned to engage targets on the other.[43] Other measures were also taken to improve cooperation. On 21 May Napier Joúston sent a liaison officer to Defensive Section 2 and, the next day, Cunliffe-Owen, Walker and Hobbs visited Section 3 and the 1st NZFA Battery observation post.[44]

On 25 May, Cunliffe-Owen issued instructions on getting artillery fire onto objectives quickly, in which it was mandated that each CRA was to remain in constant contact with his divisional commander, and the senior artillery officers in each defensive section with the relevant infantry brigadier.[45] Command and the coordination of the artillery remained at Division, but control was delegated to the extent that the artillery allotted to each defensive section was authorised to fire on section targets within ammunition restrictions. Thus, infantry commanders could make their requests for fire direct to the field artillery element supporting them, and in ordinary circumstances these would be met without further reference. Requests for support from guns in another defensive section or another division, the howitzers, and the mountain guns had to go through Division, although direct requests could be made in an emergency.[46]

Dugouts near HQ 1st Australian Division and HQ 1st Australian Divisional Artillery, illustrating the rudimentary nature of the accommodation (AWM A00873).

In this fashion the gunners gradually established a system that provided the defence with responsive close support of adequate weight. The key was the personal liaison outlined in Cunliffe-Owen's instruction. Hobbs' headquarters, which had previously been physically separate, integrated with HQ 1st Australian Division. Defensive section senior artillery officers soon had a network of observation officers and associated 'lookout men' in place, and worked closely with the trench garrisons to identify targets and pass information. Batteries registered the key targets within their zones.[47]

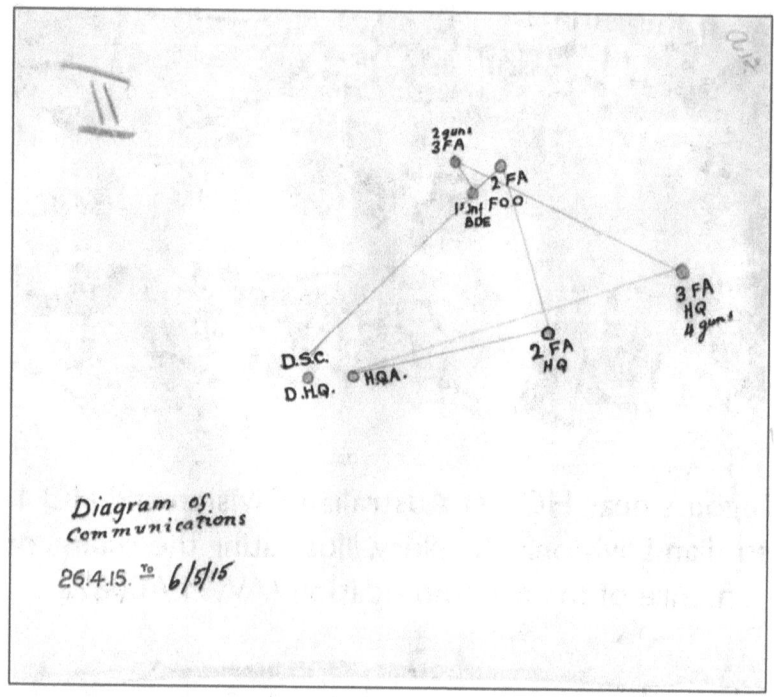

Diagram 4: Artillery Communications Diagram, 26 April to 6 May 1915. The telephone system of the Australian Divisional Artillery for the first two weeks of the campaign reflecting the limited resources ashore

The backbone of this system was a sophisticated telephone network which quickly evolved, as can be seen by the difference in the communications diagrams as at 5 May and from 16 May onwards (diagrams 4 and 5) in the 1st Australian Divisional Artillery's war diary. By mid-May all Australian batteries, their observation posts, artillery brigade headquarters and the divisional artillery headquarters were linked, and tied in with the mountain guns, HQ New Zealand

Divisional Artillery, and the naval observation officers, while direct lines ran from the respective infantry brigade headquarters to their supporting AFA brigade headquarters.[48]

Bean writes that telephone communications routed through three or four headquarters sometimes made requesting fire from another section or division a time-consuming process, citing that, on one occasion, a request for fire support did not reach the relevant officer in the other division until the next day.[49] Nonetheless, the new system worked well enough on 28 and 29 May when the New Zealanders sought fire from the Australian batteries to help defeat an attack on Quinn's Post. The officer commanding the post reported that the defence was ably assisted by fire from Sykes' 2nd NZFA Battery, Caddy's 5th AFA Battery and a mountain gun section. He attributed the repulse of the enemy largely to 'the fine shooting of the Artillery'.[50]

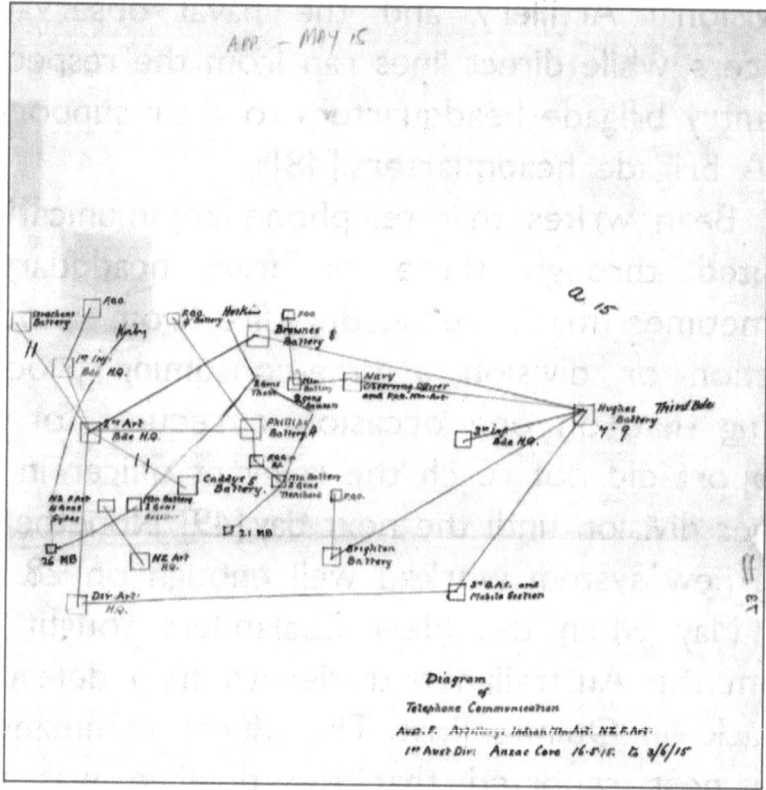

Diagram 5: Artillery Communications Diagram, 16 May to 3 June 1915. The more comprehensive artillery telephone system in place from mid May to early June showing links established from battery to brigade, and brigade to divisional artillery headquarters, but not yet directly from AFA brigade to AFA brigade.

Naval Gunfire Coordination

Another issue requiring resolution was how naval gunfire might best support a protracted defence. Many had expected it to dominate the battlefield, but the terrain restricted observation of Ottoman depth positions, the number of ships and the amount of ammunition suitable for engaging land targets was limited, the low trajectory of naval guns prevented them reaching into defiladed positions, and entrenchments provided protection against their fire. Moreover, at Anzac the ships could not fire in enfilade, the fire control equipment in the older vessels was poor, and the ships generally preferred not to anchor when firing, movement adding a further dimension to their gunnery problem. Minor issues also intruded, with Anderson noting on one occasion that a ship ceased engaging a target just as its fire became effective because it had reached its ammunition allocation for the day.[51]

The pre-dreadnought Swiftsure class battleship HMS Triumph. She was the navigation ship for the Anzac landing and, contrary to popular myth, she did not position the landing one mile (1.6 kilometres) north of the intended landing site, but in pitch darkness brought the ships carrying the troops to a position only slightly north of the proposed site. Carrying four BL 10-inch guns in twin turrets, fourteen 7.5-inch guns and fourteen QF 14-pounder guns, Triumph supported ANZAC until she was torpedoed on 25 May—in full sight of the troops ashore—with the loss of three officers and 73 sailors (Wikipedia).

On 8 May, Birdwood sent a request to Admiral Sir Cecil Thursby, commanding the 2nd Naval Squadron, requesting him to take responsibility for the zone outside the coverage of the Corps artillery and provide naval observers ashore for this purpose. Thursby replied that ammunition availability meant he could only take on batteries, bodies of troops or stores depots that were visible or located by some other means.[52] A day later, Cunliffe-Owen issued a Corps memorandum on naval gunfire support, setting out a system whereby targets identified by the forward brigades were to be sent to the flagship via Division and Corps. Observers ashore would control the subsequent fire.[53] He also warned that ships could not fire close to the ANZAC lines because 'all fire from the ships is by compass, as the map is not accurate.' Thus the artillery would take on the close targets, with the naval guns taking on targets in the 'outside zones'.[54]

As May progressed, the navy's ability to provide support was also affected by the withdrawal or loss of several battleships. The super-dreadnought *Queen Elizabeth* left for home waters, and *Queen, Implacable, London* and *Prince of Wales* were ordered to Italy. On 25 May *Canopus* departed for a refit and HMS *Triumph* was torpedoed off Anzac. Two days later *Majestic* suffered the same fate off Helles.[55]

Although on 23 May Anderson recorded that good targets were being missed because the observers ashore were having difficulty obtaining a ship to fire, naval gunfire support continued to be of great value to the Corps. Its potential reduced the possibility of an Ottoman attack or large-scale movement on Anzac's northern and southern flanks by day, it contributed to the suppression of Ottoman guns, and countered the fire of Ottoman ships in the Narrows. The presence of the cruisers and destroyers, and the monitors that joined them later, also sustained ANZAC morale.[56]

The Need for More Howitzers

As the gunners settled into their defensive tasks, completed their deployments and finalised their command and control arrangements, they experienced great difficulty in engaging the reverse slopes and valleys in which Ottoman batteries, reserves and supply routes were located. The trajectories of the high-velocity 18-pounders and naval guns were simply too flat. With an ability to manipulate their propelling charges the mountain guns fared slightly better, but their shells lacked weight.

Three days after the landing Napier JoÚston recorded, 'The country is so hilly that it is quite impracticable for field guns', adding in mid-May, 'howitzers and not guns should have been brought with a sufficiency of ammunition'.[57] Similarly, on 13 May Hobbs noted: 'We are tormented by the enemy guns and observation stations from [Hill] 971 & are subjected to heavy shell fire at once [when we open fire]. Our guns get badly knocked about & many casualties [sic]. It is impossible for us to discover [the] enemy batteries which are hidden in nullahs and behind ridges which our guns without being able to manoeuvre or with their flat trajectory cannot reach.'[58]

A gun of the 7th AFA Battery damaged on 28 June 1915 being moved to an alternative position where the affected parts can be replaced and the gun brought back into action. This occurred during the Ottoman counter-battery fire as a result of the hastily organised feints launched that afternoon by the 5th and 7th LH regiments and the 9th and 11th battalions in Defensive Section 1, in support of the British VIII Corps at Cape Helles (AWM G01061).

The artillery commanders pressed Division and Corps for more howitzers.[59] On 8 May, believing that there were BL 6-inch 30 cwt (152mm) howitzers manned by personnel of the Royal Malta Artillery on Lemnos, Birdwood requested some for Anzac.[60] Two were landed on 16 May, with one allotted to each division, where they were sited to take on targets to the north and south of the Corps beachhead.[61] The same day, Birdwood asked HQ MEF to once again seek the second 4.5-inch howitzer battery from New Zealand, a request that was passed on to the War Office even though there was some doubt that additional ammunition could be provided, or that the howitzers could be spared given their use in the training of reinforcements. In the event, the War Office advised that the second battery would leave New Zealand in the middle of June, but would require further training in theatre before being fit for service.[62]

A conference of artillery officers convened by Hobbs on 28 May considered 'if anything more than had already been done could be done for dealing with the enemy's guns and machine guns on Lone Pine and the gullies below same.' Arrangements were made for the 1st NZFA Battery from Russell's Top to engage enemy gun emplacements in gullies near Lone Pine using observation stations in the Australian sector, but Hobbs also recorded that 'all the officers ... were of the opinion that nothing but HOWITZERS [sic] could successfully deal with the gullies that the enemy causes us so much trouble with,' adding, 'I have already reported this time after time to headquarters.'[63] He sought a 5-inch howitzer battery from Australia, but Birdwood would not accede to this request as these weapons 'were not of the standard type'. There was some merit in this position as, compared to the 4.5-inchers, the 5-inchers had no effective recoil system, no on-carriage traverse, the sights had to be removed between rounds, and accuracy suffered in high winds. But the need was great and, in the circumstances, Napier JoÚston found Birdwood's view extraordinary.[64]

While further howitzers may not have been forthcoming, in May the first mortars arrived at Anzac. The initial four were Japanese, of 3-inch (77mm) calibre, with a range of around 230 metres. They fired a 28lb (13kg) projectile which was useful against both personnel and overhead cover. Each division received two. The NZ&A Division emplaced its on Russell's Top, while the Australians placed theirs towards the left of Section 2 near what became known later as Steele's Post, within reach of German Officers' Trench and JoÚston's Jolly. Ammunition supply was limited.[65]

In early June a second consignment arrived, this time Garland mortars, of 2.5-inch (63.5mm) calibre. These were primarily anti-personnel weapons throwing a 2.5lb (1kg) bomb around 180 metres. Initial testing showed them to be useful, although difficult to range because of inaccuracies in the firing tables, and subject to 10% blinds because of 'rough workmanship' in their manufacture.[66] Again, only a few were received and, as with the Japanese mortars, they constituted a very limited capability devolved to selected positions, where they were manned by volunteers and directed by the local infantry commander.

Into Action

In their section positions around Ari Burnu, the howitzers of the 4th NZFA Battery were deployed in open pits in positions shielded from Ottoman view and fire by the terrain. Positions for the field and mountain guns on the ridges and plateaus of Anzac were selected as far as was practical to be equally defiladed, but this was hard to achieve, and pits had to be dug and alternative positions found for protection. The search for the latter began almost immediately the primary positions of some of the Australian batteries were settled, with Anderson recording the identification of such positions for the 4th, 7th and 8th batteries. It appears that what were originally alternative positions for the 8th Battery ultimately became the permanent location of Jopp's element of the 9th Battery.[67]

The type of pit occupied by the field guns depended on their location and arcs of fire. On McCay's Hill with limited arcs, the guns of Phillips' 4th AFA Battery fired through embrasures from under overhead cover.

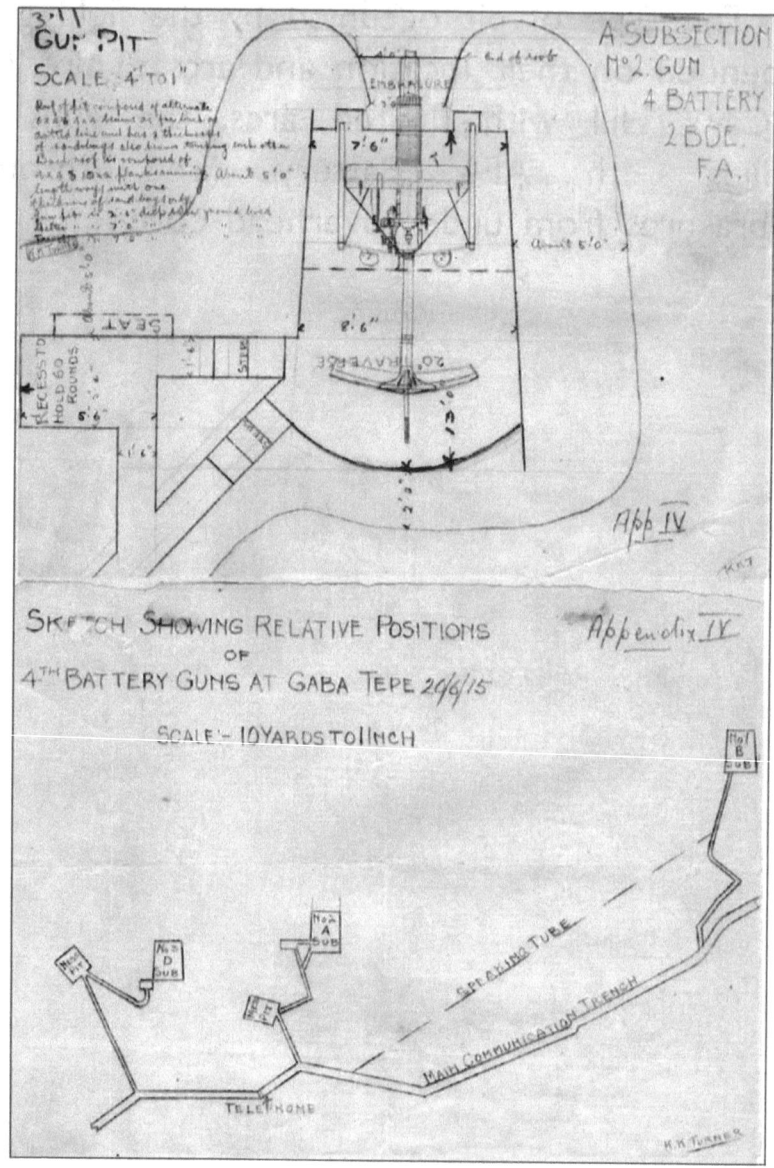

Diagram 6: A gun pit with embrasure and the relative positions of the 4th AFA Battery's guns. Diagram of the covered gun pit to be constructed for Alpha Sub-Section of the 4th AFA Battery, and of the layout of the three guns deployed by the battery on the Razor Back.

A gun of the 4th AFA Battery in a sandbagged emplacement on McCay's Hill with thin overhead cover camouflaged with vegetation. From the hill in the background, this gun appears to have had an arc of fire to the north-east covering the Nek, the Chessboard, Baby 700 and Battleship Hill, providing fire support to the New Zealand Infantry Brigade (AWM P04965.002).

One of the guns of the 4th AFA Battery in its pit on McCay's Hill. Because of its exposed position the gun has been dug into the slope and provided with overhead protection. It fired through an embrasure at the front of the pit just wide enough to allow the gun to cover a limited arc (AWM J03272).

Those of Burgess' 9th Battery further south in a slightly more defiladed position and needing to cover a larger arc, fired from open pits, as did Bessell-Browne's 8th Battery at the Pimple and Sykes' 2nd NZFA Battery on Plugge's Plateau. As a further protective measure, on 14 May Hobbs ordered all the Australian batteries to prepare covered pits into which the guns could be withdrawn if they came under fire.[68]

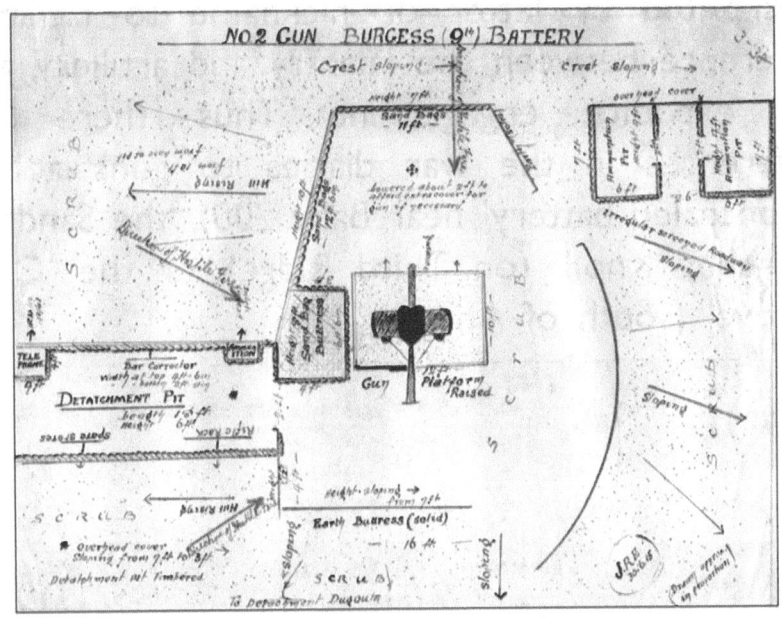

Diagram 7: Gun emplacement for No 2 Gun, 9th AFA Battery. A 9th AFA Battery gun emplacement on McCay's Hill showing the layout to achieve a larger arc of fire, and the direction from which the Ottoman artillery fire might be expected.

As each battery settled, it constructed observation posts and its guns registered the important targets within their zones, keeping a registration card in each pit for use when a particular target was ordered by the observer, who also had a list of the registrations, along with a panoramic sketch of the zone for which he was responsible. These sketches included trench lines, defensive works, hostile gun positions and other targeting aids. On each defensive section front, enduring targets were designated by letter or nickname to facilitate reference between the infantry and artillery, and to expedite engagement. Thus there are references in the war diaries to guns at 'C' ('concealed battery' near Baby 700), 'the Sandpit', 'Scrubby Knoll' (on Third Ridge), or the 'Olive Grove' (south of Anzac).

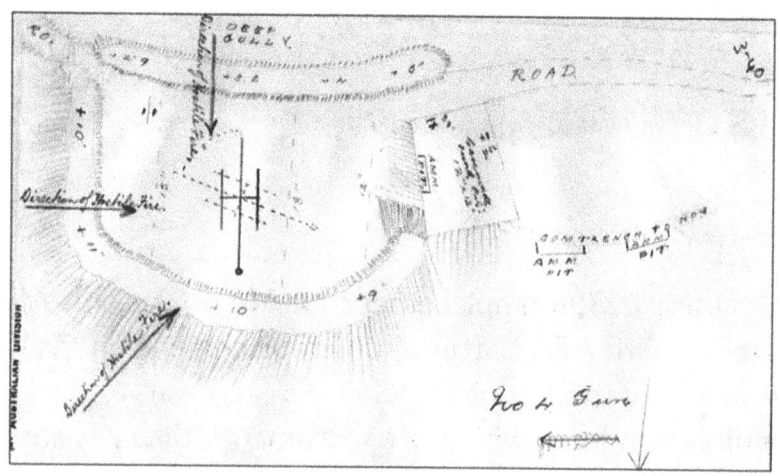

Diagram 8: Gun emplacement for No 4 Gun, 9th AFA Battery. A 9th AFA Battery gun emplacement on the Razorback.

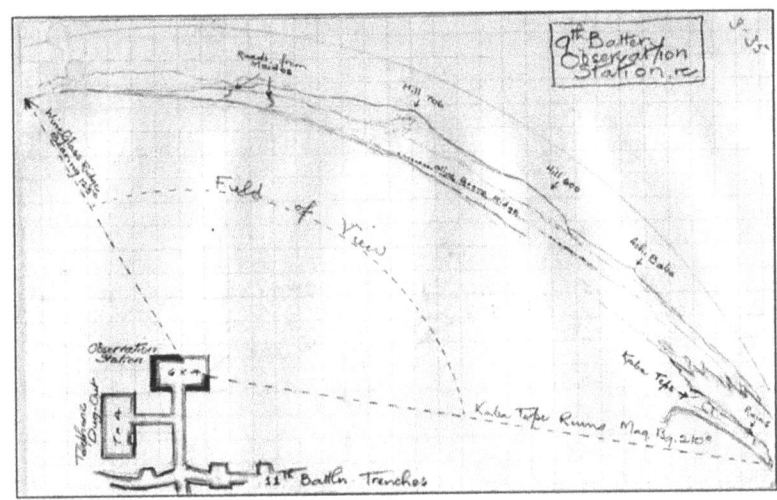

Diagram 9: Field of view, 9th AFA Battery observation station. Sketch map of the 9th AFA Battery Observation Station providing a view of the Ottoman area from Wineglass Ridge on the left to Gaba Tepe on the right with the Khilid Bahr Plateau and Achi Baba in the distance. The field of view covered is 85 Degrees from 125 degrees magnetic to 210 degrees magnetic.

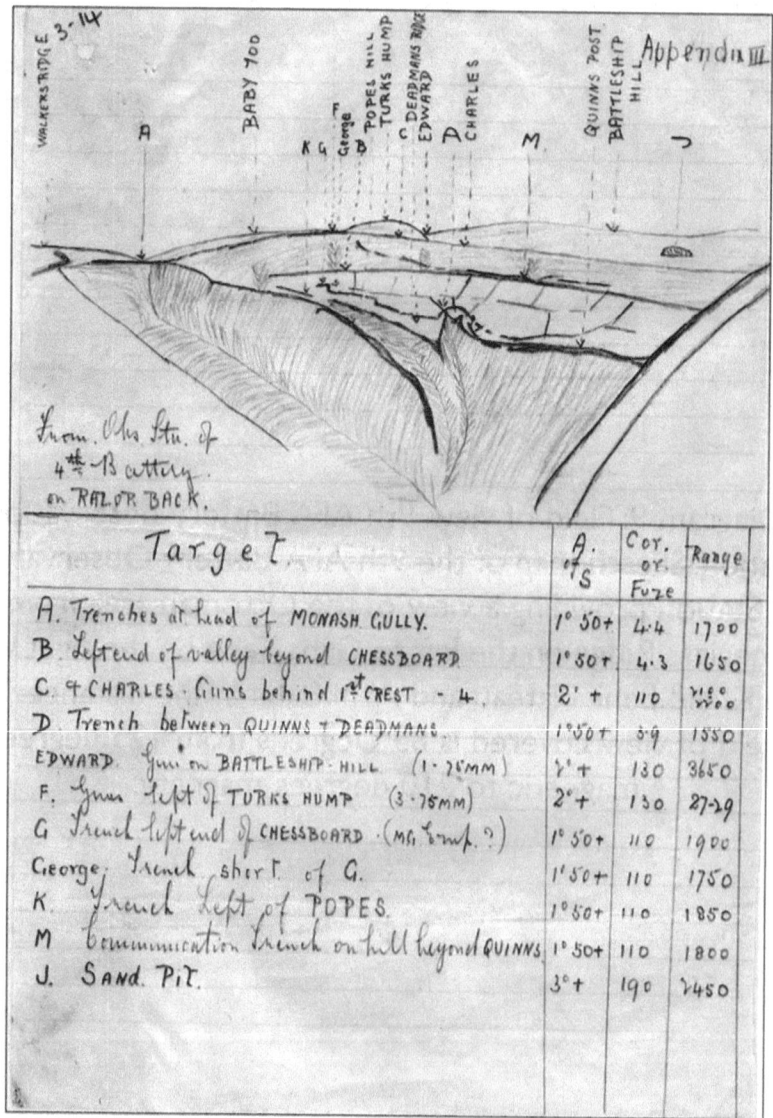

Diagram 10: Panoramic sketch from the war diary of the 4th AFA Battery observation post. This sketch was used in June 1915 by observers of the 4th AFA to facilitate the location and engagement of targets within the battery's zone. Note that the location of Turk's Hump in this sketch does not correspond to its map reference. Turk's Hump is

beyond the right hand of the sketch, being on the western end of Chunuk Bair.

The available 18-pounder registration lists indicate that, while direct fire was sometimes used, for the majority of targets a bearing, range, angle of sight, fuse setting and corrector were recorded, showing that they were engaged using indirect fire tecÚiques. This accorded with *Field Artillery Training,* which stated that 'indirect laying is the normal method employed in the field'. No registration cards are available for the howitzers, but they would also have used indirect fire. Daily reports furnished by the mountain batteries indicate that they too predominately used the same method.[69]

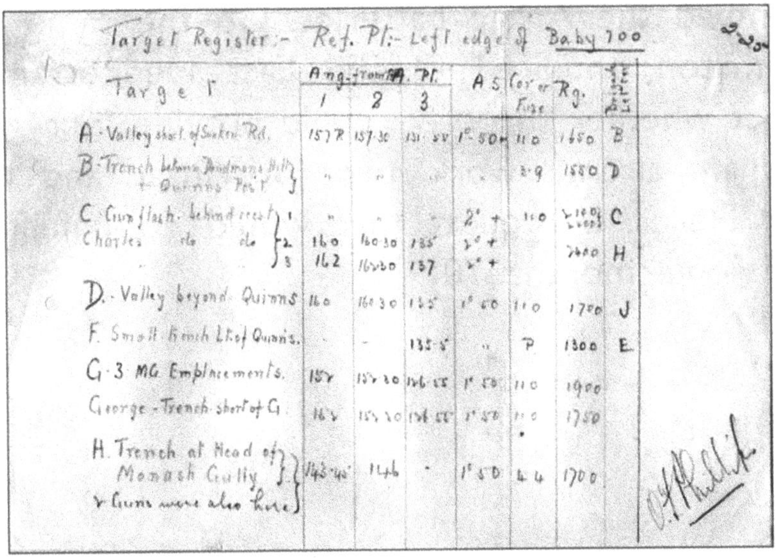

Target Register:- Ref. Pt:- Left edge of Baby 700

Target	Ang. from Ref. Pt. 1	2	3	A S	Cor or Fuse	Rg.	[illegible]
A. Valley short of Sniper Rd.	157 R	157.30	[illegible]	1° 50	110	1650	B
B. Trench between Deadmans Hill & Quinns Post	"	"	"	"	3.9	1550	D
C. Gun flash behind crest 1	"	"	"	2° +	110	[illegible]	C
Charles do do 2	160	160.30	135	2° +		2400	H
3	162	162.30	137	2° +			
D. Valley beyond Quinns	160	160.30	135	1° 60	110	1700	J
F. Small trench Lt. of Quinns.	-	-	135.5	"	P	1300	E.
G. 3 MG Emplacements.	155	155.30	136.55	1° 50	110	1900	
George - Trench short of G	165	155.30	136.55	1° 50	110	1750	
H. Trench at Head of Monash Gully & Guns were also here	143.40	146	-	1° 50	4.4	1700	

Diagram 11: Example registration card, 4th AFA Battery. Target Register used by the 4th AFA Battery in May 1915.

The data indicates that the guns engaged these targets using indirect-fire laying tecÚiques.

Although most of the field guns were, perforce, static, efforts were made to retain some sort of flexibility. As noted, early in the deployment of the 9th AFA Battery two guns formed a horse-drawn mobile battery until their permanent positions were found. Later a mobile section was formed using one un-deployed gun from each of the 4th and 5th AFA batteries. An improvised anti-aircraft capability was established on 20 May when pits were dug for the 9th Battery's mobile section, allowing the gun trails to be lowered sufficiently to enable them to fire on the enemy aircraft that had sporadically bombed the Anzac batteries. On the same day Hamilton enquired of the East Mediterranean Fleet whether the Navy could provide four guns for anti-aircraft work, two for Anzac and two for Helles, a request that would go unfulfilled for some months.[70]

Target	L.o.F	A.S.	Cor	Range	MapSquare	Remarks
						Ranging Board
				No 4 Gun Jopps Battery		
A	Direct	Zero	160	4525		Olive Grove Battery
F	"	"	160	3525	211.Pq	Kaba Tepe Brown Trench
H	"	"	160	3675		Kaba Tepe Emplacement
K	"	"	164	6025	202 J8	Four Tree Emplacement
L	"	"	164	4450	211 Z 3-6	L Trench
M	16°40'L 9up 5p 5 of 8 cape	"	168	2175	212 C6-D4	Gun Ridge Battery
E	Direct		164	4700	203 B 2-4	Howitzer "Asmak"
N	7°5'L	1°Dep	162	2175	212 C4-7	Gun Ridge "Cross Trench"
O	Direct	"	164	2625	212 H 7	Mathematical Trench
P	23°10'L	10' Dep	164	5000	213 W 2	Eski Keui-Maidos Road
S	7°10'L	30' Dep	166	5675	203 F 5	Quarry Road (2 Tree Cornfield)
T	Direct		164	3125	211 P4-5	Kaba Tepe Gun
U	10°20'L	35'Dep	164	5550	203 F 2-3	Sunken Road (new)
W	Direct		167	5375	202 D6	Yellow Bluff Trench
I	"	"	164	2675	212 H 8	The "Squirt"

Diagram 12: Example ranging board, 9th AFA Battery. Ranging Board or registration data for Number 4 Gun in Jopp's Battery, part of 9th AFA Battery. Note that some targets were engaged using direct fire, while others were engaged with indirect fire tecÚiques.

The Battles of May

After the failure of the NZ&A Division's attack on 2 May, ANZAC set about entrenching its position, in most places also developing saps and mining towards the Ottoman lines. The situation on the left of Anzac, where snipers needed to be subdued and any Ottoman advance would turn the ANZAC line on Second Ridge, remained of critical importance.

On the night of 9/10 May a sortie was made with a view to capturing the Ottoman trench 25 yards in front of Quinn's Post. After initial promise, this operation was ultimately unsuccessful, and the 2nd NZFA Battery fired 100 rounds in the early morning of 10 May to assist in holding the enemy at bay as the attackers withdrew. Heavy bomb (grenade) attacks on the post resulted in artillery engagement of the Ottoman trenches in the area on subsequent days, and another sortie, again unsuccessful, on the night of 14/15 May. Australian artillery reports indicate that the 4th and 5th AFA batteries, along with the New Zealand howitzers, supported Quinn's and Pope's on the evening of this operation, but the participation of the howitzers is not corroborated in the New Zealand records.[71]

Three days later, Anzac was subject to heavy gun and howitzer fire, chiefly falling in Section 3 and on the beach. Then, at around 4.00am on 19 May, the enemy, now four divisions strong, launched a general attack falling initially on the line between JoUston's Jolly and Quinn's Post. The 2nd NZFA, 8th AFA and sections from both mountain batteries came into action immediately, to be joined by ANZAC's other guns as daylight broke and the fighting spread along other parts of the line. The Ottoman artillery bombarded the Anzac position at around 5.00am, and shelling continued as the fighting ebbed and flowed throughout the day and into the evening and night of 19/20 May, before ceasing at dawn the next morning.[72]

The Ottoman artillery support of the first assaults was poorly managed, the heavy fire on 18 May too far divorced from the infantry action early the next morning to offer any benefit, only serving to confirm warnings of an impending attack from other sources, and removing any element of surprise. Support after daylight on 19 May appears to have been general rather than focused, perhaps because assaults in various areas were concurrent or occurred in quick succession. Success may have followed had greater artillery weight been applied to a particular sector.

The ANZAC artillery was able to generate sufficient firepower to complement that of the infantry and ensure the attacks were repulsed. Support for the New Zealanders in Section 3 from the Australian batteries and mountain guns in Section 2 proceeded satisfactorily and, as previously noted, while there were difficulties in getting a gun from the 1st NZFA Battery firing onto JoÚston's Jolly and Lone Pine, the New Zealand howitzers provided accurate fire onto these areas as required, as did some of the mountain guns. In his summary of the action, Birdwood noted that artillery fire had been responsible for a large proportion of the enemy losses and that reports from the commanders of his defensive sections showed the results obtained amply justified the ammunition expended: 1361 rounds from the 18-pounders; 143 from the 4.5-inchers; and 1410 from the mountain guns.[73] Ottoman casualties were horrendous, and an armistice was arranged four days later to cover their burial. ANZAC's gunners took advantage of this foray into no man's land to get a better lead on some previously un-located Ottoman batteries, and to scan their own area from an enemy viewpoint for defiladed areas that might be suitable as gun positions.

Although this attack marked the end of any attempt to push ANZAC into the sea, it did not mark the end of operations on the ANZAC left. NZ&A Division counter-mines were exploded at Quinn's Post on 27 and 28 May and, on the early morning of 29 May the Ottomans exploded a mine of their own, attacked the post, and captured a trench. They were driven out, but the post endured another assault before the fighting subsided. The 2nd and 4th NZFA batteries, 4th AFA Battery and mountain guns from Section 3 assisted the defence, with the officer commanding the post recording 'to the fine shooting of the artillery the repulse of the enemy is largely due.' This action was followed by sorties over the next three days to demolish enemy works to the front of Quinn's.[74]

Fighting flared again a few days later when Birdwood ordered the capture of 'Turkish Quinn's' on the night of 4/5 June, supported by a demonstration in front of Section 4 and diversionary operations by the Australians at German Officers' Trench and towards Gaba Tepe. The Australian 6-inch howitzer was to fire on the northern element of German Officers' Trench during the afternoon of 4 July, and then in immediate support of the assault, the 2nd NZFA and 4th AFA batteries along with a section of the 21st (Kohat) Battery were to fire in front of and to the left of Quinn's. At the same time, a section of the New Zealand howitzer battery was to engage the enemy communications trench leading to the post, and the 1st NZFA Battery was to bombard the northern face of Jóuston's Jolly. The guns were to commence firing at 11.00pm, the Zero Hour for the infantry. The 4th AFA Battery received its orders directly from

Napier JoÚston, who ordered it to open fire at 11.00pm at the slow rate, increase to the quick rate at 11.50pm, and cease fire at 12.40am once the trench had been captured. Why the guns should cease at this stage instead of continuing to provide some form of covering fire is unexplained.[75]

Initially the New Zealand attack at Quinn's went well, with seventy to eighty yards of Ottoman trench occupied, but the attackers were then subjected to heavy rifle and machine-gun fire. The Australian attack on German Officers' Trench failed at first and, although partially successful later, did not reduce the pressure on the New Zealanders, who retired at 6.00am in the face of an Ottoman grenade attack. The Ottomans who were counter-attacking could be seen by Australian observers but could not be engaged by Australian guns, and fire from the 2nd NZFA Battery could not stem the tide.[76]

The First Month

For the gunners, the first month at Anzac had been a period of intense adaptation: first, adjusting to static warfare, which placed a greater premium on centralised command and control of fire support, and second, operating in disadvantageous terrain which prevented them siting their field guns in depth and switching their fire along the front. It took the month to find suitable positions for all the 18-pounders, and even then some batteries were in split positions or had guns with separate arcs so that the whole front could be covered. Within that same month the telephone network linking batteries, observers, artillery and infantry brigade headquarters and the two divisional artillery headquarters was established, along with the allocations of artillery to defensive sections and the development of a flexible command and control system that delegated control to the most appropriate level and made best use of the different types of guns. The battles of May demonstrated that the arrangements made by the gunners met the day-to-day demands of the defence with an adequate weight of fire, despite restrictions on ammunition supply and the fact that the shrapnel ammunition of the field guns was not entirely suited to the situation.

Chapter Five

HOLDING THE LINE

With the major battles of the campaign now being fought at Cape Helles, from early June onwards the Anzac front essentially became static, although three advanced posts were developed to the front of Section 1: Tasmania and Ryrie's posts on Holly Ridge across Poppy Valley from Bolton's Ridge, and Chatham's Post on Harris Ridge further south. These posts were connected to the main firing line by tunnels and covered approaches.

Both sides were intent on strengthening their defences by entrenching, mining and other engineer works. As part of these activities, June saw the construction of a road within Anzac designed to ease the movement of guns and the resupply of ammunition and stores. Known as Artillery Road, it ran from the southern portion of the ANZAC line just south-east of Shell Green, passed behind the crest of Bolton's Ridge to the rear of the infantry firing line, and ran around the head of the various gullies, dipping seawards behind Lone Pine and ending at Brown's Dip, where it joined two other roads: Gun Lane running into the Pimple at Lone Pine, and an unnamed road pushing down Victoria Gully to Dawkins' Point on Brighton Beach.[1]

Together with a network of roads (see Map 10) running from Anzac Cove up MacLagan's Ridge, and up Shrapnel Valley to positions behind JoUston's Jolly and onto McCay's Hill, Artillery Road and the road that ran down Victoria Valley offered greater mobility for the artillery across the Anzac area. To take advantage of this potential, as June progressed Hobbs sought the return of the 6th AFA Battery from Helles. He envisaged that one of its sections would form a mobile battery and the other would furnish replacement guns for those in other batteries damaged by Ottoman artillery fire. The two undeployed guns from the 4th and 5th AFA batteries had already been used for the latter purpose, and at the time he was writing there were no spare 18-pounders on hand. HQ MEF agreed to the return of the 6th Battery at the end of the next operation at Helles, with no specific date set. As it happened, it would not reach Anzac until mid-August.[2]

Diggers on Artillery Road cut behind the crest of Bolton's Hill along the right half of the 1st Australian Division's line to facilitate the movement of guns and the resupply of ammunition (AWM G01054A).

Static Defence

In this environment, ANZAC's guns turned to the tasks of static defence. June war diaries for the New Zealand guns are not available, but Australian records for 16 June provide an example of the type of activity involved. During this day on which, if anything, the Ottomans were more active than normal, the guns in Section 1 fired two counter-battery missions in the early morning, two more in the early afternoon—which saw a gun in the 7th AFA Battery put out of action—and three more in the evening. In between, the same batteries engaged an enemy working party and a group of mounted and dismounted personnel. Responding to enemy shelling of the trenches in the late afternoon, the guns of Section 2 fired five counter-battery missions and engaged two observation posts. Later, the 6-inch howitzer fired a series at a gun operating from a position that remained unknown for much of the day before being located by two observers in the evening. Another big gun firing from the direction of Boghali in the north-east remained un-located, and no response was made to desultory fire from guns on JoÚston's Jolly and Gun (Third) Ridge.[3]

That same day, in response to a request from the 9th Battalion, a mountain gun from Rawson's section of the 21st (Kohat) Battery set up in the open to try to engage a trench in the Wheatfield. The attempt failed because of the unreliability of the fuses. Rawson's section later fired on a working party at Gaba Tepe, while Thom's neighbouring section fired a counter-battery mission to the north. The third section of the battery did not fire, but its observers were able to locate a gun firing from Anafarta in the north, and passed the information to the NZ&A Division.[4]

Countering the Ottoman Artillery

As exemplified by these activities, artillery reports for the month show quite clearly that the principal task for the gunners was preventing their Ottoman counterparts from materially affecting the ANZAC defence. Enemy harassing fire was a daily occurrence normally applied in 'short bursts at uncertain intervals', with the beach a regular target. Enemy counter-battery fire could be concentrated, as could preparatory fire for an attack, such as on the night of 29/30 June when, according to an ANZAC estimate, 250 shells from weapons varying in calibre from 75mm to 8.2-inch (208.2mm) fell on Russell's Top prior to an action the next morning.[5]

Determining the number and type of artillery pieces facing Anzac was an imprecise art. By mid-June the ANZAC gunners had identified forty-five Ottoman guns firing from sixteen different locations in the arc from Anafarta in the north around to Boghali and then southwards along and behind Third Ridge to Wineglass Hill in the south-east and the Olive Grove and Gaba Tepe in the south (see Diagram 8). At this time ANZAC had forty-six artillery pieces in action—twenty-eight 18-pounders, four 4.5-inch howitzers, two 6-inch howitzers, and twelve 10-pounder mountain guns—suggesting a rough balance in numbers of guns between the adversaries.[6]

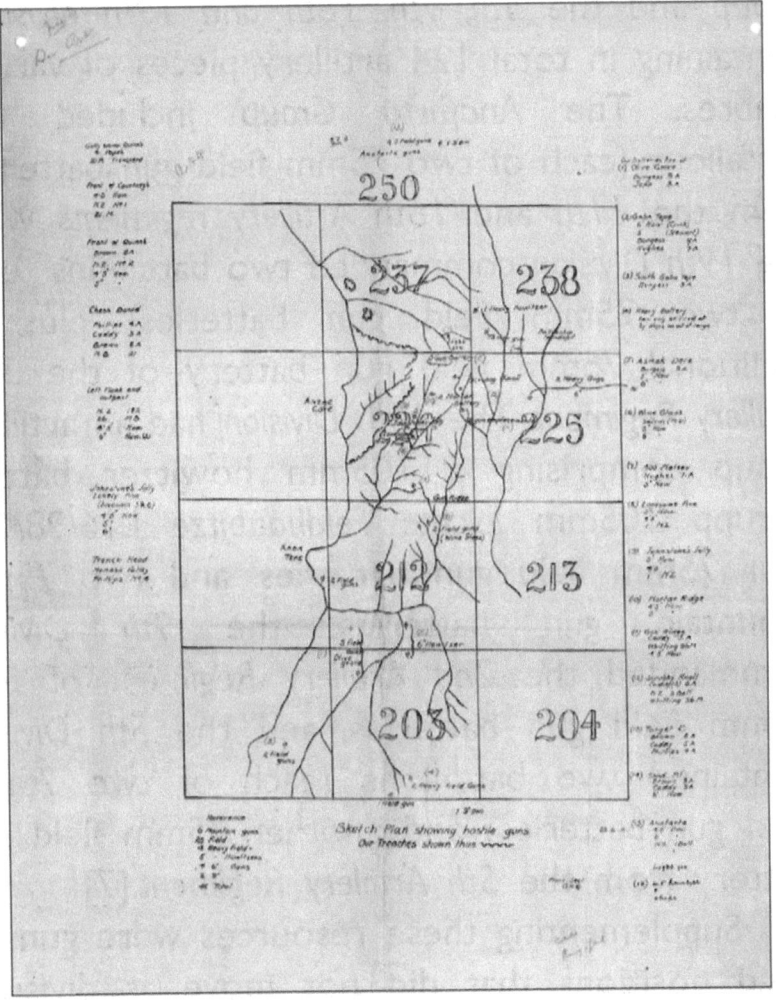

Diagram 13: Hostile batteries, June, 1st Divisional Artillery War Diary. Sketch plan from the Australian Divisional Artillery war diary showing the location, type and number of Ottoman guns identified in June 1915. The ANZAC guns capable of engaging various areas of the front are shown in the left margin, and those capable of engaging particular Ottoman gun positions in the right margin.

In fact the enemy enjoyed a considerable superiority. Their forces comprised the *Anafarta Group* and the *5th, 9th, 16th and 19th divisions*, containing in total 124 artillery pieces of various calibres. The *Anafarta Group* included two battalions (each of two 75mm field gun batteries) from the *11th* and *16th Artillery regiments* while the *19th Division* commanded two battalions (each of two 75mm field gun batteries) plus an additional 75mm field gun battery of the *39th Artillery Regiment*. The *16th Division* had an artillery group comprising a 105mm howitzer battery (Krupp 105mm *leichte Feldhaubitze* L16/98/09), four 75mm field gun batteries, and two 75mm mountain gun batteries, the *9th Division* commanded the *2nd Artillery Regiment* of four 75mm field gun batteries, and the *5th Division* contained two battalions (each of two 75mm field gun batteries) and another 75mm field gun battery from the *5th Artillery Regiment*.[7]

Supplementing these resources were guns in fixed positions that did not move as divisions rotated into and out of the line. These comprised twelve 87mm field guns, two 150mm mortars, four 120mm howitzers (Krupp 120mm *Feldhaubitze* L12/92), seven Nordenfelts, four 150mm howitzers and two 107mm guns (perhaps captured Russian 107mm K77).[8] Interestingly, the available Ottoman sources do not describe the 8.2-inch and 9-inch weapons frequently reported by Birdwood's forces.

In employing their artillery, the Ottomans held other advantages apart from numbers. Their 75mm field and mountain guns and their 105mm and 150mm howitzers were quite modern weapons. They were able to site guns and observers to the north of Anzac at Anafarta and to the south around Gaba Tepe, allowing them to fire in enfilade along the coast and shell the Anzac beaches relatively accurately. In the centre they held the high ground with its associated benefits for observation, while some of their batteries sited along the crest of Third Ridge in direct-fire positions overlooked the ANZAC guns. Throughout their area they could make use of the terrain to place their batteries in defilade to ANZAC and naval observation and fire, leaving only muzzle flash and the dust and smoke raised by firing as clues to their location. With a greater depth to their position, they also had more freedom to reposition their guns or to site guns further back so as to cover a broader arc without having to move.

However, they also faced disadvantages. While they had the high ground and thus better observation, the ruggedness of the terrain in the Anzac position made potential targets harder to locate and engage effectively. Some of the

Ottoman weapons, such as the 'Mantelli' guns and the 120mm Krupp howitzers, were older or obsolescent types, and the majority were guns rather than howitzers and so, like ANZAC's field guns and naval support, were not entirely suited to the terrain. But the critical deficiency was a shortage of ammunition, especially for the howitzers, with the Ottoman Empire having only half the desired stocks at the outbreak of the war, a very restricted domestic manufacturing capability, and no reliable supply links to Germany or Austria until Bulgaria defeated Serbia later in 1915. Quality was also an issue, with ANZAC units reporting numerous occasions on which Ottoman shells failed to explode. The actual weapon of the artillery is its shell, and the lack of sufficient stocks of reliable ammunition negated the Ottomans' potential artillery advantages. The author of the British official history of the campaign concluded that it 'prevented the enemy from making life at Anzac very nearly intolerable.'[9]

Through constant observation and the occasional use of aircraft, the Anzac gunners gradually built their knowledge of their opponent. ANZAC batteries registered and engaged those hostile batteries within their arcs of fire, and ships were often tasked to take on batteries on the flanks of ANZAC, such as the 107mm and a '9-inch' gun operating in the Anafarta area, and the '8.2-inch' and 150mm howitzers firing from the north-east. But perhaps the most troublesome Ottoman guns were those operating to the south of Anzac, field guns at Wineglass Hill towards the southern end of Third Ridge, and others at the Olive Grove, along with 150mm howitzers and a '9-inch' gun and a 120mm howitzer further south.

When the 6-inch howitzers arrived, they were positioned to take on these flanking batteries. Nevertheless, the Ottoman fire was persistent, and this may have been a factor in Birdwood's change of mind relating to the use of obsolescent 5-inch howitzers. Whereas a month before he had been reluctant to seek a battery of these weapons from Australia, when HQ MEF offered some on 23 June, they were accepted 'if ammunition can be supplied'. The 5th (City of Glasgow) Battery of the 4th (Lowland) Howitzer Brigade RFA arrived on 26 June, and was deployed near Shell Green. Men from the 3rd AFA Brigade Ammunition Column were assigned to help the battery dig in, as the Scottish gunners were as yet too soft, having just arrived in theatre.[10] This battery gave the Corps additional ability to engage concealed targets, although ammunition supply was restricted, and the wear of the howitzers' barrels caused accuracy problems. As with the 6-inch howitzers, when these weapons were assigned bombardment tasks on the forward Ottoman positions, their shells sometimes failed to explode, probably because the ranges were very short and there was insufficient time for the fuses to arm.

No.2 Gun, 9th AFA Battery, in position for firing on Gaba Tepe and the Olive Grove in June 1915. Note the open gun pit to allow for a larger arc of fire, and the use of bushes to camouflage the gun (AWM G01056).

While counter-battery fire was applied, it normally led to only temporary cessation of Ottoman fire. This is not surprising given the difficulty of accurately locating the hostile guns and the fact that because of shortages of both guns and ammunition, counter-battery missions were often allocated to one or two guns using a restricted amount of shrapnel. Therefore, only a limited area could be covered, and the fire lacked destructive or lasting effect.

Various tactics were employed to counter the Ottoman fire. Early on, immediately the guns at the Olive Grove and Gaba Tepe fired on an Anzac trench, all the ANZAC guns fired on the Ottoman trenches within their arcs. Such retaliation was intended to dissuade the Ottoman gunners, but the tactic caused Anderson to wonder whether it constituted 'perhaps a voluntary giving away of all our own carefully planned positions...' By June this tactic had been abandoned due to ammunition restrictions, and other procedures, such as the use of crossfire from two batteries, were sometimes employed.[11]

Major June Actions

After the sortie from Quinn's Post on the night of 4/5 June, ANZAC did not launch a significant offensive foray until 28 June, when diversions were staged in order to hold Ottoman forces in place while attacks were made at Cape Helles. Two afternoon sorties were made by elements of the 1st Australian Division, one from Section 1 south along Harris Ridge towards locations known as the Balkan gun pits and Echelon Trench, and the second eastwards from

Bolton's and Holly Ridge towards Sniper's Ridge, and its southern extension, the Knife Edge. These actions were launched with only a few hours' notice, and thus no time was available to implement a considered supporting artillery fire plan. Two guns of the 7th AFA Battery supported the southern thrust along with the fire of a destroyer, and the other two guns the eastern thrust.[12]

Both sorties were threatened by flanking fire from Ottoman guns around the Olive Grove and encountered stiff opposition. In response, the 8th AFA Battery fired onto Pine Ridge, the 9th AFA Battery and the 6-inch howitzer took on counter-battery tasks, a mountain section and a destroyer engaged Ottoman trenches in the south, and the New Zealand and 5-inch howitzers fired into the valley behind Lone Pine and Pine Ridge. However, neither of the two objectives was taken and the sorties were withdrawn, having incurred significant casualties. That night, to prolong the impression of a threat, HQ ANZAC ordered flares and lights to be shown in the trenches, and the mountain guns to fire star shells over Ottoman positions in the south as well as at Lone Pine, Mule Valley, the Chessboard and Baby 700.[13]

The following night, 29/30 June, Mustafa Kemal, commander of the *19th Division*, ordered an attack by the *18th Infantry Regiment* across the Nek onto Russell's Top. The action began at 12.15am on 30 June with the shelling previously mentioned and rifle fire onto the trenches on Russell's Top. At 1.00am the Ottomans assaulted, but, after some initial gains, were repulsed with the assistance of neighbouring positions and fire from HMS *Colne* on the Ottoman guns, whose fire had in any case mainly fallen behind the ANZAC positions and was thus ineffective. The NZ&A Division report on this action does not mention any significant support from the ANZAC batteries.[14]

Into July

The daily support provided by the ANZAC artillery in July was similar to that in June, as represented by the activities of the 7th AFA Battery on the 9th and 10th of the month. On the first of these days the battery's No 4 gun fired two rounds at a working party on Sniper's Ridge, followed by another three rounds at 5.30pm while, at the same time, No 3 gun despatched nine rounds at an enemy observation party near 'Cement Emplacement', four of which appeared to be effective. At 6.45pm No 4 gun engaged a machine-gun firing from Sniper's Ridge, silencing it. The next day, at 2.15pm, No 3 gun again engaged the 'Cement Emplacement' observation post with three rounds. Fifteen minutes later No 1 gun engaged a working party with four rounds, and fired on another working party at 5.00pm with three rounds. The day's firing concluded at 5.45pm with No 3 gun sending two rounds into the 'Cement Emplacement' observation post, and No 4 gun engaging another working party.[15]

More broadly, on 9 July the 5-inchers of the 5th (City of Glasgow) Battery and the 1st and 4th NZFA batteries conducted a prearranged bombardment of JoÚston's Jolly and Lone Pine designed to draw Ottoman fire and destroy overhead cover, while HMS *Chelmer* shelled Old No 3 Outpost in the spurs to the north of the Anzac position and, across the two divisions, six counter-battery missions were fired. The next day destroyers shelled the Nek and the Tabletop, the 1st NZFA Battery fired a series onto Lone Pine, the 4th NZFA (Howitzer) Battery and the 5-inchers engaged targets in Legge Valley using aeroplane observation, and the Australian batteries fired in support of Quinn's Post and onto JoÚston's Jolly and Turk's Hump—the western end of Chunuk Bair. Nine counter-battery missions were also fired.[16]

Counter-Battery Work

The amount of counter-battery work on these two days was not unusual, indicating that the primary task for the gunners remained the suppression of the Ottoman artillery. That task proved just as difficult as it had in June. Although Australian batteries endured a little less hostile battery fire than in June (thirteen times as opposed to seventeen), Hobbs reported nearly twice as many un-located Ottoman guns than in the previous month. Air observation was occasionally used in an effort to help locate and engage these weapons. Cunliffe-Owen and Napier JoUston considered the results disappointing, but Hobbs' reports to Divisional Headquarters painted a slightly more positive picture.[17]

On some occasions when under fire, the ANZAC guns covered one another. For example, on 8 July Hughes' 7th Battery fired on an Ottoman battery engaging the southern flank of the Anzac line, and was itself engaged by Turkish guns at the Olive Grove. Burgess' 9th Battery immediately engaged the Olive Grove and, in turn, was fired on by an Ottoman battery on Third Ridge which was then engaged by Bessell-Browne's 8th Battery, silencing it. This enabled the 7th Battery and two of the 9th

Battery's guns to then deal with the original Turkish battery.[18]

Understandably, frustration arose within the infantry when the ANZAC artillery could not even temporarily silence an enemy battery. Such a situation occurred in mid-July with Ottoman howitzers and field guns firing from concealed positions near Turk's Hump. Complaints from an infantry brigade led Corps headquarters to point out that enemy shelling was to be expected, the bombardment was very much lighter than might be experienced in France and, until the hostile weapons could be located and suppressed, the brigade had to deal with the problem, perhaps by temporarily reducing troop numbers in the trenches under fire.[19] For their part, the gunners responded by using aircraft to try to locate the hostile weapons, firing a series of air-observation shoots over subsequent days. In addition, an Australian observer was sent into the New Zealand sector to register a suspected enemy gun position, with direct telephone communications established between the New Zealand observers and the Australian field artillery brigade able to engage the area, and the New Zealanders were requested to provide crossfire onto the target if their zones of fire permitted. Hobbs also resorted to using retaliatory fire on the Turkish trenches opposite the Anzac trenches being targeted, a tactic he advocated throughout the campaign.[20]

A photograph taken on 30 June 1915 of Colonel Hobbs (standing left) at a 9th AFA Battery gun whose arc covered Gaba Tepe and the Olive Grove. The pit is open and the gun is covered with bushes to screen it from aeroplane observation (AWM G01055).

While the daily Ottoman shelling throughout June and July exposed ANZAC's lack of a truly effective counter-battery capability, it did not prove to be decisive. At this time the Ottomans did not attempt to maximise their artillery advantages by centralising control of their resources and employing massed fire on a particular area. Their artillery assets remained grouped with divisions, and tended to be used episodically for short periods with limited impact, reflecting the shortage of ammunition. The continual harassing fire from these weapons and their heavier brethren did not significantly interfere with ANZAC operations, although it did cause continual casualties to men and damage to materiel.

Demonstrations

ANZAC periodically conducted demonstrations in July to induce the Ottomans to expend scarce ammunition to no effect, or to divert Ottoman forces away from operations being conducted at Cape Helles. In contrast to the previous month, these actions predominately relied on activity from within the trenches, along with bombardment of the enemy positions, rather than sorties from the Anzac line.

Such an activity took place on the night of 11/12 July. Mortars and naval gunfire, but no artillery fire was used. However, the guns were used the next day in a diversion supporting an attack at Helles. At 4.30 in the morning they bombarded Lone Pine and JoÚston's Jolly for twenty minutes, and then repeated the dose at 8.15am as the infantry in the trenches simulated preparations for an attack. At the same time, in Section 1, a show was made of moving troops from the main firing line on Bolton's Ridge to Tasmania and Ryrie's posts. These actions drew a prompt response.

During the day HQ ANZAC ordered a further demonstration for that night. Consequently, between 7.45pm and 8.15pm, the left-flank destroyer shelled Baby 700 and the Nek, Section 2 directed mortars onto the trenches opposite Quinn's and Courtney's posts, Sections 3 and 4 initiated rifle fire, the mountain guns fired star shells over the Chessboard, JoÚston's Jolly and Lone Pine and engaged machine-guns on the Chessboard, the 4th and 5th AFA batteries targeted the Chessboard and the Nek, and the 1st NZFA Battery fired into Legge Valley. The batteries were ordered not to expend more than twenty rounds on this activity.[21]

Similar activities took place after ANZAC received warning of an attack on 23 July to mark the Ottoman Constitution Day. These ruses entailed movement in the trenches, artillery bombardments, the occasional firing of star shells, and periodic naval bombardments on the flanks. A growth in interdiction fire occurred in this period, with fire into Legge Valley occurring daily between 20 and 26 July.[22]

Strengthening the Artillery

As July progressed, the ANZAC artillery was gradually strengthened, although the weapons that arrived were all of obsolescent pattern. On 5 July a third 6-inch howitzer landed and was allocated to the 1st Australian Division, which then had two such weapons, one located centrally, the other in the south near the 7th AFA Battery. Five days later, a 4.7-inch (120mm) gun—nominally QF, but with separately loaded projectile and propelling charge, with no on-carriage traverse and a limited recoil mechanism—came ashore. It too was allocated to the Australians with a view to engaging targets at longer range to the south of ANZAC. From these resources Hobbs formed the 1st Australian Heavy Battery, drawing men from the brigade ammunition columns to form the gun detachments, with the battery ready for action on 18 July.[23]

Infantrymen haul the 4.7-inch naval gun from Victoria Gully to its emplacement on 17 July. The arrival of a second 6-inch howitzer and this gun enabled Hobbs to form the Australian Heavy Battery (AWM J06124).

The 4.7-inch naval gun of the Australian Heavy Battery with three of its crew in its emplacement with overhead cover. This position was located on the western slopes of the ridge between Victoria Gully and Clarke Valley. Bolton's Ridge can be seen in the background. The gun's arc of fire was to the south and south-east of the Anzac beachhead, and it frequently engaged the Olive Grove battery and other Ottoman guns south and south-east of Gaba Tepe (AWM P08097.003).

Next to arrive, beginning mid-month, were A, B, C and D batteries of the 69th Howitzer Brigade RFA from the 13th (Western) Division. Equipped with 5-inch howitzers, this brigade remained under Corps control, with batteries dispersed to positions in the rear areas of both the Australian and NZ&A divisions. The first of these batteries commenced registration of targets on 21 July.[24] At around the same time, a few more mortars were also received. They were of yet another pattern, 3.7-inch (95mm), firing a 3.5lb (1.5kg) projectile. Three were delivered, along with 600 rounds. One with 120 rounds went to the NZ&A Division for use on Russell's Top, and another went to the 1st Australian Division with a similar amount of ammunition to be sited where it could support Quinn's and Courtney's posts. The third also went to the Australians, to be deployed in the 1st Infantry Brigade area near Lone Pine.[25]

The last of the artillery units to land during the month was the 4th (City of Glasgow) Battery of the 4th (Lowland) Howitzer Brigade RFA, arriving with the Brigade Headquarters in late July to join its sister battery which had deployed a month earlier. This Brigade too remained a Corps Troops unit, with one battery allocated to each division for general support purposes. Finally, Hobbs received two replacement 18-pounders and was able to reconstitute a mobile section.[26]

A 5-inch howitzer of the 5th (City of Glasgow) Battery RFA in an open gun pit at the southern end of North Beach in August. This battery arrived at Anzac on 26 June. Initially deployed within the old Anzac beachhead, the battery moved to this location after the August Offensive and supported ANZAC until the evacuation (Alexander Turnbull Library 1/2-077923-F).

As July drew to a close, the NZ&A Division was advised that the 5th NZFA and 6th NZFA (Howitzer) batteries would soon be arriving from New Zealand and the return of the 3rd NZFA Battery from Cape Helles could be expected. This prompted a restructuring of the Division's artillery into a Divisional Artillery headquarters and two field artillery brigades, each of two 18-pounder and one 4.5-inch howitzer batteries. Napier JoÚston retained the position of CRA. Frank Symon took command of the 1st NZFA

Brigade, comprising the 1st, 3rd and 6th (Howitzer) batteries, and Francis Sykes became commander of the 2nd NZFA Brigade, comprising the 2nd, 4th (Howitzer) and 5th batteries. While this structure was put in place, the only guns available remained those of the 1st, 2nd and 4th (Howitzer) batteries.[27]

The Capture of Turkish Despair

July ended with an action to capture a section of Ottoman trench known as Turkish Despair, recently constructed in front of Tasmania Post with communications back across the Valley of Despair to Sniper's Ridge. Assisted by the explosion of mines just short of the objective and with supporting artillery fire, the 11th Battalion, 3rd Australian Infantry Brigade, attacked at moonrise, around 10.15pm, on 31 July (see Map 11).[28]

The fire plan for this attack, devised by the infantry, saw D Battery, 69th Howitzer Brigade, fire 60 rounds over two hours commencing at 4.30pm at a portion of the southern end of Sniper's Ridge containing machine-guns and a trench mortar that enfiladed the objective at a range of 274 metres, and at trenches on the ridge 183 metres east-north-east of the objective. From the commencement of the assault, this battery then re-engaged these targets and machine-gun positions on the northern end of Sniper's Ridge, while the 7th AFA Battery fired shrapnel across Harris Ridge, Poppy Valley, Sniper's Ridge and Lone Pine, the 8th AFA Battery fired into the Valley of Despair, and the right-flanking monitor shelled the Twin Trenches to the south.[29]

The attack was successful, and the commander of the 3rd Australian Infantry Brigade reported that the work of the artillery was 'of very great assistance', despite the fact that, from around 10.18pm onwards, the captured trenches came under small arms fire from adjacent Ottoman trenches, even though these trenches were under ANZAC shrapnel fire. Between 10.22pm and midnight the Ottomans shelled Bolton's Ridge and Poppy Valley behind Tasmania Post. Burgess' 9th AFA Battery responded, as did howitzers from the 4th Lowland Brigade RFA, and these resources were called on again when the captured trenches were shelled between 4.30 and 5.30am on 1 August.[30]

This fire plan, designed to cause some damage to supporting positions before the assault and then suppress surrounding Ottoman infantry positions during the attack, was only partially successful. Among its shortcomings was the application of an inadequate amount of fire to the Ottoman trenches to achieve the desired effect, along with insufficient planning to counter hostile batteries. Unfortunately, perhaps because of the minor nature of the operation and the fact that, overall, it was a success, these deficiencies apparently went unrecognised.

The First Three Months

In June and July, the ANZAC artillery refined the adaptations and innovations that had predominated in May. Battery positions at the end of July are shown in Map 12. Although greater flexibility and responsiveness may have been obtained if an Australian battery had been deployed on Russell's Top to support the 400 Plateau, and New Zealand batteries on McCay's Ridge to support Section 3, arrangements for support from neighbouring defensive sections or from Corps Troops artillery became well practised. The additional howitzers that Hobbs and Napier JoÚston requested in order to improve their ability to engage Ottoman defences and guns in defilade gradually arrived and proved generally useful. The artillery telephone network expanded as more artillery units deployed to Anzac and, by the end of July, telephone lines with built-in redundancy linked the two divisional artillery headquarters, the field artillery brigades of both divisions, the field batteries and their observation stations, the mountain guns, the Australian Heavy Battery, the howitzer batteries, and each of the divisional and defensive sector headquarters.

Static trench warfare over the period placed an emphasis on firepower and, while local success was possible, the combined infantry and artillery firepower on both sides proved sufficient to defeat any major attack. The Ottoman artillery enjoyed superior numbers and observation, but was unable to press home this advantage because its ammunition supply was restricted and its command decentralised. In countering hostile artillery fire, the best either side could achieve was the temporary cessation of the fire of the other. The ANZAC gunners were in action most days, either assisting minor infantry offensives and helping to repel the few attacks made by the Ottoman infantry or, more regularly, engaging enemy trenches and work parties, interdicting supply lines, and suppressing troublesome guns and machine-guns.

Chapter Six

THE AUGUST OFFENSIVE: PREPARATIONS, LONE PINE AND THE NEK

In the three months that ANZAC was on the defensive, Birdwood and his staff looked for options for offensive operations to improve their tactical position, sending several papers to HQ MEF on the subject. These included the possibility of exploiting the country on the left flank—difficult but lightly defended—to capture the heights of the Sari Bair Range. As the fighting at Helles became deadlocked, and with the promise of significant reinforcements, Hamilton turned to these considerations and began contemplating an offensive from Anzac, combining Birdwood's left flank option with a landing further north at Suvla Bay, which would be undertaken by the British IX Corps.[1] He made the decision to proceed along these lines on 28 June, with operations to be launched in early August (see Map 13).

ANZAC's role was the capture of the Sari Bair Range from Baby 700 to Hill 971. In outline this involved the NZ&A Division, supported by three British infantry brigades from the 13th (Western) Division, breaking out north of Anzac on the night 6/7 August in four columns. Two covering columns would seize the foothills astride the mouths of Aghyl Dere, Chailak Dere and Sazli Beit Dere, the three principal valleys running up to the high ground, allowing two assault columns to pass through and swinging around the right flank of the Ottoman defences to secure the heights of Hill 971, Hill Q and Chunuk Bair before dawn. At first light on 7 August the New Zealand Infantry Brigade would then drop down the range from Chunuk Bair to take Battleship Hill from the rear.[2] Simultaneously, the 1st and 3rd Australian LH brigades, supported by two British infantry battalions, would launch assaults from Russell's Top, Pope's Hill and Quinn's Post to eliminate the Ottoman positions on Baby 700 and the upper reaches of Second Ridge, catching the Ottoman defenders in a pincer movement from front and rear. Tactically, this would give ANZAC the high ground and flank the remaining Ottoman positions.[3] Operationally, combined with the landing of the British IX Corps at Suvla, Hamilton believed that the whole of the Ottoman defences north of the Kilid Bahr Plateau would be outflanked, enabling the British to cut the Ottoman north-south road communications, leading to the isolation and collapse of their defence of the southern part of the peninsula.[4]

The offensive would begin with the British VIII Corps at Cape Helles launching a demonstration on the afternoon of 6 August to divert Ottoman attention. That evening at Anzac, the 1st Australian Infantry Brigade would seize Lone Pine in a bid to convince the enemy that this was the main effort, drawing his attention and forces away from the heights. Later that night, the 6th Australian Infantry Battalion would take German Officers' Trench, reinforcing the impression.[5]

Preparations

The British official history notes that, in planning the offensive, Hamilton was worried about the amount of artillery support likely to be available, and prevailed on the War Office to send the reinforcing divisions with at least their full complement of howitzers, to grant the MEF temporary priority in ammunition supply, and to provide a very small number of additional modern howitzers. He was unsuccessful, leading to a dispatch to London in which he noted that, with

British stocks of guns and ammunition low and the demands of the Western Front barely being met, he realised it was no good for him to be 'crying for the moon' in terms of resources. However, he said, unless adequate resources were made available, it would be no good for London to be 'crying for the crescent', for success at Gallipoli.

The War Office did not meet all of Hamilton's requests but, during July it did send the 5-inch howitzers of the 69th Howitzer Brigade RFA and the 4th (City of Glasgow) Battery of the 4th (Lowland) Howitzer Brigade RFA. It also provided an additional 4000 rounds of ammunition of various types.[6] In theatre, ammunition was stockpiled, the plan calling for 5700 rounds of 10-pounder, 15,500 rounds of 18-pounder, 1600 rounds of 4.5-inch, 10,000 rounds of 5-inch and 2200 rounds of 6-inch ammunition, with perhaps another 3000 rounds of 10-pounder and 10,000 rounds of 18-pounder brought forward, if possible, to complete the reserve holdings.[7] The 3rd Brigade Ammunition Column reported that, on 21 July, instructions were received to increase ammunition holdings to 480 rounds per gun in the batteries and 76 rounds per gun with the column, although that may have been because an Ottoman attack was expected on 23 July. It also reported that, from

22 July onwards, it was busy assisting the offloading of rifle ammunition and, late in the month, providing men to help the new troops arriving at Anzac, presumably the 13th Division, to land.[8]

In another preparatory measure, the Navy began deception actions. On the southern flank, a destroyer regularly shelled Lone Pine, Gaba Tepe and the southern end of Third Ridge to raise suspicions of a threat to the area. On the northern flank, ships began a nightly ruse to illuminate and then shell Old No 3 Outpost and the Tabletop, both of which were objectives during the initial phase of the breakout north of Anzac. The idea was to accustom the enemy to the activity so that he would not realise when the actual attack was being launched.

Planning

During the preparations Hamilton was obsessed with secrecy. His headquarters undertook the planning for the Suvla Bay operation, while HQ ANZAC planned the seizure of the heights and the feints in the bridgehead. Considerations were held tightly, although with the arrival of additional troops it was obvious to those at Anzac that something was afoot. On 22 July the NZ&A Division recorded the preparations being made for what it deduced would be an attack of some sort on its left.[9]

Nevertheless, orders were not released until close to the event. In the 1st Australian Division a secret warning order was distributed to the infantry brigade commanders and Hobbs on 29 July. Formal Corps orders were not promulgated until 3 August, just three days before the commencement of operations. Appendix A contained the artillery tasks, with arrangements for naval gunfire support detailed on an associated sheet. The 1st Australian Division's operation orders were issued on 4 August, and the NZ&A Division's orders a day later.[10]

In his book on the August Offensive, *Climax at Gallipoli*, Rhys Crawley writes that 'High level plans were predominantly developed at army and corps level, with the CRA's [sic] being left out of the process until the last moment. This was especially pronounced in the Anzac sector.' He states that Cunliffe-Owen took on a greater than usual role in planning the artillery support, working out the specifics of the artillery program himself, and did not formally explain the detailed plans to Hobbs and Napier JoÚston until 2 August.[11]

The NZFA Brigade War Diary records that Napier JoÚston's first involvement was a conference on the morning of 3 August, the day the Corps orders were issued. This is a day later than identified by Crawley, and underpins Napier JoÚston's later claim at the Dardanelles Commission that he only had one or two days' notice of the operation. At best he had less than three days to develop the fire plans to support the NZ&A Division, which were issued on 5 August.[12]

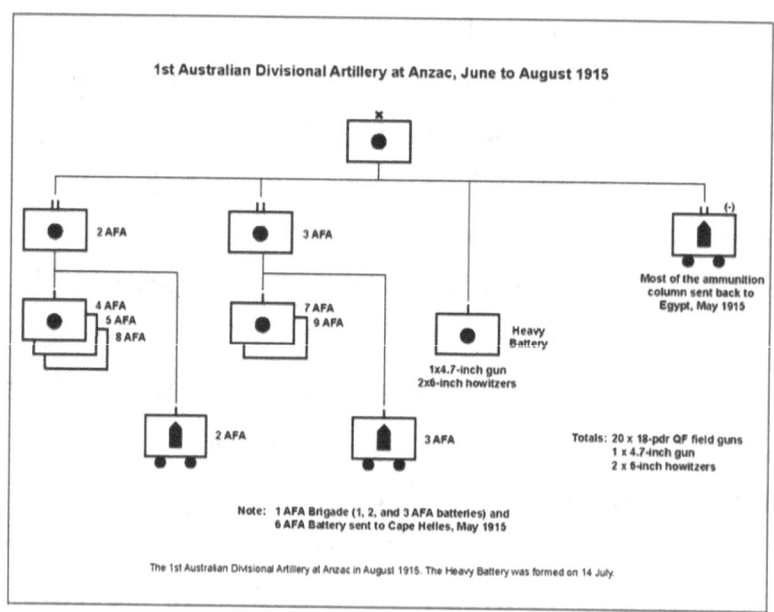

Organisation chart 4: The 1st Australian Divisional Artillery, April to August 1915

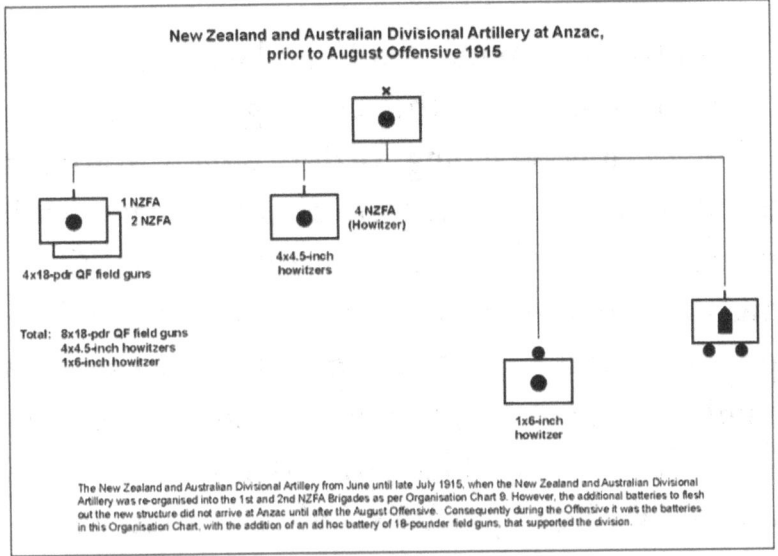

Organisation chart 5: NZ&A Divisional Artillery, prior to the August Offensive

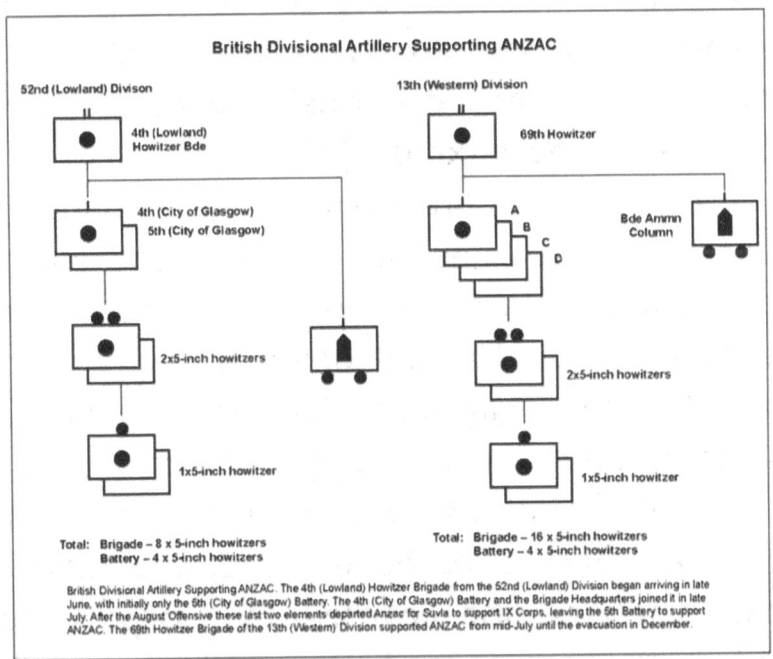

Organisation chart 6: British Divisional Artillery supporting ANZAC, 1 August 1915

Hobbs, however, had a little more time, gaining an inkling of the coming task as a result of the 29 July warning order which stated that the 'question of the degree of preliminary artillery preparation was under consideration'. On the same day he was asked for his proposals for fire support, and instructed to liaise with Cunliffe-Owen regarding the preliminary bombardment.[13] His own diary and the war diary of his headquarters indicate that he began working on supporting the offensive on 1 August, and was able to issue his orders on 3 August, the same day as Corps orders were promulgated, suggesting he had a degree of contact with Cunliffe-Owen beforehand. Further, orders were contained in the divisional operation order promulgated the next day.[14]

Even so, the involvement of Hobbs and Napier JoÚston came quite late in the planning process, with little or no opportunity to influence the outline fire plan laid down by Corps. Their relatively late engagement left both Hobbs and Napier JoÚston with barely sufficient time to make some local changes, define target areas in terms of trenches to be engaged, add tasks for those batteries not covered by Corps orders, conduct the necessary liaison with the artillery of the other division and from Corps Troops, and circulate final orders within their own formations. Equally, they had little opportunity to confirm with the attacking brigades that the nominated targets met their requirements, especially in the NZ&A Division where Napier JoÙston had to plan for both the dawn attack by the light horse on 7 August, and the assault on Sari Bair. In this regard the Corps' artillery planning processes were defective.

Fire Support Resources

To support ANZAC in the offensive, Birdwood had the fire of twelve 10-pounder mountain guns, twenty-eight 18-pounder field guns, four 4.5-inch howitzers, twenty-four 5-inch howitzers, three 6-inch howitzers, and one 4.7-inch gun. This was a parsimonious allocation to cover a potential frontage of some 5500 metres stretching from Hill 971 to the southern end of the line on Bolton's Ridge, especially as the field guns were limited in the areas they could cover, and the Corps faced the prospect of having to neutralise the Ottoman artillery at the same time as supporting the infantry.

Ammunition allocations for the offensive are not shown in the records, but the data that are available indicate that here too the resources were limited. The aforementioned stockpiles, if all were landed, equated to about 400 rounds per howitzer, 700 rounds per 10-pounder, and perhaps 800 to 900 rounds per 18-pounder, allowing that some would have been held back for contingencies. This equates to two to four hours of firing at normal rates, meaning that extensive bombardments were not possible. Fortunately, some of the 18-pounder ammunition provided was HE, which was more effective against fortifications than shrapnel.

Ammunition expenditure reports for the period are incomplete, but those that are available confirm that supplies were limited to approximate stockpile figures. The 5th AFA Battery reported firing 470 rounds per gun between 6 and 9 August, while between 6 and 10 August the 8th Battery fired 900, and the 9th Battery 600. The 3rd AFA Brigade Ammunition Column reported that, on the evening of 6 August, it received a requisition from the 7th AFA Battery for 700 rounds (175 rounds per gun) and from the 9th Battery for 1050 rounds (260 rounds per gun). Along with battery holdings this would suggest expenditure in the region of 650 to 750 rounds per gun. On 10 August the 1st NZFA Brigade recorded that no ammunition was available in the depot on the shore, indicating just how limited the supply had been.[15]

One of the two 6-inch howitzers of the Australian Heavy Battery firing from a position in White Valley. The gun has been dug into an open pit to provide some limited protection from Ottoman counter-battery fire. The photograph shows the steep terrain that restricted the availability of suitable positions for the 18-pounders and highlighted the need for howitzers, with their greater ability to elevate the barrel, to be employed at Anzac (AWM P04965.001).

Naval gunfire support was provided by the 2nd Naval Squadron comprising the cruisers *Bacchante* and *Endymion*, the monitors *Havelock*, *Humber*, *M15*, *M20* and *M33*, and the destroyers *Chelmer* and *Colne*.[16] HMS *Bacchante* carried a main armament of two 9.2-inch (233.68mm) and a secondary of twelve 6-inch (152.4mm) guns; *Endymion* a main of two 9.2-inch and a secondary of ten 6-inch and one 12-pounder (76mm). However, since the secondary guns were on either side of the vessels, only half of them could be employed at one time. Of the monitors, *Havelock* sported two 14-inch guns (355.6mm) and two 12-pounders, *Humber* had two 6-inch and two 4.7-inch (119.38mm) guns, *M15* had one 9.2-inch, one 12-pounder and one 6-pounder (57mm) gun, while *M20* carried one 9.2-inch and one 12-pounder, and *M33* had two 6-inch guns. The destroyers *Colne* and *Chelmer* each carried four 12-pounders.[17] This was an impressive array whose usefulness primarily lay in counter-battery work rather than close support, and in engaging entrenchments ahead of the assault force, along with firing on Ottoman reserves, provided they were on the seaward slopes of the hills. To perform its tasks, the squadron divided into two support groups, a northern group comprising *Endymion*, *M15* and the two destroyers to support the breakout on the left flank, and a southern group consisting of *Bacchante*, *Havelock*, *Humber*, *M20* and *M33* positioned off Gaba Tepe to support the attack on Lone Pine.[18]

The Corps Fire Plan

The Corps fire plan (see Map 14) was relatively simple. It called for periodic preliminary bombardments on 5 and 6 August to support the action at Lone Pine. These bombardments also provided an element of preparation for the attack on German Officers' Trench, and included targets in the area of the Nek, Pope's and Quinn's.[19] The fire plan then provided covering and counter-battery fire during the assault at Lone Pine, but not for the attack on German Officers' Trench, which was to be executed in conjunction with the detonation of underground mines. The final element of the plan was a light overnight preparatory bombardment, increasing in intensity as dawn approached, to support the light horse attacks.[20]

Apart from the continuation of the artillery ruse at Old No 3 Outpost and the Tabletop, there was no programmed fire in support of the seizure of the Sari Bair heights. Here the majority of the 7th IMA Brigade was to move with the assault columns but, essentially, artillery and naval gunfire was to be on call when the objectives had been seized and communications established.[21] Such arrangements are understandable in that this element of the plan was conceived as a surprise attack against what were thought to be unoccupied or weakly held positions, and any preliminary fire would alert the enemy. Furthermore, the movement of the columns at night in difficult terrain would almost certainly not proceed in accordance with a strict timetable and communications would also be unreliable while they were on the move, so a pre-planned timed program was impractical. That said, the Corps fire plan provided no contingency arrangements if the attackers had to fight their way onto the positions, or the assaults had to take place during daylight.

Lone Pine

The first attack in the Anzac area took place at Lone Pine (see Map 15) where the Ottoman trench system was some 155 metres wide and between 46 to 146 metres deep. Barbed wire covered the frontage, and the front trench had overhead protection in the form of pine logs. Immediately north, the Ottomans on the near side of Joúston's Jolly would be able to fire into the flank of the assault.

In the preparatory bombardment, Symon's 1st NZFA Battery was tasked to cut the wire at Lone Pine, Joúston's Jolly and German Officers' Trench. Initially allotted 125 rounds over a period of four days for this task, on the first day the battery fired twenty-four HE and eleven shrapnel. Achieving only meagre results, Symon pressed on methodically, using only one gun and observing from the Australian trenches near the objective, before finally achieving what was considered to be a satisfactory effect on the day of the assault, having used in the order of 380 rounds.[22] In the process, Napier JoÚston noted that 'low-bursting time shrapnel or percussion shrapnel were just as much or more effective than the H.E.'[23]

The amount of time and ammunition expended may seem excessive, but British trials on wire cutting with shrapnel conducted in France were to confirm that this was a deliberate procedure, expensive in ammunition. Special preparations had to be made at the gun to use ammunition from one fuse and propellant production lot, to make the gun as stable as possible, to ensure the barrel was close to horizontal when firing so as to minimise jump at the muzzle, and to lay carefully and accurately. Such measures were required because errors at the target of only a few yards meant the fire would be ineffective.[24]

Elsewhere in the preliminary bombardment, the fire plan directed B Battery, 69th Howitzer Brigade (5-inch), and a 4.5-inch howitzer section from the 4th NZFA Battery to fire onto Lone Pine, a similar allocation to engage JoÚston's Jolly (D Battery, 69th Howitzer Brigade, and the other section of the 4th NZFA Battery), and the 4th (City of Glasgow) Battery (5-inch) to target German Officers' Trench. They were tasked to fire a total of thirty rounds per battery in two groups onto these targets on 5 August, and a further forty rounds per battery, again in two firings, the next day. On the same days, the 4th and 5th AFA batteries and A Battery, 69th Howitzer Brigade, were directed to fire twenty rounds per battery onto areas of the Nek and the Chessboard, preferably at dawn and dusk. These tasks were to be carried out under the orders of the CRAs of both divisions, and the war diaries of the units involved indicate they were fired as planned.[25]

An 18-pounder gun being loaded near Lone Pine. This gun appears to be in the position occupied by the 8th AFA Battery at the rear of The Pimple—see Diagram 1 (AWM A03091).

This was a relatively weak preparation in terms of weight of fire. The gaps in the firing would have given the enemy an opportunity to repair any damage that might have occurred, and it is also noteworthy that two 5-inch howitzer batteries and ANZAC's 6-inch howitzers were given no bombardment tasks at a time when it might be argued that the potential fire effect should have been maximised. On the positive side, the fire was spread across the ANZAC front, should have caused some disruption to positions that might interfere with an attack on Lone Pine, and did not prejudice tactical surprise by its duration or by concentration on the actual objective, although the wire-cutting operation by Symon's battery probably alerted the Ottomans at Lone Pine.

As the final element of preparatory fire for this attack, Corps orders directed howitzer fire onto Lone Pine, JoÚston's Jolly and German Officers' Trench at the quick rate between 5.00pm and 5.30pm (Zero Hour) on 6 August. Then, until 9.00pm, all the artillery, with the exception of one 5-inch howitzer battery, was directed to provide covering fire for the assault in the form of nominated counter-battery tasks or the engagement of specified hostile trenches across the entire Anzac front. The intention was to suppress Ottoman fire and disrupt troop movements that might interfere with the capture of the position. The majority of the guns and howitzers were placed under Hobbs' orders for this period, presumably so that he could modify the tasking if required. It is of note, however, that the targets specified by Corps provided no close covering fire onto the Ottoman positions adjacent to or in depth of Lone Pine during the assault. The only nominated hostile trenches in the vicinity were those on JoÚston's Jolly, and they were to be 'watched' by the 1st NZFA Battery.[26]

In his artillery operational order, Hobbs expanded on Corps orders by specifying the times at which the bursts of preliminary fire would be applied, and defining by trench numbers the targets to be engaged on each position. He then modified the Corps plan (see Map 16) by increasing the duration of the heavier weight of fire immediately before Zero Hour to sixty minutes. This may have been intended to compensate for the fact that he had been reduced to one section of 4.5-inch howitzers and one section of 5-inch howitzers to engage Lone Pine itself.[27] In addition, Hobbs further modified Corps orders by arranging for protective fire from some 5-inch howitzers to continue on JoÚston's Jolly and German Officers' Trench and their south-eastern slopes after Zero Hour; for the howitzer fire on Lone Pine to lift onto the communication trenches to its immediate south and east; and for the 1st NZFA Battery to lift onto the trenches at Pine Ridge, immediately south of Lone Pine.[28]

The 1st Australian Division operation order reflected this tasking with some amendment. After Zero Hour the 4th (City of Glasgow) Battery firing on German Officers' Trench was returned to counter-battery duty, the 5-inch section from B Battery, 69th Howitzer Brigade, firing onto Lone Pine was absolved from firing in depth of the position after Zero Hour—making it likewise available for counter-battery duties—and the 1st NZFA Battery was switched from looking after Pine Ridge to depth duties behind Lone Pine, an area over which it had good observation. These were sensible changes. The differences between the artillery and divisional orders probably reflected the short notice of the attack, and that the Division's planning processes were still evolving.[29]

In addition, the Divisional order tasked Hughes' 7th and Bessell-Browne's 8th AFA batteries and a mobile section with firing on the Lone Pine trenches prior to the assault, after which the batteries were to switch fire onto Pine Ridge as necessary. Phillips' 4th and Caddy's 5th AFA batteries, along with the 2nd NZFA Battery, retained the covering fire tasking in the area of the Chessboard and Quinn's Post specified in

Corps orders. For counter-battery tasks, five howitzer batteries, four Australian field batteries, the Australian Heavy Battery, the New Zealand 6-inch howitzer, and one section of the 26th (Jacob's) Battery were to be prepared to engage designated hostile guns. For example, Burgess' 9th AFA Battery, Hughes' 7th AFA, the 5th (City of Glasgow) Battery, and one 6-inch howitzer and the 4.7-inch gun of the Australian Heavy Battery were allocated counter-battery tasks to the south and south-east in the vicinity of the Olive Grove and Wineglass Hill.[30]

Supplementing the ANZAC artillery were four ships of the 2nd Naval Squadron. The cruiser HMS *Bacchante* was assigned to the preparatory bombardment in the valley behind Lone Pine commencing at 5.00pm, with fire increasing to the quick rate between 5.30pm and 7.00pm, and then returning to the area between 9.25pm and 10.00pm. HMS *Humber* was tasked with shelling Ottoman batteries around the Olive Grove, and *Havelock* and another monitor were directed onto shore batteries and trenches south of Gaba Tepe.[31]

The Cressy class cruiser HMS Bacchante which supported the attack on Lone Pine by firing into Legge Valley behind the Australian's objective. She carried two 9.2-inch guns, twelve 6-inch guns, twelve 6-pounder guns, and three 3-pounders, and went on to support ANZAC throughout the campaign (Wikipedia).

When the attack went in, the fire support, along with the use of tunnels and an underground trench halfway across no man's land, assisted the 1st Infantry Brigade to break into the Ottoman position with relatively light casualties.[32] Notes in the 1st Division's war diary are critical of the howitzer fire applied to the northern section of JoÚston's Jolly, but record that the fire on the southern portion was satisfactory, and the fire on Lone Pine caused half the casualties suffered by the defenders, although it did not destroy the logs over the trenches or completely cut the wire.[33] The bombardment, which probably consisted of about 200 howitzer Lyddite rounds and a similar number of 18-pounder rounds, mostly shrapnel, was considered by the infantry to be 'intense'.[34]

HMS Havelock, an Abercrombie class monitor commissioned in May 1915 and sent to the Dardanelles in June, where she supported ANZAC during the August Offensive. Havelock carried two 14-inch guns in the twin gun turret and two 12-pounder (3-inch) guns (Wikipedia).

Other than seeking the destruction of the wire, the aim of the fire applied to Lone Pine was unspecified, but the effect achieved equated to that contained in *Field Artillery Training*, which stated that batteries engaging infantry positions should 'endeavour temporarily to disturb the enemy's aim and reduce the volume and effect of his fire so as to afford its own infantry the opportunity of gaining ground.'[35] In other words it should achieve suppression rather than destruction. The fire had done that by forcing the defenders under cover and, on this occasion, unlike 2 May at Baby 700, they were unable to emerge in any strength before the attackers reached them.

A 6-inch, 30-cwt howitzer known as 'the Kanga', preparing to fire on the Ottoman gun at the Olive Grove known as 'Beachy Bill' from White's Valley in August 1915. The 1st Australian Heavy Battery had two of these obsolescent howitzers. The shape of the sandbags to the front indicates that this howitzer had a relatively limited arc of fire from this position (AWM H15735).

Throughout the attack and the initial defence of Lone Pine, Hobbs suffered from the decisions of HQ 1st Australian Division and the NZFA Brigade to change locations on that very day, with the consequent disruption to telephone communications. Nevertheless, he was able to respond to calls to engage troublesome targets, in the end reporting that 'the arrangements for neutralising the enemy artillery and machine gun fire, for supporting the rifle fire of our own infantry and keeping down the enemy rifle fire needed little or no alteration, in so far as allotting batteries to previously discovered objectives was concerned. It was, however, found necessary on a few occasions to concentrate more guns on a single objective temporarily to relieve the pressure on the infantry.'[36]

The infantry were less phlegmatic, noting that counter-battery fire after Zero Hour failed to prevent the Ottoman artillery maintaining a 'very rigorous bombardment' on the ANZAC trenches and gun positions, 'fire from Turk's Hump, Sandpit, "C" and un-located guns in rear of Scrubby Knoll being heavy.' The response from the 18-pounders was thought to be good, but howitzer shooting contained 'perceptible lulls, giving the impression the men were tiring'.[37]

The areas engaged by the Ottoman artillery in response to the attack at Lone Pine included Steele's Post, from which the 6th Battalion was to assault German Officers' Trench at midnight.

This fire caused severe damage. As noted, neither Corps nor Divisional Artillery orders provided specific preliminary or covering fire for the attack on this objective, which was to be made in conjunction with the explosion of three underground mines. It appears, however, that separate arrangements were made, as the 4th (Lowland) Howitzer Brigade ordered its 4th Battery to bombard German Officers' Trench from 7.15pm until dark and then apply six rounds every half hour until 11.30pm, for which purposes 150 rounds of Lyddite were allocated. In the event, the attack proved unsuccessful. Two of the mines were intentionally fired early, and this drew a bombardment from the Ottoman artillery that further damaged the Australian trenches and tunnels and delayed the attack. The failure was a setback because the capture of the position was an important precursor to the assault at the Nek. The 6th Battalion was ordered to make a second attempt, but this too failed.[38]

No.4 Gun, 9th AFA Battery, on McCay's Hill firing at an Ottoman supply train in the vicinity of the Olive Grove. The gun is camouflaged with leaves attached to netting. The pit behind the two gunners facing the camera was used to store ammunition (AWM A00830).

Meanwhile, fierce fighting continued at Lone Pine, the beginning of a struggle that was to persist for three days characterised by incessant combat at close quarters from the morning of 7 August onwards, during which the 1st Australian Infantry Brigade and its reinforcements suffered severe losses. The Australian defenders were ably supported by the 1st NZFA Battery on Russell's Top, guns from Hughes' 7th AFA Battery with fields of fire across the southern slopes of Lone Pine, and some of the howitzers, which together helped to break up counter-attacks. Observation officers located in the captured trenches controlled much of this fire. Other guns and howitzers continued to engage hostile batteries, while a mountain gun section fired star shells over Owen's Gully between Lone Pine and JoUston's Jolly throughout each night.[39] The support was marred on at least two occasions when howitzer rounds fell within the Australian-held entrenchments, but the commander of the 1st Australian Division formally recorded that 'the assistance given by the artillery was continual and effective—the gunners sparing no effort likely to help their comrades.'[40]

The Nek—Tragedy at Dawn

With battle joined at Lone Pine, the breakout to the north of Anzac began after dark on 6 August. As already mentioned, the plan was that, having captured Chunuk Bair by dawn, the New Zealanders would move down the range and secure Battleship Hill while the light horse would launch an attack to seize Baby 700 and the upper reaches of Second Ridge catching the Ottoman defenders in a pincer. However, the tactical situation in the early hours of 7 August was vastly different from that envisaged in Birdwood's plan (see Map 17). Lone Pine had been captured, but German Officers' Trench had not fallen and, critically, the New Zealanders were short of Chunuk Bair. There could be no concentric attack on Baby 700 at dawn, but Birdwood and Godley decided to press ahead with the light horse action against Baby 700 with the revised aim of supporting the endeavours to take the Sari Bair heights. As Lieutenant Colonel Andrew Skeen of HQ ANZAC told Bean at the time, he was 'not worried about the light horse, but the New Zealanders. He thought the Light Horse wd [sic] be alright but he hoped that what they were doing would assist NZ in the more difficult task.'[41]

The intention was for the 8th and 10th LH regiments from the 3rd LH Brigade to take the Ottoman trenches on Russell's Top before pushing on through the Nek to the seaward slopes of Baby 700 and the upper reaches of the Chessboard (see Map 18). Supporting them, the 8th Royal Welsh Fusiliers climbing out of the head of Monash Valley, and the 8th Cheshires, moving behind the light horsemen, would take the rest of Baby 700 and consolidate the position. Immediately south, at Pope's Hill, the 1st LH Regiment, scaling Waterfall Gully, would seize the Ottoman trenches on Dead Man's Ridge, while the 2nd LH Regiment would attack the Ottoman trenches opposite Quinn's Post.[42]

When the attacks went in, the 1st LH Regiment at Pope's was able to get into the first three lines of Turkish trenches before being driven out after two hours, sustaining 154 casualties out of the 200 men who attacked. Elsewhere, the assaults were swept away. The attack at Quinn's was stopped immediately, but that at the Nek continued, despite calls by the Commanding Officer of the 10th LH Regiment, Lieutenant Colonel Noel Brazier, to have it abandoned. Over a period of twenty minutes, four waves of light horsemen from the 8th and 10th regiments were destroyed before reaching the Ottoman trenches, which lay between thirty-five and forty-five metres away, while the leading platoons of the Royal Welsh Fusiliers were shot and bombed back into Monash Valley before gaining the top of the steep incline.[43]

'Poor Light Horse, Artillery and Naval Coordination?

The failure at the Nek has long been attributed to poor coordination among the artillery, the supporting ships and the light horse, resulting in a seven-minute delay between the preliminary fire ceasing and the attack commencing. Bean's *Official History* claims the bombardment, planned to cease at 4.30am, stopped when the watches of the light horse read 4.23am, speculating that this was due to faulty synchronisation.[44] This has been accepted without question by succeeding historians and was graphically portrayed in Peter Weir's 1982 film *Gallipoli*. However, the available evidence questions Bean's assertion, and his view was first challenged by the late Graham Wilson. Not entirely convinced by Wilson's argument, the authors of this book undertook their own examination of the available evidence.[45]

The seven-minute delay was asserted by Lieutenant Wilfred Robinson in three 1924 letters to Bean, and these seem to be the only basis for it in the *Official History*. In his second letter, Robinson discussed the reaction in the trench when the bombardment ceased, and the conversation that ensued with the Commanding Officer and others, all of whom he names, and who charged with the first line. Robinson concludes, 'But I am sure that the bombardment ceased at 4.23 according to Redford's time and mine [that is, the time according the 8th LH Regiment watches set the evening before], and that the attack was launched seven minutes after the bombardment ceased.'

Despite his firm belief in the delay, the accuracy of Robinson's recollections could be called into question on three counts. First, as

Jeff Pickerd has noted, Robinson's troop, which was in the second line to attack, was late getting into position. Sergeant Charles Lyon, Robinson's troop sergeant, wrote, 'Owing to a misunderstanding my troop was late in moving up and just as we got into the front line our troop officer [Robinson] was shot through the hand and retired. I was left in charge and being unable to jam past the men, jumped up and ran round to the front sap calling on them to follow, but just as we got out the line fell back nearly all wounded.' Lyon's account implies Robinson and his troop only entered the front trench after the first line had gone. Robinson also describes being shot through the hand as he left the trench.

Second, Robinson asserts that, after the bombardment ceased, 'for three minutes hardly a shot came from the Turks & then a scattered rifle fire broke out above which could be heard distinctly the rattle of about ten shots as each Turk machine gun was made ready for action.' No other account mentions this. Indeed, a good many state that immediately or just after the bombardment ceased a tremendously heavy rifle and machine-gun fire broke out, with 8th LH survivors recounting that this happened immediately the first line charged. Lieutenant Colonel Brazier of the 10th LH drew a vivid parallel: 'A thousand sticks rattled across a thousand sheets of corrugated iron at the rate of a thousand revolutions per minute would barely give a conception of what the sound of the gun [sic] was like.' Others described it as 'a terrific fire', 'a hail', 'a fierce crackle of fire', 'a solid wall of lead' and 'murderous'.

Third, in his second letter to Bean, Robinson claimed, 'The work of the Brigade staff as arrangements for the attack of the 8th &10th regiments were concerned was disgraceful, beyond being given the time for the attack we officers were practically left to make our own arrangements.' Yet the brigade operation order, running to eight pages, is a very detailed and comprehensive document which clearly specifies how the operation was to be undertaken down to the actions and objectives of all four lines, together with all logistic and administrative requirements, including clothing to be worn.[46]

Even so, there are others whose testimony supports the notion of some delay between the bombardment ceasing and the first line charging. Captain Leslie Hore, who commanded the right wing of the 8th LH Regiment's second line, implies that the bombardment ceased at 4.25am, when he wrote 'At 4a.m. we stood to arms; the bombardment started: in 25 minutes it stopped. Immediately a fierce crackle of fire came out of the Turkish trenches.... At 25 minutes past 4 we stood on the banquets of our trenches and in a few minutes the crackle of musketry turned into a roar.' While this implies a five-minute delay, Hore does not specify such a delay, which would have been an eternity for those waiting to assault, and he writes that the fierce crackle of fire broke out immediately the bombardment ceased.[47]

In a letter to Bean, Wilfred Kent Hughes of the 3rd LH Brigade headquarters, wrote, 'As far as I can remember the bombardment did stop early, but at a time when seconds are minutes, & minutes seem like hours I should hardly like to hazard a guess at the length of time.' Sergeant Francis Boyle, in a letter written on 18 September 1915, recalled, 'At 3.10a.m. on 7/8/15 our battle-ships bombarded the trenches in front of our lines which we were to take, and continued until 3.55. Almost as soon as they stopped firing the Turks opened with their machine guns, playing on the secret sap ... At 4am we charged forward.' While clearly Boyle's recollections of the timings are incorrect, his account nonetheless suggests a five-minute delay.[48]

Conversely, observing the bombardment, Lance Corporal Cyril Lawrence of the 2nd Field Company mentioned that it reached its highest pitch at 4.29am and, when it ceased, was followed by a silence of not more than a minute before a roar of Turkish rifle and machine-gun fire erupted. Trooper JoÚ Faulkner recorded, 'Just before the first peep of day (about 4.30am) [brackets and time in the original] the bombardment began to *slacken* [emphasis added] and Lieutenant Colonel White looked at his watch. He passed the word along. "Five minutes to go" then "three minutes to go" and then "Get Ready", and finally "Jump Parapet!" His orders followed in quick succession. In an instant our first line eagerly leapt over the parapet ... and as soon as our heads appeared above, the Turks opened fire with machine-guns and rifles.' Although Faulkner mentions that the bombardment slackened, he does not say that it ceased.[49]

Bean's diary entries at the time make no mention of a delay, simply noting (some of it in shorthand) '4-4.30 heavy bombardment ... Attack 4.30 when bombardment ceased', and a later entry 'Bomb. [sic] ceased 4.30 on tick. Last shell fell after 1st man over parapet.' In a dispatch dated 15 August 1915 recounting the light horse attack and published in *The Register,* he reported, 'The bombardment stopped at 4.30pm, as if cut short by night [sic], and at that instant there broke out such a rattle of rifle and machine gun as was never heard before. Into that fusillade, at that instant, our men went out.... The moment the bombardment stopped, the first line, on a signal given by the officers with their watches in their hands, jumped over the parapet.' In an historical note on file written while working on the second volume of the *Official History,* Bean says he witnessed the bombardment and that 'my impression from not far away at about halfway through the bombardment, was that it was a very heavy one for Gallipoli.' If he witnessed the bombardment, it is curious that he makes no mention of a lengthy delay in his diary entries or his 15 August dispatch. In a later diary, recording an interrogation from a prisoner of the *18th Infantry Regiment,* he makes the first mention of a delay. The Turk stated that the fire did no damage to the front-line trenches, and that there was a delay between the bombardment and the attack which, according to the prisoner, took place at around 8.00am, three and a half hours later than the actual time, which Bean rightly questioned. In addition, Tim Travers claims that the journalist Phillip Schuler told Bean the artillery stopped three minutes early.[50]

None of the brigade or regimental war diaries mentions a delay of any sort. That of the 1st LH Brigade states, '4 to 4.30am Heavy artillery bombardment', the 3rd LH Brigade simply records, 'at 4.30am assaulted NEK', similarly the 8th LH War Diary says, 'At 4.30am we led the attack on the TURKISH trenches on the NEK.' The 9th LH War Diary records, 'Attack on "Baby 700" after heavy bombardment by howitzers. 9th Regt formed Brigade Reserve & gave fire support to 8th &10th who were unsuccessful', while the 10th LH Regiment notes, 'The destroyer opened fire in the direction of the NEK at 4am & continued to 4.30am, with apparently little effect. Bombardment ceased at 4.30am & almost immediately & before the 1st line of ours [8 LH] had left our trenches, enemy rifle and machine gun fire opened on our parapet. 1st and 2nd lines, who were in the firing trenches, then sprang forward to the assault and were mown down before allowing the 3rd & 4th lines to assault...' According to Tim Travers, HMS *Endymion*'s log states that the bombardment ceased at 4.30am.[51]

Significantly, the post-action report of the 8th LH Regiment, written by Major Arthur Deeble, who survived the charge, states that 'A bombardment by field and naval guns proceeded during the night 6/7 and up to 0430 this morning upon the enemy's trenches to our front. In accordance with the orders issued to this regiment, two lines of 150 men each dashed from our trenches on the Nek to seize the enemy's trenches opposite our front at 0430.' The report concluded that the attack failed because: 'the bombardment failed to demoralise the enemy and to weaken materially his defences; while his machine guns had not been put out.' Deeble makes no mention of any discrepancy in timings, or a delay between the bombardment ceasing and the regiment attacking; indeed his report states that the bombardment ceased and his regiment attacked at 4.30am.[52] Similarly, in his report dated 7 August, Brigadier General Frederic [correct spelling] Hughes, GOC 3rd LH Brigade, wrote that 'the Navy and Artillery shelled the NEK and CHESSBOARD from 0400 to 0430 with increasing rapidity.... At precisely 0430 the 1st line, followed by the 2nd (8th L.H.) jumped out of the saps and trenches in the face of an overwhelming rifle and MG fire,...'[53] He makes no mention of a delay between the cessation of the bombardment and the 8th LH assaulting. As Hughes had observed the whole action from a forward observation post and, like Deeble's, his report was written the day of the attack, there is little doubt he would have mentioned a delay, and certainly one extending over seven minutes.

The 10th LH Regiment's post-action report records that 'the bombardment continued 4.30 [sic] when a murderous machine gun & rifle fire upon our parapets commenced' while, in his personal diary entry for 7 August, Brazier states, 'Bombardment started at 4am & ceased at 0430. A hail of shrapnel, machine gun & rifle fire hit the parapet of trenches. Word came that the 1st & 2nd lines had gone.' The 9th LH report mentions that it provided covering fire 'during the five minutes prior to the time laid down for the assault', but makes no mention of any delay in the assault. The NZ&A Division's post-action report states that 'all available guns, assisted by the guns of H.M. ships being engaged from 4.20 to 4.30am; heavy rifle and machine gun fire was also directed to the same objective. At exactly 4.30am an assault by the 8th Light Horse Regiment was delivered from the trenches.'[54]

Responding to a draft of the British *Official History* in 1931, Brazier gave an account of the action that contradicted his earlier 1915 war diary entry, post-action report and entry in his personal diary. Writing to Bean he stated: 'The bombardment proceeded principally from the war ships, and was to cease at 4.30am. Noticing the cessation of the firing and thinking it was a temporary lull, Colonel White said "There are seven minutes to go." Still waiting for a continuation of the fire he said "Two minutes to go", then just "Go." This seven minutes gave the Turks time to man their parapets and no fire was directed by our machine guns.'[55]

This version, written sixteen years after the event, uses almost the same words as those in Bean's Volume II of the *Official History* published in 1924. However, Brazier implied that he was not in the front trenches with White when the latter was purported to have spoken, noting that he did not see the annihilation of the 8th LH until he entered the trenches with his own men, put up a trench periscope and observed 'the Eight's line all flat on the ground in a row.' This is supported by his personal diary entry that 'word came that the 1st & 2nd lines had gone.' Moreover, the 3rd LH Brigade orders and plan for forming up prior to the attack stipulated that the 10th LH was to occupy the communication trenches and enter the front-line trench after the first line, and thus White had gone, so he could not have heard what White said. Not only does his 1931 letter contradict his 1915 accounts, his reference to no fire being directed by friendly machine-guns contradicts the 9th LH Regiment's war diary. It would seem that his 1931 recollections were influenced by Bean's account in the *Official History*.[56]

Several accounts written by 8th LH participants soon after the charge report that the attack was launched immediately after the bombardment had ceased. Private David McGarvie, a survivor from the first line, wrote that 'During the night the gunboats ... gave them a terrible bombardment from 9pm to 4:30am.... At 4a.m. the bombardment increased. Word came along "3 minutes to go". We got ready; the bombardment slackened off, then "2 minutes to go." The bombardment ceased and then came the word "Go", and out we went. No sooner were we out than they opened fire on us.' According to Jeff Pickerd, McGarvie told his family that Bean had got much of his account in the *Official History* wrong. Private Frank Merrit recorded, 'At the very moment the shelling stopped, we all went over the top...', while Lieutenant Andrew Crawford remembered, 'As soon as they stopped shelling in the morning, we advanced. It was just half-past four in the morning of the 7th August that the first line got out,...', a view supported by Private Clifford St Pinnock: 'At half past four to the second the battleships stopped their fire and we got the order to "Give it to them Boys!" Well we all got over and cheered but they were waiting ready for us and simply gave us a solid wall of lead.'[57]

Sergeant George Fuzzard wrote in his field service notebook sometime after the event, 'Our attack at this point was commenced about

3.30a.m. of the 7th by a heavy artillery fire concentrated on the small frontage of Turkish trenches immediately on our front. At 4.30a.m. this fire stopped and our first line, which was already in the saps in front of our trenches, attempted to rush their line.' Private Alex Meldrum wrote, 'At midnight our warships started shelling ... The bits of flying shells were hitting all around us.... At 4 o'clock just breaking day our red light signal flashed up to stop the bombardment. In an instant we were all out of our trenches and off dashed the first line.' Similarly, a 1916 article believed to be written by Major Alan Love, the Second-in-Command of the 10th LH, recounted, 'At 4am, just as the first streaks of dawn were visible, the destroyer again opened fire on the trenches to our front, and continued to 4.30am.' After discussing the forming-up arrangements and objectives for both regiments, he continued, 'At 4.30am the first line rose out of the trenches and rushed forward, followed by the second line.'[58]

In all of the available accounts written by 8th LH survivors, there is no mention of a significant time gap between the artillery and naval fire ceasing, and the first line launching its assault. However, some participants record a short delay associated with climbing out of the trench before the order to charge was given.

The diary of Major Thomas Redford of the 8th LH, who was killed in the charge, is continued after 7 August by another author, presumed to be Squadron Quartermaster (later Major) William McGrath. He wrote, 'At 0400 on the morning of the 7th a short bombardment by Howitzers and warships which did no damage was succeeded by the word being passed around for the attack. B Squadron (100 bayonets) plus 50 bayonets from A [Squadron] took from the extreme left to the top of the ridge. Every man sprang out of the trench eagerly and crawled carefully for a few yards. Suddenly as they stood up to run forward and got sillouetted [sic] on the skyline a terrific fire from machine guns swept everything down ... never before have I heard such a terrific volume of fire.' Private Jack Dale, in the first line, wrote, 'At 4.30a.m. we got the order to get on the parapet. A few minutes later we advanced and all of a sudden the Turks opened up with a murderous machine gun fire.' Lance Corporal Ernie Mack recollected, 'As soon as the guns stopped firing and we got out of the trenches to wait for the signal to charge, our worst fears were realised. The Turks opened up immediately the most terrific fire it has been my misfortune to hear.' Similarly, Sergeant William Cameron of the 9th LH recorded, 'The eighth was the first out. We saw them climb out and move forward about ten yards and lie flat.' There is a note on the forming-up plan regarding those on the left: 'B-C 1st line-lying full length in front of saps, 2nd line-75 standing in saps'. Thus there is the possibility the 1st line may have climbed out before the bombardment stopped, rather than crawling out after it ceased.[59]

In examining the primary source evidence two common points stand out. The first is that the majority of the accounts mention that the Turks opened with a tremendous fire immediately or just after the bombardment ceased. Second, most of the 8th LH survivors state that this fire commenced as soon as they advanced. This indicates that the charge occurred very soon after the artillery and naval guns ceased firing. Thus the weight of evidence suggests that, while there may have been a short delay of a minute or less between the attackers climbing over the parapet and lying down before they charged, there was not a lengthy delay, and certainly not one of seven minutes. Furthermore, if the delay occurred between the first line climbing over the parapet to lie down after the bombardment ceased and charging, this suggests there was no discrepancy in timings between the light horse and the artillery.

The reports and war diaries consistently indicate that the bombardment from the artillery and naval guns ceased at 4.30am, implying that, if there was a problem with watch timings as Bean asserts, it lay with those of the 8th LH. Kent Hughes told Bean that his watch was synchronised with all other brigade watches. Therefore, it follows that, when the synchronisation was effected, the watches of the representatives of the three regiments would have shown the same time, and this would have carried forward to the respective regimental synchronisations. Given that the watches were synchronised at brigade headquarters, and Frederic Hughes and Brazier both recorded that the bombardment ceased at 4.30am, then it seems improbable that the 8th LH watch settings would have been so different from those of the brigade commander and the Commanding Officer of the 10th LH Regiment. But if the 8th LH watches were seven minutes slow, then why didn't Deeble, Hore and Crawford who, as officers, would have had their watches synchronised, record the bombardment ceasing seven minutes early? Such a lengthy delay would have had a profound influence on their accounts. It is also inconceivable that, on seeing or hearing the attacks at Pope's and Quinn's begin immediately after the artillery bombardment ceased, the 8th LH would wait a full seven minutes before attacking—an eternity under combat conditions, as Kent Hughes suggests. Nor do the accounts of survivors, other than Robinson, mention a problem with the watches. It would appear that, rather than a seven-minute delay between the cessation of the bombardment and the light horse assaulting, other factors contributed to the disaster and these included deficiencies in the supporting fire plan.[60]

The Nek Fire Plan

For the attack at the Nek, Corps orders placed the artillery of the NZ&A Division plus A Battery, 69th Howitzer Brigade, a 5-inch section of B Battery, 69th Howitzer Brigade, and the 4th, 5th and 8th AFA batteries from the 2nd AFA Brigade under Napier JoÚston's orders from 9.00pm on 6 August onwards. The orders specified that a preliminary bombardment would begin at 9.30pm. The three Australian batteries would open on the Chessboard, one New Zealand battery would take on the trenches in front of Pope's and the other the trenches in front of Quinn's, while two 5-inch howitzer batteries, including one under Corps orders, would engage Baby 700. Fire was to be sustained throughout the night at a rate of one round every five minutes. At 4.00am, naval gunfire was to join the artillery bombardment, with HMS

Endymion and a monitor engaging the Nek and Chessboard, and the destroyers *Colne* and *Chelmer* taking on the Nek. From this hour as well, artillery fire was to increase to the quick rate until 4.30am, when it was to cease. The NZ&A Division was authorised to add other serials if required.[61]

Unlike the attack at Lone Pine, Corps orders did not make significant provision for wide-ranging covering or counter-battery fire after Zero Hour, perhaps reflecting a planning assumption that, with the loss of Lone Pine, German Officers' Trench and Chunuk Bair, and with the New Zealand infantry advancing on Battleship Hill, the Ottoman defences would be in disarray. The only potential covering fire prescribed required HMS *Endymion* and the monitor to engage the east side of the Chessboard and Battleship Hill from 4.30 to 5.30am, although this may have been preparatory fire to assist the New Zealanders take Battleship Hill. As for the artillery, the orders were for the batteries that had been involved in preparatory fire to be ready to fire on Battleship Hill, presumably in support of the New Zealanders advancing on it.[62]

The final artillery orders for this attack are contained in the NZ&A Division Operation Order Number 11 issued on 5 August. Interestingly, although three batteries of the 2nd AFA Brigade were under Napier JoÚston's orders for the operation, neither the 1st Australian Division, nor Hobbs' headquarters, nor the 2nd AFA Brigade's headquarters, nor the batteries themselves are shown on the distribution list of this document. The records suggest that, instead, the Australian batteries fired on orders contained in Hobbs' operation order of 3 August, which was circulated to the NZ&A Division and Napier JoÚston. This would not have mattered had the two sets of orders aligned, but in some ways they did not.[63]

The New Zealand orders modified the Corps fire plan in that a 5-inch battery was taken off bombardment of Baby 700 and given a counter-battery role, the field battery engagement of the trenches in front of Pope's was omitted, and the 4.5-inch howitzers, along with a section of 5-inch howitzers, engaged the Nek before the overnight bombardment began.[64] It was in the detail of this latter bombardment that the differences with the Australian orders first arose.

A 4.5-inch howitzer of the 4th NZFA (Howitzer) Battery in action on North Beach below Walker's Ridge (Alexander Turnbull Library PAColl-0914-1-16-2).

The NZ&A Division plan for preliminary fire is shown at Map 19. Faithful to the Corps fire plan, both sets of orders contained a slow bombardment commencing on the night of 6/7 August, and running until 4.00am the next morning. Napier JoÚston's orders had the 2nd NZFA Battery engaging the enemy trenches opposite Quinn's, while the 4th AFA Battery and the 4.5-inch howitzers of the 4th NZFA Battery took on the Ottoman trenches on Russell's Top, a section of 5-inch howitzers from B Battery, 69th Howitzer Brigade, engaged the Nek itself (which lay about 55 metres behind the Ottoman front line), the 5th and 8th AFA batteries engaged specified areas of the northern

Chessboard below Baby 700, and A Battery, 69th Howitzer Brigade, took on counter-battery tasks. The Australian orders corresponded in the detail of the targets to be engaged, but identified a section from a different 5-inch battery (C Battery) as being involved, and showed the overnight fire commencing for some batteries as early as 9.00pm. Under the New Zealand orders the 4.5-inch battery and the 5-inch section began at 10.10pm with an engagement of the Nek, and the full preliminary bombardment began at 11.30pm. Further, while the Australian orders specified the rate of fire as one round every two and a half minutes (battery fire two and a half minutes), the New Zealand orders specified a rate of one round every five minutes, as did the Corps fire plan. At 4.00am, both sets of orders showed the rate of fire increasing to 'a more normal rate for preliminary bombardment' under the New Zealand orders, and to one round every fifteen seconds (battery fire fifteen seconds) under the Australian orders. In the latter, fire from 4.27am onwards was applied at the intense rate. In both sets of orders, the preliminary bombardment ceased at 4.30am.[65]

The most significant difference in the two sets of orders then came into play. The Australian orders showed no further serials, but the New Zealand orders contained a task requiring the Australian batteries to join the New Zealand howitzers between 4.30 and 4.33am in firing on the Chessboard at the intense rate (see Map 20).[66] The evidence indicates that the Australian batteries did not fire this serial.

It is difficult to understand why these differences occurred. The Australian orders were not simply extracted from the Corps fire plan without reference to the NZ&A Division, because the Australian and the New Zealand orders used exactly the same trench numbers to define the various target areas, a detail not included in Corps orders. There had obviously been some degree of liaison between the two artillery headquarters—perhaps at or following the conference on 3 August—making it surprising that the additional serial was not added to the Australian orders, and that timings and rates of fire were inconsistent. Given that the Australian orders were issued two days before the New Zealand orders, perhaps the Australian orders did not reflect Napier JoÚston's final decisions. But this should have been noticed when the Australian orders were circulated to the New Zealand artillery headquarters and, in any case, the final New Zealand orders should have been circulated to the Australian batteries under Napier JoÚston's control.

Deficiencies in the Fire Plan

Setting these differences aside for the moment, the fire plan itself contained some significant deficiencies. First, the overnight bombardment was quite weak in terms of rate of fire coupled with the large target areas allotted to the two Australian batteries firing on the Chessboard. A battery effectively covers an area in breadth equating to its frontage plus an allowance on either side for the lateral effect of a shell burst, and in depth equating to any depth at the gun position along the line of fire, plus an allowance for the zone in which the rounds will fall at the range in question, plus an amount for forward and rearward shell effect. As a guide, the indicative coverage of a four-gun field battery would be approximately 90x110 metres. Larger areas could be covered by moving the fire around, but this would increase the time between rounds falling in the same area.[67] Coverage of lesser size could be achieved by converging the lines of fire of each gun onto a point, or a limited area. The area on Russell's Top allotted to Phillips' 4th AFA Battery (three guns) was approximately 46x46 metres, well within its normal coverage. However, the 5th (three guns) and 8th (normally two guns covering this zone) AFA batteries were allotted an area of approximately 183x160 metres on the northern Chessboard, larger than their normal coverage.

No 1 Gun, 8th AFA Battery, in action at the Pimple on the Lone Pine lobe of the 400 Plateau. This position was immediately behind the infantry firing line and the gun pit was one of five for the battery's four guns (see Diagram 1 for a plan of this position). At this time the 8th AFA Battery was under command of the 2nd AFA Brigade, located in Defensive Section 2 (AWM P05603.004).

Given the weakness of the overnight bombardment, it is presumed that its primary purpose was to further distract Ottoman attention from the columns approaching Chunuk Bair, rather than to suppress the positions or cause significant damage or casualties. However, following the attacks at Lone Pine and German Officers' Trench, the fire potentially also served to signal that yet another assault was planned, and it certainly caused the Ottoman artillery to shell the light horse trenches.[68]

The second deficiency in the fire plan was that, according to the orders, only the 4th AFA Battery and the New Zealand howitzer battery were to engage the Ottoman trenches on Russell's Top. The other batteries and the navy were directed onto the Nek itself, or areas further back. The amount of fire on the foremost trenches was thus relatively light. To exacerbate matters, there are also reports, including the one from the Ottoman prisoner interviewed by Bean, that the front trench was not touched by the bombardment.

These reports are somewhat surprising, as the Nek had been engaged many times previously by the batteries involved. If they were true, it may have been that the batteries did not register accurately, but it is also possible, especially in the case of the howitzers firing overhead of the light horse, that the fire was displaced for safety reasons. The trenches were only 36 to 45 metres apart and, if howitzer fire had been centred on the Ottoman front trench, shells falling at the bottom of the battery's normal zone of fire would have fallen on friendly troops. Other considerations may also have intruded, such as the incident on 14 July when variations in the weight of shells supplied to the howitzers—variations resulting from deficiencies in the manufacturing process—caused fire directed in this area to differ by as much as 90 metres. Such factors may have led to the mean point of impact of the howitzer rounds being placed behind the front trench, close enough perhaps to force the defenders under cover while shells were falling, but reducing the weight of fire on the foremost defences. The field guns did not have this problem to the same degree, as their line of fire was oblique. A separate issue was that one small section of the Ottoman front line (known to ANZAC as Trench A2) was excluded from the list of targets to be engaged, although it may well have received some fire directed at adjacent areas.[69]

A third and major defect in the fire plan was coverage. The target areas did not include hostile machine-guns on Battleship Hill identified in the 3rd LH Brigade operation order for the attack, and left other machine-guns on Baby 700 on their periphery.[70] As it also transpired, the preparatory artillery bombardment probably did not extend sufficiently to encompass Ottoman machine-guns enfilading the Nek from the southern area of the Chessboard. Moreover, to destroy a machine-gun post would have required a direct hit with HE which, given the resources allotted to the objective, was highly improbable.

These defects might be attributed to poor targeting caused by the lack of preparation time allowed Napier Joúston, combined with the allotment by Corps headquarters of too few batteries for the task. However, it is of note that the Corps fire plan showed two 5-inch batteries allocated to Baby 700 (A and D batteries, 69th Howitzer Brigade) while in the NZ&A Division plan this was reduced to one (D Battery), and the New Zealand orders also omitted the task in the Corps fire plan for some New Zealand field artillery fire on the southern end of the Chessboard near Pope's.

Finally, as previously noted, this fire plan lacked the wide protective covering and counter-battery fire during the assault that was implemented at Lone Pine. Better coverage would have been provided to some degree had the Australian batteries joined the New Zealand howitzers in firing the last New Zealand serial, but its duration was only three minutes, which would not have been enough to keep the machine-guns in check while the light horse and British infantry completed their missions. Providing further evidence that the NZ&A Division tasking the Australian batteries to engage the Chessboard after Zero Hour did not reach them, Brazier's 1931 letter to Bean stated that 'Bessell-Browne, of a Western Australian Artillery unit [8th AFA

Battery], told me some days later that they had watched the Light Horse go over and wondered what was going on, and that he could easily have helped the attack had they been informed.'[71]

The overall deficiency in the density, coverage and duration of the supporting fire plan is reflected in the after-action report of the defenders, which states: 'all of the attackers were knocked down by our infantry and machine-gun fire opened both from our front and from the trenches marked 15, 16 and 17, which enfiladed Sergeant Mehmed's front [on Russell's Top] and from trench 18.' Similarly, the Ottoman prisoner whose account Bean recorded mentions 'a heavy rifle fire direct & a cross fire from a machine gun on the right was opened...'[72]

An Ottoman trench map, albeit at very large scale and thus difficult to interpret definitively, indicates that Trench 18 was on the Ottoman right flank and Trench 17 in depth in the area of Baby 700, both probably on the edge of the fire plan target areas. Trenches 15 and 16, which enfiladed Russell's Top, were on the western and south-western edges of the Chessboard respectively, Trench 15 seemingly within the preliminary bombardment area, and Trench 16 most likely not. It is probable that Trench 16 was Trench C6b shown on the ANZAC trench diagram, an extension of Trench C6a, both of which were part of the forward trench on the Chessboard and in direct enfilade to no man's land on Russell's Top. Prior to the charge, HQ 3rd LH Brigade had identified, among others, a machine-gun in C6a and its probable impact, noting, 'As all these have alternative emplacements it is not likely that all can be put out of action easily.'[73]

It is apparent from the Ottoman reports that, rather than a seven-minute delay, the destruction of the light horsemen at the Nek, as Deeble reported on 7 August, can be attributed to a failure to suppress the machine-guns that covered the ground over which they were to assault. Other factors also contributed by alerting the enemy to an impending attack. A heightened state of Ottoman watchfulness would naturally have followed the assaults at Lone Pine and German Officers' Trench. It would not have been lessened by Godley's instructions for his forces to keep the Turks on their toes at Quinn's, Pope's and Russell's Top by fire and bombs during the night in order to draw attention away from the columns moving to secure the heights.[74]

A post-war photograph of an Ottoman machine-gun position with overhead protection on Baby 700. The arc of fire of this gun covered the Nek. Machine-gun positions at the time of the light horse attack may not have been so well protected (AWM G01876).

After the attack, Brigadier General Frederic Hughes and Colonel JoÚ Antill, the Commander and Brigade Major of the 3rd Australian LH Brigade respectively, sought to lay blame on the Australian batteries for not firing on the enemy trenches. Hobbs refuted this, writing: '4, 5, 8 batteries obeyed the orders they read and ceased fire at 4.30am.'[75] His retort indicates that the additional New Zealand serial had not been passed to him, or to the Australian batteries.

The matter was also investigated by Walker, now GOC 1st Australian Division and a professional, no-nonsense British regular. He too absolved the Australian batteries, noting that Hughes' complaint 'must therefore apply to the period after 0430. But both the New Zealand artillery timetable and Appendix A III [to Corps orders] lay down that fire was to stop at 0430.' He then went on to say that 'correction (a) to the latter order states that "other objectives may be given by the senior New Zealand artillery officer at Anzac." If therefore further support was required from Colonel JoÚston's [2nd AFA Brigade] batteries, I submit it may be fairly urged it should have been ordered by the senior New Zealand Artillery officer at Anzac.'[76]

Walker's statement is somewhat mystifying as the NZ&A Division did order a serial after 4.30am, and a copy of its operation order containing this serial is in the 1st Division's war diary. It may be that the order was sent to Walker after his report was received as evidence of the additional serial. Whatever the explanation, there was clearly a breakdown in the distribution of the additional New Zealand serial, and in the liaison between the two divisional artillery headquarters. This may reflect the limited time both artilleries were given to prepare for the offensive, or simply inadequate coordination. In passing it is also noteworthy that, in lodging their complaint, Hughes and Antill made no mention of the artillery ceasing fire early, or of a significant delay between the bombardment finishing and the 8th LH attacking, especially as Hughes had observed the assaults from a forward sap.[77]

Reflections

In terms of fire planning for support of the feints from Anzac and the concentric attack at the Nek, ANZAC staff processes were deficient in that the initial details were conceived by Cunliffe-Owen without detailed consultation with Hobbs and Napier JoÚston, who would have to implement them. The orders were then issued quite close to the event, leaving these men little time to determine and implement the additional detail required.

As to effectiveness, the arrangements finally struck at Lone Pine were satisfactory, strengths being the width of the coverage and the provision of some close covering fire after Zero Hour. The resources and their tasking were sufficient to suppress the defenders, especially those on JoÚston's Jolly adjacent to the attack, and to help ward off the subsequent counter-attacks. The arrangements for the Nek lacked the adequate allocation of resources, coverage and close support attributes of Lone Pine, the consequential effect being exacerbated by the formation commanders deciding to attack using the same resources in far less satisfactory tactical circumstances than first envisaged. The fire plan was insufficient to suppress the Ottoman positions and their supporting machine-guns. That said, there were elements of one or both of these fire plans that would prove sound in the light of later experience. These included the attempts to suppress the enemy immediately before the assault, provide covering fire during the assault, interdict enemy reinforcements, and incorporate a counter-battery plan.

Chapter Seven

THE AUGUST OFFENSIVE: THE ATTACKS ON SARI BAIR

The Terrain

The ground over which the breakout by the NZ&A Division to the north of Anzac would occur was tortuous (see Map 21). The northern flank of the Sari Bair Range is precipitous—its sides plunge sharply into the numerous valleys and gullies that cut deeply into its flank. Multiple spurs and ridges run off to the north and north-west, and in most cases they drop steeply from the crest of the range. Many are short, presenting a difficult climb, even for fit infantry, others are longer, running away to the coastal strip or falling to the Anafarta Valley. At their head they are narrow and steep sided and, while some remain so for their entire length, others broaden out with several significant spurs running off either side, creating a confusion of gullies and re-entrants. The terrain poses significant problems in deploying artillery, especially in the country closer to Sari Bair.

From Hill 971 towards the coast, of the principal ridges concerned with the planned breakout, the first is the long Abdul Rahman Bair which slides off that feature and runs due north to the Anafarta Valley. Initially narrow and straight for half its length, it then splits into several broader spurs that fan out to overlook the valley.

Next is Damakjelik Bair slipping from the north-eastern corner of Hill Q. Dropping sharply at first, it makes its way north-west, broadening out and throwing off numerous large spurs along its western flank as it approaches Hill 100; there it divides into two. Continuing north-west is Yauan Tepe, a broad spur gently sloping to an insignificant knoll three kilometres from the coast, known to the Anzacs as Hill 60 and Kaiajik Aghala to the Ottomans, which overlooks the Anafarta Valley to its north. From Hill 100 the main ridge swings west, where a prominent spur thrusts west into Aghyl Dere, the largest valley in the area, and forms the southern shoulder of what became known as Australia Valley—a large re-entrant that cuts north-east from the main valley: Aghyl Dere. Continuing west, the crest of Damakjelik Bair generally flattens out with four more spurs jutting into Aghyl Dere before ending some 1200 metres from the sea at the mouth of the Anafarta Valley on one side, and the entrance to Aghyl Dere on the other.

Further along, from Hill Q to Chunuk Bair, several short spurs drop steeply from the seaward slope of the main range either side of a longer ridge which creates a fork in Aghyl Dere 1100 metres north of Chunuk Bair. Next is Rhododendron Ridge. Narrow and steep sided for its entire length, it runs west from Chunuk Bair for 400 metres to the Apex, where it then divides in two. The equally narrow and steep-sided Cheshire Ridge heads north-west before broadening out into the long Bauchop's Hill, and eventually finishes at Walden Point, a low, rounded feature some 900 metres from the coast which sits on the southern entrance to Aghyl Dere. A narrow gap, Taylor's, separates Bauchop's Hill from Walden Point. From the Apex, Rhododendron Ridge itself continues generally west and north-west, steadily falling for another 1200 metres until it reaches the Tabletop, a flat feature with almost perpendicular sides and rising around 120 metres above sea level. From there the ridge drops sharply to a razor-thin footway which continues for around 150 metres before reaching a long hill which thrusts west, ending some 200 metres from the coast. At the seaward end of the hill ANZAC occupied No 2 and No 3 Outposts, while the Ottomans held Old No 3 Outpost further inland.

More spurs and ridges fall steeply from Baby 700, intermixed with a tangle of gullies that run into Sazli Beit Dere, a narrow, winding valley that runs from the coast to the foot of Chunuk Bair. Two of these ridges are long, with the inland one ending at the mouth of Sazli Biet Dere opposite No 2 Outpost, and the seaward one terminating at No 1 Outpost. The final ridge is the previously mentioned Walker's Ridge that drops to North Beach 650 metres north of Anzac Cove and was the ANZAC front line.

Within this area are four main valleys. From east to west, the first is Asma Dere, sliding between Abdul Rahman Bair and the upper reaches of Damakjelik Bair and running north to the Anafarta Valley. Next, the largest of the four, is the aforementioned Aghyl Dere. With its broad entrance lying between Damakjelik Bair and Walden Point, it runs south-east before being split in two, one fork continuing towards Chunuk Bair, the other heading east before splintering into a series of gullies below Hill Q and the upper reaches of Damakjelik Bair. Throughout its length, numerous gullies and re-entrants cut into the main ridges either side of the dere. Third, Bauchop's Hill and Rhododendron Ridge form the shoulders of the entrance to Chailak Dere which runs up to the Apex, the hollow at the head of the valley where Cheshire Ridge splits from Rhododendron Ridge. Finally, on the southern flank of Rhododendron Ridge is the previously mentioned Sazli Beit Dere which, after intermingling with the series of spurs and gullies falling from Baby 700, shuffles between the main range and Rhododendron Ridge to the foot of Chunuk Bair.

Navigation along the valleys is difficult, especially at night. Nor could horse-drawn field guns and howitzers negotiate them, except along the coastal strip and the lower reaches of Chailak Dere and Aghyl Dere. The only artillery that could accompany the infantry to the crest of the main range were the mule-packed mountain guns of the 7th IMA Brigade.

For further artillery support the attackers would be reliant on the ships and the guns in the Anzac beachhead. The field and remaining mountain guns of the NZ&A Division had limited coverage of the heights, while those of the 2nd AFA Brigade could engage targets with observed fire on the crest and southern shoulders of the main range as far as Chunuk Bair and Third Ridge. Beyond that they could fire using data predicted from map coordinates. The arcs of all these batteries would generally provide fire in enfilade to the attackers approaching the crests from the principal ridges. The ships could engage the Nek, Baby 700, Battleship Hill and the crests and seaward slopes of the main range with observed fire, while the howitzers could also engage these areas and the southern slopes.

The Breakout Plan

In detail, the plan for the breakout to the north of Anzac (Map 13) involved four columns: two covering forces to seize the lower slopes of the ridges overlooking the entrances to Sazli Beit Dere, Chailak Dere, and Aghyl Dere; and two assault columns which would then pass through and seize the heights on the Sari Bair Range. Leading off along the coastal strip, the Right Covering Force, the NZMR Brigade, was tasked with seizing Destroyer Hill near the mouth of Sazli Beit Dere, Old No 3 Outpost and the Tabletop at the foot of Rhododendron Ridge, along with Bauchop's Hill, thereby clearing the way for the Right Assault Column to advance on Chunuk Bair. Following behind, the Left Covering Force (the British 40th Infantry Brigade) was to move along the coast past Bauchop's Hill and Walden Point, pass over the mouth of Aghyl Dere and occupy the southern end of Damakjelik Bair to protect the Left Assault Column from

Ottoman interference from the north and north-east. Together with the New Zealanders on Bauchop's Hill, they would secure the entrance to Aghyl Dere, along which the Left Assault Column would initially move towards its objectives.[1]

Next would be the New Zealand Infantry Brigade, the Right Assault Column which, once the NZMR Brigade had secured its objectives, would pass through and advance up Sazli Beit Dere and Chailak Dere, either side of Rhododendron Ridge, to capture Chunuk Bair. Having secured the height, a portion of the brigade would then move down the range onto Battleship Hill as part of the concentric attack on Baby 700 at dawn (4.30am) on 7 August. Last was the Left Assault Column, comprising the 4th Australian Infantry Brigade and the 29th Indian Infantry Brigade, which would go around Walden Point and advance up Aghyl Dere before splitting. The 4th Australian Infantry Brigade would detach two battalions to Damakjelik Bair to link up with the right-hand portion of the British 40th Infantry Brigade, and project that line further up the bair. On reaching the main fork of Aghyl Dere, two Gurkha battalions of the 29th Indian Infantry Brigade would be detached to seize Hill Q, while the rest of the column turned north-east, swinging left over Damakjelik Bair, crossing Asma

Dere and climbing onto Abdul Rahman Bair. There they would turn right and, advancing up the bair, would take Hill 971. All of this was expected to be completed by dawn on 7 August.[2]

Birdwood's timetable was highly ambitious given the complexity of the operation, especially the advance of the Left Assault Column, and the terrain over which the assault columns had to pass in the dark. To add to the difficulties, the New Zealanders, Australians and Indians involved had been fighting on the peninsula since late April, with many of the men weakened and wracked by dysentery and diarrhoea. Reinforcements in these formations were not well trained, with some only arriving on the peninsula a week or two before the offensive. For the newly landed brigades of the 13th (Western) Division, a Kitchener New Army formation raised from the rush of volunteers in late 1914, this would be their first operation. Furthermore, if the timetable was to be achieved it depended on little or no opposition both in the area through which the assault columns had to pass, and on the three heights to be captured.

The Ottoman Defensive Arrangements

Anchored on Russell's Top and Baby 700, which were held by the *18th Infantry Regiment*, the main Ottoman defensive line paralleled the ANZAC front along Second Ridge, the 400 Plateau, and Bolton's Ridge to the coast north of Gaba Tepe. Further back along Sari Bair, and guarding the right flank, the *1st* and *3rd battalions* of the *72nd Infantry Regiment (1/72nd Infantry* and *3/72nd Infantry)* occupied Battleship Hill and the ridges running north-west off the feature, while the *14th Infantry Regiment,* less its *2nd Battalion (2/14th Infantry),* lay south-west of Battleship Hill in reserve. Further along the spine of Sari Bair, the three main heights—Chunuk Bair, Hill Q and Hill 971—had only rudimentary trenches and were undefended, save for the *1st Battalion, 32nd Infantry Regiment (1/32nd Infantry),* encamped near Hill 971. Across the tangled terrain north of Sari Bair extending to the Anafarta Valley, and through which the ANZAC assault columns would pass to outflank the Ottoman defensive line, was a thin screen provided by the *2/14th Infantry.*[3] Punching through this screen quickly without alerting the remainder of the Ottoman defenders, and securing the objectives behind the Ottoman defensive line before they could deploy reinforcements to the threatened heights was essential to the success of the operation. This was a big ask.

As previously mentioned, other than the nightly ruse of illumination and sequenced fire on Old No 3 Outpost and the Tabletop to accustom the Ottomans to the activity and lull them into a sense of complacency, there was no Corps fire plan to support the assaulting columns. Instead, artillery and naval gunfire was to be on call when communications were established. To facilitate this, telephone cable would be laid behind the advancing troops. Nor did Napier JoÚston issue a fire plan, which was understandable since pre-planned fire support was impracticable for an operation in which timings could vary. While both the Australian and New Zealand guns remained in their current positions, two sections (four guns) of the 26th (Jacob's) Battery would travel with the New Zealand Infantry Brigade, and two sections of the 21st (Kohat) Battery would move with the Left Assault Column. In essence, from an artillery perspective, the assaults on the heights would be a silent attack, with any immediate fire support required being provided by the Indian mountain guns travelling with each assault column. Heavier fire support could only occur once communications had been established between the forward observers and the relevant artillery headquarters.

Breaking Out of Anzac

Leading off soon after nightfall on 6 August, the NZMR Brigade set off along the narrow coastal strip past No 1 Outpost. The ruse at Old No 3 Outpost and the Tabletop worked. Creeping up below Old No 3 under cover of the bombardment, the Auckland Mounted Rifles seized the position with ease as the destroyer, supported by howitzers, switched to the Tabletop and fired for half an hour. Delayed, the Wellington Mounted Rifles clawed their way up the sheer sides of the feature an hour after the bombardment had ceased to find it unoccupied.[4] By 1.10am, two hours later than planned, the Right Covering Force had seized all its objectives, clearing the way for the Right Assault Column to advance on Chunuk Bair.[5]

Behind schedule, the Otago and Canterbury battalions of the New Zealand Infantry Brigade set out for Chunuk Bair along the Chailak Dere and Sazli Beit Dere respectively. The Otagos faced opposition from elements of the *2/14th Infantry* in the Chailak Dere and along Rhododendron Ridge as the Ottomans conducted a fighting withdrawal towards Chunuk Bair. In the Sazli Beit Dere the leading companies of the Cantabrians became increasingly lost in the confusion of gullies running into the valley, and the timetable fell further behind; they eventually turned back to scale Rhododendron Ridge inland from the Tabletop, and ascended the ridge towards the Apex. By dawn the New Zealanders were well short of Chunuk Bair. As the sun climbed higher the Otagos, followed by the Wellington and Auckland battalions, reached the Apex, some 500 metres short of Chunuk Bair.

Meanwhile the British 40th Infantry Brigade had secured the mouth of Aghyl Dere, but in an effort to make up time, and on the advice of a local Greek guide, the 4th Australian Infantry Brigade took a short cut through Taylor's Gap. This proved to be unfortunate as the narrowness of the path reduced the frontage of the column to single file, and they were regularly sniped at by riflemen of the *2/14th Infantry* who had evaded the New Zealanders on Bauchop's Hill and Walden Point. This delayed the column further and, when the men finally debouched into Aghyl Dere, the Australians were unsure how far up the valley they were. As the leading battalions moved up the dere, they were fired on from Damakjelik Bair by elements of the *1/32nd Infantry*. Instead of an unopposed advance, they had to clear their way, and by daybreak had occupied the bair astride Australia Valley.[6] Following behind the Australians, the 29th Indian Infantry Brigade swung up Aghyl Dere, but in the confused terrain its battalions split up, and by daylight were in an arc occupying the spurs and ridges south of the Australians, with the 2/10th Gurkha Rifles drifting into the left of the New Zealanders.

7 August

By the early morning of 7 August, the original plan to seize the Sari Bair heights had unravelled (Map 17). On reaching the Apex, Colonel Earl Joúston halted the New Zealand advance. He thought it would be unwise to move on Chunuk Bair without artillery support to counter enfilade fire from Ottoman positions on Battleship Hill and Turk's Hump, or subdue the defenders on Chunuk Bair, which loomed some 500 yards to the New Zealanders' front. Earl Joúston may not have fully realised it at the time, but his caution had merit.

Contrary to the accepted belief that the heights were open for the taking, elements of the *2/14th Infantry* had retreated to Chunuk Bair, and Mustafa Kemal, commanding the Ottoman *19th Infantry Division* and the Ottoman Anzac

Sector, had ordered the *1st Battalion, 14th Infantry Regiment* (*1/14th Infantry*) to Hill 971, and another two companies of the same regiment to Hill Q. Separately, the *1/72nd Infantry* had sent two companies to Chunuk Bair, while sometime between 6.00 and 7.00am the advanced elements of the *64th Infantry Regiment* also reached Chunuk Bair and Hill Q, and began occupying the heights. When the *25th Infantry Regiment* arrived afterwards to reinforce the Ottoman positions, it too was directed towards Chunuk Bair.[7]

Unaware of this and on learning that Earl Jo'Uston had halted, General Godley immediately ordered him to seize Chunuk Bair, leaving Napier Jo'Uston to hurriedly organise fire support (see Map 22). The latter's resources, according to Byrne, were 'so small as to be almost insignificant'. He had the two reduced batteries of mountain artillery travelling with the assault columns (eight guns total) and, firing from old Anzac, two 4.5-inch howitzers of Falla's 4th NZFA (Howitzer) Battery (the other two were supporting the defence of Lone Pine), the 6-inch howitzer on Walker's Ridge, perhaps a section of mountain guns, and an uncertain number of 18-pounders, most probably six but perhaps up to ten, two from either McGilp's 1st or Hume's 2nd NZFA batteries, four from an ad hoc battery that had been formed under Captain Groves

Daniell of the NZFA using spare Australian and New Zealand gunners and borrowed Australian and British guns, and perchance four from a similarly formed ad hoc battery under Captain H.J. Daltry of the 4th NZFA Battery. Napier JoÚston could also call on naval gunfire support, assistance from George JoÚston's 2nd AFA Brigade, and probably the fire of the 5-inch batteries from the British 69th Howitzer Brigade in Corps Troops.[8]

The Edgar class cruiser HMS Endymion. She and her sister ship, HMS Grafton, supported ANZAC during the August Offensive and until the end of the campaign. She carried two BL 9.2-inch Mk VI guns, ten QF 6-inch guns, and twelve 6-pounder guns (Wikipedia).

With limited time and with telephone line communications back to old Anzac tenuous at best, Napier JoÚston had little chance of implementing a coordinated fire plan. He discovered that the mountain guns of the 26th (Jacob's) Battery had been pushed practically into the firing line on Rhododendron Ridge and were not in a position to support the operation. Instead, from 8.00am onwards, at a range of 1370 to 2290 metres, they fired across the front of the 29th Indian Infantry Brigade as it pushed up Aghyl Dere against un-entrenched Ottoman infantry towards the Farm, a shelf lying below Chunuk Bair. However, the guns of the 21st (Kohat) Battery in Aghyl Dere were available, and fired some 240 rounds in support of the New Zealanders.[9] The navy also responded, and for two hours HMS *Endymion*'s 6-inch guns smothered Battleship Hill, and *Bacchante*'s 9.2-inch guns fired on Chunuk Bair. Both ceased at 9.30am, ninety minutes before the attack went in.[10]

A gun of the 4th NZFA (Howitzer) Battery being readied to fire. The detachment sergeant is adjusting the trail of the howitzer (Stower Collection WF-007559-424).

The contribution of the New Zealand artillery and the 5-inch howitzers firing from old Anzac is uncertain as the war diaries are not available or contain insufficient detail. Of the Australian batteries, the 5th AFA engaged the Ottoman infantry on Battleship Hill and Turk's Hump during the day, while the 8th AFA engaged both Battleship Hill and the north-western slopes of Chunuk Bair. However, it appears these batteries were engaging opportunity targets rather than participating in a fire plan.[11]

At 11.00am, three companies of the Auckland Battalion rushed along the narrow ridge, losing heavily under fire from Chunuk Bair, Turk's Hump and Battleship Hill. Reaching the Pinnacle,

400 metres short of Chunuk Bair, they scurried into an Ottoman trench, and could go no further. A second attempt by some of the Cantabrians achieved similar results, and it was decided to call it a day.[12] The fire support had been ineffective, which is understandable as the gap between the naval bombardment and the assault gave the Ottoman defenders warning, along with ample time to work around any damage that had been caused. The only effective close fire support Earl JoÚston's men might have received would have come from whatever New Zealand 18-pounders and howitzers were available. Napier JoÚston recorded somewhat optimistically 'both attacks very nearly succeeded, but there was not sufficient artillery support. The ships' guns did not do much damage. They did their best, but there were only two destroyers. The NZ howitzers fired over 1200 rounds in 28 hours.'[13] It would seem that Napier JoÚston was unsure of the naval support provided, highlighting the rushed nature of the fire plan and the inadequate time allowed for him to put it together.

8 August

Godley decided to renew the offensive at dawn on 8 August (see Map 23). The 4th

Australian Infantry Brigade was to advance from Damakjelik Bair, descend into Asma Dere before climbing onto Abdul Rahman Bair, and advance up the latter to Hill 971; in the centre the 29th Indian Infantry Brigade, reinforced by the British 39th Infantry Brigade, would push for Hill Q; and the New Zealand Infantry Brigade, reinforced by two British battalions, would assault Chunuk Bair.[14] To support the attacks, Napier JoÚston had available the same artillery as on the previous day, supplemented by the two 5-inch batteries from the 4th (Lowland) Howitzer Brigade, and two 6-inch howitzers from the Australian Heavy Battery which (along with the 4th, 5th and 8th AFA batteries) had been ordered by Hobbs to register areas along the top of the range on the afternoon of 7 August.[15] To this was added the 9.2 and 6-inch guns of HMS *Bacchante*, and the fire of the destroyers with lesser armaments ranging from 4-inch to 12 and 6-pounder guns.

Registration orders for the Australian batteries show that their fire was spread between Hill 971 and Chunuk Bair, a distance of around 1650 metres.[16] Because the relevant war diaries are unavailable, it is not known whether the New Zealand guns, the howitzers, or the ships were tasked to fire on the same area as the Australians or to spread the fire onto Battleship Hill and Turk's Hump. As it was, the registration orders for the Australian guns created difficulties in that some of the batteries involved had no observation over their allotted target areas. The 5th and 8th AFA batteries, along with the 6-inch howitzers of the Heavy Battery, resorted to firing on compass bearings (there is no August 1915 war diary for the 4th AFA Battery).[17]

The fire plan for the attack was to involve a bombardment of the heights between 3.30am and 4.15am.[18] The 2nd AFA Brigade diary makes no specific reference to the bombardment, and the 5th and 8th AFA battery diaries only record firing throughout the night. The clearest reference to what might have been asked of the Australian guns is found in the war diary of the Heavy Battery. Its allotted zone lay adjacent to Hill 971, and its 6-inchers were tasked to fire one round every thirty minutes into this area before participating in the bombardment. It fired six rounds until 3.10am on the 8th, and another sixteen in the bombardment between 3.30 and 4.15am. Interestingly, this was the first time the 6-inchers had fired at night. It fired another nine rounds into its zone at 6.11am.[19]

For the 4th Australian Infantry Brigade, approximately 2800 metres from its objective, the bombardment proved of little use. Moving at 3.00am, the brigade crossed over Kaiajik Dere and onto Yauan Tepe, the branch spur jutting off Damakjelik Bair at Hill 100. Erroneously believing it had crossed Asma Dere and was on Abdul Rahman Bair, it swung right and began advancing. An Ottoman machine-gun company on a spur of Abdul Rahman Bair dominated Yauan Tepe with grazing fire and, as dawn broke, these guns engaged the head of the Australian column, forcing the men back into Kaiajik Dere, where the advance stalled.

In the centre, Brigadier General Herbert Cox, commanding the 29th Indian Infantry Brigade, divided his and the British 39th Infantry Brigade's battalions into three columns. The left column (two battalions) attempted to advance on the 4th Australian Infantry Brigade's flank, but was unable to cross the valley to its front. The centre column (three battalions) clawed its way up the gullies, reaching a position some 230 metres below the dip between Chunuk Bair and Hill Q, where at 2.00pm the men dug in. The right-hand column (three battalions) managed to reach the Farm below Chunuk Bair, but could get no further.

Clearly the duration of the bombardment of the two northern objectives was too brief and too distant to support the long advance of the Australians and Cox's two brigades through difficult country, and the lack of suitable communications meant adjustments could not be made to the fire support to take account of the local fighting. More useful assistance was provided during the day by the eight Indian mountain guns which supported the advance of Cox's columns.[20]

With a shorter distance to travel, the New Zealanders fared better. Their assault was launched in darkness with the Wellington Battalion leading and two British battalions, one each from the Gloucestershire and the Welsh regiments, following on behind. At 4.15am the Wellingtons set off for the crest 365 metres away in a close phalanx. Expecting a fiery reception, to everyone's surprise they found the height unoccupied and quickly gained the feature. The bombardment had done its job. Bean claimed the Wellingtons had found the Ottoman defenders asleep, but that is odd. Other than overrunning an Ottoman picquet on the north-west slope, the Wellington Battalion history stated that no other Turk was seen. Nor does it seem likely that the defenders would have slept through a forty-five minute bombardment. Most probably they withdrew, as their shallow trenches, no more than knee deep, would have provided little or no cover from artillery shells. A report received at the Ottoman *III Corps HQ* at 4.45am stated that their troops were retreating from the feature.[21]

The 7th Battalion, the Gloucestershire Regiment, and the 8th Battalion, the Welsh Regiment, were not so fortunate. By the time the Glosters set off it was becoming light, and the bombardment had probably ceased. They suffered heavy casualties from Ottoman infantry fire from Turk's Hump and Battleship Hill. Reaching the summit, the survivors fanned out to the left of the Wellingtons. When the 8th Welsh advanced it was fully daylight, and they suffered even more severely, with only a handful reaching the right of the Wellingtons.

At daybreak Bessell-Browne's 8th AFA Battery reported observing the enemy 'launching an attack over the north and southern slopes of Battleship Hill' and fired on them.[22] These were probably Ottoman reinforcements, and the battery's engagement, while useful, would not have materially assisted the Glosters or the Welsh, as the Ottoman riflemen and machine-gunners on the northern slope of the feature facing Rhododendron Ridge would have been in defilade to the 18-pounders. In another twist, at daybreak on 8 August, Caddy's 5th AFA Battery noted that it also fired two rounds at troops on Battleship Hill but, on seeing them waving red and yellow flags, identified them as friendly and ceased firing.[23]

Within a few hours of Earl JoÚston's forces gaining the crest of Chunuk Bair, the Ottoman *25th* and *64th Infantry regiments* counter-attacked, followed later by the *33rd Infantry Regiment*.[24] The 6-inchers of the Australian Heavy Battery fired twenty rounds at Baby 700 at 7.35am and the 5th AFA Battery recorded seeing Ottoman infantry attacking up the west slope of Battleship Hill and engaged them, noting that, after some time, the friendly troops withdrew. Whether the 5th's diarist mixed up Battleship Hill with Chunuk Bair, and the battery was in fact supporting the Wellingtons on the latter feature is unknown.[25]

The Ottomans pushed into the flanks of the Wellingtons' forward trench and, after fierce fighting over a few hours, annihilated the New Zealanders, whose few survivors fell back to the reserve line on the seaward slopes above the junction with Rhododendron Ridge. Turning their attention to this line, the Ottomans attacked downhill repeatedly, only to be stopped by the desperate fire from the surviving Wellingtons, Welsh and Glosters, while artillery, including support from the two mountain gun batteries, and naval gunfire brought down on the crest, helped break up the attacks.[26] At 4.00pm, 130 men of the Auckland Mounted Rifles reinforced the survivors, but were then subjected to heavy Ottoman shellfire and another attack, which was again beaten off. Towards the end of this engagement, rounds from friendly artillery burst over the Wellingtons killing several men, including their Commanding Officer. That evening the few surviving Wellingtons, Glosters and Welsh were relieved by the Otago Battalion and the Wellington Mounted Rifles.

9 August

Abandoning any idea of taking Hill 971, Godley ordered another attempt to capture Hill Q and regain the crest of Chunuk Bair for the morning of 9 August (see Map 24). On his left, the 4th Australian Infantry Brigade fell back to Damakjelik Bair where, along with the British 40th Infantry Brigade, it formed a defensive line facing north-east. In what would prove to be a tragic lack of foresight, no-one thought to occupy Hill 60, the knoll at the foot of Yauan Tepe, which overlooked the entrance to the Anafarta Gap, and provided a potentially solid junction point with IX Corps at Suvla.[27]

Zero Hour for the next attempt on the heights was set at 5.15am, forty-five minutes after dawn. The 29th Indian and 39th Infantry brigades were to renew their assault on Hill Q, while a composite brigade of four British battalions under Brigadier General Anthony Baldwin (GOC 38th

Infantry Brigade) was to make the main assault through Chunuk Bair north to Hill Q. Godley called a conference at Earl Joúston's headquarters to discuss how the task might be achieved, but never turned up. Consequently, Joúston chaired the meeting and counselled Baldwin against an assault along the ridge, given that it would be made in broad daylight and swept by fire from the crest of the main range. Instead he suggested Baldwin move across country to a forming-up place east of the Farm. This would involve a move along an un-reconnoitred route through difficult terrain in darkness but, after seeing the ground for himself, Baldwin agreed.[28]

Historians have roundly criticised Earl Joúston for recommending the alternative route, but they have ignored the fact that, with the assault to occur forty-five minutes after dawn, to move up Rhododendron Ridge in broad daylight would have brought enfilade fire from the right flank. Previous attempts to use this approach in daylight had been cut to pieces. Furthermore, Godley's orders issued at 8.30pm that evening directed Baldwin to 'advance on a line east of The Farm' to take Hill Q, while Joúston's New Zealanders were to 'hold and consolidate the ground [already won], and in cooperation with the other advancing troops, to gain the whole of the Chunuk Bair position extending as far as possible to the south and east', indicating that Godley also accepted Johnston's recommendation.[29]

Looking east from the Tabletop towards Chunuk Bair (the highest crest) and the Farm (the cleared area below Chunuk Bair). Rhododendron Ridge swings away to the right in the foreground. The right-hand side of the Apex can be seen in the top right of the photograph, with Cheshire Ridge dropping away to the left and running down through the middle portion of the photograph. A portion of Hill Q can be seen on the left skyline. Aghyl Dere lies just beyond Cheshire Ridge and below the Farm. The sheer-sided spur this side of Cheshire Ridge drops off Rhododendron Ridge into Chailak Dere (AWM P07906.069).

Again the attack was to be preceded by a forty-five minute bombardment of the crest of the range commencing at 4.30am. With a smaller target area—roughly 730 metres in length—a heavier weight of fire could be brought down than on the previous morning. According to the British official historian, the crest of Chunuk Bair was not included in the bombardment, the New Zealanders being too close. The NZ&A Division orders directed that 'at 5.15am, the Naval [sic] fire will be switched off to the flanks. As regards the Field Artillery those batteries under the direct control of CRA NZ and A Division will raise their trajectory and fire on the reverse slopes of the objective to engage the reverse slopes of the objectives. The remaining guns will be directed on the flanks by order of the CRA NZ and A Division.'[30]

These orders were issued at 8.30pm on 8 August for dissemination overnight. Reflective of the lack of inclusion of the artillery in planning an attack, and limited combined-arms training pre-war, Napier JoÚston complained, 'The G.O.C., an infantry officer, did not appear to realise that to concentrate the fire of so many land and naval guns required careful preparation, and not, as had been done, arranged in three quarters of an hour.'[31] To assist the navy identify its targets in the pre-dawn darkness, two New Zealanders crept out over Cheshire Ridge and placed a battery-operated lamp facing the sea on the north corner of the Farm. Although not mentioned in the NZ&A Division's orders, throughout the night of 8/9 August the 4th, 5th and 8th AFA batteries sprinkled the Sari Bair Range from Chunuk Bair to Hill 971 with fire at a rate of one round from each battery every ten minutes, increasing their rate of fire 'for few minutes' at 5.10am, apparently in support of the infantry assault. The Australian Heavy Battery did not fire in support of this attack.[32]

At 4.00am on 9 August, before Godley's assault began, the Ottomans launched another attack against the New Zealanders on Chunuk Bair. They failed to break the thin defensive line and were driven back after fierce fighting. Further disruption occurred when at 5.00am three HE shells burst among the New Zealanders. The source has never been established. Bean says they were almost certainly from the howitzers to the right rear, while Colonel William Meldrum of the Wellington Mounted Rifles thought they were naval shells. In the chaos, the Otago Battalion and a portion of the Wellington Mounted Rifles fell back down the hill, abandoning their shallow trenches. Crisis was averted when, rallied by their officers, the New Zealanders regained their position.[33]

New Zealand gunners of the 4th NZFA (Howitzer) Battery and their 4.5-inch howitzer in an open gun position on North Beach during the summer. Russell's Top is in the background with the Sphinx jutting above the ridge. From here this gun could cover most of the Anzac beachhead, and during the August Offensive it could fire along the spine of the main range in support of the infantry attacks on Chunuk Bair (Stower Collection WF-007559-423).

To the north, and moving up close to the bombardment, the 1/6th Gurkha Rifles and a portion of the 6th Battalion, the South Lancashire Regiment closed with the bombardment before storming Hill Q and, after a brief but vicious fight, wrested it from the Ottoman defenders. As the troops consolidated on the feature, HE shells landed among them, inflicting casualties and throwing the troops into confusion. The survivors fell back down the slope, leaving Hill Q unoccupied. Who fired these shells is still debated. At the time it was believed to be the navy, with HMS *Bacchante* the culprit; Birdwood thought so and Napier JoÚston noted his view that she had fired for too long. Others have suggested it was howitzer fire, pointing out that the shells had landed on the reverse slope which, with their flat trajectory, the naval guns could not have reached, and that the howitzers had been tasked to lift their fire to the reverse slope after Zero Hour. The highest point of Hill Q is nearer the seaward slope and the inland portion is broader, which lends credence to the view that the howitzer fire did the damage. Irrespective of who fired, it was another tragic incident of friendly fire, this time with adverse tactical repercussions.[34]

The crew and 5-inch howitzer of the 5th (City of Glasgow) Battery RFA in action on North Beach during the August Offensive. The gunners in the foreground are setting the fuses of the shells. Walker's Ridge can be seen in the background, and to the left in the distance is No 1 Outpost (IWM Q13623).

Further south, the 2/10th Gurkha Rifles and the 9th Battalion, the Royal Warwickshire Regiment, were to take the saddle between Hill Q and Chunuk Bair, but had been told not to move forward until Baldwin's brigade began to come into line to their right. However, Baldwin was fatally delayed. At 5.15am he was nowhere to be seen, and it was not until 6.00am that his troops began to advance from the Farm. Attacking across that small, open flat, with the fire support long since ceased, they suffered heavily, under fire from the Ottomans lining the crest of the range. Baldwin, seeing the futility of progressing further, withdrew them to the northern lip of the Farm plateau. Throughout the day the 4th, 5th and 8th AFA batteries again engaged targets of opportunity from Turk's Hump to Battleship Hill.[35]

The third attempt to take the Sari Bair heights had failed. As on 8 August, the lack of immediate communications between the attacking infantry and the guns meant the fire plan could not be adjusted to meet changing circumstances brought about by Baldwin's delay. This was a situation that was to bedevil all armies throughout the Great War and after, until radios were of a sufficient size and reliability to be carried by the gunners with the attacking infantry.

10 August

Fortuitously for the New Zealanders, their ordeal on the slopes of Chunuk Bair was over. At midnight on 9/10 August they were relieved by the raw, untried and exhausted 6th Battalion, the Loyal North Lancashire Regiment, and 5th Battalion, the Wiltshire Regiment, who were soon to be engulfed in another tragedy. Forming up on the reverse slopes of the Sari Bair Range from Hill Q to Chunuk Bair were sixteen

Ottoman battalions from the *7th, 8th, 9th* and *12th divisions*. At 4.30am on 10 August they swept over the crest in dense waves overwhelming the two British battalions. A little to the north, descending on the Farm, the Ottomans routed Baldwin's force, killing around 1000 men, including Baldwin himself. The attack was only stopped by the combined machine-guns of the New Zealand Infantry Brigade firing from the Apex, which cut the Ottoman infantry down in swathes, and fire from the NZFA batteries and the 69th Howitzer Brigade RFA. At the same time the 4th, 5th and 8th AFA batteries opened a rapid fire on the succeeding waves moving up the inland slope of Chunuk Bair. Both Indian mountain batteries continued to fire on the attackers throughout the day.[36]

The Attacks in Retrospect

The Ottoman counter-attack on 10 August brought the August Offensive to an end. Looking back on the previous four days, there was much to reflect on. In the end, forced to proceed with the artillery on hand, augmented by the five 5-inch howitzer batteries that arrived in July, the commanders had banked on surprise, sequencing the actions so that the feints at Lone Pine and German Officers' Trench preceded the attempt on the heights, potentially allowing a good proportion of the Corps Troops howitzers to be available to support the latter if required. However, when surprise was lost, there were insufficient batteries and ammunition to cover the potential tasks.

At the Dardanelles Commission, Napier JoÚston was critical of Birdwood and Cunliffe-Owen for not making contingency artillery plans in case the assault on the heights initially failed, and for not deploying the 6-inch and 9.2-inch howitzers he believed were in Egypt.[37] Whether these guns and suitable ammunition stocks were available and whether suitable positions for them could have been found while maintaining surprise are moot points. However, Napier JoÚston was able to form ad hoc batteries from resources already at Anzac, and this raises the question as to why more senior planners had not examined similar possibilities, or indeed the use of the 18-pounders of the 13th (Western) Division's artillery that were ashore at the time.

Firing into the Sari Bair heights created potential difficulties for the gunners. The difference in altitude between many gun positions and their targets made it essential that compensating adjustments to elevation be applied if potential errors in range were to be averted.

Observation was another problem, with many areas defilade to ANZAC observers. Napier JoÚston also made the point that some of the fire support was not the optimum type. The ships' guns could only engage targets on the seaward slopes. Field guns faced similar problems, although those firing in enfilade from the old Anzac beachhead gave some coverage of the inland slopes.[38]

The bombardments supporting the assaults on the Sari Bair heights proved unsuccessful, with the exception of those supporting the Wellingtons' attack on Chunuk Bair on the morning of 8 August, and the 1/6th Gurkhas and 6th South Lancs on 9 August. In the other attacks there were difficulties with communications, the time available for planning, the distance between the attackers and the objectives when fire lifted, and casualties caused by friendly fire.

With the limited artillery resources available, the question arises as to whether the continued fighting to hold Lone Pine robbed the NZ&A Division of critical fire support. The evidence indicates that Napier JoÚston lost the fire of a field gun section and a 4.5-inch howitzer section from his divisional artillery, a battery of 5-inch howitzers from Corps Troops artillery, and the two Australian 6-inchers, except for the morning of 8 August. It is unlikely these few resources would have redressed the underlying problem the New Zealanders faced. It might also be argued that the fighting for Lone Pine assisted the NZ&A Division in some measure by preventing the Ottomans focusing their complete attention on Sari Bair. It is also evident from the war diaries that those guns in the 1st Australian Division that could reach into the Sari Bair Range provided support for Godley's troops.

In his report on the offensive, Godley was complimentary about the contribution of the gunners, recording that 'the artillery of the Force, and the guns of the 1st Australian Division, at all times gave efficient support, and not only rendered material assistance to the infantry in repelling Turkish counter-attacks, but were responsible for the infliction of severe loss on the enemy.'[39] Birdwood was even more effusive, encouraging the troops to never forget the 'enormous self-sacrificing assistance the infantry have received throughout from 40 every gun.'[40]

At the gun positions, the gunners of both divisions gave a good account of themselves under Ottoman counter-battery fire. The Corps War Diary records that, on 7 and 8 August, 600 shells of 75mm, 9-pounder, 4.2-inch and 5.9-inch calibre fell on Hughes' 7th and Phillips' 4th AFA batteries, noting also that a proportion of the larger shells failed to explode. The 2nd AFA Brigade War Diary confirms the heavy engagement of the 4th Battery, recording that one gun received a direct hit and two gun pits were collapsed. Hughes' 7th AFA Battery recorded being constantly under fire, with No 2 gun being knocked out temporarily, No 3 gun being forced to withdraw from its pit, and the parapets blown in on the morning of 9 August. McGilp's 1st NZFA Battery was under heavy fire on 6 August, its emplacements badly knocked about and No 1 and 2 guns temporarily out of action. On 8 August the 8th AFA Battery's No 4 gun was destroyed, and the buffer of its No 1 gun was severely damaged.[41]

No 4 Gun, 8th AFA Battery, behind the Pimple, destroyed by Ottoman counter-battery fire around noon on 8 August, killing Gunner Charles Barber and wounding Gunners

Thomas Ewing and Harry Belcher, both of whom survived their wounds. Barber is buried in the Shell Green Cemetery at Anzac, Ewing returned to Australia in June 1916, and Belcher died of wounds in France on 31 January 1917 (AWM P01251.005).

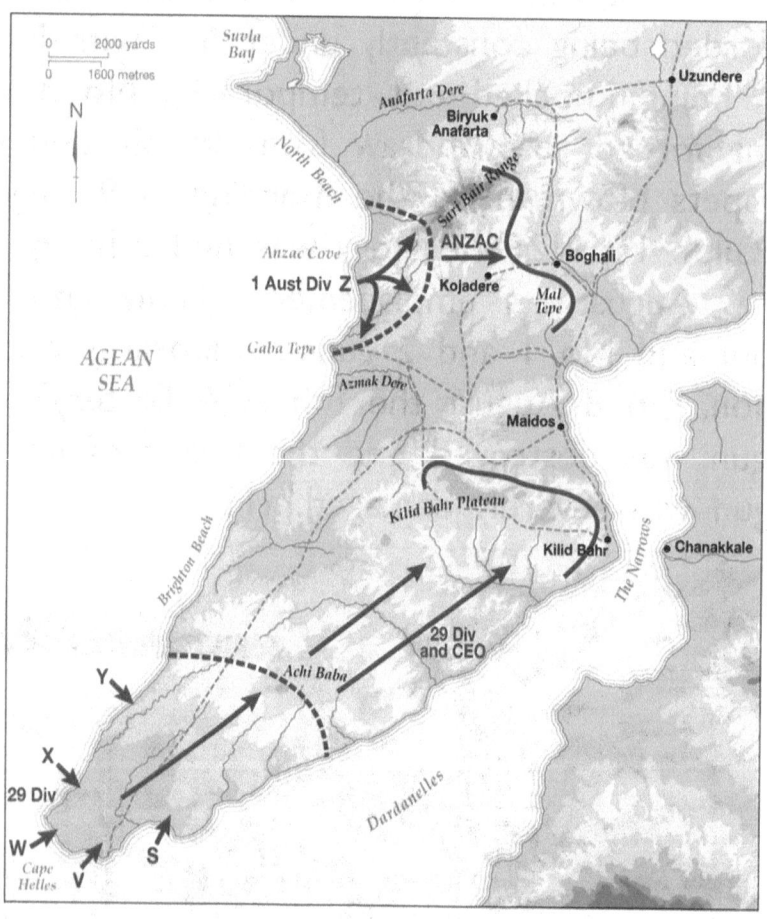

Map 1. General Hamilton's plan. The main assault would be undertaken by the British 29th Division landing on five beaches (S, V, W, X and Y) at Cape Helles and take Achi Baba. Reinforced by the French Corps Expeditionnaire D'Orient (CEO), they would then strike north to seize the Kilid Bahr Plateau and the Ottoman batteries on the

western shore of the Dardanelles. North of Gaba Tepe the 1st Australian Division would land at Z Beach and capture the Sari Bair Range. Once the whole Corps was ashore ANZAC would advance east and secure the Mal Tepe Ridge to cut the north-south road communications.

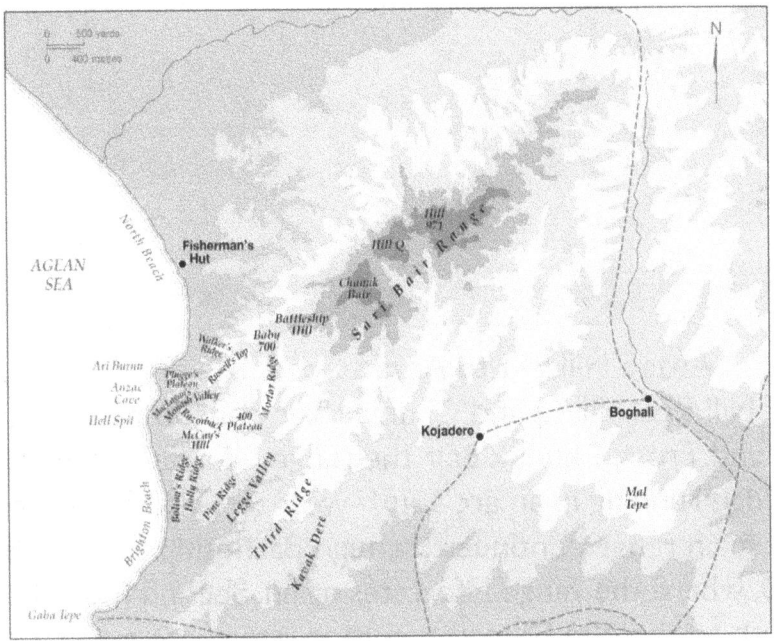

Map 2. The Sari Bair Range. Running from its foot at Anzac Cove, the Sari Bair Range climbs to the north-east through the principle heights of Baby 700, Battleship Hill, Chunuk Bair, Hill Q to Hill 971. To the north of the range, the ground drops steeply in a tangle of ridges, spurs, valleys and gullies, while to the south the principle ridges slip more gradually to the Gaba Tepe-Maidos plain. ANZAC's ultimate objective is the ridge dropping from the Sari Bair range east of Hill 971 to Mal Tepe.

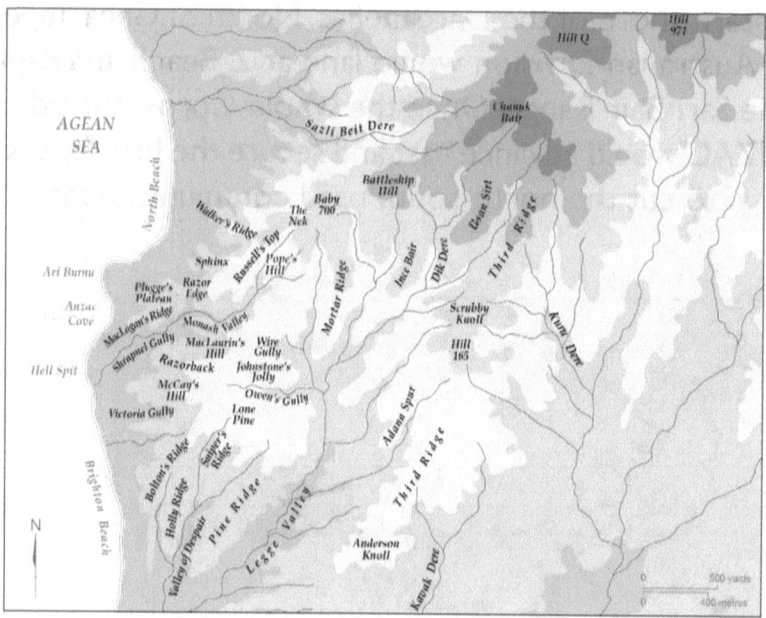

Map 3. Anzac: Hill 971 to Anzac Cove. The principal heights of Hill 971, Hill Q and Chunuk Bair constitutes the vital ground. From Chunuk Bair the range bifurcates with Third Ridge running in an arc south-west to Gaba Tepe, while the main range continues through Battleship Hill and Baby 700, where the range bifurcates again. Second Ridge heads south to the 400 Plateau before splitting into a number of spurs, the principal ones being McCay's Hill running west to Brighton Beach, Bolton's Ridge paralleling the coast above the beach, its subsidiary Holly Ridge, and further inland Pine Ridge overlooking Legge Valley. From Baby 700 the range continues as Russells Top to Plugge's Plateau overlooking Anzac Cove. Horse drawn artillery can only move along the beach, up Legge Valley, along Third Ridge to the main range, and across the open country inland from Gaba Tepe.

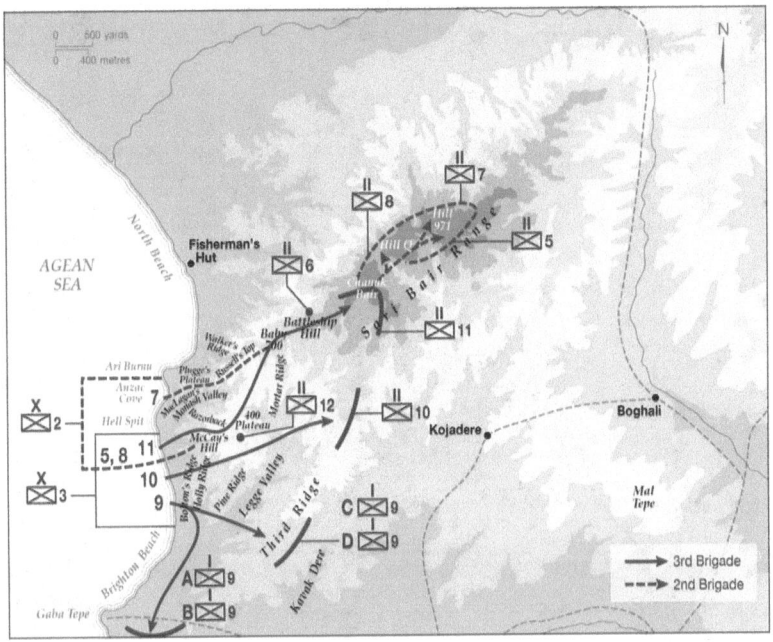

Map 4. The 1st Australian Division's objectives, 25 April 1915. Landing immediately south of Anzac Cove the 3rd Brigade will capture a covering position with the 11th Battalion taking Chunuk Bair and the head of Third Ridge, the 10th taking the central portion of Third Ridge, and the 9th in two groups taking the lower end of the ridge and Gaba Tepe. The 12th Battalion will form the brigade reserve. Following on, and echeloned slightly north to include Anzac Cove, the 2nd Brigade will push up the main range through the left flank of the covering force and take Hill Q and Hill 971 with 5th, 7th and 8th battalions, while the 6th will be in reserve on Battleship Hill.

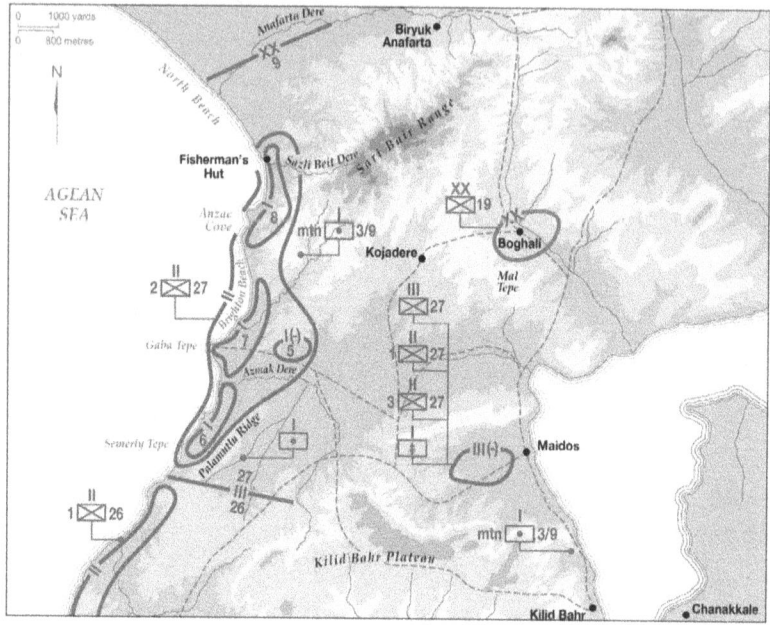

Map 5. The Ottoman defensive dispositions in the Sari Bair-Gaba Tepe area, 24 April 1915. The dispositions of the 27th Infantry Regiment on 24 April 1915. Deployed forward the 2nd Battalion (2/27th Infantry) has three rifle companies (6th, 7th and 8th) covering the 12 kilometres of coast between Semerley Tepe and the Fishermans Hut, with the 5th Company in reserve two and half kilometres east of Gaba Tepe. The remainder of the regiment, the 1/27th Infantry, 3/27th Infantry and the machine gun company are in reserve near Maidos. A battery of four mountain guns of the 3rd Battalion, 9th Artillery Regiment (3/9th Artillery) is at Lone Pine. The other mountain battery of the 3/9th Artillery is south of Maidos, and a battery of four 15cm heavy guns is behind the Palamutlu Ridge. Two obsolete 87mm field guns (not shown), of which one was inoperable, were also positioned at Gaba Tepe. The 39th Artillery Regiment is with the 19th Division (the 5th Army reserve) at Boghali, but can only be released on the authority of Liman von Sanders.

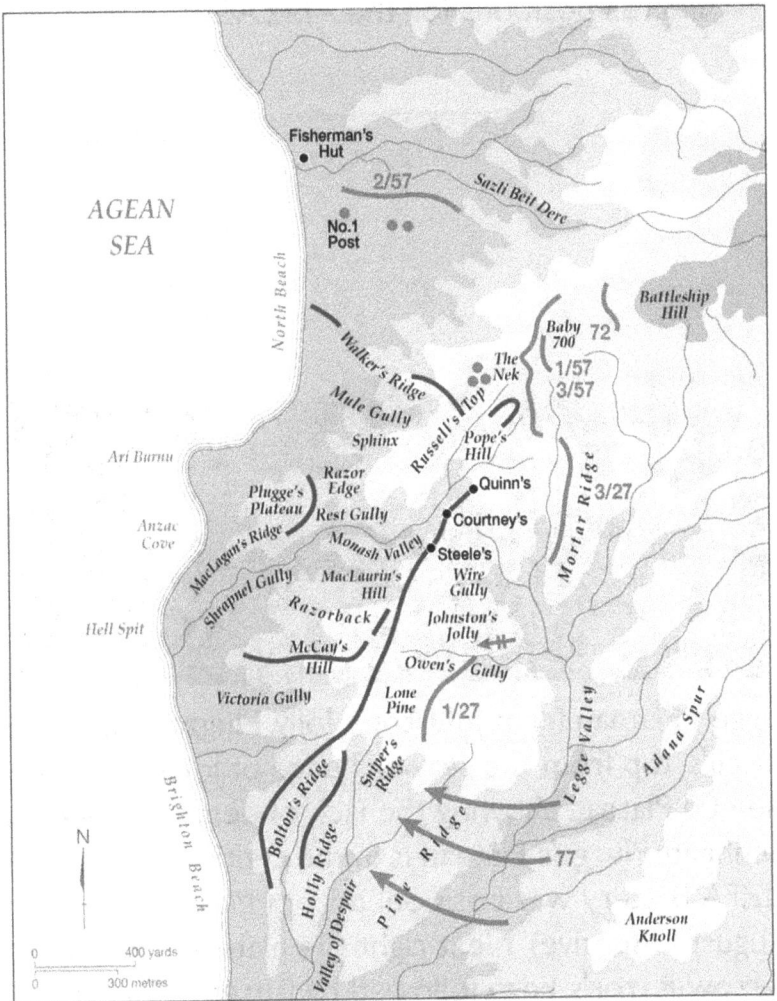

Map 6. The situation at Anzac on the evening of 25 April 1915. Initially attacking with five battalions (three of the 57th Infantry Regiment and the 1st Battalion 27th Infantry Regiment) against fourteen ANZAC battalions the Ottoman's have seized the ground of tactical importance around Baby 700 and and driven the Australians back across Lone Pine. Near dusk they are reinforced by the 1st Battalion, 72nd Regiment and the 1st and 2nd battalions of the 77th Infantry Regiment. This results in a shallow

beachhead of no tactical importance with no depth and limited positions for the ANZAC field guns.

Plugge's Plateau from JoÚston's Jolly. Plugge's Plateau and Russell's Top from the seaward edge of JoÚston's Jolly on the 400 Plateau showing the lack of depth in the Anzac beachhead. Plugge's Plateau is in the centre (where the 2nd NZFA Battery was positioned from May until after the August Offensive). Next right the plateau drops to the narrow Razor's Edge followed by Russell's Top running away to the Nek at the right, (marked by the stand of trees). The Sphinx is peeping above the Top. The 1st NZFA Battery and a section of 26th (Jacob's) Battery were located to the right of the Sphinx in the vicinity of the two single trees on the crest of the Top. (Glenn Wahlert Image)

Second Ridge. The ANZAC line along Second Ridge from Russell's Top. The camera is looking across the upper reaches of Monash Valley. On the extreme left is the Nek (marked by the pine trees). The high feature to the right of the Nek with the long stand of trees is Baby 700, to it's right is the Chessboard, with Pope's Hill marked by the yellow soil in the foreground. Waterfall Gully is to its right. This area was the scene of the disastrous attack by the 13th, 16th and Otago battalions on the evening 2 May. Further right, marked by the white monument, is Quinn's Post. In the far distance above the white road is the 400 Plateau, with McCay's Hill running off to the right of the photograph. ANZAC occupied the lower half of Pope's Hill, with a gap between it and Russell's Top, and another gap between Pope's and Quinn's Post. The line then clung to the seaward edge of the ridge to the 400 Plateau. This view shows how the 1st NZFA Battery on Russell's Top could fire in enfilade across the front of the 1st Australian Division trenches on the plateau, and the impossibility of siting 18-pounders along Second Ridge. (Chris Roberts Image)

400 Plateau from Turk's Hump. View of the 400 Plateau taken from the southern side of Turks Hump. The white monument (marked by the red circle), is on Lone Pine and JoÚston's Jolly is the flat northern lobe below the monument and the trees to its right, and across which the road runs (marked by the red arrow). From April to August the Australian front line was on the left hand side of the clump of trees (The Pimple) on Lone Pine, and to the right of the road on JoÚston's Jolly. After the attack on 6 August 1915 the Australian front line on Lone Pine was at the monument. Battleship Hill is on the far right of the photograph where the dark green trees are, with Ince Bair running down to the left. This was the furtherest inland the group of Australians of the 11th Battalion under Captain Tulloch reached on the morning of 25 April 1915, until they were driven off by the Ottoman counter-attack around 1pm. Gaba Tepe is the first promontory jutting out into the sea. This photograph shows the superior ground held

by the Ottomans, and the clear fields of observation they had over the ANZAC beachhead.

Bolton's Ridge from Lone Pine. Looking south from Lone Pine. Bolton's Ridge runs from the far right of the photograph above the sea, with its extension Harris Ridge running down past the green triangle. The Valley of Despair climbs towards the camera from the foot of the triangle. Holly Ridge can just be discerned branching off to the right of the hump on Bolton's Ridge in the centre of the photograph. The first promontory jutting out into the Aegean Sea is Gaba Tepe, the foot of Third Ridge. (Chris Roberts Image)

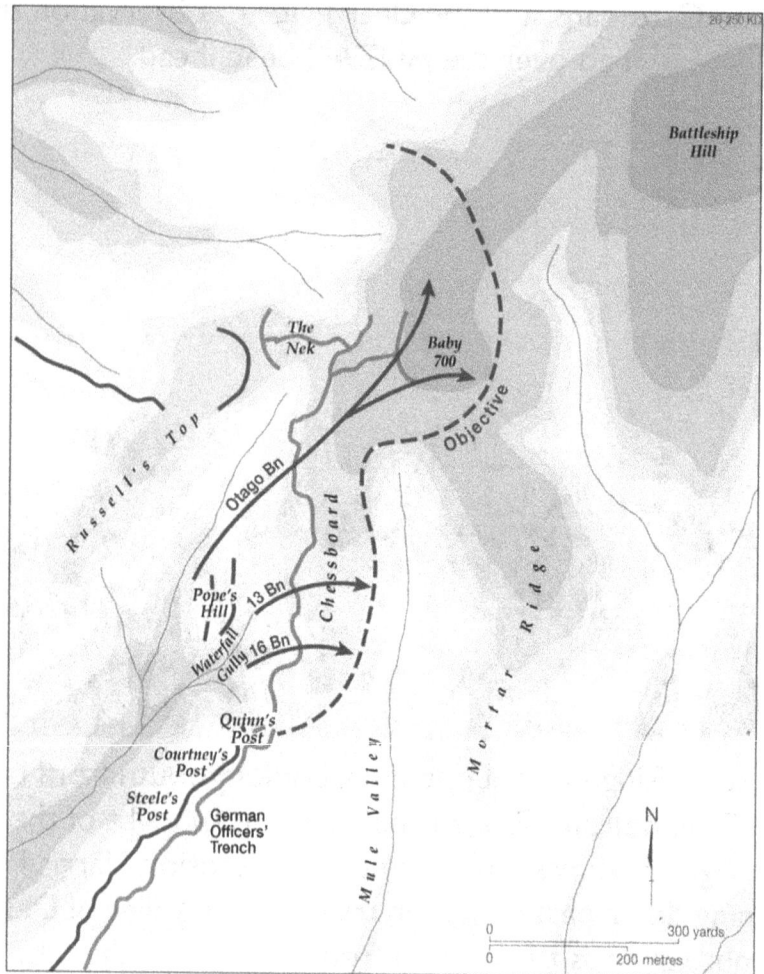

Map 7. Plan for the attack on Baby 700, 2 May 1915. Attacking in echelon from south to north the 16th and 13th Australian infantry battalions attack up the steep sides of Monash valley with the intention of seizing the upper reaches of Second Ridge. Further north the Otago Battalion was to seize Baby 700.

The head of Monash Valley. The head of Monash Valley from Braund's Hill to the bifurcation at Pope's Hill, which is the spur slipping towards the camera in the centre of the photograph. Waterfall Gully runs to the right while the northern arm climbs to The Nek lying between the gap in the trees, indicated by the solitary tree on the horizon (marked by red arrow 1). Running across the horizon from the left is Russell's Top to The Nek. Above Pope's Hill lies The Chessboard, marked by the trees and the white monument rising above them (marked by red arrow 2). Further left, marked by the smaller white monument (marked by red arrow 3), is Quinn's Post, while the rear of Second Ridge towers over the valley on the right. During the attack on 2 May 1915 the 16th and 13th battalions climbed out of Waterfall Gully and assaulted the The Chessboard to the left of Quinn s Post. Further left the Otago Battalion struggled up the right fork of the valley past Pope's Hill and assaulted Baby 700 to the righi of The

Nek. The lack of suitable gun positions in this area is evident. (Chris Roberts Image)

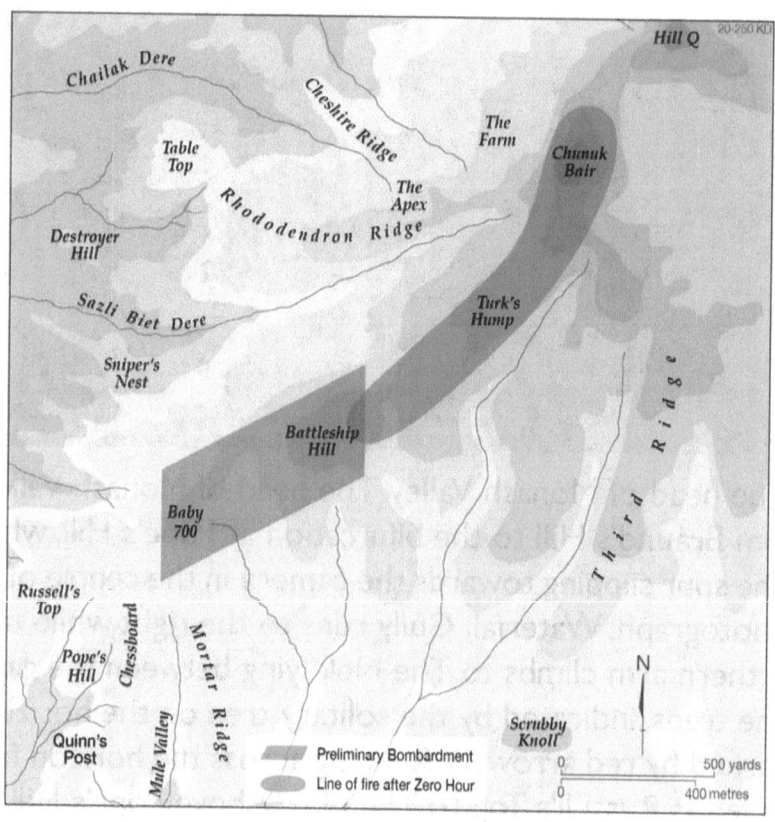

Map 8. Fire Plan for the attack on Baby 700, 2 May 1915. The NZ&A Division wanted the Navy, its divisional artillery ashore (two 18-pounder batteries, a 4.5inch howitzer battery and an attached mountain battery), and, if possible, the guns of the 2nd AFA Brigade along with the mountain battery attached to the 1st Australian Division, to conduct a preliminary bombardment between 7.00 and 7.15pm into a parallelogram, the forward line of which ran for some 384 metres north-south across Baby 700 and onto Mortar Ridge, and the rear line across Battleship Hill. At 7.15pm the fire

was to lift to cover the ridge between Battleship Hill and Chunuk Bair while the attackers captured Baby 700.

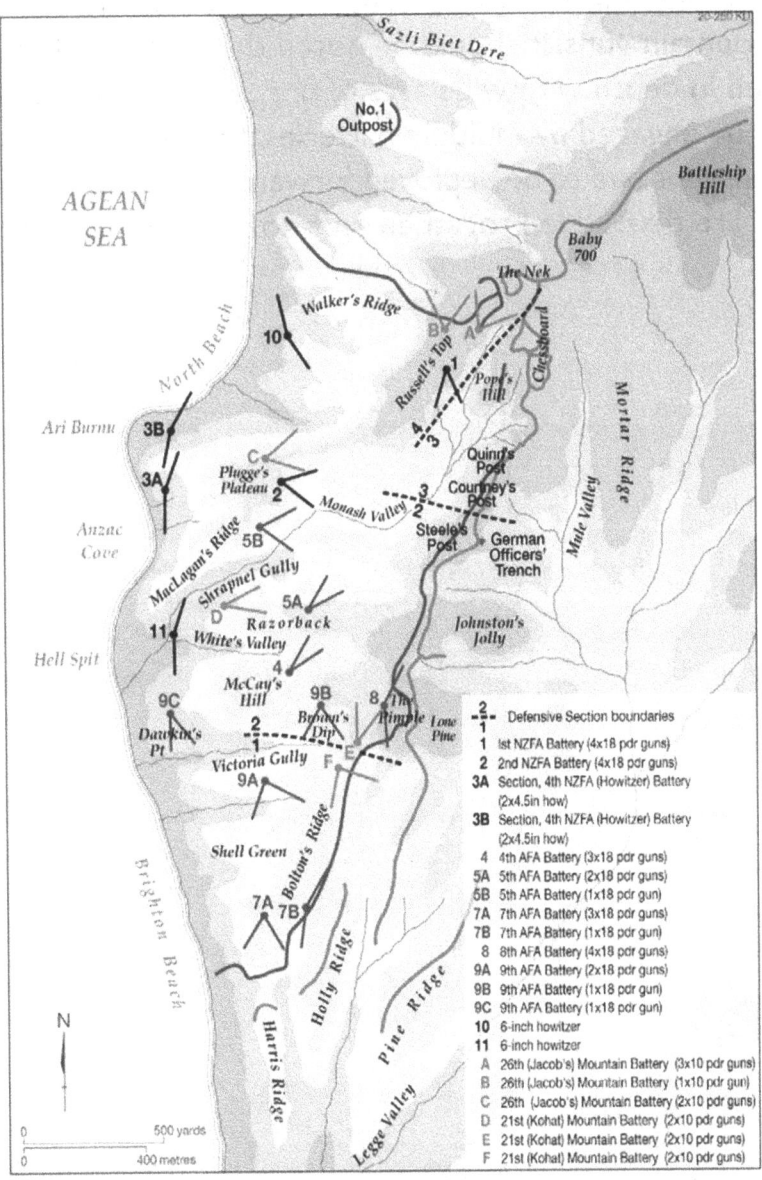

Map 9. Battery positions and defensive sections, 25 May 1915. In late April Birdwood divided the beachhead into four defensive sections. The location of the guns and their

respective batteries are shown as at 25 May 1915, after all of the allotted fire units had been brought ashore and interim deployments, designed to test the feasibility of potential firing positions. In relation to the field and mountain guns, it should be noted that instead of being sited in depth with wide arcs of fire and targets thus able to be engaged by multiple batteries, the terrain dictated these guns had to be deployed forward with restricted arcs of fire that, added together, gave coverage of the whole front.

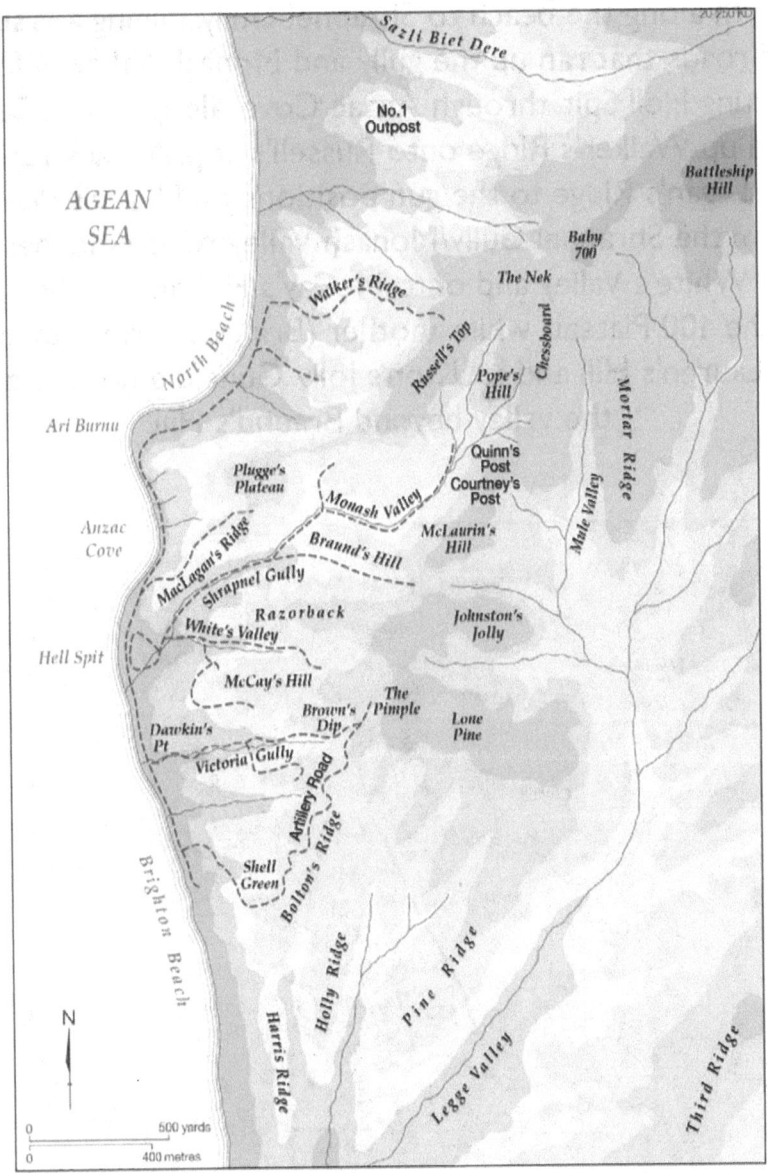

Map 10. Roads constructed within Anzac. The road system eventually established within the Anzac beachhead that facilitated the movement of guns and mobile batteries. Artillery Road ran along the rear of Bolton's Ridge to the rear of the 400 Plateau, where it joined the unnamed road running down Victoria Gully to Dawkin's Point. A track ran

north along the beach to Shrapnel Gully, joining a system of roads that ran up the gully and Monash Valley, before skirting Hell Spit, through Anzac Cove, along North Beach and up Walker's Ridge onto Russell's Top. A track run up MacLagan's Ridge to the gun positions on Plugge's Plateau. From the Shrapnel Gully/Monash Valley road, branches ran up White's Valley and onto McCay's Hill, and to the rear of the 400 Plateau, while another (Bridge's Road) ran up to McLauren's Hill and JoUston's Jolly. Guns did not travel up the valley beyond Braund's Hill.

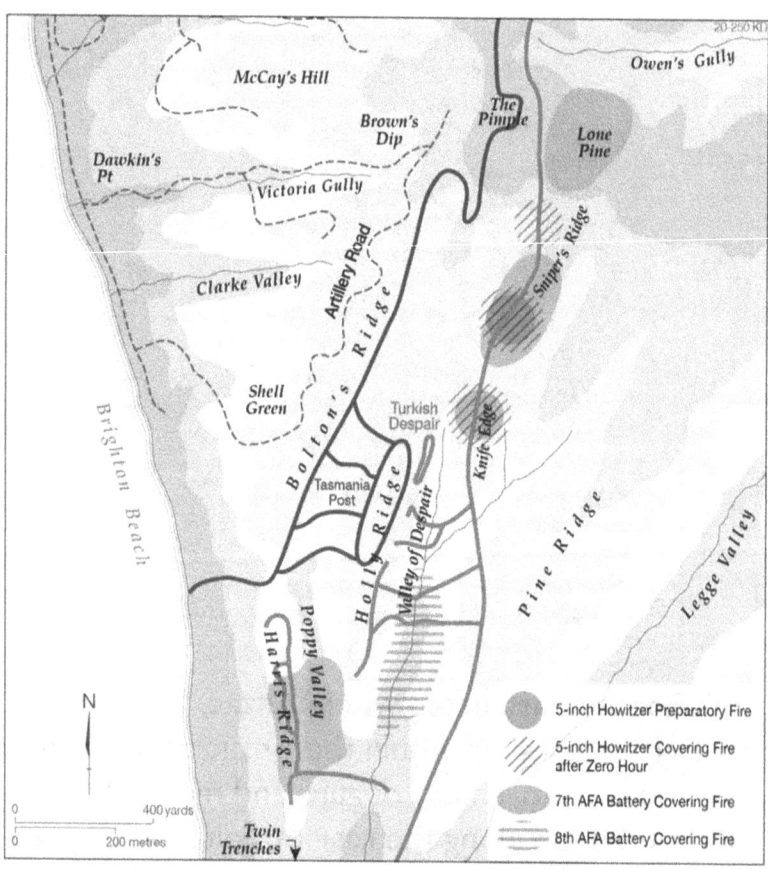

Map 11. Fire plan for the capture of Turkish Despair, 31 July 1915. The plan called for preparatory howitzer fire

commencing at 4.30pm on the southern end of Sniper's Ridge and trenches east-north-east of the objective. At Zero hour howitzers would re-engage those targets and the northern end of Sniper's Ridge, while field guns fired shrapnel onto surrounding ridges, Lone Pine and into the Valley of Despair, and naval monitors shelled other targets to the south.

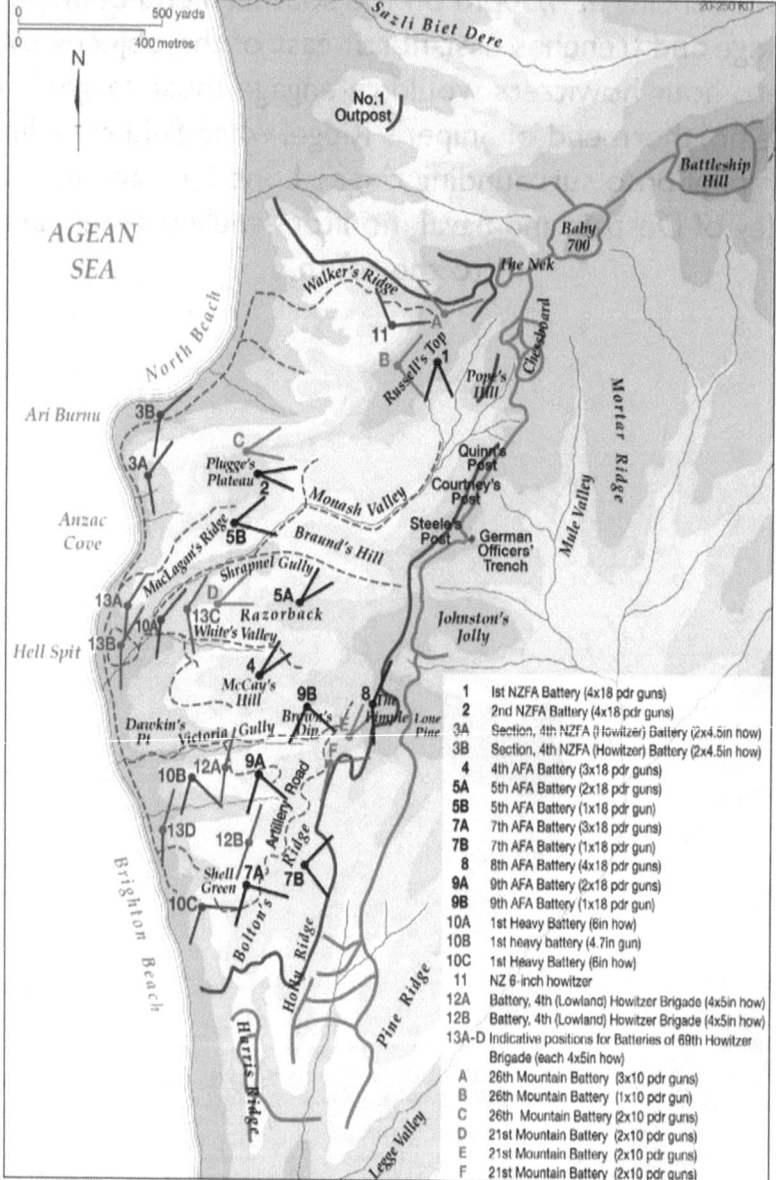

Map 12. Battery positions at the end of July 1915. The positions occupied by the Corps' artillery have changed little since late May, but this map now shows the positions occupied by the newly created 1st Australian Heavy Battery, and the reinforcing batteries from the 4th (Lowland) and the 69th Howitzer brigades.

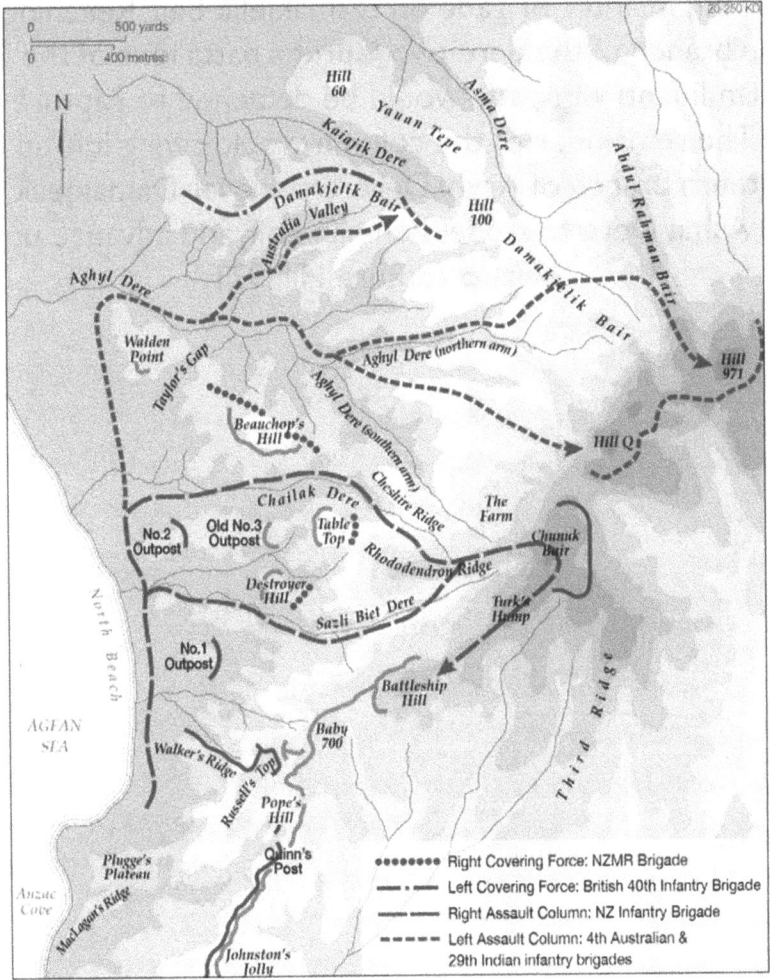

Map 13. Plan for the breakout and capture of the Sari Bair Range, night 6/7 August 1915. Initially the NZMR and 40th Infantry brigades would seize the foothills covering the entrances to the principal valleys. The New Zealand Infantry Brigade would pass through the NZMR Brigade via Sazli Biet Dere, Chailak Dere and the upper reaches of Rhododendron Ridge and take Chunuk Bair, whereupon elements would advance down the range to assault Battleship Hill. The Left Assault Column would go around Walden Point into Aghyl Dere before the 4th Australian Infantry Brigade would detach two battalions to link up with

the 40th Infantry Brigade on Damakjelik Bair. Reaching the main branch of the dere two Gurkha battalions of the 29th Indian Infantry Brigade would be detached to capture Hill Q. The remainder of the column would swing left up the southern branch of Agyhl Dere, cross over Damakjelik Bair and Asma Dere to Abdel Rahman Bair, and advance up the bair to capture Hill 971.

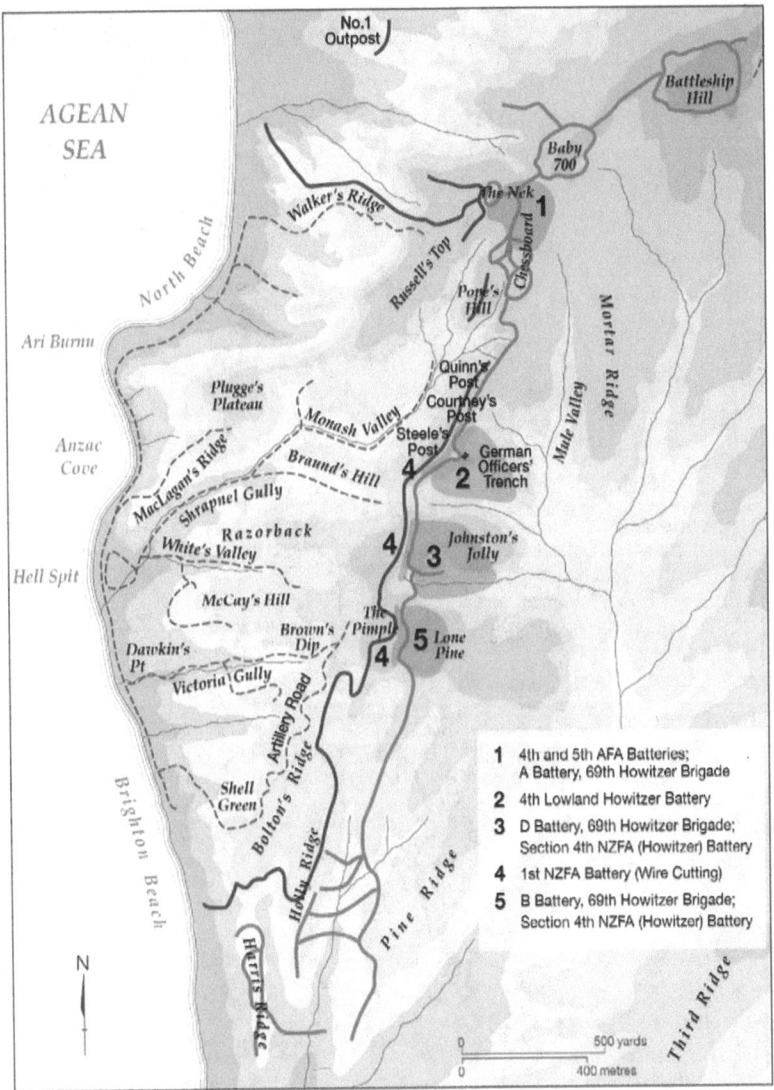

Map 14. Corps fire plan for the August Offensive. The targeting of preparatory fire in accordance with Corps Orders prior to the attacks from the ANZAC position on the night 6/7 August. Wire cutting was to take place between 3 and 6 August.

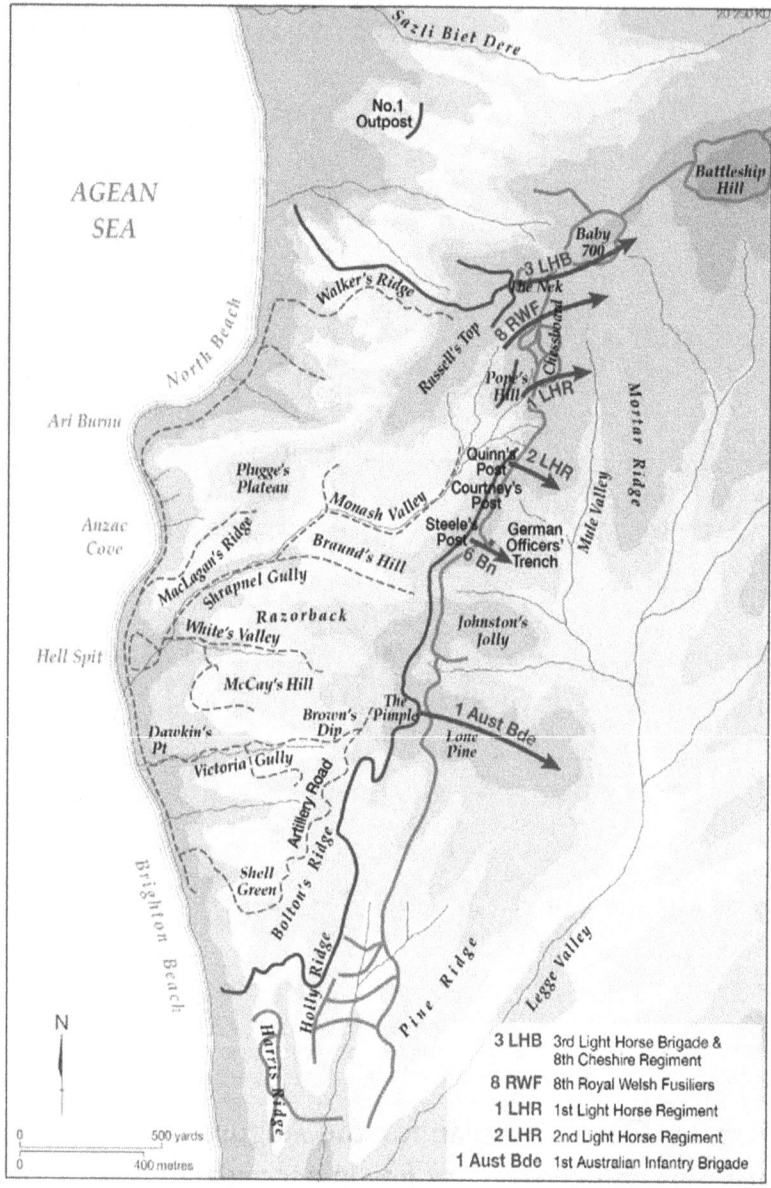

Map 15. Australian attacks at Lone Pine, German Officer's Trench, Quinn's Post, Pope's Hill and the Nek 6/7 August 1915. Assaulting on the evening 6 August the 1st Australian Infantry Brigade would create a diversion by capturing Lone Pine. Later that night the 6th Australian Infantry Battalion would attack German Officer's Trench to keep Ottoman

attention in the south. At dawn on 7 August the 2nd Light Horse Regiment would capture Turkish Quinn's, the 1st Light Horse Regiment would capture the Chessboard, while the 3rd Light Horse Brigade, supported by two British infantry battalions, would seize Baby 700. At this time the New Zealanders were expected to be attacking Battleship Hill.

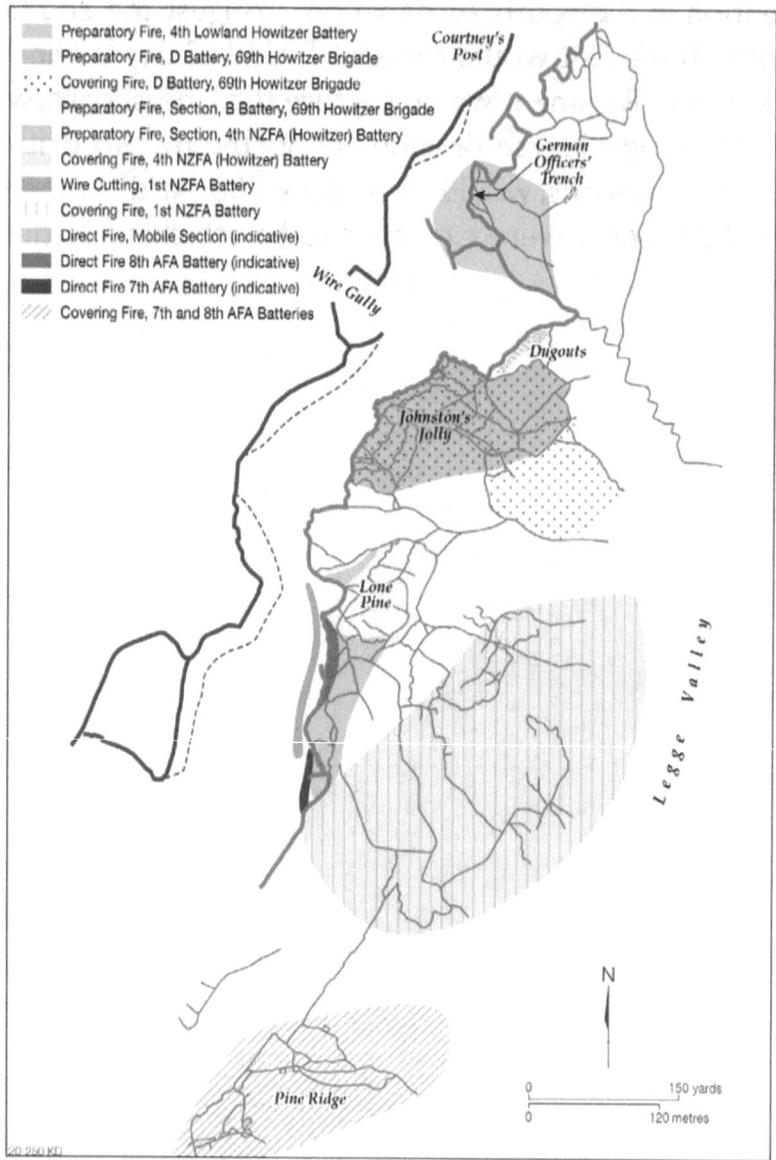

Map 16. Fire plan for the attack at Lone Pine. The location of preparatory fire and then covering fire for the attack at Lone Pine in accordance with orders issued by Corps and modified by the CRA 1st Australian Division. Final preparatory fire was to occur between 4.30 and 5.50pm (Zero Hour) on 6 August, after which the batteries would lift to their covering fire tasks on the approaches to Lone

Pine, or the Ottoman Trenches that overlooked it. Across the broader ANZAC front, other batteries and naval gunfire were tasked with engaging enemy trenches, movement and guns as gains at Lone Pine were consolidated.

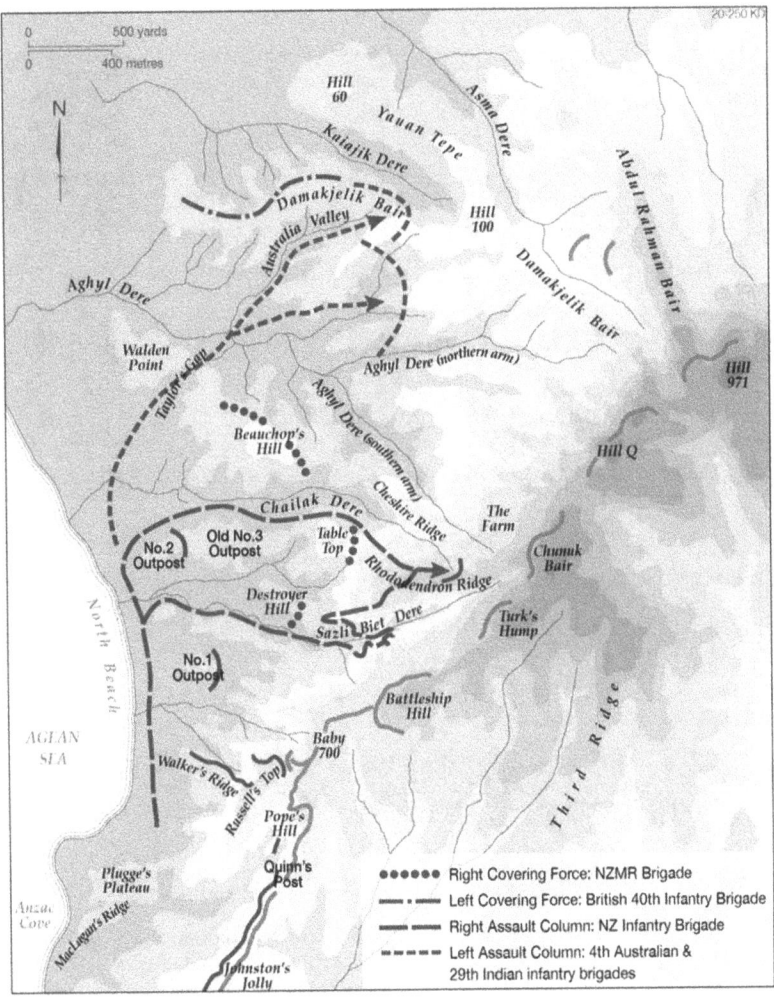

Map 17. The situation north of Anzac early morning 7 August 1915. The NZMR and 40th Infantry brigades have captured their objectives. The New Zealand Infantry Brigade has reached the Apex on Rhododendron Ridge, 500 metres short of Chunuk Bair. Having taken a short cut through

Taylor's Gap to make up time, the Left Assault Column is well short of its objectives, with the 4th Australian Infantry Brigade on Damakjelik Bair to the right of the 40th Infantry Brigade, while the 29th Indian Infantry Brigade is strung out in an arc to the Australian's right.

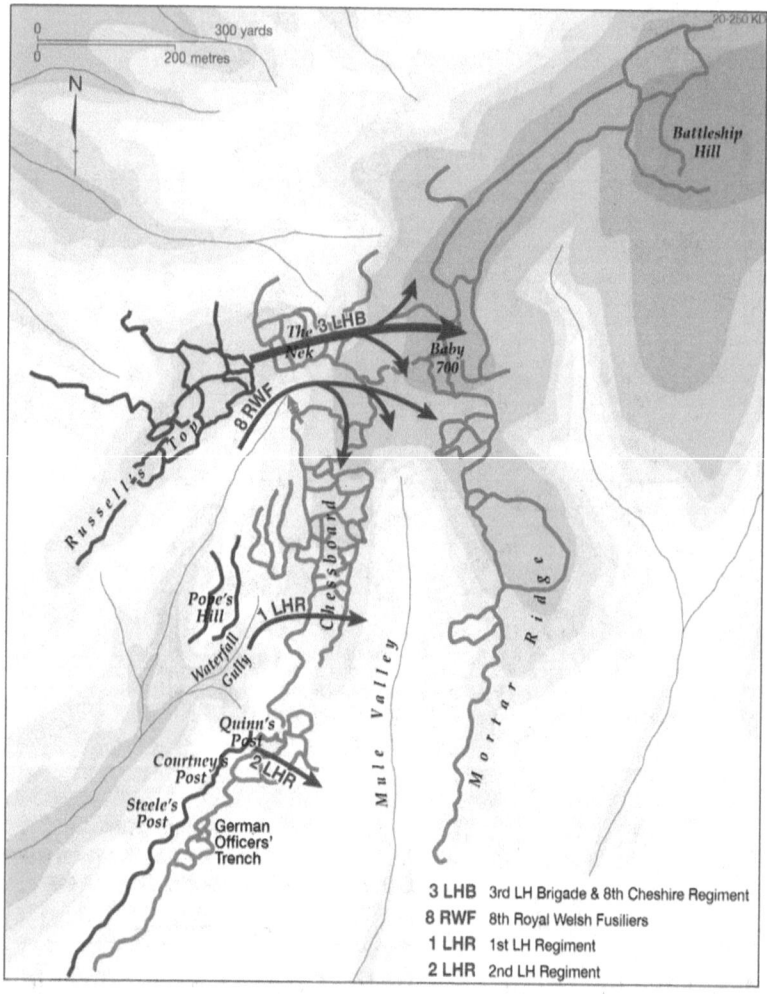

Map 18. Plan for the Light Horse attacks at Quinn's Post, Pope's Hill and the Nek, 7 August 1915. With the New Zealanders advancing down the main range to capture Battleship Hill, the 3rd Australian Light Horse Brigade,

supported by two British battalions, would assault across the Nek to take Baby 700. To their south the 1st Light Horse Regiment would attack out of Waterfall Gully and seize the Chessboard, while the 2nd Light Horse Regiment would capture Turkish Quinn's. Shown is the machine gun position that enfiladed no-man's land on Russell's Top from the Chessboard.

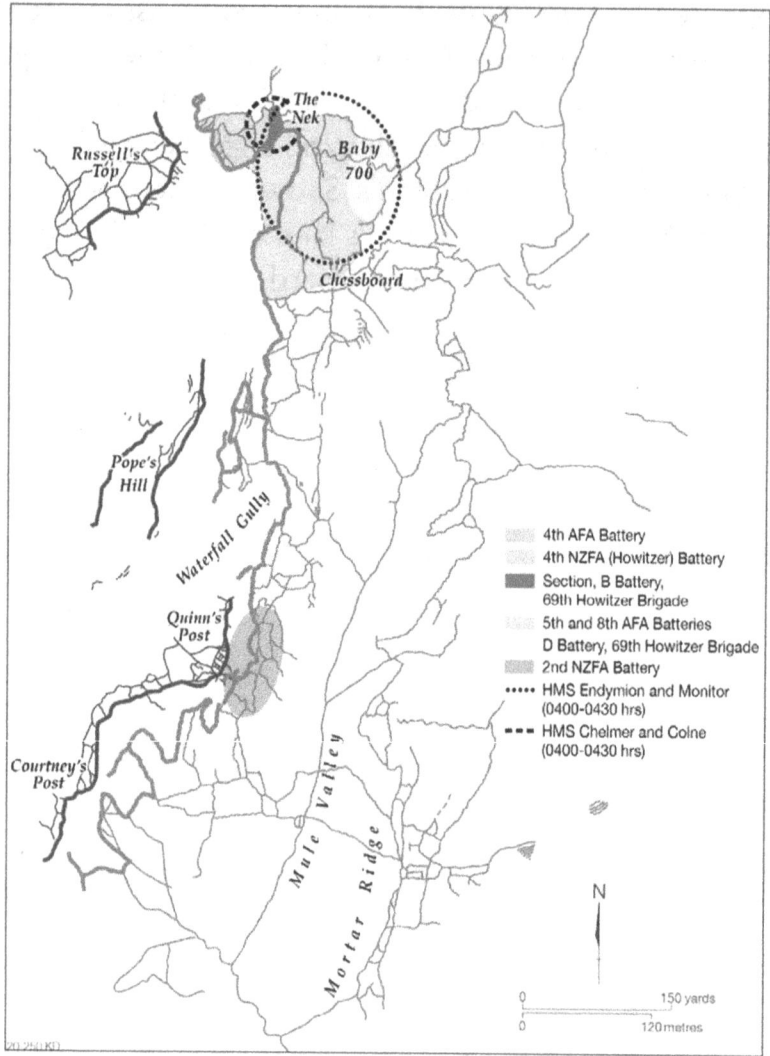

Map 19. Preparatory fire plan for the Light Horse attacks, night 6/7 August 1915. The targeting of preparatory fire for the attack on the Nek in accordance with orders issued by Corps and supplemented by the CRA NZ&A Division. For the batteries involved, the orders imposed a very slow rate of fire (typically one round per battery every five minutes) from 11.30pm 6 August onwards, and a much higher rate (typically one round per battery every fifteen seconds) from 4.00 to 4.30am (Zero Hour) on 7 August. Naval gunfire

would join in for this final period. It can be seen from the coverage that the fire did not extend to the southern extremity of the Chessboard opposite Pope's Hill, from which enfilade fire in support of the Ottoman positions on Russell's Top could be provided.

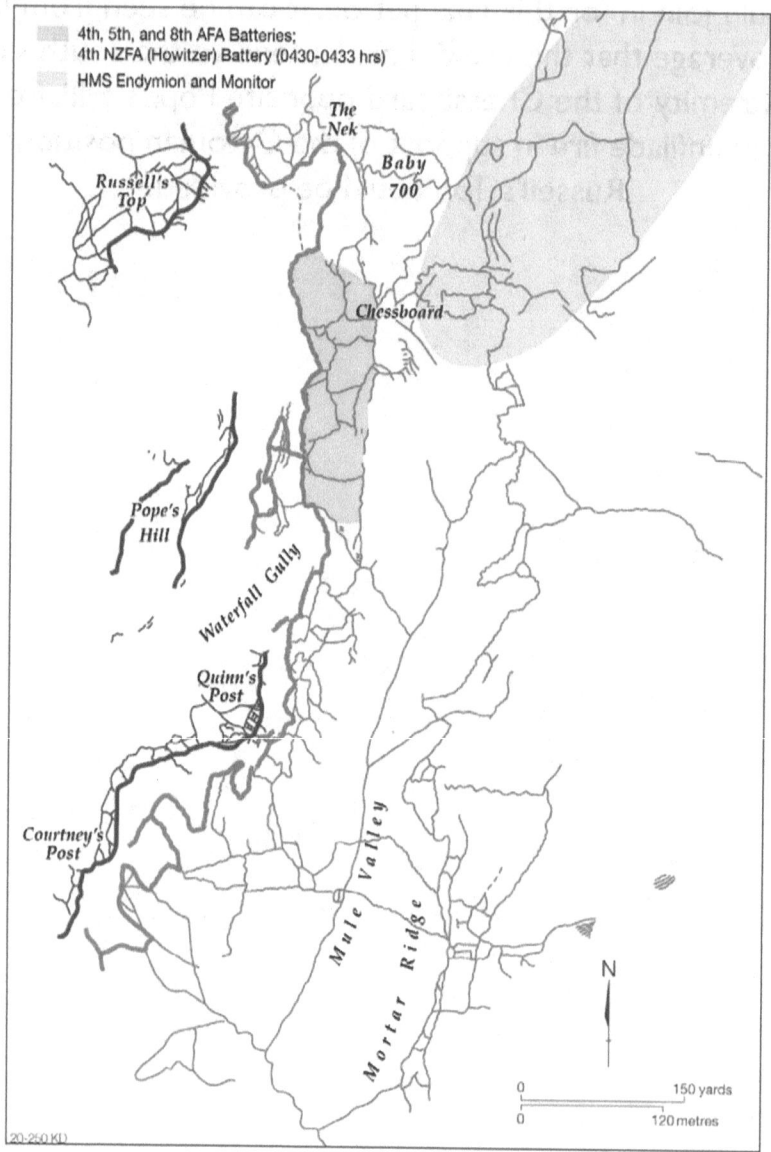

Map 20. Supporting fire for the Light Horse attacks, 7 August 1915. The location of covering fire tasks between 4.30am and 4.33am 7 August as contained in Corps and NZ&A Division orders. The evidence shows the Australian batteries did not receive the field-gun orders, which were issued by the NZ&A Division, and thus did not fire the serial, which was, in any case, of a very limited duration.

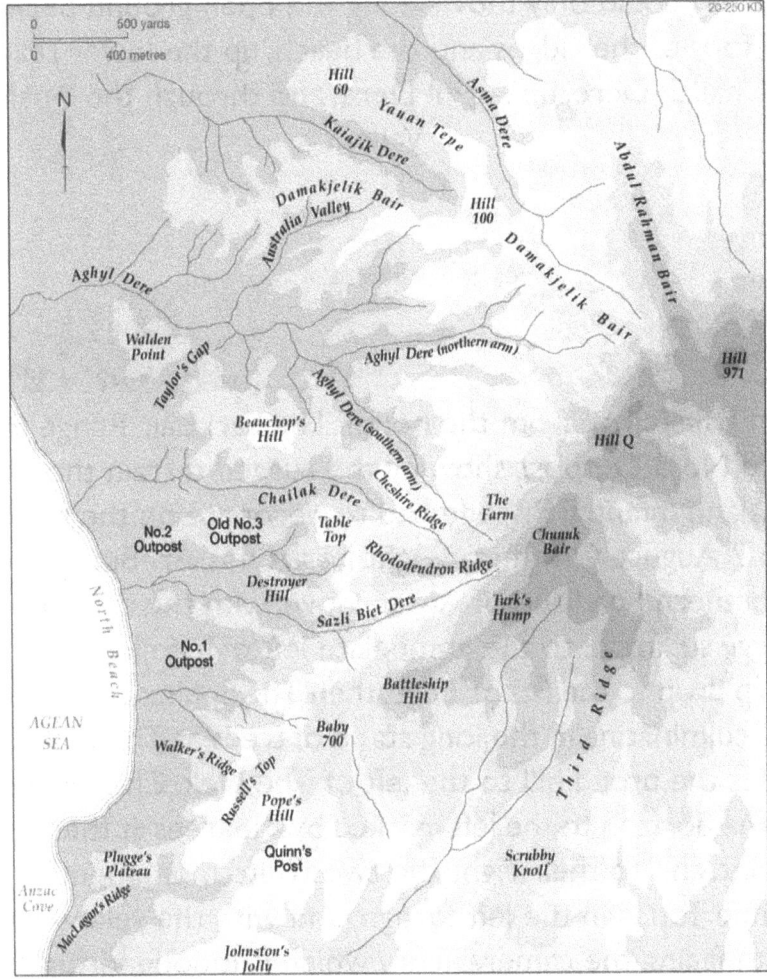

Map 21. The terrain north of Anzac. Highlighted are the principal ridges-Abdul Rahman Bair, Damakjelik Bair and its subsidiary spur Yauan Tepe, Cheshire Ridge branching off Rhododendron Ridge and ending at Bauchop's Hill and Walden Point, with Rhododendron Ridge continuing through the Table Top and ending at No 2 Outpost. Another long ridge runs from Baby 700 to No 1 Outpost, while Walker's Ridge runs from Russell's Top to the coast. Between them are the principal valleys-Asma Dere, Aghyl

Dere, Chailak Dere, and Sazli Beit Dere. Horse drawn artillery could only move along the open ground between the foot of the ridges and the beach, up the lower reaches of Chailak Dere, up Agyhl Dere, and through the Anafarta Valley.

Sari Bair Range from the north. The Sari Bair Range from Old No 3 Outpost showing the rugged terrain the New Zealand Infantry Brigade had to negotiate on the night of 6/7 August. On the far right horizon is Ari Burnu, the northern headland of Anzac Cove, with the flat topped Plugge's Plateau to the immediate left of it, followed by the sharp drop to the Razor Edge, then The Sphinx and Russell's Top culminating in the long stand of trees at The Nek. Baby 700 is the broad hill to the left of The Nek. Chunuk Bair is on the horizon to the left marked by the trees at the highest point, and to their right the two white monuments. The Table Top is in the left foreground with the yellow bare earth facing the camera, from which Rhododendron Ridge swings away to the right, the middle reaches of which can be seen where the yellow track curves to the left below the horizon. From there it runs up to Chunuk Bair. Sazli Beit Dere is the low valley running from the right of the photograph. disappearing behind the hill in the middle foreground and Rhododendron Ridge, ending at the foot of Chunuk Bair. Chailak Dere is to the left of the Tabletop ending at The Apex which is marked by the trees below and to the right of the two white monuments. (JoÚ Lafferty Image)

The lower portion of Rhododendron Ridge. On the far left the hill at the foot of the ridge overlooking the sea is the location of No 2 Outpost with Old No 3 Outpost being on the inland end of the hill, marked by the two clear areas dropping from the near side of the hill. Next along the ridge is the Table Top. From there the while track follows the crest of Rhododendron Ridge across the photograph, and up to the position of the camera. Chailak Dere is to right of and below Rhododendron Ridge. Beyond it on the right is Bauchop's Hill with the road curving up its southern flank, with Walden Point above it-the low treed area above the last curve in the road. To the right of Walden Point is the mouth to Aghyl Dere. Suvla Bay and the Salt Lake are in the far distance on the right. (Chris Roberts Image)

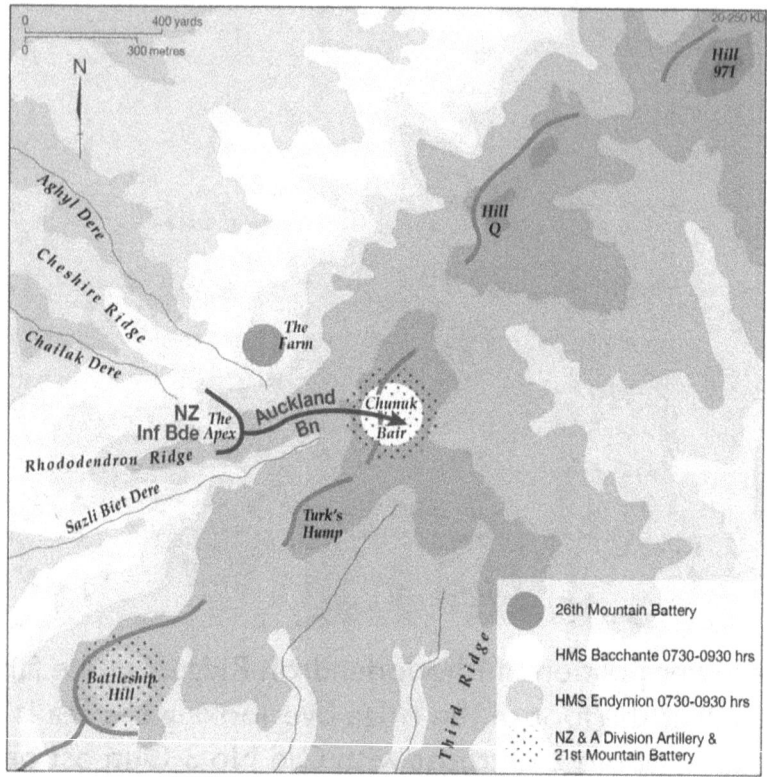

Map 22. Fire plan and New Zealand attack on Chunuk Bair, 7 August 1915. The Auckland Battalion was to attack along the crest of Rhododendron Ridge from The Apex and seize Chunuk Bair. As best can be determined from incomplete records, the hurriedly organised fire support consisted of a naval bombardment of Battleship Hill and Chunuk Bair ending some ninety minutes before the attack went in, and artillery support from four mountain guns, two 4.5inch howitzers, a six-inch howitzer, probably six but perhaps ten 18-pounders and some 5-inch howitzers onto the same targets immediately prior to Zero Hour.

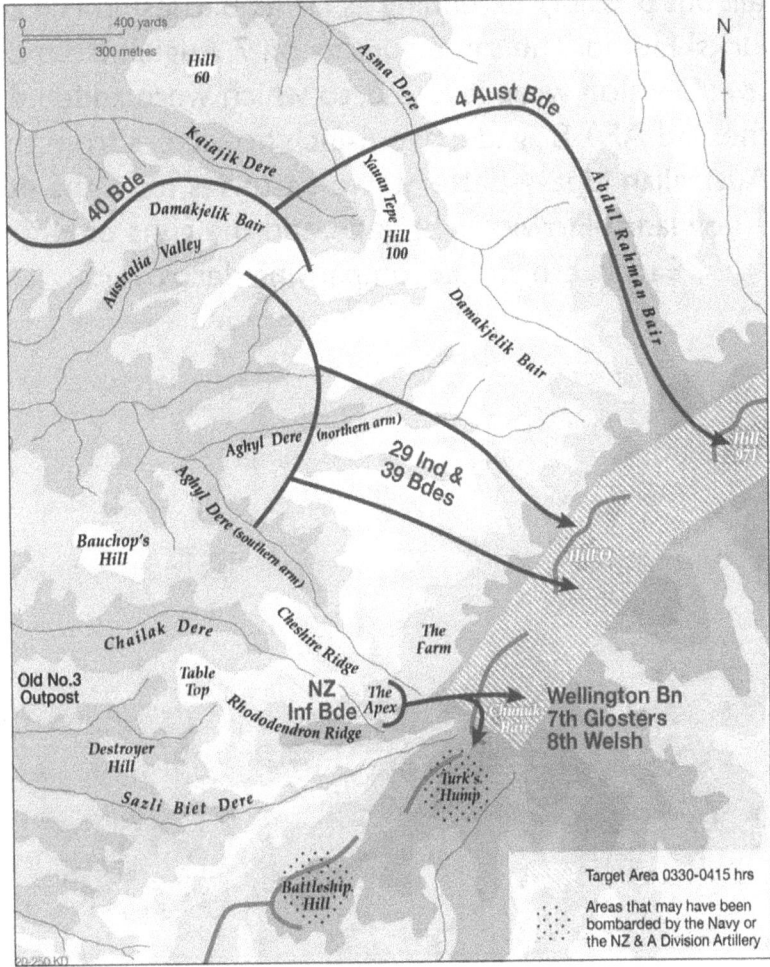

Map 23. Fire plan and attacks on Sari Bair, 8 August 1915. The 4th Australian Infantry Brigade was to move across to Abdul Rahman Bair and swing up the ridge to capture Hill 971. The 29th Indian and British 39th infantry brigades were to attack up the ridges between the two branches of Aghyl Dere and take Hill Q. The Wellington Battalion, 7th Battalion the Gloucestershire Regiment, and 8th Battalion the Welsh Regiment were to attack along Rhododendron Ridge from The Apex and seize Chunuk Bair. The fire support plan called for a bombardment between 3.30 and 4.15am of the heights between at least Hill 971 and Chunuk

Bair, but possibly extending as far as Battleship Hill and Turks' Hump. The same guns as on 7 August from the NZ&A Division were involved, to which were added those the 2nd AFA Brigade, two 6-inch howitzers from the Australian Heavy Battery, two batteries from the 4th (Lowland) Howitzer Brigade, and the guns of HMS Bacchante and accompanying destroyers.

Chunuk Bair and Hill Q from Hill 971. Chunuk Bair is the feature surmounted by the monuments and trees to the right of the bird. Running off to the left is Turk's Hump and further left is Battleship Hill. In the foreground the road curves down to Hill Q, marked by the clump dark green trees on the rounded crest to the right of Chunuk Bair.

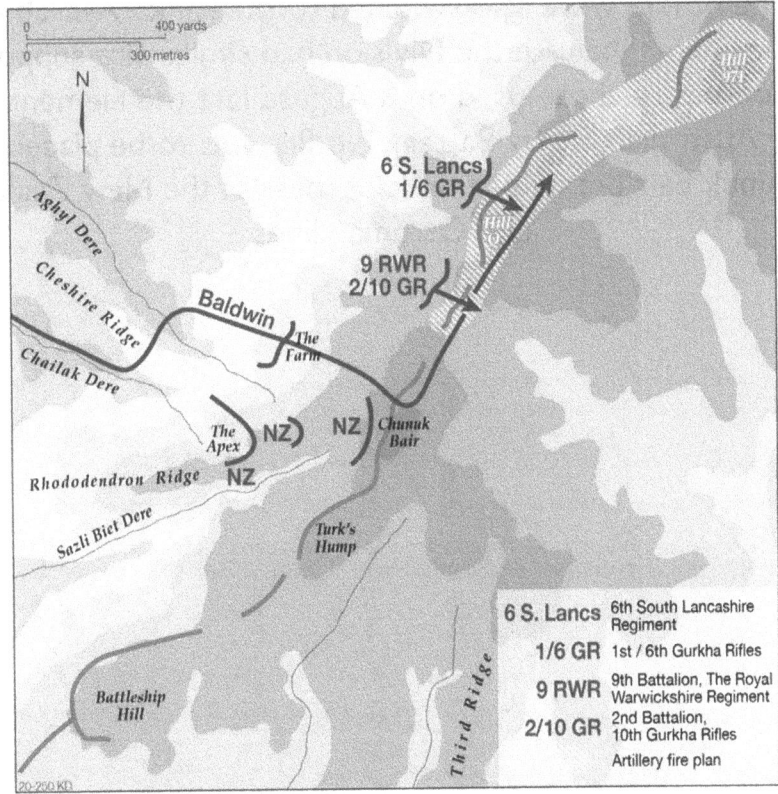

Map 24. Fire plan and attacks on Chunuk Bair and Hill Q, 9 August 1915. The 6th Battalion South Lancashire Regiment and 1st Battalion 6th Gurkha Rifles were to seize Hill Q while the 9th Battalion, The Royal Warwickshire Regiment and the 2nd Battalion 10th Gurkha Rifles attacked via the saddle between Hill Q and Chunuk Bair. Baldwin's force (a mixture of the 38th and 29th Infantry brigades) would attack from the Farm and clear the main range from Chunuk Bair to inclusive Hill Q. The fire support plan envisaged a forty-five-minute bombardment of the crest of the range from Hill 971 to the saddle between Hill Q and Chunuk Bair commencing at 4.30am until 5.15am (Zero Hour), after which naval fire would be switched to the flanks, and some NZ&A Division guns, presumably the howitzers, would engage targets on the reverse slopes of the range, while

the others were also switched to the flanks. Available documents indicate the Division had similar fire support resources to those used on 8 August, less the elements of the Australian Heavy Battery. No fire was to be placed on Chunuk Bair because of the closeness of the New Zealand and Ottoman lines.

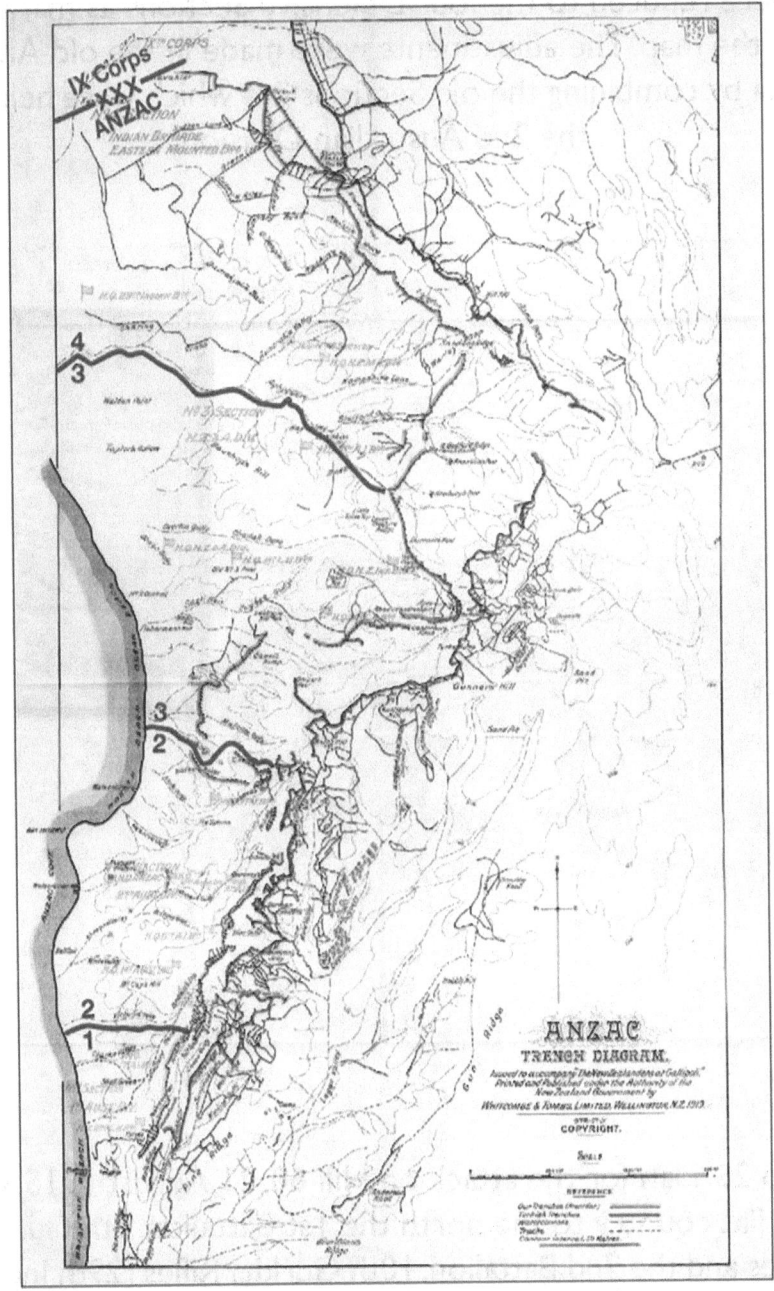

Map 25. The enlarged Anzac area and defensive sections. The enlarged Anzac beachhead following the August Offensive. Initially the Nos 5 and 6 Defensive Sections were added north of old Anzac, but on 30 September 1915 these

were reduced to the four Defensive Sections as marked on the map. The adjustments were made in the old Anzac area by combining the old Sections 2-4 which were held by the 2nd Australian Division.

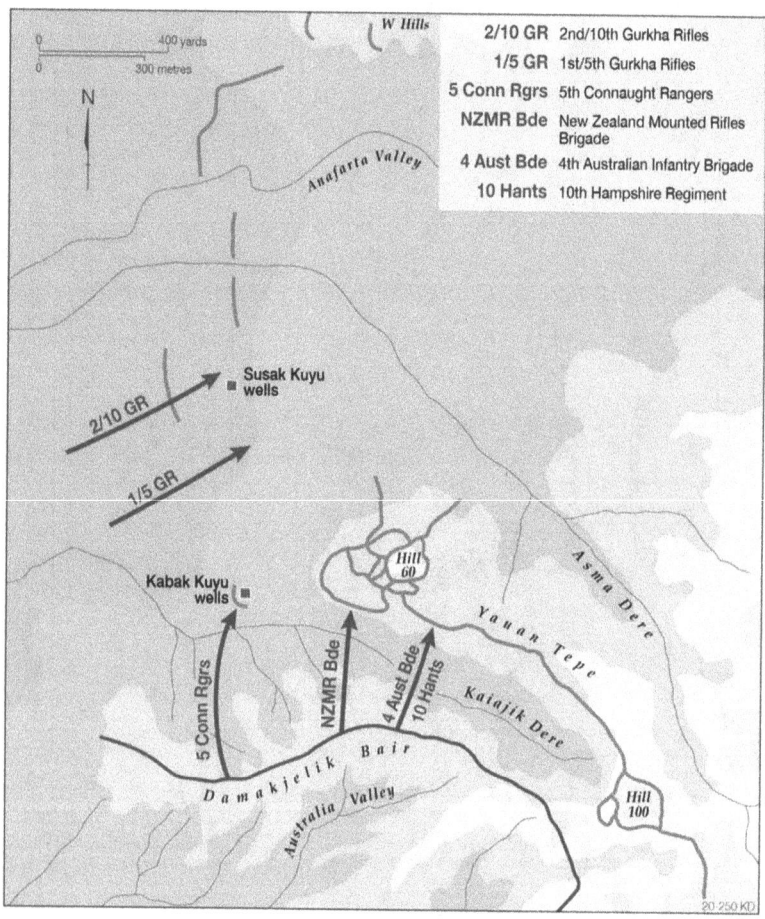

Map 26. Plan for the attack on Hill 60, 21 August 1915. On the flat country to the north the 1st Battalion, 5th Gurkha Rifles and the 2nd Battalion, 10th Gurkha Rifles (29th Indian Infantry Brigade) were to capture the Susak Kuyu well, and the 5th Battalion, Connaught Rangers (British 29th Infantry Brigade) was to take Kabak Kuyu. The depleted NZMR Brigade was to cross Kaiajik Dere and seize Hill 60, while

to their east the depleted 4th Australian Infantry Brigade, supported by the 10th Battalion, the Hampshire Regiment (British 29th Infantry Brigade), was to assault across the dere and take the portion of Yauan Tepe east of Hill 60.

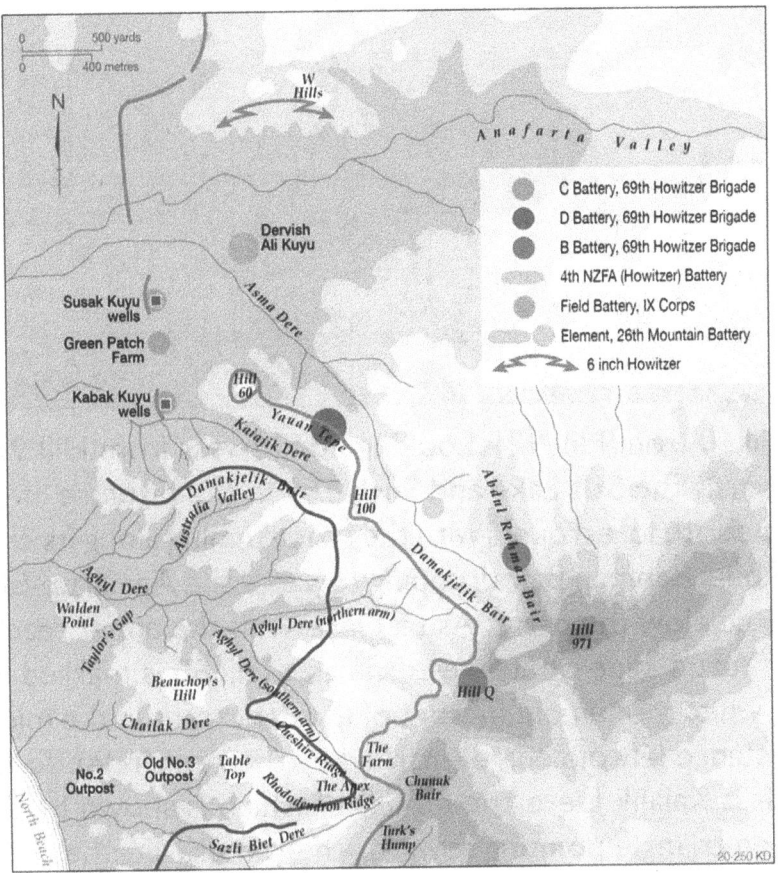

Map 27. Fire plan for the attack on Hill 60, 21 August 1915. The location of preparatory fire tasks for the first attack at Hill 60 as deduced from the 54th Division's orders, the report of the CRA NZ&A Division, and returns from the artillery brigades and batteries involved. The support provided insufficient coverage of the face of Hill 60, and of Yauan Tepe and Hill 100 that enfiladed the attacking forces.

Hill 60 from Hill 971. Looking north-west from Hill 971 towards the Salt Lake and Suvla Bay in the distance. In the immediate foreground, with the road running along its crest, is Abdul Rahman Bair dropping towards the Anafarta Valley. Next, below the bair, is Asma Dere, with the upper reaches of Yuaun Tepe on its western flank. Hill 60 is marked by the white monument in front of the dark trees in the middle distance left of centre (marked by the red circle). To its left is Kaiajik Dere, the mouth of which is shown by the green triangle pointing towards the camera. Further left is the scrub covered lower reaches of Damakjelik Bair, which curves around to the left towards the camera. Yuaun Tepe runs from Hill 60 directly towards the camera before curving left to join Damakjelik Bair at Hill 100, the slight rise looking down Kaiajik Dere. On the right of the photograph in the middle distance is the mouth of the Anafarta Valley, above which are the distinctive W Hills. This photograph shows the extent of the observation Hill

971 provided, with the same extent afforded to the south of Sari Bair. The ground over which the 4th Australian Infantry Brigade came to grief on 8 August lies hallway between the monument and where Yuaun Tepe curves to the left. The scene of of the attack across the lower reaches ol Kaiajik Dere by ihc NZMR and ith Australian Infantry brigades attacked, from left to right across the green triangle, on 21 August, together with the enfilade fire allorded the Ottoman machine guns on Hill 100, can be clearly seen.

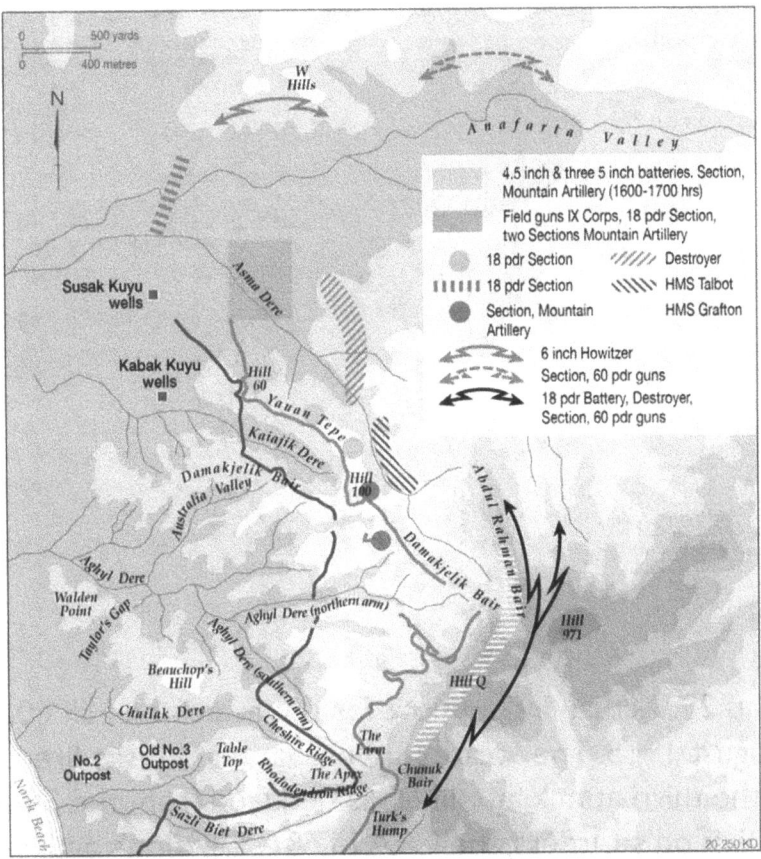

Map 28. Fire plan for the attack on Hill 60, 27 August 1915. The location of preparatory fire tasks for the third attack

at Hill 60 as shown in the 54th Division's orders as amended by the artillery timetable issued by the CRA NZ&A Division. The tasking represents a more deliberate attempt to use both artillery and naval gunfire to engage the objective, its approaches, and supporting defences. However, planned suppression of Yauan Tepe and Hill 100 was weak.

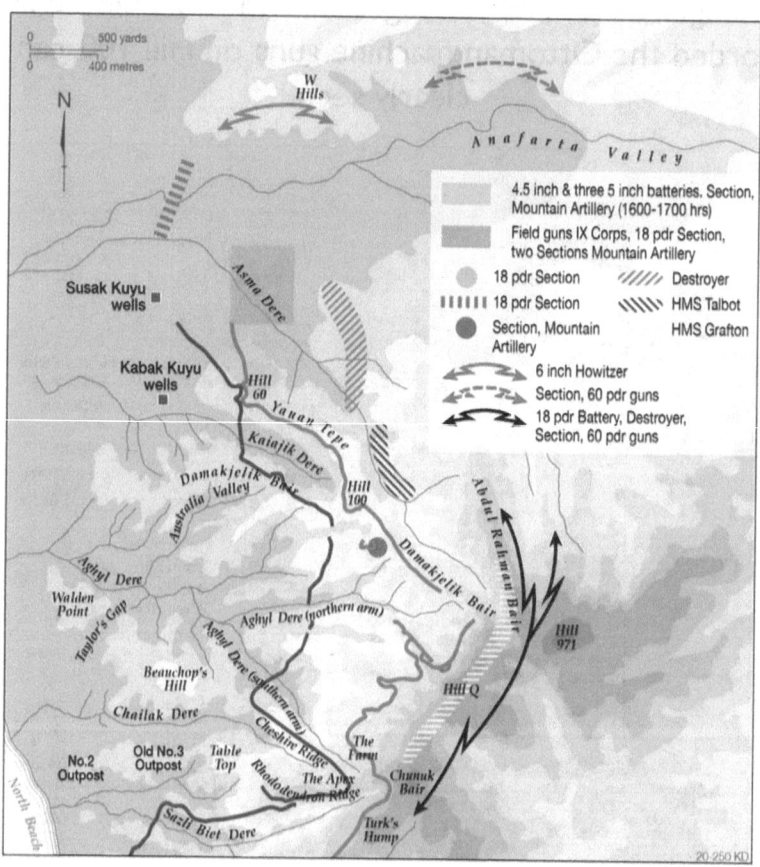

Map 29. Actual fire support for the attack on Hill 60, 27 August 1915. The location of preparatory tasks fired for the third attack at Hill 60 as deduced from the 54th Division's Orders, the CRA NZ&A Division's artillery timetable, and reports from the artillery brigades and batteries involved. The difference from the planned fire

shown in Map 28 is that the two field gun section targeted on Yauan Tepe actually fired on Hill 60, and the mountain gun section targeted on Hill 100 did not fire its serial. This left the attack vulnerable to enfilade fire from the right.

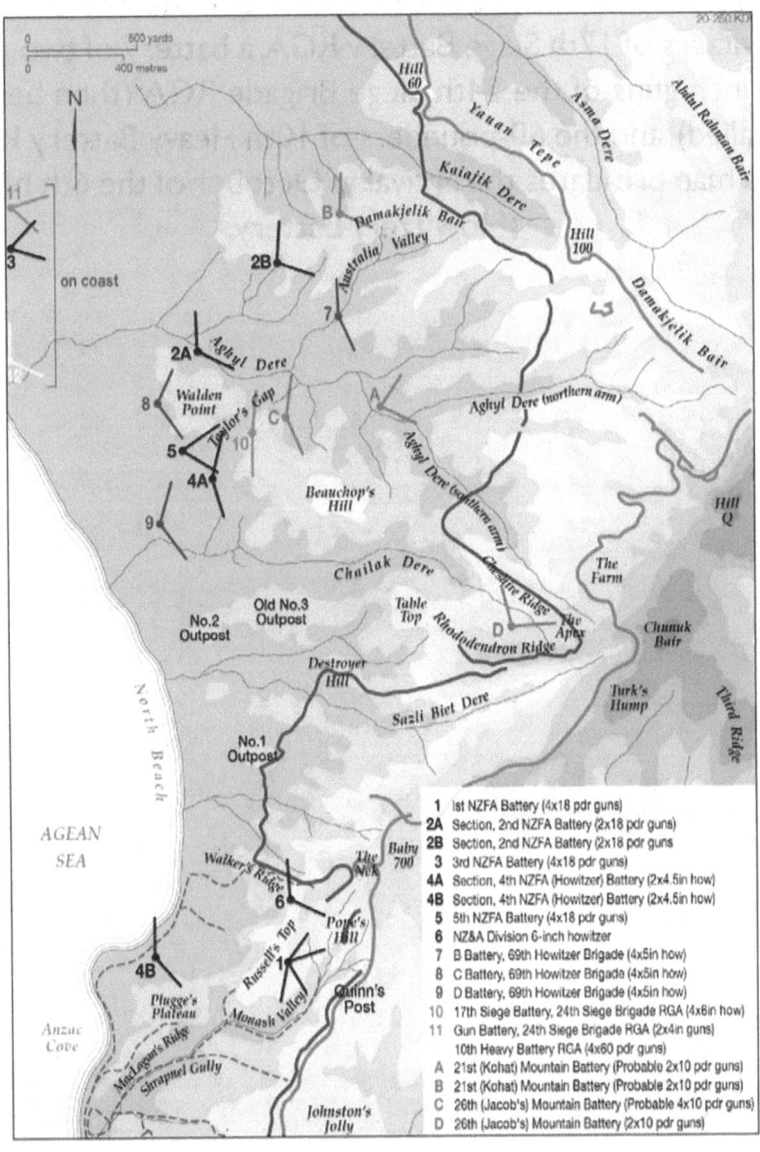

Map 30. NZ&A Divisional Artillery battery positions, September 1915. Most the division's guns have been moved

into the ground won during the August offensive. They have been strengthened by the return of the 3rd NZFA Battery from Cape Helles, and the arrival of the 5th NZFA Battery from Egypt. General support is provided by the 7th Indian Mountain Brigade, less a Section, three 5-inch howitzer batteries from the 69th Howitzer Brigade, the 6-inch howitzers of 17th Siege Battery RGA, a battery of two naval 4-inch guns of the 24th Siege Brigade RGA (then being installed), and the 60-pounders of 10th Heavy Battery RGA. This map pre-dates the arrival in October of the 6th NZFA (Howitzer) Battery.

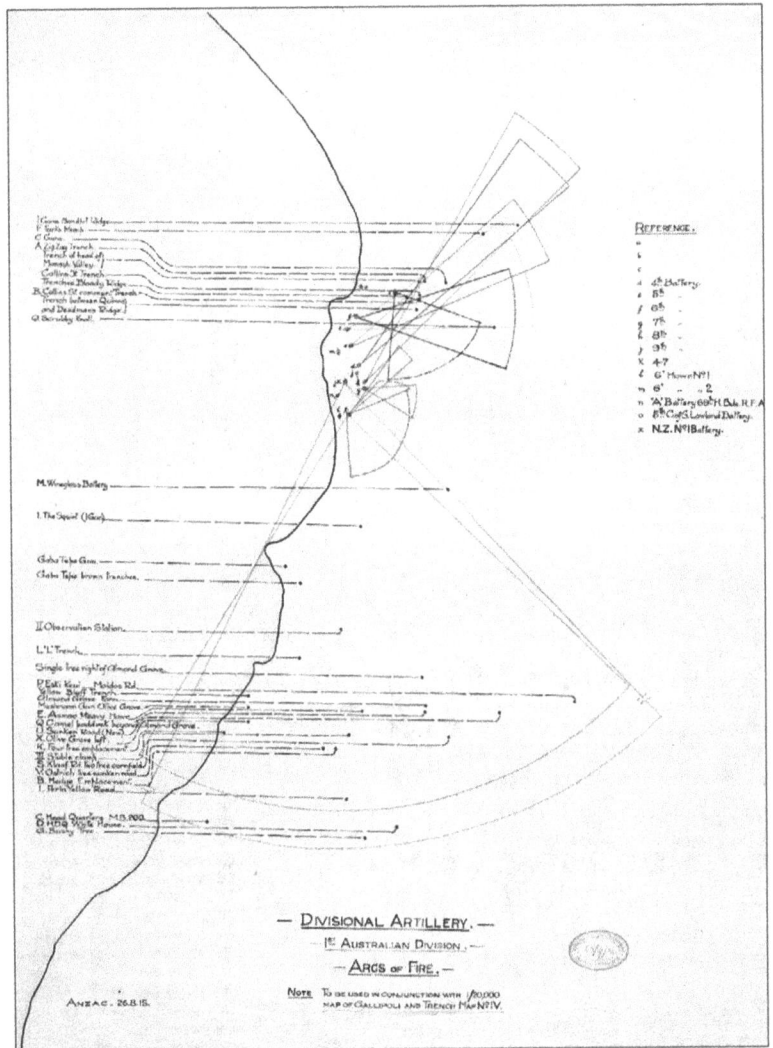

Map 31. Sketch map of Australian battery positions and arcs of fire, late August 1915. This map shows the location of the artillery supporting the division in late August, the arcs of fire from each of the gun positions, and the targets, including some of the hostile batteries, commonly engaged.

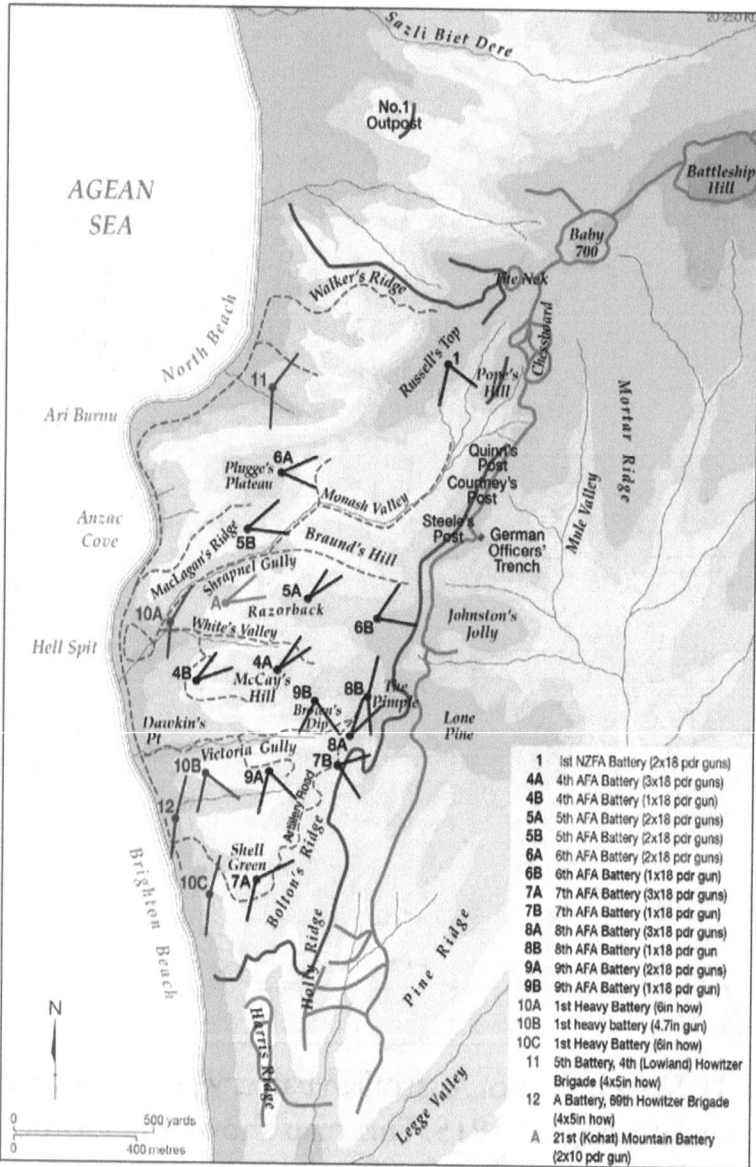

Map 32. 1st Australian Divisional Artillery battery positions, September 1915. The positions occupied by the artillery supporting the 1st and 2nd Australian divisions in early September. By this time the 6th AFA Battery had returned from Cape Helles, but the 1st AFA Brigade had not yet arrived. The six field batteries and the 1st Australian Heavy

Battery in the divisional artillery were supported by a section of the 1st NZFA Battery on Russell's Top, a section of 21st (Kohat) Battery from the 7th Indian Mountain Brigade, and two batteries of 5-inch howitzers. The gun positions are essentially the same as those of late July, except for individual gun deployments by the 6th and 7th AFA Batteries, and the shift of the majority of the 8th AFA Battery to a position immediately south of its former location.

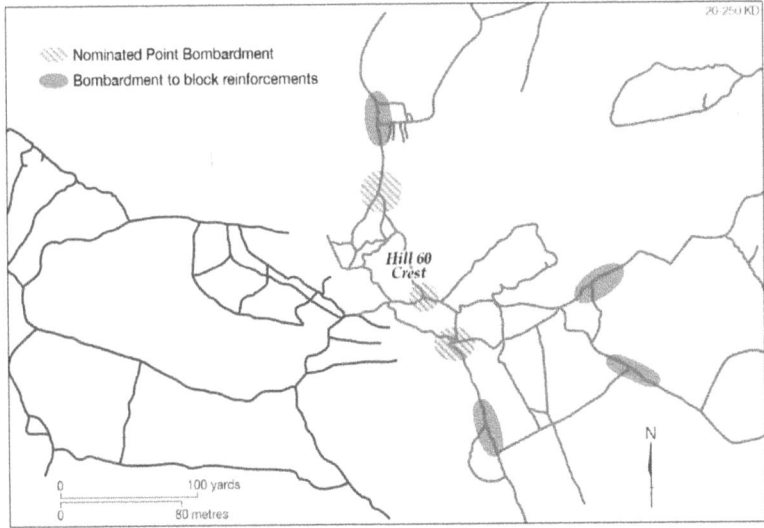

Map 33. Fire plan for a putative attack at Hill 60 by the 54th (East Anglian) Division on 7 November 1915. In late 1915, the 54th Division made a series of plans to capture the Ottoman trenches on the crest of Hill 60, for which purpose mines were also dug under the Ottoman lines. This shows the outline fire support arrangements for the second of those plans, intended for implementation on 7 November. In the end, no attack was made, and the mines were exploded on 15 November, accompanied by a limited artillery engagement of the enemy position

Chapter Eight

HILL 60

When the fighting around Chunuk Bair subsided, the Ottomans held the high ground across a torn and battered landscape littered with recent dead. For all the effort and loss of life, ANZAC had gained little of operational or tactical significance (see Map 25). To the north of its original position, it now held a front that swung from the foot of Walker's Ridge across Sazli Beit Dere to the south-western spurs of Rhododendron Ridge before climbing along that feature to the Apex. From here it slid along the crest of Cheshire Ridge, before cutting north across Aghyl Dere and the intervening spurs to Damakjelik Bair opposite Hill 100. From there it topped the bair running north-west to the foot of the ridge opposite Hill 60, before running, as yet indeterminately, north across the low ground to join the line of IX Corps at Suvla.

This newly won territory was divided into Sections 5 and 6 of the Corps position, and the NZ&A Division assumed responsibility for them. Napier JoÚston began redeploying his guns, taking advantage of the greater expanse of flat terrain between the lower ends of the recently captured spurs and the coast. A section of Falla's 4th NZFA (Howitzer) Battery moved from Anzac Cove to Taylor's Hollow below Bauchop's Hill, and on 14 August two guns of Hume's 2nd NZFA Battery left Plugge's Plateau, joining Daniell's Battery on the flat near the mouth of Chailak Dere. On the 19th the remaining two guns of the 2nd NZFA Battery joined the other section, and Standish's 3rd NZFA Battery arrived from Helles, taking post in Taylor's Hollow. McGilp's 1st NZFA Battery remained on Russell's Top with the left section facing north-east to support Section 5, and the right section continuing to support Section 2 and the Australians. The New Zealand 6-inch howitzer remained near Walker's Ridge. Major George Stevenson's 6th AFA Battery redeployed from Helles on the night of 18/19 August, one section replacing the New Zealanders on Plugge's Plateau on the night 20/21 August, the other temporarily forming a mobile section before occupying new gun pits on Plugge's on the night of 20/21 September.[1] B, C and D batteries of the 69th (Howitzer) Brigade RFA were allotted in support of the NZ&A Division.

Soon after the NZ&A Division's artillery had completed this redeployment it was called on to assist in attacks aimed at Hill 60 (Kaiajik Aghala), the small indistinct knoll at the western end of

Yauan Tepe. Separated from the western portion of Damakjelik Bair by the low ground of the Kaiajik Dere, Yauan Tepe ran parallel to it for about 920 metres before terminating at Hill 60, which Birdwood and Godley wanted to capture to consolidate the ground that had been gained in the August Offensive and create a more secure junction with IX Corps. Hill 60 would also provide ANZAC with observation over Ottoman positions to the north-east, including the mouth of the Anafarta Gap.[2]

A New Zealand 18-pounder gun of the 3rd NZFA Battery in a sandbagged open gun position with sandbagged overhead protection located in the vicinity of Taylor's Hollow following the August Offensive. This battery had served at Cape Helles from May until mid-August. On returning to Anzac it joined the 1st NZFA Brigade, which had been formed in late July. Note the camouflaged ammunition limber on the left of the photograph (AWM P01116.065).

21 August, The First Attack

The first attack took place on the afternoon of 21 August in conjunction with an attempt by IX Corps in the Suvla beachhead to gain the W Hills (Ismail Oglu Tepe) immediately to the north (see Map 26). Within Anzac, under the newly promoted Major General Herbert Cox, the plan was that two Gurkha battalions and a battalion from the Connaught Rangers would seize Susak Kuyu, Green Patch Farm, and Kabak Kuyu in the low ground west and north-west of Hill 60, and then press on to the line between Dervish Ali Kuyu and the northern slopes of Hill 60. Meanwhile, the Canterbury and the Otago Mounted Rifles from the NZMR Brigade, assaulting across Kaiajik Dere, would take Hill 60, exploiting to its northern slopes. Immediately to their east, 500 men of the 4th Australian Infantry Brigade, supported by a battalion of the Hampshire Regiment, would also attack across the dere and seize the lower portion of Yauan Tepe.[3] To support this attack, Napier JoÚston had available the 18-pounders of Hume's 2nd and Standish's 3rd NZFA batteries, along with Daniell's Battery (now two guns). He also had the 4.5-inch howitzers of Falla's 4th NZFA Battery, at least two mountain gun sections, three 5-inch howitzer batteries from the 69th Brigade

RFA, and his 6-inch howitzer. He was further allotted a field battery from IX Corps and some naval gunfire support.[4]

Napier JoÚston attended a conference on the attack at Cox's headquarters on the evening of 20 August. Cox's orders issued that day set Zero Hour as 3.00pm on 21 August. Beforehand, from 2.15pm onwards he wanted howitzer fire on Hill 60, Yauan Tepe and Hill 100 (which enfiladed Kaiajik Dere), two locations close to Hill 100, and the positions in the low ground at Susak Kuyu, Green Patch Farm and Kabak Kuyu. After Zero Hour, he wanted shrapnel fire to continue on these latter positions until the attackers approached, and then lift gradually to the line between Dervish Ali Kuyu and Hill 60. At Hill 60, the fire was to lift at Zero Hour, but on Yauan Tepe and Hill 100, 'howitzer and shrapnel' fire was to be maintained until the troops attacking Hill 60 had captured that feature and dug in.[5]

Given the number of targets to be engaged and the length of Yauan Tepe, the reference only to howitzer fire in Cox's orders is surprising. There is no direct reference to field or mountain guns, although mention of the use of shrapnel creates a degree of ambiguity, in that all types of artillery weapons fired this projectile. Napier JoÚston should have had the opportunity to clarify the matter and, indeed, to press for the use of the full range of artillery at the conference. However, any artillery orders he may have subsequently issued have not survived in the written record.

On the day of the attack, plans had to be altered when the ANZAC artillery was tasked with thickening up the fire support for the adjacent IX Corps operation. Consequently, Zero Hour within Anzac was put back by thirty minutes to 3.30pm, and the duration of the preparatory bombardment was reduced from forty-five to thirty minutes (3.00 to 3.30pm).[6] When the attack went in, the Gurkhas and the Connaught Rangers on the left captured the objectives in the low ground, although they were unable to exploit to Dervish Ali Kuyu, and it subsequently took some time to effect a link between Susak Kuyu and IX Corps on the left. In the centre the New Zealanders gained a portion of the lower trench on the south-western slope of Hill 60, but could go no further. On the right, the first line of Australian attackers was annihilated by enfilade machine-gun fire from Hill 100, with only about forty of the 150 men reaching the lip of Yauan Tepe, where they huddled under the slope. The following two lines also suffered heavily from the enfilading machine-gun fire, the third being prevented from crossing at all until after dark. Unable to advance further, the eighty to 100 survivors began digging in under the lip of Yauan Tepe near the 'Big Tree'.[7] The fire plan had not materially assisted the Australians and New Zealanders.

The divisional artillery report covering the attack (see Map 27) shows that Napier JoUston assigned the ships, the 6-inch howitzer, one battery of 5-inch howitzers (B Battery, 69th Howitzer Brigade), and the field battery from IX Corps to counter-battery and depth targets, reasonable tasking given the need to suppress Ottoman batteries as far as practical, the unsuitability of the heavier weapons and ships' armaments for close-support work, and the range limitations on the IX Corps battery.[8] This left three howitzer batteries, two field batteries, a field section, and two mountain gun sections with which he could have provided preparatory and covering fire.

Looking down Kaiajik Dere showing a view similar to that enjoyed by enfilading Ottoman machine-guns on Hill 100 during the ANZAC attack on 21 August. Yauan Tepe is on the right and Damakjelik Bair on the left. Hill 60 is the minor protrusion at the end of the dere, with the Salt Lake in the distance and beyond it Suvla Bay (AWM G01860).

The report also states that, at 3.00pm, once support for IX Corps ceased, all guns were switched to cover the targets nominated by Cox.[9] However, artillery brigade and battery records reveal that only the howitzers undertook the preparatory and covering fire tasks on or adjacent to the objectives. The 7th IMA Brigade War Diary notes that fire from the 26th Battery was directed at trenches east of Hill 100 and along the Sari Bair heights from the upper reaches of Abdul Rahman Bair to Hill Q. The 21st Battery was asked to fire at Yauan Tepe only after the attack at 6.10pm, and then could not do so effectively. Reports from the field guns show that they fired in support of IX Corps until 3.00pm, and then at opportunity targets in depth from around 3.40pm onwards. There are no reports of these guns firing in the preparatory fire period between 3.00 and 3.30pm or providing covering fire on Hill 60 or Yauan Tepe thereafter.[10]

Conversely, reports from the 4th NZFA (Howitzer) Battery record that its 4.5-inchers fired from 3.00pm onwards on Hill 60, lengthening their fire after 3.30pm as the infantry advanced, and also occasionally firing on Hill 100, a target nearby, and Abdul Rahman Bair. The 69th Howitzer Brigade reported that, from 3.00pm onwards, the fire of its C and D batteries turned to support General Cox's attack, but described the targets only as 'trenches'. The exact locations engaged are not specified, but both batteries had previously registered targets in the map squares covering the objectives in the low ground and Hill 60, and D Battery had also registered targets along Kaiajik Dere, that is, the area of Yauan Tepe and Hill 100.[11]

Shells falling on Hill 60 (white smoke burst) and in the mouth of the Anafarta Valley (black column of smoke), with the foot of Damakjelik Bair in the foreground. The W Hills are behind and to the right of the white smoke of the bursting shell. IX Corps occupied the ground to the left of the black column of smoke (Stower Collection WF-007559-413).

In summary, in the preparatory fire phase it is evident that the 4.5-inch battery fired on Hill 60, and it appears that the 5-inchers took on the targets in the low ground and along Yauan Tepe. It is also clear that, after Zero Hour, the field guns and 4.5-inch howitzers did not fire onto the Yauan Tepe area, apart from the occasional 4.5-inch engagement of Hill 100. The probability is then that only one 5-inch battery was firing on the spur. Logically, this battery would have been directed by sections or even individual guns onto known target areas along the spur, but regardless of how the fire might have been distributed, this was too sparse an allocation to subdue all the defenders. This explains why the attackers suffered heavily from enfilade fire as they crossed Kaiajik Dere.

A 4.5-inch howitzer of the 4th NZFA (Howitzer) Battery at full recoil during a fire mission from its new location in Taylor's Hollow below Bauchop's Hill, which is in the background. This section of the battery moved there immediately after the August Offensive, leaving the other section in its original position on North Beach (AWM P10637.071.002).

Coverage was also a problem on Hill 60. According to Christopher Pugsley, the mounted rifles watching from Damakjelik Bair felt that very few of the ANZAC shells landed on the Ottoman trenches. Their view was supported by a report in the NZMR Brigade War Diary, which stated 'an hrs.[hour's] v. poor preparation by arty. took place.'[12] The divisional artillery report does not comment on the density or accuracy of the preparatory fire, noting only that, after the assault began, the 4.5-inch battery bombarded 'the trenches on the Kaiajik Aghala [Hill 60] where considerable resistance was being offered', and that the shooting was 'good' according to the testimony of prisoners.[13]

Battery records offer a clue as to why the 4.5-inch fire was ineffective. Major Falla's report reveals that he engaged a line running from north-west to south-east across the crest of the hill. This line was some 275 metres behind the approximate position of the forward Ottoman trenches and around 460 metres long, effectively dispersing the fire, when the principal target area was approximately 230 metres across. After Zero Hour and until 7.30pm the battery lengthened its range—that is, moved to the north-east—as the infantry advanced, and also engaged targets in the area of Hill 100. Between 3.00 and 7.30pm it fired 289 rounds.[14]

It is difficult to see why Falla did not choose a more concentrated preliminary bombardment of Hill 60, other than to speculate that he might have been attempting to support not only those attacking the hill itself, but also the troops who were to approach Dervish Ali Kuyu to the north-west of the feature through the objectives in the low ground. Prima facie, there were no significant safety constraints in engaging the forward slopes of Hill 60. His fire was overhead of the attackers, and no man's land was some 275 metres wide. Nevertheless, he may have been concerned because the NZMR commander, Brigadier General Andrew Russell, ordered his troops to move out into no man's land during the preparatory fire in order to reduce the distance to be covered when the artillery fire ceased.[15]

In retrospect, the fire plan for the attack on 21 August appears to have been poorly conceived by Cox, the infantry commander. By limiting support tasks to the howitzers, he did not make use of the full range of available resources. On Hill 60 itself, this failing was exacerbated by the poor targeting of the battery involved, with the result that Ottoman positions able to influence the course of the attack were insufficiently suppressed. Better use of the guns should have flowed from the conference before the attack, but the outcome is suggestive of infantry considerations dominating, with insufficient regard for artillery capabilities or the lessons of recent operations.

22 August, A Second Attempt

With the New Zealanders and Australians clinging precariously to their hard-won toeholds, Russell urged a second attack on the knoll that same night. The 4.5-inch howitzer battery was directed to continue to fire on the objective, and subsequently fired fifteen rounds at the main Ottoman communication trench leading to the hill.[16]

With a lack of immediate reserves, the raw and inadequately trained 18th Australian Infantry Battalion, which had arrived at Gallipoli just two days before, was pressed into service. Orders were issued at 2.00am for an attack beginning at 4.15am on 22 August.[17] Leaving from close to Anzac Cove, the battalion hurried to the area, arriving after Zero Hour, only to be informed that it was to attack immediately. Unable to carry out a reconnaissance, let alone properly disseminate orders, the men assaulted the feature from the west in the early daylight of 5.00am. D Battery, 69th Howitzer Brigade, provided some fire support to the east of the hill, and also later fired on Ottoman reinforcements moving towards the fighting, but essentially the battalion attacked without any supporting artillery fire.[18]

Pushing their way through gaps in a thick hedge and then moving across open ground, the attackers were met with rifle and machine-gun fire, but succeeded in taking the first trench and then managed to extend somewhat the ground won by the New Zealanders before they could go no further, subsequently losing some of their gains to strong opposition and fierce counter-attacks.[19] The most serious defect of this attack was its rushed nature, which gave neither the battalion nor the gunners sufficient time to plan and prepare adequately.

27 August, A Third Attack

As ANZAC troops consolidated the line across to Susak Kuyu and their toehold on the lower slopes of Hill 60, the gunners fired into the area to inhibit the development of the Ottoman defences. A third attempt to capture the feature was made on the evening of 27 August, again under Cox, the objectives this time were the Ottoman fire trenches on the south-west slope of the knoll, along with the communication trenches running up the slope and across the crest and, on the right, trenches linking to the Australians at the 'Big Tree', an area approximately 275 metres square.

Napier JoUston's assets for this operation were the field guns from the 2nd, 3rd and 5th NZFA batteries, plus one section from the 1st NZFA Battery; the 4.5-inchers of the 4th NZFA Battery, the 5-inchers of B, C and D batteries, 69th Howitzer Brigade; 10th Heavy Battery RGA (60-pounders), a 6-inch howitzer; eight mountain guns; field gun support from IX Corps; and the fire of four ships: the cruisers HMS *Grafton* and *Talbot*, and two destroyers.[20] The exact ammunition allocation is unknown, but reflecting the shortages of ammunition that plagued the gunners throughout the campaign, Birdwood ordered them to be 'sparing of 5-inch shell, which is very scarce'.[21]

Cox opted again for an afternoon attack, with Zero Hour at 5.00pm, an hour or so before nightfall. In his operation order, he noted that an artillery plan had been arranged whereby from 4.00pm until dark all the resources, except four howitzer batteries and a mountain gun section, were directed onto roads at the rear of Hill 60 or allocated to counter-battery tasks, with the exception that some field and mountain guns would provide intensive fire along Yauan Tepe from 4.35 to 5.00pm. Between 4.00 and 5.00pm the four howitzer batteries were to fire onto the objective, but also periodically engage the spur, and after Zero Hour they were to switch permanently to the spur. One mountain section was to fire point blank into Hill 60 until Zero Hour.[22]

This fire plan was an improvement on its predecessor in its use of the full range of artillery available, its attempt to isolate Hill 60 before and after the assault, its concentration on the primary objective in the preparatory phase, and its greater allocation of resources to suppress Ottoman defences along Yauan Tepe after Zero Hour. The use of mountain guns in the direct fire role mirrored a tactic used by the Australians at Lone Pine, and may have been instituted because the proximity of the front-line trenches posed a real problem of safety from friendly fire. Cox was aware of the potential danger, and ordered all forward troops, except for a few sentries, to sit at the bottom of their trenches during the preliminary bombardment.[23]

An artillery timetable to support the attack was issued on 27 August, the day of the assault (see Map 28). While it generally reflected Cox's operation order, there was one significant difference. Cox's order showed a twenty-five minute burst of field and mountain gun fire along with occasional howitzer fire on Yauan Tepe during preparatory fire, but the timetable placed only the fire of two field sections, one each from the 2nd and 3rd NZFA batteries, on the spur in this period, with a mountain gun section tasked to engage Hill 100 and some ground to its south. The reason for the change is unclear, especially as the four field and two mountain guns involved could not have covered the full target area. Somewhat contrary to Birdwood's injunction to be sparing with the use of 5-inch ammunition, the timetable also specified that, in their bombardment of the 'lower spur of Kaiajik Dere and Kaiajik Aghala [Hill 60]', the howitzers would fire a total of 500 rounds, 200 from the 4.5-inch battery, and 100 each from the three 5-inch batteries.[24] Apparently this figure was the result of an estimate by the assaulting infantry of the rounds required.[25]

When the attack went in, the New Zealand commander reported, 'Though the bombardment looked to be fairly effective, immediately the assault began at 1700 every trench appeared to be full of Turks, & our men were v. strongly opposed.'[26] The ANZAC war diary noted that the 'launching of the attack drew heavy fire of enemy shrapnel, machine guns and rifles—followed in short time by heavy shell onto the knoll, where enemy shrapnel burst all over the position, including the trenches still occupied by the Turks.'[27] On the left the objectives were gained initially, but subsequently lost to Ottoman counter-attack. On the right, the Australians were immediately checked by machine-gun fire. The trenches opposing them appeared to have been missed by the preliminary bombardment, and only two shells of small calibre were said have fallen on the Ottoman defences.[28] In the centre, after much fighting, some gains were made and, by next morning, the line had been advanced on a narrow front almost to the crest of the knoll.[29]

A 5-inch howitzer and crew of D Battery, 69th Howitzer Brigade RFA, firing in support of the NZ&A Division in the expanded Anzac beachhead. This battery provided support for the attacks on Hill 60 (Alexander Turnbull Library 1/4-058091-F).

In three of its aspects, the fire plan had been unsuccessful. The first was the counter-battery arrangements, which had not held hostile batteries in check, reflecting once more the lack of capability to accurately locate Ottoman guns, and the allocation of too few resources to the task: the 5th NZFA Battery, one 6-inch howitzer, the 10th Heavy Battery and a destroyer.[30] The second was the attempt to isolate Hill 60, which proved insufficient to prevent the Ottomans reinforcing the position during the night and conducting numerous counter-attacks. The third aspect in which the fire plan was unsuccessful was its support for the Australians on the right. An examination of the records reveals the reasons (see Map 29). First, the 7th IMA Brigade War Diary indicates that the section tasked with engaging Hill 100 did not fire its allotted serial.[31] Second, neither of the field artillery sections allotted to Yauan Tepe, a totally inadequate allocation in any case, fired on the area before Zero Hour. The section from the 2nd NZFA Battery instead swept and searched the east and north-east slopes of Hill 60. The section from the 3rd NZFA Battery could not register the spur before the cut-off time in the timetable and so resorted to firing on communication trenches on the crest of Hill 60 itself.[32]

The situation did not improve after Zero Hour. The field guns remained elsewhere while the 5-inch howitzers, which were supposed to switch to Yauan Tepe, reported that 'a slower rate of fire was continued as required, more particularly on the north-east slopes of Hill 60, and the communication trenches running east to Anafarta.' Some of their fire may have been directed at the spur, but the emphasis was clearly placed elsewhere. The targeting of the 4.5-inch howitzer battery after Zero Hour is unspecified, inferring that it engaged the spur as per orders. However, its fire, even combined with that of a few 5-inchers, would have been insufficient to suppress the Ottoman defenders.[33]

The reasons for the failure of some guns to follow the timetable are not shown in the records, except in the case of the section that could not complete its registration. However, it is noted that Cox's orders were issued as late as the evening before, and the artillery timetable came out on the day of the assault. This left little time for dissemination of fire plan orders and subsequent preparations at lower levels, indicating that the requirements of the supporting artillery were, once again, not completely understood and that, on the part of the artillery, inadequate procedures were in place to ensure batteries were ready to participate as planned.

With regard to the final aspect of the fire plan, support for the infantry in the centre and on the left, the fire plan was successful in that it suppressed the enemy sufficiently to allow the attackers to leave their trenches and advance on their objectives, even though their initial gains were subsequently curtailed or lost to counter-attack. What it did not do was destroy the Ottoman defences, which may well have been the outcome sought by the infantry when they asked for 500 rounds to fall in the area before Zero Hour.

There are two potential reasons for this failure. First, while the four howitzer batteries assigned to the hill could reasonably have covered the 230x275-metre target area, there may have been issues with the distribution of their fire. The selection of the actual target areas was delegated to two artillery brigade commanders, raising the potential for a lack of coordination, and these commanders may also have had to displace the fire somewhat because of the proximity of the trench lines, leaving the forward edge of the defences only lightly covered.[34]

The second and more likely reason was that in each target area the rounds were probably not directed onto specific trenches, and even if they were, because of the zone of the gun and perhaps variations in atmospheric conditions—5-inch howitzer fire was particularly affected by wind—too few would have fallen on the actual works to achieve the desired effect. To exacerbate matters in this regard, during the preliminary bombardment the 4.5-inch battery reported firing only 136 rounds instead of the 200 ordered.[35] In 1915 it was not yet fully realised that achieving destruction using indirect fire entailed considerable ammunition expenditure. British experience published later in the war indicated that, as a rough guide, sixty-five rounds from a 6-inch howitzer were required to destroy a machine-gun emplacement, and between fifty and 100 rounds from a 9.2-inch howitzer to destroy a strongpoint.[36]

In the aftermath of this third attempt to take Hill 60, Cunliffe-Owen wrote to the divisional commanders concerning the availability of artillery ammunition. He advised that 937 rounds of 18-pounder, 361 of 4.5-inch, 704 of 5-inch, and five of 6-inch howitzer had been used and that, while the holdings at the batteries still seemed adequate (400 rounds per gun for the field guns and 200 for the 5-inchers), the reserves on the beaches were down to fifty rounds per gun for the 18-pounders, 250 for the 4.5-inchers and twenty for the 5-inch howitzers. This was the reason, he explained, that he had asked Hobbs and Napier JoÚston a few days previously to limit normal daily expenditure to ten rounds per 18-pounder and five per howitzer, and to attach a short explanation in their daily reports if these amounts were exceeded.[37]

A 5-inch howitzer and crew of D Battery, 69th Howitzer Brigade RFA. The battery was moved to this location following the August Offensive and before the attacks on Hill 60. It was under Napier JoÚston's control for the remainder of the campaign (Alexander Turnbull Library 1/4-058090-F).

A Final Attempt

The final assault on Hill 60 took place on the night of 28/29 August when, in a silent attack without artillery support, the 10th LH Regiment seized further trenches. The crest remained in

Ottoman hands, but an acceptable line was reached. Artillery engagements continued on and around the hill, but offensive action ceased for the time being.

The success of the light horse action raises the question of whether, from an artillery perspective, the planners had chosen the optimum time of day for the attacks on 21 and 27 August. For the 27th, Russell, GOC NZMR Brigade, had urged a night attack, although another assault in the late afternoon was ultimately selected, perhaps to allow for artillery registration in the morning, or for consolidation of any success during the night, free from Ottoman observation. But the proximate onset of darkness also limited the time Ottoman counter-attack forces were open to observation and interdiction. With greater experience, later in the war many attacks were mounted around dawn, allowing the infantry to advance in the half-light to minimise casualties, and the gunners to use the daylight to maximise observation over counter-attack forces.

In retrospect, the fire plans at Hill 60 on 21 and 27 August suffered from a lack of sufficient fire units to cover the objectives, their flanking defences, counter-attack routes and the enemy artillery. This led to only partial success on both occasions, the defects compounded on 27 August by some batteries apparently not following orders. The formation and artillery commanders' plans indicated that they understood the areas that should be covered, but in the first attack there was an over-reliance on howitzer fire, and on both 21 and 27 August a lack of experience and understanding of the weight of fire required to achieve suppression of a determined foe, let alone achieve destruction, if that was indeed the aim of the allocation of 500 rounds to Hill 60 on the latter date. The lack of adequate artillery support for the attack by the 18th Battalion on the morning of 22 August reflected the haste with which it was mounted, leaving Napier Joŭston no time to prepare a proper fire plan.

Indeed, all attacks were mounted at short notice with seemingly little time for Napier Joŭston to plan, disseminate his orders, and complete the artillery preparations. This was another indication that formation commanders did not as yet fully recognise the need to allow time for artillery preparations as part of battle procedure. On the Western Front things were changing in this regard. Operations were analysed for lessons learned.[38] The Battle of Loos in September 1915 was preceded by a four-day bombardment 'so that all fire could be carefully aimed and no shell would be wasted.'[39] While this was positive recognition of the importance of firepower, it reflected a movement away from concepts of suppression towards the destruction of wire, trenches, strongpoints and dugouts in attempting to support the infantry. Perhaps such a step was unavoidable in coming to terms with trench warfare, but it would ultimately prove nugatory. A focus on suppression returned from late 1916 onwards with the use of creeping barrages, and from late 1917 with preliminary bombardments of increasingly shorter duration.

Chapter Nine

EXPANSION AND CONSOLIDATION

As the fighting for Hill 60 was winding down, the British 54th (East Anglian) and the 2nd Australian divisions arrived to assist in garrisoning the expanded ANZAC area. Neither brought any artillery.[1] The 54th Division's guns stayed behind when it left Britain. The 2nd Division—hastily formed in Egypt under Major General James Legge by grouping the independently raised 5th, 6th and 7th Australian Infantry brigades—had no guns because there were insufficient in either Australia or Britain to equip its artillery.[2] The 54th Division went into the line on the left of Anzac on 1 September, obtaining its fire support through Napier JoUston. HQ ANZAC allotted the 2nd Australian Division to Sections 2, 3 and 4 of the defence, and on 27 and 28 August the 5th Australian Infantry Brigade began taking over these parts of the line from the NZ&A Division. The 2nd Australian Division's artillery support was to be provided by the 1st Australian Division, although it could also call on support from some of the New Zealand guns if required.

On 20 September HQ ANZAC changed the defensive section arrangements, reducing the number from six to four. Under the revised allocation, (See Map 25) the 1st Australian Division, together with the 2nd LH Brigade, occupied Section 1, which ran from the sea in the south to Brown's Dip, just south of Lone Pine. The 2nd Australian Division held Section 2, from Brown's Dip to Russell's Top and then down Walker's Ridge. Section 3, the responsibility of the NZ&A Division, ran from the foot of Walker's Ridge through No 1 Outpost and the Camel's Hump to Rhododendron Ridge and thence up to the Apex and along Cheshire Ridge to Aghyl Dere. The line in Section 4, occupied by the 54th Division, crossed Aghyl Dere to Damakjelik Bair, and then ran down that feature before slicing across the lower end of Kaiajik Dere and the western portion of Hill 60 to the boundary with IX Corps.[3] Hobbs coordinated the fire support in Sections 1 and 2, and Napier JoÚston the artillery in Sections 3 and 4.

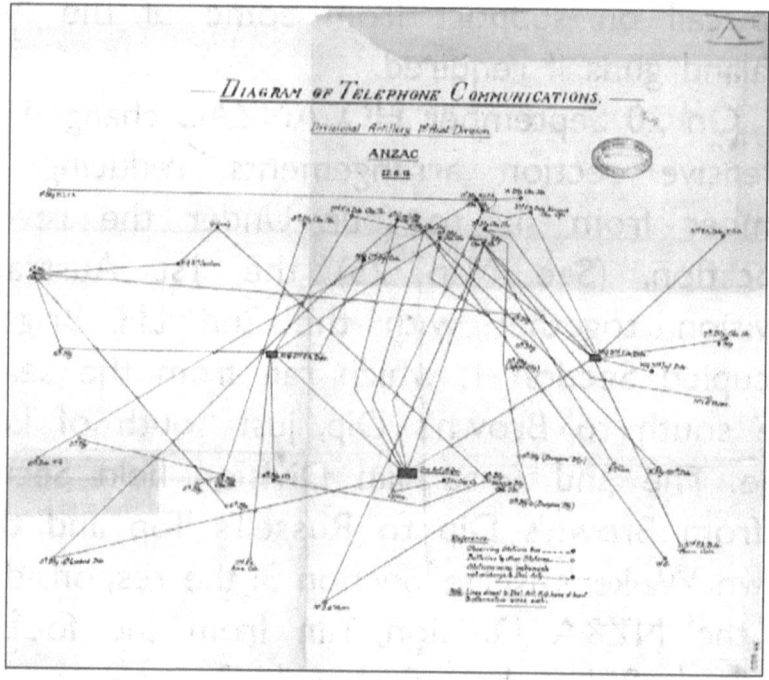

Diagram 14: Artillery communications, 27 August 1915. The fully mature 1st Australian Divisional Artillery telephone system established after the August Offensive. It links all AFA and infantry brigade headquarters, AFA field batteries, the 1st Australian Heavy Battery, artillery brigade and battery observation stations and forward observation officers, AFA Ammunition Columns, W5 Radio Station, the 1st NZFA Battery (a section of which with observer provided coverage of the 400 Plateau), the 5th (City of Glasgow) Battery RFA and A Battery and Headquarters 69th Howitzer Brigade RFA.

Between August and October additional artillery arrived at Anzac. In mid-August the 3rd NZFA and 6th AFA batteries returned from Cape Helles, the 5th NZFA Battery arrived from Egypt, and two HotcSiss 3-pounders (2-inch, 47mm) and the 60-pounder (5-inch, 127mm) guns of the 10th Heavy Battery RGA of the 11th (Northern) Division were landed.[4]

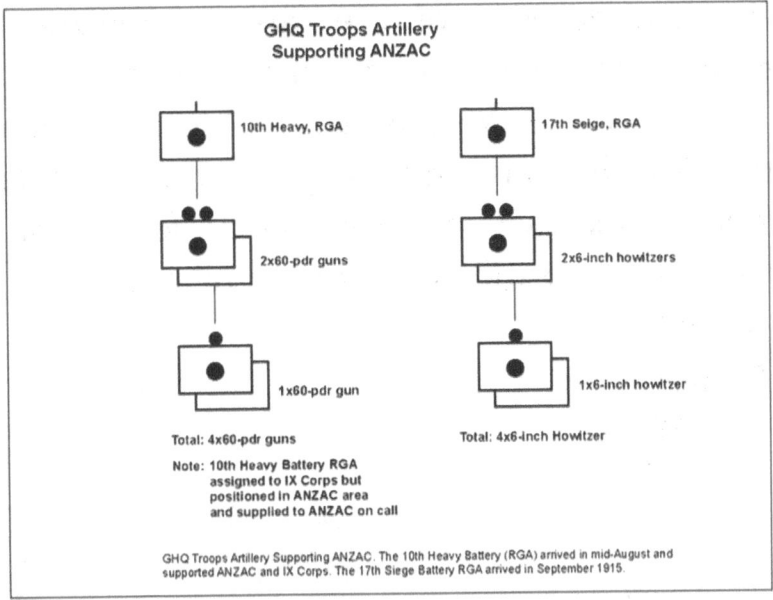

Organisation Chart 7: British GHQ artillery units supporting Anzac, October-November 1915

September brought the 6-inch (152mm) howitzers of the 17th Siege Battery, 24th Siege Brigade RGA. In October a 12-pounder (3-inch, 77mm) anti-aircraft gun was deployed; the 1st AFA Brigade returned from Helles; a battery, again from the 24th Siege Brigade, comprising two naval 4-inch (102mm) guns came into action; and the 4.5-inchers of the 6th NZFA (Howitzer) Battery arrived, completing the complement of the two NZFA field artillery brigades.[5]

Other weapons were available to the MEF, but not deployed, including a 15-inch (381mm) howitzer and a battery of 9.2-inch (234mm) howitzers. On 3 September Hamilton turned down the delivery of the larger howitzer and the offer of further naval batteries, noting that he was currently keeping the 9.2-inch howitzers, some 6-inch guns and 'large amounts of Field Artillery' inactive in Alexandria for want of suitable gun positions on the peninsula.[6]

A 60-pounder gun and crew of the 10th Heavy Battery RGA near Walden Point. The battery disembarked at Suvla on 9 and 10 August, and moved south to Anzac, initially being positioned on North Beach near No 2 Outpost. On the night of 17 August it moved to a position west of Walden Point, a portion of which can be seen on the right of the photograph just above the right-hand corner of the tarpaulin and sandbags. The foot of Damakjelik Bair is in the distance, with the mouth of Aghyl Dere in the middle distance. The gun is facing north into the IX Corps area at Suvla. In September the NZ&A Division reported the battery was located on the coast (AWM P05859.005).

To provide support for Sections 3 and 4, the New Zealand and some Corps Troops artillery moved into the newly won area, their former positions in old Anzac filled by Australian guns. The 1st NZFA Battery, however, remained on Russell's Top, with one section providing support to the New Zealanders, and the other section supporting the Australians. Interestingly, in late September, one of the battery's guns was removed for use in an ingenious effort to provide close-range enfilade fire on some trenches on Hill 60. A tunnel was driven through a feature nearby, with a firing chamber at the end from which an embrasure could be broken out in the cliff side when it was desired to open fire. The 18-pounder was taken through the tunnel piece-by-piece and reassembled in the chamber, but it was never used.[7] Map 30 shows the battery positions in the NZ&A Division's sector in September.

A HotcŠiss QF 12-pounder, 12 cwt Mk I anti-aircraft gun on a garrison mount emplaced near Shrapnel Gully. This gun arrived in August. One of the officers shown is believed to be Lieutenant Terence Garling, the officer in charge (AWM C01627).

Artillery Allocations

The NZ&A and 54th divisions were routinely supported by the two NZFA brigades, a 6-inch howitzer, B, C and D batteries of the 69th (Howitzer) Brigade RFA, the two mountain batteries, less one gun and, once deployed, the 10th Heavy Battery RGA, a section of the 17th Siege Battery RGA, and the 4-inch naval gun battery of the 24th Siege Brigade. Broadly speaking, for field gun coverage the 1st NZFA Battery watched over the Chunuk Bair area, the

5th Battery the Sari Bair heights, and the 2nd and 3rd batteries the area to the north of the defensive sections. The howitzers and larger calibre weapons ranged over the whole NZ&A and 54th division's front. All batteries engaged opportunity targets, registered hostile areas, shelled defensive works and machine-guns, and undertook infantry support tasks and counter-battery work. The latter included the engagement of enemy batteries and their observation posts, as well as retaliatory shelling of the Ottoman lines.[8]

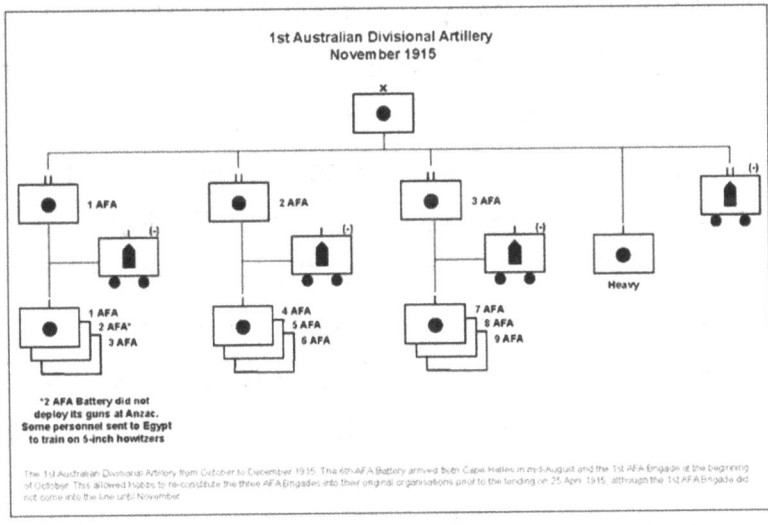

Organisation Chart 8: NZ&A Divisional Artillery, October–December 1915

Until the 1st AFA Brigade came into the line in November, artillery support for the Australian defensive sections was provided by the 2nd and

3rd AFA brigades and the Australian Heavy Battery of the 1st Australian Divisional Artillery; and from Corps Troops artillery, the 5th (City of Glasgow) Howitzer Battery RFA; A Battery, 69th Howitzer Brigade RFA; a mountain gun; and a section from the 17th Siege Battery RGA. The field guns covered the same areas as before the August Offensive (see maps 31 and 32), with the responsibilities of the 2nd AFA Brigade expanded to include the guns on Plugge's Plateau where, in mid-August, the 6th AFA Battery replaced the 2nd NZFA Battery, and then Russell's Top in early October when a section of the 3rd AFA Battery replaced the New Zealand section that had been supporting the Australian infantry on the 400 Plateau. Two HotcŠiss guns were also deployed on Russell's Top and Walker's Ridge, one earmarked for trench duties, the other for anti-aircraft purposes until it was sent to the NZ&A Division in early September. Deployed in the 3rd AFA Brigade area, the Australian Heavy Battery predominately undertook counter-battery work around the Olive Grove to the south, and the Corps Troops howitzers ranged across the Australian front.[9] To assist with the use of these assets, when Legge's division deployed, Hobbs took the opportunity to issue revised copies of his notes for the guidance of artillery officers and on infantry-artillery cooperation.[10]

By this stage adjustments to some of the Australian gun positions had also been made. The 6th AFA Battery kept a section on Plugge's Plateau and deployed a gun opposite JoUston's Jolly. The 7th had a gun on Bolton's Ridge with fields of fire over the south of Lone Pine, Legge Valley and Pine Ridge, with its other three guns further south. The 8th Battery likewise left a gun in its original position near the Pimple at Lone Pine, and deployed its other guns around 200 metres further south, with arcs of fire to the north-east as before.[11]

Prior to this period, the Australian batteries had experienced difficulties with the training of reinforcements, prompting Hobbs to visit Egypt in early September. He reported that there was no satisfactory method of instructing the artillery personnel arriving from Australia, largely because of a lack of guns and equipment. He proposed an artillery training camp, adding that, if guns for its use could not be sourced from elsewhere, he recommended that two be sent from Anzac. Walker, commanding the 1st Australian Division, supported him and forwarded the proposition to Birdwood who disagreed, believing that two guns could not be spared, and the reinforcements should be trained in matters such as gun drill and fuse setting after being posted to a battery at Anzac. The lack of a suitable artillery base in

Egypt was also evident in the numbers of NCOs and men proceeding to Gallipoli without authorisation. Thirty-three reinforcements for the 1st AFA Brigade (then located at Helles) had left Alexandria in August and their whereabouts remained unclear.[12]

On Anzac itself the cumulative effect of combat casualties and arduous campaigning began to show on health and morale. Arrangements were made on 10 September to continue sending groups to Lemnos for rest. By the end of the month constant changes to subordinate command in the 1st Division's artillery caused by casualties or illness also led to cessation of the practice of referring to artillery brigades and batteries by the name of their commanders. Thereafter, they were designated simply by number.[13]

Ammunition Supply

The increase in the number of guns from August onwards was not accompanied by an improvement in ammunition availability. On 28 August Hobbs complained in his diary again about the shortage of ammunition, writing: 'owing to the lack of ammunition we have had to restrict our fire for the last four or five days and it has been the same nearly all the way through. The infantry and others are continually asking urgently for artillery support that I could not properly give on account of the shortness of ammunition and lack of aeroplane assistance in spotting for us.'[14] HQ MEF monitored daily expenditures, and on 8 September chided IX Corps for its greater use of 18-pounder ammunition over the previous three days (13.9 rounds per gun versus 3.2 in ANZAC), noting that, 'with more activity on the part of your infantry, it may be possible to do with a smaller expenditure of artillery ammunition which, as you know, is so difficult to replace.'[15]

However, with winter coming, and the possibility of rough seas disrupting supply, HQ MEF began pushing gun ammunition ashore, announcing in early September a plan to fill up the divisional units, double the authorised corps reserves, and position three-quarters of the supplies in the Lines of Communication on the beaches. Within ANZAC, this represented a delivery of an additional nineteen thousand, five hundred 18-pounder rounds, eight hundred and fifty 4.5-inch howitzer and fifteen hundred 6-inch howitzer shells. For the other weapons there was no such 'surplus'. While the increases may appear generous, the catch was that each corps then had to manage the balance between expenditure and the establishment of a winter reserve. HQ MEF stressed the need for strict economy in expenditure so as to create this reserve. It advised that ammunition in the Lines of Communication would only be available in an emergency.[16] Perhaps these machinations explain why, on 24 September, the 3rd AFA Brigade Ammunition Column reported that holdings at the front were reduced to 252 rounds per gun in gun pits, and 126 rounds per gun in the columns.[17]

On 25 September Hamilton cabled London concerning ammunition, noting that in August the War Office had despatched the equivalent of eleven rounds per 18-pounder per day, and seemed to be basing provision on expenditure rather than previously promised amounts, frustrating his efforts to economise on expenditure in order to build up reserves for winter and future operations. He requested a fixed minimum rate of supply on which to base his planning.[18] The response to this cable is not in the war diaries, but the correspondence provides some insight into the restrictions at the gun lines experienced by the gunners throughout the campaign.

Artillery Support Arrangements

In their defensive sections the four divisions inherited arrangements for artillery support that provided the commander of each section with some artillery at call, and some on request to divisional artillery headquarters.[19] Thus it was, for example, that when the 2nd Australian Division assumed responsibility for old defensive Sections 2, 3 and 4, Legge was advised that he would find both New Zealand and Australian guns stationed in his area, but in terms of immediate fire support, the fire of two guns of the 1st NZFA Battery and those of the 5th and 6th AFA batteries were available 'to assist' him. If he required additional support, then thirteen 18-pounders, one 10-pounder, one 6-inch howitzer, and two 4.5-inch howitzers would be available, although he would have to apply directly to the division concerned, with the request repeated to HQ ANZAC. Requests for naval gunfire support from the 3rd Naval Squadron could be sent through HQ ANZAC, although in an emergency he could send them directly to the ships through W6 Signal Section, each message to begin with the word 'Urgent' and conclude with 'LEGGE' to enable the navy to recognise the sender. Similar arrangements for providing fire support prevailed in other defensive sections.[20]

Support arrangements in new Sections 1 and 2 changed on 7 November when Hobbs issued orders designed to bring the 1st AFA Brigade into the line, minimise the split battery positions that had prevailed for some months, and place batteries under their parent field artillery brigade headquarters so as to simplify command relationships.[21] Up until this time the 1st AFA Brigade, having returned from Helles in early October, had been in reserve in Shrapnel Gully, apart from the section of the 3rd Battery on Russell's Top. The men were employed on general duties, manning the anti-aircraft gun, or providing reliefs for other batteries.[22]

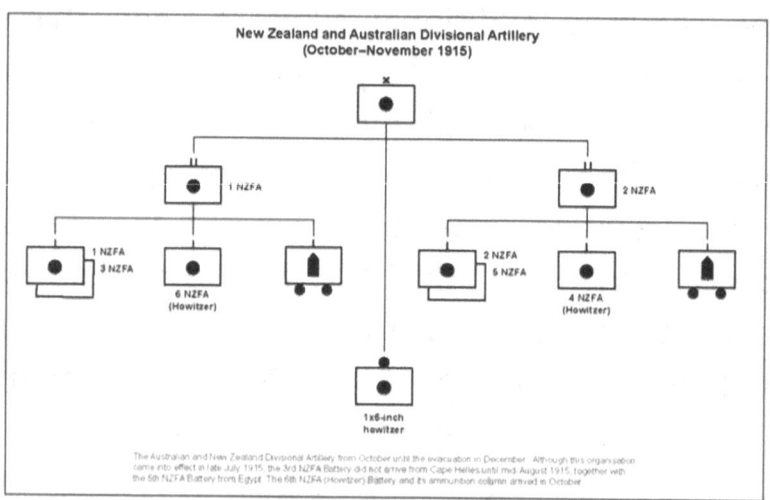

Organisation Chart 9: The 1st Australian Divisional Artillery, October-December 1915

Under the new arrangements, the 1st AFA Brigade became responsible for the batteries on the Australian left, with its 3rd Battery deployed on Russell's Top, and the 1st AFA Battery forming a three-gun battery on Plugge's

Plateau/MacLagan's Ridge by swapping its guns for those previously manned by the 6th and 5th AFA batteries respectively. The 2nd AFA Brigade was consolidated in the centre, with the 5th AFA Battery on the Razorback, the 4th AFA Battery remaining on McCay's Hill, and the 6th AFA Battery taking over the 8th AFA Battery's positions and guns just behind Lone Pine. On the right, in the 3rd AFA Brigade, the 7th AFA Battery remained in position, while the 8th AFA Battery moved to McCay's Hill, where it assumed command of two of the 9th AFA Battery's guns and completed its position with two guns previously held by the 6th Battery. The 9th AFA Battery also acquired two guns from the 6th, adding them to its own two guns in a battery position on the spur running west of the junction of Bolton's and Holly ridges.[23]

The swapping of guns, stores and ammunition holdings cleverly resolved the very practical problem of completing the reorganisation speedily in difficult terrain. In the process, Hobbs took the opportunity to form a mobile section using un-deployed guns from the 1st and 4th batteries. The 2nd AFA Battery was not included in the reorganisation because when it departed Helles, two officers and eight other ranks were sent to Alexandria to train on 5-inch howitzers.[24] The intention was that the battery would become a howitzer sub-unit when further 5-inchers arrived at Anzac in late November. Events, however, intervened. The transport carrying the guns arrived off Anzac on 24 November, by which time contingency planning for the evacuation had commenced, and the howitzers were not disembarked.[25]

In mid-November, Napier JoÚston issued a memo to all the infantry brigade commanders in the NZ&A Division, listing the artillery allotted to the Division, the allocations to sections of the line, the characteristics and positions of the weapons, the duties of forward observation officers, and artillery communications.[26] This document preceded by four days a Corps circular designating, for each part of the firing line in the four defensive sections, the batteries to provide immediate and additional support. The circular aimed to ensure close cooperation between the artillery and the infantry. Its underlying principle was that the artillery of the divisions would remain under command of the CRA under the orders of the divisional commander, but control of the fire of a limited number of guns would be allotted to the artillery commanders in the defensive sections to provide immediate support. These artillery commanders would be in direct communication with the infantry in each defensive section, and could obtain further fire support through artillery channels. Whether that additional support would be provided depended on the overall situation at the time, but artillery brigade commanders were given latitude to employ guns that were available in the interim between receiving the request from the defensive sections and getting instructions from the CRA.[27]

The principles behind the new tables (see Tables 2, 3 and 4) were very similar to those governing the previous allotment of guns, and it appears that the November circular, which was the result of collaboration between Cunliffe-Owen, Hobbs and Napier JoÚston, represented the Corps' formalisation of divisional practice, and growing recognition of the need for Corps coordination of fire support where practical. Napier JoÚston's memo supported the circular by adding detail relevant to the NZ&A Division.

In the Australian defensive sections, the November tables would have been very similar to their predecessors. On the left of Section 2 where the lines were close and the danger greater, the 5th and 7th Australian Infantry brigades (Walker's Ridge to Wire Gully) could draw on the immediate support of the 1st, 4th, 5th and 6th AFA batteries, and additional support from A Battery, 69th Howitzer Brigade, the 17th Siege Battery and one mountain gun. On the right, again a high-risk area, the 6th Infantry Brigade (Wire Gully to Lone Pine inclusive) had immediate support from the 1st, 3rd and 7th AFA batteries together with elements of A Battery, 69th Howitzer Brigade. The remainder of A Battery was nominated to provide additional support if available, along with the 17th Siege Battery and a mountain gun.

In Section 1, where the threat was less imminent, on the left the 1st and 3rd Infantry brigades (Holly Ridge and upper Bolton's Ridge) were provided with a lower level of immediate support, that of the 7th AFA Battery only, with additional support coming from the 5th (City of Glasgow) Howitzer Battery and, in the case of the 1st Infantry Brigade, one gun from the 6th AFA Battery. On the right, the remainder of the line to the coast, the 2nd LH Brigade had immediate support from the 6th and 8th AFA batteries and the 5th (City of Glasgow) Battery, while the 17th Siege Battery RGA was allocated to provide additional support as required. The nomination of the 6th AFA Battery to provide immediate support, when it was also assigned to provide the same for the northern end of the line, and no mention of Burgess's 9th AFA Battery in the tables is odd. This may have stemmed from a typographical error. While the 6th Battery, positioned behind Lone Pine, may have been able to cover both areas, it could not provide immediate support to both at the same time. The 9th Battery, located in Defensive Section 1 within the 2 LH Brigade's area facing south was perhaps better placed to provide immediate support to the 2nd LH Brigade.[28]

In Defensive Sections 3 and 4, the arrangements also reflected a greater level of immediate support to the more vulnerable sections of the line. On the right of Section 3, the two light horse brigades holding an area of low risk between Walker's Ridge and Rhododendron Ridge had only the immediate support of a section of 5-inch howitzers, plus a section of 4-inch naval guns. In the centre of the defensive section, encompassing the higher risk area of Rhododendron Ridge, the Apex and Cheshire Ridge, the 4th Australian and New Zealand infantry brigades had the immediate support of one and a half 18-pounder batteries plus a 4.5-inch howitzer section, with additional support from six 4.5-inchers, three batteries of 5-inchers, a section from 17th Siege Battery, the two-gun naval battery, and a section of mountain guns.

The New Zealand Mounted Rifles took over the front from Aghyl Dere to Damakjelik Bair on 26 November. Here, where the risk was moderate to high, its left flank had the immediate support of a section of 5-inchers, with additional support from an 18-pounder battery, two 4.5-inch batteries, two sections of 5-inchers, the 4-inch gun battery, and a section each from the 17th Siege Battery and the 26th (Jacob's) Battery. The right of the Brigade could call on immediate support from B Battery of the 69th Howitzer Brigade plus a section from the 21st (Kohat) Battery, with supplementary support from the two 4.5-inch batteries, an 18-pounder battery, two 5-inch batteries and, similar to the left flank, a section each from the 17th Battery and the 26th (Jacob's) Battery.

In Section 4, held by the 54th (East Anglian) Division, around the hotly contested area of Hill 60, the brigade in the line could immediately call on a field battery, six 4.5-inchers, a section each of 5 and 6-inch howitzers, and six mountain guns, with another field battery and 5-inch howitzer battery providing additional support. On the left, in the lower risk area out to Susak Kuyu, the defenders could call on a field battery and 5-inch section, with substantial additional support if required.[29]

Besides the allocations of guns to defensive sections, the 22 November circular also stipulated that guns detailed for immediate support of the infantry should be laid at nightfall on suitable enemy trenches, with arrangements made for them to be able to fire immediately. Thus, for example, two 18-pounders of the 4th AFA Battery were laid on the Ottoman front-line trenches on Russell's Top, two from the 5th AFA Battery were laid on the trenches opposite Pope's Hill, two from the 1st AFA Battery were laid on Turkish Quinn's, and so on down the line to the right flank.[30] Napier JoÚston's memo contained details of the night lines for his artillery. They represented the gestation of the immediate defensive fire tasks familiar to gunners and infantrymen in more recent times.

Naval Gunfire Coordination

As well as coordinating its own fire support, in the period between August and November, HQ ANZAC revised the arrangements for support from the navy, and made arrangements with IX Corps for support along the inter-corps boundary. The agreements struck with the 3rd Naval Squadron provided on-call and prearranged support on a 24-hour basis, with the cruiser HMS *Bacchante* remaining in support at Kephalo Bay at Imbros Island, and the cruisers *Endymion* and *Grafton* rotating every seventy-two hours between Kephalo and the left flank of Anzac. The monitors *Humber* and *M33* would rotate every forty-eight hours to a station off ANZAC's right flank during daylight hours, principally to deal with the Olive Grove battery. During the night they were to anchor to the south-west of Nibrunesi Point at Suvla, unless required for night firing.

Monitors *M19*, *M18*, *M20* and *M28* were kept in reserve at Kephalo, one to be ready for sea at a moment's notice, while two destroyers, drawn from *Colne, Chelmer, Bulldog* and *Mosquito*—stationed at Mudros—would stand off Anzac on forty-eight hours' rotation, one of them retiring to Kephalo during daylight hours. This was later changed in November to *Colne, Chelmer* and *Pincher,* with two operating off Anzac during darkness and one in reserve at Mudros, while during daylight hours the second destroyer off Anzac was to be at Kephalo unless otherwise required. Cunliffe-Owen at Corps headquarters controlled all routine requests for naval gunfire and allotted targets from day to day, generally selecting hostile works and gun emplacements that could be better engaged from the sea. In emergencies however, an ANZAC defensive section commander could signal direct to the warship through Signal Station W6. For the observation of naval gunfire, observers on shore were in telephone contact with W6, which then transmitted the necessary message to the ships.[31]

The monitor HMS Humber. The first of her class, Humber arrived off Gallipoli in June. She carried two 6-inch guns and two 4.7-inch howitzers, and supported ANZAC from then until the evacuation in December (Wikipedia).

Naval gunfire support during autumn was generally prearranged on areas that could be readily engaged without endangering ANZAC troops. It was intermittent in its application. During September, the ANZAC war diary records the navy providing fire support on eight days. On 4 September the right-flank destroyer shelled Harris Ridge supporting a demonstration by the 5th LH Regiment at the extreme south of the line, and the cruiser *Endymion* shelled trenches at the Nek. On the 11th, the destroyer *Chelmer* assisted with shelling during the day and, on the evening of the 16th, two destroyers participated in a ruse to test the enemy's strength, *Colne* firing on Harris Ridge and *Bulldog* on Baby 700. On 21 September, *Colne* shelled working parties on Harris Ridge while *Bulldog* engaged Battleship Hill and, three days later, *Chelmer* again engaged Harris Ridge. On the night 28/29 September the destroyer *Colne* put one shell into Bird Trench on the extreme southern flank and, the following day, *Endymion* shelled the enemy support trenches and upper works at the Nek, apparently causing considerable damage. That evening and the following, *Chelmer* shelled enemy trenches opposite the 1st Australian Division's sector.[32]

The River class destroyer HMS Chelmer. She supported ANZAC from the beginning of the campaign, carrying the tows of the second wave at the landing, and providing naval gunfire support until the evacuation in December. Chelmer carried one QF 12-pounder 12 cwt gun, three 12-pounder 8 cwt guns, and five 6-pounder 5 cwt guns (authors' image).

In his memoirs, Commodore Roger Keyes, Chief of Staff to Admiral de Robeck, the Naval Commander, noted the improvements in naval gunfire that had evolved by this stage of the campaign. 'The enemy's batteries, trenches, bivouacs, etc', he wrote, 'were fixed by aerial photography and other means, and excellent maps were issued to the firing ships. Indirect fire was developed to a high degree of accuracy, with the aid of aerial and shore observation. Mark buoys were laid, and aiming points, ranges and deflections were registered onto any position on which fire was required by the Army; indirect fire could then be opened at short notice without waiting for aerial observation.'[33]

Wireless Station W5, one of three wireless stations established at Anzac (W4, W5 and W6) located in the 1st Australian Division area which provided communications to the Royal Navy ships offshore and through which the

1st Australian Divisional Artillery sent requests for naval gunfire support (AWM A05781).

Following several discussions in October and November, procedures and prearranged targets were laid down with the navy in the event of a sudden Ottoman attack. Depending on the area being attacked, and whether the attack occurred by night or day, these procedures listed the targets allotted to the various ships on station. They stated that, if the attack were to be made against ANZAC's right flank, the cruiser on station would engage the Olive Grove guns, the right-flank destroyer the Twin Trenches along Harris Ridge at the southern extremity of the ANZAC line, and the left-flank destroyer Baby 700. In case of an attack from the Nek, the cruiser would engage the Sari Bair Range from Chunuk Bair to Hill 971, the left-flank destroyer would fire on the Nek, and the right-flank destroyer would engage Legge Valley and Scrubby Knoll.[34] The reasoning for selecting some of these targets, well away from the point of the attack, seems odd. However, it was acknowledged that these were preliminaries, and when observation was practicable the ships were to engage the best target they could locate.

Cooperation with IX Corps

In contrast to the agreements with the navy, the arrangements for artillery cooperation between ANZAC and IX Corps were longer in coming. They were initiated at the end of October and agreed in early November at a meeting attended by Cunliffe-Owen and Brigadier General Brudenell White, by then the Brigadier General General Staff (BGGS)—the principal staff officer at HQ ANZAC. Why it took so long to reach agreement is unknown, especially as the arrangements themselves were limited. Essentially, both corps agreed to support the infantry brigades on either side of the inter-corps boundary by allowing them to call on nominated batteries from the other corps if attacked. If both brigades were attacked simultaneously, which was a distinct possibility, support would be provided by the parent corps, and the agreement would have no effect.

The 2nd and 6th NZFA batteries within ANZAC were allocated to support the flanking IX Corps brigade while, within IX Corps, A and B batteries, 55th Howitzer Brigade RFA, were to support ANZAC. Embarrassingly, following the conference it was discovered that the 2nd NZFA Battery could not reach all the targets it might be called on to engage. After a flurry of messages the 3rd NZFA Battery took over the role. Direct communications between Napier Jo(u)ston and the CRA of the flanking division were established, as were communications between the flanking infantry brigades and their supporting batteries.[35]

Support Tasks

With a stalemate existing across the expanded front, the artillery reverted to the daily missions associated with the niggling tussles of defensive trench warfare. Curiously, given Hamilton's concern about ammunition, after ten days of relatively little firing by the New Zealand 18-pounders, during which some batteries fired no rounds for two or three days in a row, Napier Jo(u)ston received orders on 21 September that all New Zealand batteries were to expend their daily allowance of ammunition. If no important targets were identified during the day, the rounds were to be fired in the evening at the Ottoman trenches or known reserve locations. That afternoon, the 3rd NZFA Battery fired its daily allowance of forty rounds onto Ottoman works in front of the 29th Indian Infantry Brigade in two missions two hours apart, and the next day threw another forty rounds at them in three missions between 2.22pm and 5.16pm.[36]

More typical of a day's firing from then on were the 2nd NZFA Battery's missions on 3 October. At 7.00am two rounds were sent into a working group building emplacements, and eleven rounds were fired at intervals into troops at Chakajak Kuyu. At 4.00pm four rounds searched for a gun north-east of Chunuk Bair, and an hour later seven rounds were fired into the same emplacement engaged earlier in the day. In the last mission of the day, nine rounds were expended engaging a gun north-east of Chunuk Bair, making a total of thirty-three rounds fired, eight per gun. That same day, at 5.45pm, B Battery, 69th (Howitzer) Brigade, fired six rounds onto a trench near the Pinnacle, its only mission of the day.[37]

Similarly, on 15 October, Burgess' 9th AFA Battery engaged a convoy on the main road near the Kilid Bahr re-entrant with fifteen rounds at 7.15am, followed by six rounds into an Ottoman observation station at 10.30am. Three rounds were fired at a party of dismounted men at 2.15pm, followed by another four rounds at the same target twenty minutes later. At 5.50pm the battery engaged a 6-inch howitzer, the right section of the Olive Grove battery, and trenches, with a total of five rounds from three guns.[38]

Numerous missions such as these, with limited ammunition expenditure, are common in the battery and artillery brigade war diaries for the period.

Counter-Battery Work

Counter-battery work remained a high priority for the ANZAC gunners as indicated by Map 31, which shows the identified hostile batteries in the Australian area in late August and the ANZAC batteries that could cover them. Enemy shelling of both the New Zealand and Australian sectors was an almost daily occurrence, with the Ottoman gunners undertaking the same tasks as their ANZAC counterparts. The shelling was generally limited, but exceptions occurred when a demonstration was mounted to test the ANZAC reaction, such as occurred on 18 September and 4 and 27 October, or when efforts were made to silence particular ANZAC guns. On 19 September, for example, the Olive Grove batteries fired more than fifty rounds at one of the guns of the 9th AFA Battery. The gun was not hit and only two men were wounded. On 27 September, 150 rounds were fired at No 2 gun of the 4th AFA Battery, damaging the weapon and forcing it to move to a new position on Artillery Road. On 28

September approximately 200 rounds were fired at the 6th Battery on Plugge's Plateau, knocking the pits around and causing some temporary damage to the guns. The same battery was targeted again on 5 October, but by this stage the Australian batteries commonly made use of shelter pits, known as 'run-out positions' or 'funk holes', into which the guns could be withdrawn when the firing emplacements came under fire. Fifty to sixty shells were fired at the naval battery on 20 November. This battery was put out of action on several occasions, and the 60-pounders of the 10th Heavy Battery became so badly damaged by hostile gunfire that eventually they were sent away about a month before the evacuation.[39]

Suppressing the Ottoman batteries remained a tricky proposition. Location was generally reliant on ground observation of flash and dust. Air reconnaissance began to make a useful contribution with, for example, the NZ&A Division receiving three aerial reports of gun locations in September. Nevertheless, in early October Hobbs lamented that it was 'practically hopeless to silence enemys [sic] guns firing from ... concealed positions ... unless the assistance of aircraft is obtained for spotting our fire.' The war diaries record two to four instances of air observation each month, usually with indifferent results because of factors such as limited visibility or poor communications.[40]

Temporary suppression was generally only achievable when the hostile batteries or their observation stations could be seen or had been registered. On many occasions hostile guns began firing again shortly after the ANZAC counter-fire ceased, or hostile shellfire came from un-located or poorly located guns that were not susceptible to direct engagement. Moreover, possessed of ample supplies of timber and labour, scarce commodities at Anzac, the Ottomans built innumerable covered locations that protected their guns from ANZAC fire or served as alternative positions.[41] Accordingly, Hobbs advised his batteries that, from experience, 'the best method of preventing the enemy from shelling our trenches, is to retaliate by shelling his.' Reflecting what was by then common practice, in late September he directed artillery commanders to bring immediate fire onto the Ottoman trenches nearest the point being shelled, noting that 'the infantry must take the necessary steps to guard against possible danger from our shell fire, which may, at times, necessarily be in very close proximity to our own trenches.' The New Zealanders also used retaliation and, as an interesting pointer to its potential effect, recorded on 12 September that the NZ&A Division guns were asked not to fire on Ottoman trenches, apart from those on Hill 100, in case Ottoman retaliation disrupted the reliefs taking place in the friendly trenches.[42]

New Zealand artillerymen operating a 4.5-inch howitzer of the 4th NZFA (Howitzer) Battery in Taylor's Hollow behind Bauchop's Hill following the August Offensive. One section of the battery had moved into this position by 12 August, the other section remained in its original position on North Beach near Anzac Cove. These guns were sited in open pits to allow a wide arc of fire. The high, arching trajectory of their shells allowed them to be positioned behind hills and ridges, shielded from Ottoman view by the intervening terrain (AWM H15383).

Perhaps the most difficult hostile batteries to suppress throughout the campaign were those located south of the Australian sector at the Olive Grove and nearby positions. The Australian Heavy Battery War Diary records that the

Ottoman guns sited there fired on all but a handful of days each month. The 9th AFA Battery, the Heavy Battery and the 5-inchers responded as appropriate, but were never able to shut the positions down for any length of time. On the few occasions it was attempted, air observation was unreliable.[43] Naval engagements proved equally unsuccessful.

The 6-inch, 30 cwt howitzer of the Australian Heavy Battery known as 'the Kanga' is laid for line in its pit in White's Valley prior to firing on an Ottoman gun known as 'Beachy Bill', located in the Olive Grove (AWM H15736).

The persistence of 'Beachy Bill' and the Olive Grove gunners caused some of their Australian counterparts to speculate as early as August that the guns they sought to silence were deployed in tunnels. Cunliffe-Owen took a similar tack in his presentation to the Royal Artillery Institution after the war, opining that these guns were located in multiple positions on the reverse slope of a deep ravine, where they were mounted on rails and fired through tunnels. An examination of the area by Bean in 1919 found no sign of such works. His view was that the guns had simply been sited cleverly in protective pits on a reverse slope, and this was sufficient to prevent the ANZAC gunners achieving an accurate location or causing lasting damage.[44] This is a logical explanation. There are, after all, numerous accounts in the artillery war diaries of Ottoman fire searching for and failing to find ANZAC gun positions, or causing damage to guns and emplacements, but achieving little more than a temporary suspension of fire.

An Artillery Demonstration

On 16 October the ANZAC artillery participated in a demonstration along the front for the purposes of alarming the enemy, drawing fire to test the strength of the opposing lines, and 'to accustom troops new to the trenches to an outburst of enemy fire'. Commencing at 4.00am, it involved both infantry and artillery firing for ten minutes. The Australian artillery was limited to fifteen rounds per field battery and ten rounds per howitzer battery, while

Napier JoUston's four field batteries and four available howitzer batteries (4th NZFA and three of the 69th Howitzer Brigade) fired eight rounds each, and the 17th Siege Battery four.[45] Whether the ammunition expenditure was worth the effort, and whether the demonstration achieved its purpose, are questionable. Opposite the Australians the greatest volume of Ottoman fire was reported to have come from Lone Pine; there was very little from the right or JoUston's Jolly, and the Ottoman machine-guns remained silent. The 1st Australian Division reported that it 'drew a certain amount of fire ... but not as much as usual', indicating that at least the first two reasons for the undertaking failed.[46]

The third purpose, however, was achieved, although it is doubtful the Anzac infantry subjected to the subsequent shelling appreciated the intent. The Ottoman artillery retaliated, firing on the NZ&A Division's trenches along Rhododendron Ridge all day, leading to the expenditure of more than 100 rounds in retaliatory fire. Further south, Ottoman guns at the Olive Grove and behind Third Ridge shelled the Australian trenches commencing at 11.45am. The batteries there answered, and the line was ablaze with gunfire for the best part of an hour. In all, Hobbs' guns and howitzers expended 391 rounds, one of the heaviest expenditures of artillery ammunition at Anzac after the August offensive.[47] Given the concerns over the artillery ammunition supply, the consequent restrictions normally placed on firing, and the lack of practical result, the reasons for undertaking this demonstration are highly questionable.

Trench Mortars

As the campaign drew on, different types of targets began to appear. An increase in Ottoman use of trench mortars was noted, along with occasional barrages of 'stick bombs', which were reported as cartridge cases from QF guns stuffed with explosive and bullets, mounted on a stick, and fired from some form of trench mortar.[48] Their introduction resulted in increased calls for artillery retaliation, which was difficult to provide effectively as the artillery observers were often not in a useful location, and the offending weapons were usually sited behind ridges quite close to the ANZAC line. While Hobbs noted a few rounds from a howitzer generally sufficed to silence these weapons, he believed fire from ANZAC trench mortars would have been a preferable countermeasure had ammunition for them been more readily available. The 1st Australian Division had a total of ten mortars in

November, while the 2nd Australian Division had seven 3.7-inchers and an unstated number of the other two types. As Hobbs had intimated, ammunition supply was limited.[49]

In the Australian divisions the mortars were formed into 'batteries' made up of men drawn from a variety of units and deployed under the orders of the divisional commander (1st Division) or brigade commanders (2nd Division). Corresponding detail applicable to the NZ&A Division is lacking, although Napier JoÚston noted on 12 October that he had been given responsibility for the trench mortars and their crews and tecÚical inspection of mortar ammunition. This signals, perhaps, a different approach to that of the Australian divisions, but thereafter Napier JoÚston's daily artillery reports make no reference to trench mortars, the overall lack of which led to such expedients as large India-rubber powered slingshots capable of hurling grenades about 150 yards with reasonable accuracy.[50]

Further Plans for Hill 60

While the records show that ANZAC launched no major attacks after August, behind the scenes from late September onwards the 54th (East Anglian) Division planned another attempt to take the crest of Hill 60. Its initial concept was to conduct a series of preliminary bombardments, spaced to preserve surprise, in which Ottoman wire would be destroyed. Then, on the day of the attack, mines would be exploded under the first line of enemy trenches. The infantry would immediately advance to secure this line, then seize the second, supported by a fire plan designed to achieve four objectives: block the trenches through which the Ottomans might counter-attack, prepare a further section of trench for capture, suppress enemy fire from Yauan Tepe and Hill 100, and neutralise hostile batteries. Napier JoÚston produced artillery instructions in support of this concept. A program for wire-cutting in September and October was implemented, but suspended after early firings when the infantry reported that the required effect had been achieved.[51]

Over the next few weeks the concept firmed into the 54th Division's Operation Order Number 2 of 4 November for an attack envisaged for around 7 November. Revised instruction from Napier JoÚston on 2 November accompanied the order. When Napier JoÚston sought approval for the ammunition expenditure envisaged in this fire plan (see Map 33), Corps headquarters requested a report on progress from the Division, which resulted in the advice that the mines should be ready to be blown by 15 November, along with a copy of a new operation order (Number 3 of 5 November), reducing the action to blowing the mines under the Ottoman front trench and attempting, by the insertion of barricades, to prevent the enemy reoccupying it. This plan too was abandoned when Birdwood queried the amount of ammunition required for the associated fire plan, and sought to have a flanking formation moved forward a little before any operation went ahead. Eventually, to circumvent Ottoman counter-mining, the mines were simply exploded on 15 November, causing considerable casualties to the enemy, but no loss of position. Some of Napier JoÚston's batteries also fired for a while on adjacent Ottoman trenches within their daily ammunition allowances.[52]

Examination of the various documents suggests that the orders for this potential operation were developed in consultation between the gunners and the infantry. Perhaps because of this, it is evident from the fire plans that lessons from earlier actions had been learnt. Measures were taken to ensure registration and wire-cutting did not prejudice surprise. Target areas were quite specific, the guns nominated to engage them could have covered them effectively, and adequate resources were allotted to Yauan

Tepe. Even so, counter-battery arrangements still contained weaknesses. More resources were devoted to this task than in earlier attempts on Hill 60 and the nomination of target areas suggested that the location of hostile batteries had improved. However, each fire unit was tasked to cover multiple locations and would have struggled to suppress them if more than one opened simultaneously.[53]

Perhaps the most noticeable feature of these fire plans was the amount of ammunition to be expended. The plan in support of Operation Order Number 2 typically called for fifty to sixty rounds in the first twenty minutes from the heavy and howitzer batteries, and 200 rounds over the same period from the field and mountain batteries. This appears to have been an attempt to increase the weight of fire that had previously proved deficient. But, while Cunliffe-Owen thought such expenditure warranted, Birdwood was not convinced, his argument being that, if the position was to be taken essentially by mining, then significant artillery preparation and covering fire was not required, except for engaging counter-attack forces. He noted that artillery ammunition was in short supply and the provision of more at an early date could not be counted on. In the end, Godley of the NZ&A Division, after consulting with the commander of the 54th Division and considering the reduced scope of Operation Order 3, authorised an expenditure only slightly exceeding the normal daily allowance.[54]

As if to underscore Birdwood's concern, shortly afterwards, HQ MEF altered once more the methods of accounting for gun ammunition. The instruction that had been issued in September placing an increased amount of ammunition ashore was set aside, and HQ ANZAC was advised that, from 15 November, a specified number of rounds per gun (for example, thirty-five for the 18-pounders and five for the 4.5-inch howitzers) would be the daily scale provided, and the Corps was to build a winter reserve based on savings in expenditure from this scale. The stock already ashore was to be drawn down until fresh supply was required, and henceforth Corps was to provide a weekly report recording the daily expenditure, the ammunition on hand and the amount in the Corps reserve. The weekly amount on hand would be forwarded to the War Office as the basis for resupply.[55]

The Period in Review

For the ANZAC gunners, the period between mid-August and November 1915 was one of expansion, consolidation and static trench warfare, during which each side harassed the other with sniping and shelling, adding to a relatively low, but steady toll of dead and wounded for no apparent gain. With a larger beachhead providing more suitable gun positions, artillery reinforcements were steadily introduced. The five Anzac batteries sent to Helles in May returned, two further New Zealand batteries arrived from Egypt, and much-needed howitzers and heavy gun batteries were landed. This gave the Corps an increased weight of fire and a better counter-battery capability, although the difficulties in accurately locating hostile batteries remained. Ammunition supply was still limited, exacerbated by the need to create a winter reserve.

In terms of command and control, Napier JoÚston consolidated his batteries into two NZFA brigades and Hobbs, having regained the 1st AFA Brigade, was able to restructure his support arrangements and return batteries to their parent units. Corps arrangements for providing responsive fire support were refined, and provisions introduced for immediate defensive fire tasks, with designated batteries laid on specific targets during the night. Revised agreements for naval gunfire support saw nominated cruisers, monitors and destroyers on station on a rotational basis, and included provision for an immediate response on prearranged targets should the Ottomans attack. In addition, arrangements for mutual support between the right flank of IX Corps and the left flank of ANZAC were eventually agreed, although an Ottoman attack against these flanks at the same time would negate them. These evolving procedures reflected the growing capabilities of the gunners as resourcing improved somewhat and as they gained experience.

Chapter Ten

EVACUATION

Preliminaries

On the evening of 22 November 1915, Brigadier General White at HQ ANZAC was handed a pink sheet of paper torn from a signal pad. Written on it was the message 'Genl Birdwood to Genl White begins. my [sic] views unlikely to be accepted inform Genl Godley and start future plans immediately.'[1] These plans were for the evacuation of ANZAC from the Gallipoli peninsula.

Termination of the campaign had first been mooted when the Dardanelles Committee met in London on 11 October. Afterwards, Lord Kitchener, as Secretary of State for War, signalled Hamilton for his estimate of the numbers he would lose in an evacuation.[2] By now London had lost confidence in Hamilton and, when he was replaced as GOC MEF by General Sir Charles Monro a few days later, Kitchener sent Monro to the peninsula with special instructions to review the military situation and advise whether it would be better to evacuate or to continue operations.[3] On arrival Monro inspected the battlefields and, after consulting his corps and divisional commanders, recommended evacuation, detailing his reasons in a lengthy telegram on 31 October.[4] Of the three corps commanders, only Birdwood opposed the withdrawal.

One of the reasons behind Monro's recommendation was that the entry of Bulgaria into the war on the side of Germany and Austria-Hungary and the subsequent defeat of Serbia had opened reliable rail resupply routes between the Central Powers and the Ottomans. It was expected that this would pave the way for significant amounts of gun ammunition and heavy artillery to reach Liman von Sanders and the Ottoman *Fifth Army* at Gallipoli, making the success of future offensive action by the MEF more uncertain, and threatening the existing defences. These changing circumstances had already caused HQ ANZAC to issue a special order on 23 October calling for units to improve their defences by constructing dugouts that would provide better protection against artillery bombardment.[5]

An unidentified 18-pounder gun following the snowstorm on the night of 27 November (AWM P00821.011).

Monro's recommendations were received with consternation in London. In early November he was reappointed to command at Salonika, and Birdwood took his place as GOC MEF. Kitchener was despatched to Gallipoli to assess the situation for himself. After inspecting the defences and discussing the situation with all concerned, on 22 November he came to the same conclusion as Monro, telegraphing his views to the government that evening. The Dardanelles Committee accepted his recommendation, but a divided Cabinet procrastinated, and it was not until 7 December that an evacuation was formally approved.[6]

While this process was in train, the expected increase in Ottoman capability began to materialise. The first shipments of long-coveted gun ammunition arrived, with Liman von Sanders expressing the hope that the Ottoman artillery, previously inhibited by inferior shells, could now produce more than limited results. An Austro-Hungarian heavy howitzer battery, equipped with 240mm (9.2-inch) Morser (mortar, but howitzer in British nomenclature) went into action at Anafarta on 27 November, able to reach into the Suvla and Anzac areas.[7] HQ MEF operations staff noted that Ottoman artillery fire had ceased to be 'of promiscuous character with rapid variation of objectives' and become more systematic and controlled, which perhaps reflected Liman von Sanders' placement of the Ottoman artillery under the command of a German officer with Western Front experience from September onwards. HQ MEF also noted that, along with the 240mm howitzers, a few 105mm howitzers and a 12-incher had also made an appearance, commenting that these weapons had only fired on one day to that point, causing considerable damage at Lone Pine. The war diaries suggest that this was the bombardment of that position on 29 November.[8]

Planning the Artillery Embarkation

While London deliberated, in theatre HQ MEF began contingency planning, producing an outline scheme on 16 November. It envisaged an evacuation consisting of preliminary, intermediate and final stages, noting that the preliminary stage (all troops, animals and material not required for a winter defensive campaign) could be implemented 'without comment before definite sanction to a withdrawal is received'. The intermediate stage could then 'begin directly the policy of withdrawal is accepted.'[9]

It was perhaps this thinking that led to a secret memorandum from HQ MEF to HQ ANZAC on 18 November requiring eight of the Corps' 18-pounders to be withdrawn to reserve in Mudros as soon as practical, along with all non-essential artillery wagons and limbers. No reason was given. The memo also advised ANZAC that, on the arrival of the 5-inch howitzers for the 2nd AFA Battery, the 5th (City of Glasgow) Howitzer Battery was to be transferred to Suvla.[10]

At HQ ANZAC planning began in earnest after Birdwood's message to White on 22 November, and a detailed proposal was submitted to HQ MEF on 27 November.[11] It appears that the requirements of the MEF memorandum of 18 November were overtaken by the developing ANZAC proposal, for the 2nd AFA Battery's 5-inch howitzers were not landed, although its four 18-pounders and one of the 1st Battery's were taken off Anzac on 23 November.[12]

ANZAC's plans included deception arrangements designed to condition the Ottomans to a reduction in activity. These began before the Corps' evacuation proposal was submitted and included a 'silent stunt' from 6.00pm on 24 November until midnight on 27 November, during which there would be no firing. The ANZAC guns did not open fire until towards the end of this period, but infantry engaged Ottoman patrols approaching the front lines and Hobbs' war diary notes that HMS *Endymion* engaged the Olive Grove on 25 November, a navy monitor fired on enemy positions just south of Anzac the next day, and HMS *Grafton* engaged Ottoman guns further to the south on the last day. Napier JoÚston's reports show that his guns began firing again at 1.30pm on 27 November with an engagement of Chunuk Bair.[13]

The ANZAC proposal of 27 November divided the evacuation into two stages, reflecting the intermediate and final stages of the MEF outline plan. In Stage One everything surplus to the requirement to resist an attack would be withdrawn, and in Stage Two the remainder of the Corps would be evacuated over two nights (instead of the MEF outline plan of four nights), with materiel likely to be of use to the enemy destroyed. The proposal noted that, of the guns and howitzers then currently ashore, thirty-four could be removed immediately, leaving sixty-three in place. Of the latter, a further thirty-three would be removed during Stage One, together with a proportion of the ammunition. In Stage Two, 'a certain number of guns' would be removed, and the remainder destroyed.[14] In a preliminary move, the 54th (East Anglian) Division was withdrawn from Anzac. As he left, the divisional commander sent a note to Napier JoUston thanking him very heartily for his cooperation and assistance, 'and for the effective help your guns have always afforded us'.[15]

With London finally agreeing to the withdrawal from Anzac and Suvla on 8 December, Dardanelles Army, the new title of the former MEF, ordered the commencement of the intermediate stage, and followed this with an instruction released on 10 December. This listed 104 guns and howitzers, of which eight 18-pounders had already been evacuated; however these numbers did not account for one 6-inch howitzer and the 60-pounders of the 10th Heavy Battery, the latter being evacuated under IX

Corps arrangements. Of the remaining weapons, it was suggested that sixty-four be withdrawn during the intermediate period, and twelve 10-pounders on the first night of the final stage, with seventeen 18-pounders and four 5-inch howitzers left behind at the completion of the evacuation.[16] In practice, the evacuation of the artillery bore little resemblance to this instruction.

Pre-empting it, on 8 December, White instructed the NZ&A Division to prepare nineteen guns and howitzers for embarkation at short notice. The 1st Australian Division was told on 10 December to embark fifteen guns and howitzers, and the batteries from which they were to come.[17] It seems the senior gunners were kept somewhat in the dark. On 26 November Napier Joŭston, in his first reference to a withdrawal, recorded, 'Brig-General Cunliffe-Owen informed me this morning that half my guns must be withdrawn, which means no more fighting here.' On 9 December he wrote, 'In accordance with instructions issued orders for withdrawal of certain guns, commencing with 4-inch guns, to be placed on the beach ready for embarkation in a night', and on 11 December, 'Very nearly half my guns have been sent into Anzac for embarkation tonight. It looks very much like evacuation.'[18] The 1st Australian Divisional Artillery War Diary for

December is missing, and that for November makes no reference to planning for the guns to be evacuated.

With the need for secrecy paramount, it seems the detailed planning was undertaken at HQ ANZAC with Cunliffe-Owen advising on artillery matters, and the CRAs being told when and how many guns were to be withdrawn each night during the period 11 to 18 December. No detailed plan for the embarkation of the guns appears to have been drawn up. Instead, in three handwritten memos, issued by White one or two days before each stage of evacuation, Hobbs was told which guns were to be withdrawn for specific nights, and the batteries from which they were to come. Napier JoÚston received his instructions the same way. This suggests that, either the CRAs were left out of the planning, or the numbers had been arrived at through verbal discussions. Discrepancies between the number of guns nominated in the ANZAC instructions and the weapons listed as being withdrawn each night in the war diaries of the NZ&A Division and those extant AFA battery diaries suggests it was the former.[19]

Leaving Anzac

Likewise, the artillery brigade and battery commanders were taken by surprise. The 5th AFA Battery War Diary noted on 10 December, 'Orders received for 2 guns 1 officer & 20 men to leave and embark tomorrow night. No destination or reason furnished.' The 2nd AFA Brigade recorded on 11 December, 'During the night 11-12th-by orders from H.Q. 2 guns & personnel of this brigade (with others) were embarked for-destination unknown.' In the 8th AFA Battery, No 1 and 2 guns were taken from their newly constructed pits 'from which they had never fired' with 'a good deal of discussion taking place as to the nature of the move.' The next day, when its mess chef returned from Imbros, the battery discovered that he had been advised not to take any stores back to Anzac as 'we were going to evacuate'. On 12 December the 5th AFA Battery recorded, 'orders received entanglements of Turks are not to be destroyed. Indications point to a withdrawal from this position' and on 13 December, 'Evacuation expected but no orders.'[20]

The anomalies in the records, and several missing battery diaries, make calculating the number and timing of the guns withdrawn difficult. Tables 5 and 6 are based on the extant

AFA battery war diaries, the 1st AFA Brigade War Diary, and the NZ&A Division War Diary. In accordance with the 8 December directive, on the night 11/12 December, fifteen of the 1st Australian Division's guns and howitzers were embarked as instructed, while the NZ&A Division recorded that it embarked eighteen of the nineteen nominated.[21]

Presumably in an attempt to disguise the reduction in the number of guns, on 12 December the 1st Australian Division issued instructions that, in the event of an Ottoman general bombardment, howitzer batteries and concealed 18-pounders would retaliate vigorously on any enemy communications and rear trenches within the respective batteries' fire zones, while 18-pounders in open positions would remain inactive, but ready to fire in the event of an enemy assault. In addition, any battery commander locating hostile guns in action within his zone was to engage them immediately. As a means of preserving the impression of normality, gunfire was regulated to maintain the usual daily rate of fire from the reduced number of guns and, as weapons were withdrawn, some batteries erected dummy guns in the vacated pits.[22]

Following the embarkation of thirty-three guns and howitzers on the night of 11/12 December, the remainder of the ANZAC artillery was thinned out over a period of five nights commencing on the night of 14/15 December. Similarly, the headquarters staffs of the divisional artillery and AFA brigades began leaving on 11 December. Lieutenant Colonel Bessell-Browne, now commanding the 2nd AFA Brigade, assumed command of the remaining divisional artillery on the morning of 16 December, with the last members of the headquarters of the 1st and 3rd AFA brigades departing that evening. Napier JoÚston left on 18 December, embarking on HMS *Grafton* to supervise the ship's covering fire during the final stages of the evacuation. Bessell-Browne and his staff departed on the night of 18 December, presumably leaving control of the guns on the last day to each of the remaining battery commanders.[23]

Over the night 14/15 December, the NZ&A Division recorded that it withdrew two 4.5-inch howitzers and three 18-pounders, and on 15/16 December, three 4.5-inch howitzers and two 18-pounders. On 16/17 December two 6-inch howitzers, three 4.5-inch howitzers and seven 10-pounders embarked, while one 18-pounder was taken off on the night 17/18, and a 10-pounder the following night. According to the NZ&A Division this left six 5-inch howitzers, two 18-pounders, four 10-pounders and one 3-pounder HotcŠiss gun, and it recorded evacuating all except one 5-inch howitzer and the Hotcšiss gun, which were destroyed and rendered inoperable respectively, on the final night.[24] However, in instructions dated 18 December to the Rearguard Commander, Major General Andrew Russell (now GOC NZ&A Division), HQ ANZAC advised that there were three 5-inch howitzers remaining in the NZ&A Division sector, one each from B, C and D batteries of the 69th Howitzer Brigade RFA and two in the Australian sector.[25] These discrepancies highlight the apparent lack of an overall and detailed plan for the evacuation of the artillery, and the consequent inability of Corps headquarters to keep an accurate track of the number of guns and howitzers being withdrawn. This could have had consequences on their embarkation, with insufficient lighters and shipping available for the task on any one night.

Lines of 18-pounder gun limbers await evacuation near Williams Pier on North Beach. The steamer Milo is at the end of the pier, having been grounded there on 26 October to act as a breakwater. Suvla is in the far distance (AWM P01436.004).

In the 1st Australian Division, with one of the Heavy Battery's two 6-inch howitzers withdrawn in the initial evacuation on the night 11/12 December, the battery destroyed the 4.7-inch naval gun on the afternoon of 15 December and withdrew its remaining howitzer that evening.[26] Two of the four remaining 5-inch howitzers were also withdrawn. Interestingly, this program meant that, in the three days before the final withdrawal, there would be no 6-inch howitzer fire. These weapons played a prominent part in counter-battery duties, particularly around the Olive Grove, and their absence constituted a potential risk to the secrecy of the operation. The planners must have calculated that this was acceptable, as there had been previous periods when these weapons had not fired for a couple of days.[27]

The 4.7-inch naval gun of the Australian Heavy Battery following its destruction on the afternoon of 15 December. The right-hand wheel has been blown off, the barrel at the muzzle has been ruptured for several feet with an explosive charge, and the breech block has been removed to be taken off Anzac or dumped in a latrine. The barrel is now in the Australian War Memorial (AWM G01280).

The remaining 18-pounders of the AFA batteries were thinned out over the four nights 14/15 to 17/18 December. In the 1st AFA Brigade, only four guns remained: the 2nd AFA Battery's guns and one of the 1st Battery's had left the peninsula on 23 November, and on 11 December the 3rd AFA Battery had handed over two of its remaining guns on Russell's Top to the 1st AFA Battery, embarking the other two and one from the 1st Battery that night. This left the 1st Battery with four guns, two of its own on Plugge's Plateau and two of the 3rd Battery's on Russell's Top. One gun was withdrawn from Plugge's on 15/16 December, and one each from the plateau and Russell's Top on the night of 17/18 December, leaving one 18-pounder on the Top, along with one from the 1st NZFA Battery. In the 2nd AFA Brigade, the 5th AFA Battery withdrew one of its remaining two guns on 14/15 December, while the 6th withdrew its four guns one at a time over the four nights commencing on the night 14/15 December. The 4th AFA Battery's records are missing but ANZAC directed its remaining two guns be taken off on the night 16/17 December. In the 3rd AFA Brigade, the 7th AFA Battery withdrew its remaining three guns one at a time over the three nights commencing 15/16 December, while the 8th AFA Battery withdrew one of its two remaining guns on the night of 15/16, and the 9th Battery did the same on 14/15 December.[28]

By 18 December, only two 5-inch howitzers, four 18-pounders, a 3-pounder HotcŠiss and the

12-pounder anti-aircraft gun were left to cover the elements of the 1st and 2nd Australian divisions remaining in the old Anzac area. Of these, A Battery, 69th Howitzer Brigade RFA, and the 5th (City of Glasgow) Battery RFA each provided a howitzer, while the 1st, 5th, 8th and 9th AFA batteries provided one 18-pounder each.[29] With what remained in the NZ&A Division area, across the whole ANZAC frontage a thin screen of seven 5-inch howitzers, six 18-pounders, four 10-pounder mountain guns and two 3-pounders supported the remaining infantry in the event the Ottomans attacked.

The final day dawned foggy before becoming cloudy but fine and, as it passed, the Ottoman and Australian artillery shelled various points of their opposing sectors, while in the afternoon a hostile aircraft was driven off by the anti-aircraft gun.[30] The ANZAC gunners expended much of their remaining ammunition, with the three guns of the 5th, 8th, and 9th AFA batteries firing 242 rounds between them, and the other guns and howitzers an unknown amount. At 5.05pm the last artillery rounds were fired from Anzac, when the 8th AFA Battery sent '3 HE farewell rounds' into their old opponents in the Olive Grove battery.[31]

The 9th AFA Battery's No 1 Gun firing off its ammunition on 19 December 1915. During the day the gun fired 109 rounds (eighteen HE and ninety-one shrapnel), with the firing of the last nine rounds commencing at 4.40pm (AWM P00046.041).

Being largely emplaced in the relatively flat terrain, the New Zealanders were able to get the majority of their remaining guns away on the last night, manhandling the 18-pounder down Walker's Ridge from Russell's Top at 6.00pm. With positions on the steep ridges of old Anzac, the Australians were ordered to destroy their remaining 18-pounders and one of the 5-inch howitzers. The 1st AFA Battery gunners felt they could have taken their gun with them, but were refused permission, and a request by the 9th

AFA to bring off its gun was also rejected, the weapons in each case being old and worn. The guns were disabled by the removal of key components, some buried or dumped in the latrines, others, such as breech-blocks and sights, carried away by the detachments. Finally, engineers placed an explosive charge, not louder than that made by the discharge of a gun firing, in the breech and detonated it once the last party of infantry had passed the gun locations between 3.00am and 3.25am on 20 December.[32]

Altogether ANZAC reported that 99 guns and howitzers had been evacuated and ten destroyed in situ, although a detailed study of the documents suggests that 98 were embarked, including those which left prior to 11 December. Irrespective, it was an impressive achievement, especially with the CRAs seemingly left outside the planning process and receiving their instructions for each phase of the withdrawal at such short notice. Of the ten weapons left behind, the 4.7-inch gun, one 5-inch howitzer, four 18-pounders, a 3-pounder HotcŠiss and the anti-aircraft gun were destroyed by the 1st Australian Division, and a 5-inch howitzer was destroyed and a 3-pounder HotcŠiss rendered useless by the New Zealanders.[33]

The crew of the 9th AFA Battery's last gun (No 1) at Anzac on 19 December. At this stage the battery had two officers and ten other ranks in the Anzac beachhead (AWM P00046.032).

The gunners had been able to mask the reduction in the number of guns over the last week by maintaining a regular fire program with the few guns and howitzers remaining, and in some instances replacing withdrawn weapons with dummy guns. Liman von Sanders recorded after the war, 'One or another [Ottoman] artillery commander had noticed that in the last few days some batteries had fired one gun only or not at all, but no importance was attached to the fact, which therefore was not reported to superiors.'[34] According to Associate Professor

Mesut Uyar, Ottoman documents show that the commanders facing Anzac were unaware of the evacuation, a view echoed by Liman von Sanders: 'We of course knew nothing of the intended withdrawal and did not learn of it up to the last minute.... the very skilful beginning and execution of the withdrawal prevented its being seen from the front line of Turks.'[35] It had been a remarkable effort all round, with Napier JoÚston recording with some satisfaction that he had got all his guns, horses and mules away.[36]

CONCLUSION AND LESSONS

The Gallipoli campaign was a testing introduction to war for the Australian and New Zealand artilleries, a period of adaptation, innovation and education under arduous conditions. Expecting a campaign of manoeuvre, the gunners had to adjust quickly to a static battle waged day after day from positions that were largely overlooked by Ottoman observers. With a limited number of guns and a restricted ammunition supply they established satisfactory defensive arrangements before the attempts to capture the Sari Bair Range in August 1915 provided them the opportunity for offensive fire support, a challenge that was met with varying levels of success. A second period on the defensive followed before the campaign finished with a well-executed withdrawal.

The ANZAC artillery that regrouped in Egypt was a different force from the hastily trained body that had set out for the peninsula nine months earlier. It had encountered, but not fully resolved, many of the issues facing the successful employment of artillery in trench warfare: communications, command and control at division and corps, the importance of counter-battery work, and effective fire planning for the attack.

The limited resources that could be deployed in the beachhead and the terrain of Anzac meant there was little opportunity to gain experience with the massing of fire. There was still a lot to be learnt.

The limited time for training before the start of the campaign reflected government decisions pre-war to base the Australian and New Zealand armies on part-time forces raised through compulsory training. The schemes had been in operation for less than four years when the conflict broke out, and there had been little opportunity for unit or combined-arms training in any depth. In any case, legislation precluded members of these schemes being deployed overseas, and so when expeditionary forces were offered, they had to be raised from scratch and manned by volunteers. The commanders of the resulting AIF and NZEF artillery had significant permanent or militia experience, although not at the level demanded of them in their expeditionary appointments. At more junior levels a good number of former part-time gunners joined, but their experience was probably limited to battery procedures. The field artillery brigades and batteries of the expeditionary forces had little or no time for training at home before embarking for the war, and were reliant on the orderly and sequential training conducted in Egypt from December 1914 to March 1915 to develop the essential skills. The artillery commanders were satisfied with the standards reached, but even so, the training was limited by ammunition restrictions and the early deployment of the Corps to the Dardanelles.

For the campaign at Gallipoli both the 1st Australian and the NZ&A divisions were poorly resourced in terms of artillery. With a combined total of forty 18-pounder field guns, four 4.5-inch howitzers, and no heavy guns, the two divisions had less than four-fifths of the field guns and less than a quarter of the howitzers of a single British infantry division. In the event, the shallow and narrow Anzac beachhead with its steep terrain made finding suitable positions extremely difficult, and not all the field guns that were on hand could initially be landed, further limiting the support the gunners could provide. The paucity of howitzers severely restricted them in countering the enemy artillery, or providing a heavier weight of fire against the Ottoman entrenchments.

Many assumed naval gunfire would be able to provide the heavier and longer range fire required, but the assumption proved only partially valid. The front lines were too close for the ships to engage the forward Ottoman trenches, a situation exacerbated by the original maps of the area being insufficiently accurate for naval gunfire use. Ship ammunition supplies were also restricted, and some types were not useful for land targets. Throughout the campaign the navy was confined to the engagement of depth targets and hostile batteries, where it provided useful assistance. Close support remained the preserve of the artillery.

The landing of the Australian guns at Anzac Cove was beset by confusion, with the batteries trickling ashore over a period of thirteen days. The New Zealand landings were more orderly, perhaps reflecting the smaller number of batteries involved, perhaps more effective command arrangements, perhaps less difficulty in finding the fewer positions required.

The shallowness and ruggedness of the Anzac beachhead prohibited the field guns from adopting positions in sufficient depth to make best use of the 18-pounders, and thus robbed the artillery commanders of the potential to concentrate the fire of multiple batteries along the front line. To cover the front the 18-pounders had to be deployed on the ridge lines in a series of positions with restricted arcs of fire, and it took until early June before suitable locations were finalised. When they were, the weight of fire that could be developed at any one point was adequate but low, and further constrained by restricted ammunition supply.

In these positions the 18-pounders were not entirely suitable for the tasks facing them. They had no HE ammunition until August and, while their shrapnel was useful against exposed troops making an attack or moving in the open, and in support of a friendly attack could force Ottoman defenders under cover, it caused little or no material damage to their trenches. In addition, their flat trajectory—as with the flat trajectory of the naval guns—prevented them placing effective fire on Ottoman positions and guns concealed behind ridges and spurs. The artillery commanders recognised very early that additional howitzers were required and pressed Birdwood for them. They began arriving in limited numbers in mid-May with more in July, but they were of an obsolescent pattern and also suffered from ammunition restrictions.

The Ottomans held the high ground at Anzac, and the advantages this conferred in observation meant the Anzac guns could not be deployed in the open. ANZAC was fortunate that the Ottoman artillery suffered under ammunition restrictions, but even so it was quite capable of inflicting serious damage on visible targets. The ANZAC artillery was thus forced to adopt concealed and semi-concealed positions, using terrain to provide defilade, complementing this on the ridge lines by digging pits for the guns and dugouts for the detachments and ammunition. *Field Artillery Training* was prescient in noting that batteries would need to adapt their gun positions to the ground and use concealment in the defence.

In the first week at Anzac control of artillery fire largely resided at battery, section or even sub-section level. Faced with static trench warfare, and operating with two divisions in a confined beachhead, these practices dissipated the ability of the Corps artillery to effectively support the infantry across the whole front. A better system was required if the artillery of both divisions and the 7th IMA Brigade were to employ their fire to best effect and this led to calls for more centralised control of fire.

The problem in providing effective field gun fire was that the limited arcs of the batteries, combined with the benefits of using fire from a flank when the trench lines were so close, meant that front-line infantry brigades often got their most effective support from guns deployed in another infantry brigade area, or in another division. For howitzers, which could fire from depth positions and range across sections of the front, the problem was arranging access to their fire while retaining the ability to decide between competing demands. With its emphasis on mobility, pre-war artillery doctrine gave little consideration to centralised command and control and, with their minimal staffs, the Corps artillery adviser, Cunliffe-Owen, and the two divisional artillery commanders, Hobbs and Napier JoUston, were ill equipped to tackle the issue.

Despite this, each CRA initially established arrangements to provide support for the defensive sections manned by their division. Control across the divisional boundaries was attempted through coordination conferences between the two CRAs and Cunliffe-Owen for prearranged fire. Gradually an effective system developed based on command of the artillery at divisional level with delegation of control of fire such that each defensive section, with direct liaison between the local infantry and artillery commanders, could call directly on the fire of nominated artillery batteries with others on call through divisional arrangements. This system was effected through a comprehensive telephone net with redundancy of lines linking all the artillery headquarters, gun positions, infantry brigade headquarters and observation stations. It was not entirely efficient, in that it was based on cooperation between the two divisional artillery headquarters rather than overall Corps command, but it was the best that could be done.

Cunliffe-Owen was an adviser, not a commander, and he lacked the staff and resources to provide effective coordination.

As noted, while overall command and the coordination of the artillery remained at Division, control of the fire of field guns, and sometimes howitzers, was delegated to brigades to provide responsive support to the infantry within their defensive section. Infantry commanders could make their requests for fire direct to the field artillery brigade headquarters supporting them. Requests for support from the howitzers, the mountain guns, the Australian Heavy Battery and the guns of the other division had to go through the divisional artillery headquarters, although direct requests could be made in an emergency. These arrangements generally proved effective and were applied when additional howitzers of the RFA and heavy guns of the RGA arrived, and were progressively refined and expanded to cover the territory gained in the August Offensive. Fresh instructions on allocations of guns to support defensive sections were issued as late as 22 November 1915.

Manoeuvre at Anzac was inhibited by the terrain and within a week the front was stabilised with entrenchments along Second Ridge, Russell's Top and Walker's Ridge. Hamilton's decision in early May to place ANZAC on the defensive and concentrate offensive operations at Helles limited the Corps to defensive operations. Firepower became the dominant factor on the Anzac battlefield, and both sides showed they held sufficient within their entrenched infantry and its artillery support to repel the attacks of the other; ANZAC was assisted in this regard by naval gunfire support. Limited gains were achievable, but neither side could develop the superiority necessary for significant success.

In the employment of artillery, the Ottomans held a clear advantage in observation and the ability to conceal their guns and occupy different gun positions. They used their artillery not only to support their own attacks and repel those launched by ANZAC, but also to harass the ANZAC lines, headquarters and supply routes. Counter-battery fire thus became an important role for the Anzac gunners, one that assumed a level of importance unexpected in pre-war doctrine.

The ANZAC artillery responded as best it could. It was not well suited to the task in terms of equipment, but the concept of the time was that hostile batteries should be subdued rather than destroyed, and for this purpose proximate field gun shrapnel and howitzer fire had some utility. Every effort was made to locate Ottoman guns using flash and dust raised by firing, map appreciation and, occasionally, aeroplane spotting. Guns and howitzers registered the Ottoman battery locations within their arcs of fire. Crossfire from different batteries was used to try to increase effectiveness, and one battery would sometimes fire on the hostile batteries engaging a sister battery. More howitzers were gradually brought in to assist, an ad hoc heavy battery was formed within the 1st Australian Division primarily for counter-battery purposes, and further heavier artillery was landed after the August Offensive when the bridgehead enlarged. Naval gunfire was used throughout the campaign in the counter-battery role.

When the hostile batteries themselves could not be located, the Australian and New Zealand artilleries resorted to retaliatory shelling of the Ottoman lines. Overall, the best effect normally achieved was a temporary cessation of enemy fire. As long as the Ottoman ammunition supplies were not prolific this was an acceptable outcome, but it would not have sufficed in the face of the arrival of heavy howitzers and more plentiful ammunition resupply from Austria-Hungary and Germany from late November onwards. This deficiency was one of the reasons behind the decision at that stage to evacuate the Anzac position.

With the switch to offensive operations at Anzac in August 1915, another deficiency in early British doctrine was exposed by the nature of trench warfare and its stress on firepower. Pre-war, the artillery was considered to be an auxiliary arm, and this allowed infantry plans to be developed without consideration of the artillery's ability to adequately support them. Some such thinking had been evident in the plans for the landing itself, and it arose again in the planning for the August Offensive, where the Corps plans were developed with little real consultation with the divisional artilleries. The late issue of orders for the offensive, the decision to press ahead at the Nek with the original artillery support despite the changed tactical circumstances, late amendments to the fire support for the original attack at Hill 60 and the late issue of orders for the third attack, and Napier JoÚston's comment that General Godley, a divisional commander, had insufficient knowledge about the time it took to prepare a fire plan, were further indicators of a lack of appreciation on the part of commanders of the requirements necessary to provide effective fire support.

It is clear from the fire plans at Lone Pine, the Nek, Sari Bair and Hill 60 that the ANZAC formation and artillery commanders were on a steep learning curve in relation to planning fire support for assaults against entrenched positions, a problem their counterparts on the Western Front also confronted at this stage of the war. Detailed examination of the plans has identified instances in which the orders were not correctly implemented, reflecting the evolving nature of artillery staff work and a lack of understanding of the time necessary to implement a deliberate fire plan. At a more general level, with perhaps the exception of Lone Pine, all fire plans experienced difficulties in providing adequate coverage of essential targets and the weight of fire necessary to achieve the desired aim.

While it is easy in hindsight to identify such deficiencies, it should be acknowledged that the commanders were breaking new ground and elements of their plans were often sound in the light of later experience: suppression of the enemy immediately before the assault; covering fire during the assault, if possible against all the positions that might influence the point of engagement; interdiction of enemy reinforcements; and incorporation of a counter-battery plan. What told against them was a paucity of resources, as yet unrefined tecÚiques for locating the hostile batteries, a want of ammunition such as HE and smoke for the field guns, and a lack of experience—shared with the infantry—of the amount of fire required to at least neutralise an entrenched and determined foe.

The August Offensive took place at a time when pre-war concepts of suppression of the enemy to assist an attack were beginning to give way to attempts at destruction of the wire and fortifications protecting the enemy's firepower. The fire plans of the August Offensive and at Hill 60 probably aimed for suppression, which was perhaps the best that could be expected from the guns and ammunition available. However, there was some evidence of the emerging trend towards destruction in the explosion of mines at German Officers' Trench, the application of 500 rounds of howitzer fire to Hill 60 in the third attack, and the use of mines once more in the 54th Division's proposed plans for Hill 60 in November. For the formation and artillery commanders involved, this was the beginning of a period of trial and error in the application of offensive fire support that extended well into 1916 before the concept of suppression prevailed, per the medium of the creeping barrage.

Overall, the ANZAC artillery commanders performed competently, although Cunliffe-Owen has attracted criticism in some quarters for his lack of coordination of fire in the early days. This is valid to some extent but, as noted, he was an adviser without staff, not a commander, and lacked the means to take control. He also spent considerable time coordinating naval gunfire support, a necessary task for which the Corps had no other resource.

Napier Jo∪ston and Hobbs proved to be very solid divisional artillery commanders, determined to provide the best fire support possible with the limited resources and gun locations at hand. Their subordinate field artillery brigade and battery commanders played a similar part. It is fair to say that the ANZAC artillery commanders adapted quickly to difficult terrain and the conditions in which they found themselves and, learning both from doctrine and operational experience, developed innovative solutions to the problems and hostile artillery fire that confronted them. Together these officers would provide the backbone of the Australian and New Zealand artillery command structure over the remaining three years of the war, many rising to higher ranks and responsibilities (see Appendix 6). The gunners they commanded earned the admiration of their colleagues as guns and ammunition were hauled up onto the ridges, positions were developed in unfavourable terrain, and support was provided even while under fire. Mistakes were made, occasional rounds landed short, but overall the ANZAC gunners built confidence and trust in their arm.

The experiences at Anzac showed that forces should be thoroughly trained before being committed to operations. For the artillery, technical training forms the foundation, but technical proficiency must be accompanied by tactical proficiency, and the whole command and control system must be trained and exercised in a variety of operational scenarios if fire support is to be rendered effectively and quickly. Indeed, as with infantry and armoured tactics, various artillery tactics need to be considered and practised during training.

Anzac demonstrated the need for coordination between the artillery commands of different formation headquarters and nationalities. There is also a need to ensure that commanders at all levels understand the capabilities and tactical employment of the fire support available. The gunners should play a pivotal role in planning for operations, and be integrated into the initial planning teams. For their part, the gunners must keep abreast of emerging developments in fire support and consider how the artillery might adapt both organisationally and tactically.

To underpin training and education there is a requirement for well-considered doctrine. The exact circumstances of the next deployment cannot be predicted, and doctrine will not accurately reflect how to fight in a future conflict. Nonetheless, thoughtful guidance will provide a sound platform on which to start, and from which to adapt under operational conditions. Just as the flexibility in *Field Artillery Training* proved useful at Gallipoli, modern doctrine needs to be supple enough to cover a range of operational scenarios and provide a sound framework for intelligent thought and action appropriate to the tactical situation, noting Kiggell's remarks that 'the problems of war cannot be solved by rules, but by judgement based on a knowledge of general principles.' In developing it, robust and continuing debate is required, based on pragmatic assessments of the conditions under which the artillery is likely to fight, and the weapons they are likely to employ. This debate should not be confined to the gunners alone. It needs to be undertaken in an all-arms and joint service environment and involve senior commanders, for it is they—like Birdwood and Godley, Bridges and Walker—who are ultimately responsible for the employment of effective fire support.

It is remarkable that, since the Vietnam War, no guns from the RAA or RNZA have been deployed in support of Australian or New Zealand troops, even when allied contingents have included artillery. Why has this been so?

Perhaps the deployed forces have been too small. Perhaps other nations or services have supplied the firepower required. A reason related to one of the authors by a very senior Australian officer was that the guns were not accurate enough, an extraordinary statement in light of the advent of guided munitions, British and American deployment of guns to recent Middle East operations, and the attachment of Australian gunners to British batteries in Afghanistan. It suggests a lack of understanding of current artillery capabilities that needs to be addressed in all-arms education and training, in the development of tactical doctrine, and in operational planning processes.

The principal lesson from the Gallipoli campaign was the need for adaptation and innovation. While sound training, adequate resources and well-considered doctrine will provide a firm basis for a deployment, they will not cover everything. As Cunliffe-Owen, Hobbs, Napier JoÚston and the artillery brigade and battery commanders found, new challenges will always emerge. The ability of today's gunners to adapt and bring innovative solutions to problems will be crucial in providing effective fire support.

APPENDIX I

GUNS AND HOWITZERS USED AT ANZAC

The BL 10-pounder mountain gun (AAHU image).

BL 10-Pounder Mountain Gun

Calibre	2.75 inches (70 millimetres)
Barrel lengt	76.4 inches (1.9 metres)
Weight	762 pounds in action (345.63 kilograms)
Breech Action	Three-motion interrupted screw
Recoil System	Nil
Ammunition	Separately loaded propellant charge and projectile
Shell Type	Common, Shrapnel, Star
Shell Weight	10 pounds (4.54 kilograms)

Elevation	-15 to +25 degrees
On-carriage Traverse	Nil
Range	Shrapnel 3700 yards (3383 metres); HE 6000 yards (5486 metres)
Rate of Fire	Not recorded in data book. Served using a bag charge, fired with a friction tube and no recoil system, it would leap back after firing, slowing the potential rate of fire
Detachment	One NCO and five gunners

The BL 10-pounder mountain gun was introduced in the early 1900s to replace the 2.5-inch Rifled Muzzle Loading (RML) mountain gun, which was outranged during the South African War. The barrel came in two pieces which were screwed together when coming into action. When carried on pack animals the gun was broken down into four loads: two for the barrel, one for the trail and one for the wheels. These guns were organised into six-gun batteries and were normally used in the direct-fire mode.

The QF 18-pounder Mk I and Mk II field gun (AAHU image).

QF 18-pounder Mk I and Mk II Field Gun

Calibre	3.3 inches (83.8 millimetres)
Barrel length	97 inches (2.46 metres)
Weight	2821 pounds (1281 kilograms)
Breech Action	Single motion interrupted Welin screw with case extractor
Recoil System	Mk I Hydro-Spring; Mk II Hyrdo-pneumatic
Ammunition	Fixed cartridge case and projectile
Shell Type	At Anzac Shrapnel, and later HE
Shell Weight	18.5 pounds (8.39 kilograms)
Elevation	-5 to +16 degrees
On-carriage Traverse	4 degrees left and right
Range	Shrapnel 6525 yards (5966 metres)

Rate of Fire	20 rounds per minute maximum, 4 sustained
Detachment	One NCO and nine gunners for gun, two limbers, ammunition wagon and two horse teams.

The 18-pounder QF field gun was used by the RFA to support the infantry, while the QF 13-pounder gun of the Royal Horse Artillery supported the cavalry. Introduced in the early 1900s, the gun and its ammunition limber were drawn by a six-horse team and could be brought into action quickly. It could be manhandled if required and quickly repositioned. Since it was a gun as opposed to a howitzer, it had a relatively high muzzle velocity and correspondingly flat trajectory. It could be used in either the direct or indirect fire role.

The QF 4.5-inch howitzer (AAHU image).

QF 4.5-inch Howitzer

Calibre	4.5 inches (114 millimetres)
Barrel length	70 inches (1.78 metres)
Weight	3010 pounds (1365 kilograms)
Breech Action	Horizontal sliding block
Recoil System	Hydro-Spring with variable recoil. Recoil varied with elevation. Maximum of 40 inches at horizontal, reducing to 20 inches at 45 degrees.
Ammunition	Separately loaded cartridge case with variable charge weight, and projectile
Shell Type	At Anzac, HE and Shrapnel
Shell Weight	35 pounds (15.9 kilograms)
Elevation	-5 to +45 degrees
On-carriage Traverse	3 degrees right and left
Range	7330 yards (6700 metres) with streamlined shell. Non-streamlined had a maximum range of 6,600 yards (6035 metres)
Rate of Fire	4 rounds per minute
Detachment	One NCO and five gunners with four gunners in reserve to prepare ammunition and replace casualties.

The Ordnance QF 4.5-inch howitzer was the standard British field howitzer during the Great War. Unlike the field gun, the howitzer had relatively low muzzle velocity and fired at a reasonably high trajectory, allowing it to engage targets close behind ridges and in dead ground.

Introduced in 1909, the weapon was drawn by six horses. Along with its ammunition limber, it could be quickly brought into action.

The BL 5-inch howitzer Mk I (Wikipedia).

BL 5-inch Howitzer Mk. I

Calibre	5 inches (127 millimetres)
Barrel length	49 inches (1.24 metres)
Weight	2673 pounds (1212.45 kilograms) weight in action. Gun & breech 1,077 pounds (498 kilograms) and the total weight of gun and limber with 21 rounds, as towed by the horse team, was 5,216 pounds (2,216 kilograms).
Breech Action	Three motion, six segment interrupted screw
Recoil System	Hydro-spring and ground drag shoes
Ammunition	Separately loaded propellant bag and projectile
Shell Type	HE, Shrapnel, Case Shot, Star.

Shell Weight	50 pounds (23 kilograms) and 40 pounds (18 kilograms)
Elevation	-5 to +45 degrees
On-carriage Traverse	Nil
Range	4800 yards (4400 metres) 50 pound; 6500 yards (5900 metres) 40 pound
Rate of Fire	Not recorded in data book. Served using a bag charge, fired with a friction tube and the four spring recoil buffer was insufficient to halt movement. The sight was removed before each round was fired, then remounted and after which the gun was re-laid. These considerations slowed the potential rate of fire.
Detachment	One NCO and nine gunners, which includes the manning of the second horse team towing a limber and an ammunition wagon. Six at the gun during firing.

The BL 5-inch howitzer served with the RFA from 1896 to 1908, and with the Territorial Force Artillery before and during the Great War. It was introduced to provide the field artillery with a capability to fire explosive shells when the decision was made to arm field guns only with shrapnel. As the war progressed, the 5-inch howitzer was gradually replaced by the more modern 4.5-inch howitzer, which overcame these deficiencies.

The QF 4.7-inch gun (Wikipedia).

QF 4.7-inch Gun

Calibre	4.724 inches (119 millimetres)
Barrel length	194.1 inches (4.93 metres)
Weight	8418 pounds (3820 kilograms)
Breech Action	Single action Welin screw
Recoil System	Hydro spring supplemented by spring spade in ground
Ammunition	Separately loaded cartridge case and projectile
Shell Type	HE, Shrapnel
Shell Weight	46 pounds (20.8 kilograms)
Elevation	-6 to +20 degrees
On-carriage Traverse	Nil
Range	11,800 yards (10,790 metres)
Rate of Fire	5-6 rounds per minute

Detachment	One NCO and nine gunners.

Originally designed for naval and fortress use, the QF 4.7-inch gun was mounted on land carriages during the South African War, and thereafter remained in service as the heavy gun of the Territorial infantry divisions. Regular divisions were equipped from the early 1900s onwards with the BL 60-pounder gun, which gradually replaced the 4.7-inch gun in all divisions as the war progressed.

The 4.7-inch gun was not an easy gun to serve because of its weight and its relative instability on firing. Its lack of on-carriage traverse meant it had to be physically repositioned to make adjustments to the bearing required, and this was complicated by its use of a spade, which dug into the ground to help absorb the force of recoil.

The BL 6-inch, 30 cwt howitzer Mk I (Wikipedia).

BL 6-inch 30 cwt Howitzer (Mk I)

Calibre	6 inches (152.4 millimetres)
Barrel length	94 inches (2.39 metres)
Weight	7728 pounds (3506 kilograms)
Breech Action	Three motion interrupted straight screw
Recoil System	Hydro-spring and anchor stay to carriage wheels; optional drag shoes.
Ammunition	Separately loaded propellant bag and projectile
Shell Type	HE, Shrapnel, Star
Shell Weight	100 pounds (45.36 kilograms); 122.6 pounds (55.6 kilograms)
Elevation	-10 to +35 degrees mobile carriage; +35 to +70 degrees siege mount

On-carriage Traverse	Nil
Range	7000 yards (6400 metres) for the 100 pound projectile; 5200 yards (4755 metres) for the 122.6 pound projectile.
Rate of Fire	2 rounds per minute
Detachment	One NCO and nine gunners

Introduced in 1896 for siege work and to supplement the field howitzer, the BL 6-inch 30 cwt howitzer could be fired from its travelling carriage or from a static siege mount. As a high-trajectory weapon it was suitable for engaging targets in defilade or behind cover. Only a limited number of these guns were available when the Great War broke out, and they were gradually superseded in the heavy artillery by the more modern 6-inch 26 cwt howitzer.

The BL 60-pounder Mk I field gun (Wikipedia).

BL 60-Pounder Mk I Field Gun

Calibre	5-inch (127 millimetres)
Barrel length	13 feet 3 inches (4.04 metre)
Weight	9856 pounds (4470.5 kilograms)
Breech Action	Single motion, Welin screw with shot guide.
Recoil System	Hydro-spring constant
Ammunition	Separately loaded cartridge case and projectile
Shell Type	At Anzac HE, Shrapnel.
Shell Weight	60 pounds (27 kilograms)
Elevation	-5 degrees to +21.5 degrees
On-carriage Traverse	4 degrees left and right
Range	10,300 yards
Rate of Fire	2 rounds a minute
Detachment	One NCO and nine gunners

The BL 60-pounder Mk I entered service in the British Army in 1905, replacing the QF 4.7-inch gun. At nearly four and a half tons it was at the upper limit of what could be called a field gun drawn by horses. To distribute the weight of the gun during travel, the barrel and cradle could be slid to the rear.

One battery of four 60-pounders was allotted to the Divisional Artillery of the infantry divisions of the Regular Army. Neither the Australian

Citizen Force nor the New Zealand Territorial Force was equipped with these, and thus the Divisional Artillery of the 1st Australian Division lacked a 60-pounder battery.

APPENDIX 2

BREECH-LOADING AND QUICK-FIRING ARTILLERY

By the turn of the twentieth century, artillery pieces were loaded at the breech rather than the muzzle. This made loading faster and meant that the gun crew was less exposed. The major problem to be solved with breech loading was obturation: sealing of the breech to ensure that none of the gases generated by the burning propellant escaped rearwards.

Two solutions were developed. The first was the use of a partly threaded block that could be advanced into the breech and then rotated to engage threads in the breech itself. These blocks carried a compressible (obturator) pad to seal the breech face on firing. The alternative was to place the propellant charge in a metal cartridge case, which was inserted into the breech, held in place with a sliding breech block or a simple breech screw, and then ejected when the breech was opened after firing.

The Royal Artillery designated guns and howitzers using breech screws and obturator pads, such as the 5 and 6-inch howitzers used at Anzac, 'breech-loading' (BL) weapons.

In BL weapons the projectile and propellant, contained in fabric bags, were loaded separately. This was a practical solution for larger calibre weapons with their heavier projectiles, and for howitzers, where the use of propellant bags facilitated the use of differing charges to enable them to lob their shells onto a target. But, combined with other factors such as the need to swab out the breech between rounds, separate loading meant that rates of fire were relatively slow.

For the field artillery with its lighter projectiles, the impetus to field weapons with a higher rate of fire was provided by the introduction of the French 75mm cannon in 1898. This gun could fire fifteen rounds per minute. Other nations were quick to follow the tecŪology, which was initially based on the use of a propellant cartridge case fixed to the projectile and loaded as one piece, combined with a simple screw or sliding breech block mechanism to hold the complete round in place, an on-carriage recoil and recuperation system that meant the gun did not move on firing, and smokeless propellant that did not obscure the sights. Later versions allowed for the cartridge case to be loaded separately, or to be detached from the projectile so that the charge could be altered and then reattached before loading.

In British service, weapons using cartridge cases to seal the breech were designated 'quick firing' (QF). Examples used at Gallipoli were the QF 18-pounder, the QF 4.5-inch howitzer and the QF 4.7-inch gun.

Earlier BL weapons, such as the 5 and 6-inch howitzers, were not fitted with recoil mechanisms as effective as those on QF weapons, which again contributed to a slower rate of fire. This deficiency was addressed later in the war as more modern BL weapons were fielded.

APPENDIX 3

BRITISH ARTILLERY AMMUNITION

The Royal Artillery entered the Great War using anti-personnel shrapnel shells for its field guns, and both shrapnel and explosive rounds for its howitzers.

Shrapnel projectiles consisted of a thin-walled steel case with a time fuse in the nose and a metal tube, filled with compressed gunpowder pellets, running through the centre to a bursting charge in the base. The shell case was filled with balls manufactured from 'mixed metal', a compound of one part antimony to seven parts lead, set in resin. The 18-pounder shrapnel contained 375 such balls. When the fuse functioned a flash travelled through the central tube setting off the bursting charge, which blew off the nose of the shell and ejected the contents. The spin of the projectile caused the balls to fan out in a cone shape and strike in the target area at a similar velocity to the shell at time of burst.

Shrapnel was designed for use against troops in the open. In trench warfare it had little effect against fortifications or entrenched troops. But it could be used to cut barbed wire—although this was a slow and imprecise process—and to neutralise enemy defenders by forcing them to stay under cover. Attackers could move quite close behind a shrapnel barrage as the balls all travelled forward, no craters were created, and the smoke of the burst and the dust from the ball strike tended to obscure enemy vision.

Explosive shells became the preferred ammunition in trench warfare because of their destructive effect. In British service the shells consisted of a steel-walled body filled initially with gunpowder (common shells), then Lyddite (common Lyddite shells), and finally TNT mixtures (HE shells). These rounds were normally fitted with a fuse that activated on impact, although early in the war the rounds actually penetrated a little before fuse action was complete, particularly in soft or boggy ground, with the result that the blast was channelled upwards and caused cratering. The effectiveness of HE shells was enhanced when instantaneous fuses were introduced in late 1916, causing rounds to detonate at the surface. The shell walls then tore into fragments projecting in all directions, scything through wire and flesh.

Experience showed that entrenchments, deep dugouts and concrete emplacements were hard to destroy, even after protracted HE bombardment, which had the added disadvantage of cratering the battlefield and inhibiting the mobility of the attacking infantry. With the advent of the creeping barrage from 1917 onwards, HE was used more for neutralisation than destruction. Troops could not advance quite so close behind an HE barrage because some fragments were thrown rearwards.

The first 18-pounder HE rounds were produced in September 1914. Trial allocations arrived at Anzac in June 1915, and service allocations in August. Even then they were not large. Throughout the campaign the field guns were forced to rely on shrapnel, despite its limitations. At Gallipoli, both types of ammunition also suffered from manufacturing defects, a reminder that the campaign coincided with the rapid expansion of the munitions industry. During this period the quality of the shells and their fuses was often poor.

As the war progressed other types of rounds, such as smoke, star (illumination) and gas were also introduced into the field artillery.

APPENDIX 4

BRITISH ARTILLERY AT ANZAC

Equipped with 18-pounder field guns and only one 4-gun battery of 4.5-inch howitzers, and without the 60-pounders in a regular British infantry division, the Australian and New Zealand artillery at Anzac lacked the capability to effectively counter Ottoman batteries in defilade positions behind the hills and ridges or firing from long ranges. To correct this deficiency, Hobbs and Napier JoÚston lobbied for more howitzers and heavy guns to be sent to Anzac. On 16 May two 6-inch howitzers arrived, with one allotted to each division. Eventually another 6-inch howitzer and a 4.7-inch gun arrived, enabling Hobbs to form an ad hoc heavy battery as part of his divisional artillery. Clearly these weapons were insufficient and the shortfall was made up with artillery brigades and batteries from the British Army, the first of which arrived at Anzac on 24 June. These units from the Royal Field Artillery (RFA) and the Royal Garrison Artillery (RGA) fought alongside the Anzac gunners.

4th (Lowland) Howitzer Brigade RFA, 52nd (Lowland) Division

Formed on the creation of the British Territorial Force (TF) in 1908, the brigade comprised two batteries: the 4th (City of Glasgow) and 5th (City of Glasgow), both of which were equipped with four 5-inch howitzers. The brigade was allotted to the TF Lowland Division which, after the outbreak of war, became the 52nd (Lowland) Division. Initially employed on defence duties in the United Kingdom, the division's units sailed for Gallipoli between 18 May and 8 June. The 5th (City of Glasgow) Battery arrived at Anzac on 26 June, and the 4th (City of Glasgow) Battery and the brigade headquarters arrived in July. Incorporated into ANZAC, the brigade provided fire support to the 1st Australian and the New Zealand & Australian (NZ&A) divisions during the August Offensive. After the offensive the 5th (City of Glasgow) Battery was placed under the direct control of Hobbs and supported the 1st Australian Division, while the brigade headquarters and the 4th (City of Glasgow) Battery was sent to Suvla to support IX Corps.

69th Howitzer Brigade RFA, 13th (Western) Division

With the rush of volunteers to enlist following the declaration of war, units known as Kitchener's New Army were raised, the first flush known as the 'K1' units. Among these was the 69th Howitzer Brigade RFA, equipped with the old 5-inch howitzers originally organised into three 6-gun batteries. It was assigned as the howitzer brigade for the New Army 13th (Western) Division's divisional artillery. In February 1915 the brigade was reorganised into four 4-gun batteries designated A, B, C and D. With the impending August Offensive, the brigade was sent ahead of the division, arriving at Anzac from 15 to 19 July. A and C batteries were temporarily under command of the 1st Australian Division, and B and D under the NZ&A Division, where they supported ANZAC during the August Offensive. With the expansion of the beachhead, A Battery remained to support the 1st Australian Division, while B, C and D batteries moved into the enlarged area supporting the NZ&A Division.

10th Heavy Battery RGA, 11th (Northern) Division

The 10th Heavy Battery was a New Army unit raised in September 1914 and equipped with 60-pounder guns. Mobilised for war service in July 1915, it was despatched to the Dardanelles, arriving at the enlarged Anzac beachhead in early August 1915. Initially located near No 2 Outpost, it moved further north to a position west of Walden Point near the coast. Although it fired in support of the IX Corps attack on 21 August, it was not included in the NZ&A Divisional Artillery fire plan for the attack on Hill 60. Nonetheless, it supported ANZAC during the remainder of the campaign. The battery embarked from West Beach in the Suvla area over the period 4 to 6 December.

17th Siege Battery RGA

The 17th Siege Battery was formed on 1 February 1915 by the conversion of the Regular Army 17th Company RGA. Equipped with 6-inch howitzers, it departed the United Kingdom in July 1915 and arrived at Mudros in early August. The battery was sent to the enlarged Anzac beachhead in mid-September where it occupied a position in Taylor's Hollow in the enlarged

Anzac beachhead. From there one section primarily supported the 1st Australian Division, and the other the NZ&A Division until it was evacuated in December.

APPENDIX 5

THE ROYAL NAVY AT ANZAC

Other than the part it played prior to the commitment of military forces to Gallipoli, and at the landings on 25 April, the role of the Royal Navy has largely been forgotten in the subsequent historiography of the campaign. Yet throughout the next eight months ships of the Royal Navy's 2nd and 3rd naval squadrons supported ANZAC, and the latter covered the evacuation in December. Primarily they provided naval gunfire support. Due to the flat trajectory of the armaments the ships carried, the weight of shell thrown ashore, inadequate maps of the type required for close fire support, limited communications and difficulties with observation, this support was limited to engaging targets that could be seen from offshore, or targets in depth that were not concealed close behind the ridges and spurs.

Yet even with these limitations, the fire support the ships provided could be tactically decisive on occasions. During the major Ottoman counter-attacks on 27 April, HM Ships *Queen* and

Queen Elizabeth broke up the attack by two battalions of the *64th Regiment* as they swept over the crest of Baby 700 before they could engulf the most fragile portion of the ANZAC defence. Prior to the August Offensive the ruse at No 3 Outpost enabled the Auckland Mounted Rifles to seize the position with ease.

The ships that initially supported ANZAC comprised five battleships, one cruiser, eight destroyers, a seaplane carrier, a balloon ship, a submarine depot ship, and four trawlers. After the torpedoing of two battleships in late May, the remaining battleships were withdrawn from the theatre, and the job of supporting the troops ashore was undertaken by the cruisers and destroyers, with monitors arriving in June to provide a heavier weight of fire in lieu of the withdrawn battleships. Those ships known to have supported Anzac at one time or another are listed below.

Battleships

HMS *Canopus.* The lead ship of the Canopus class pre-dreadnought battleships, HMS *Canopus* was launched in 1897 and commissioned in 1899. Arriving in theatre in early 1915 she participated in the attempt to force the Dardanelles on 18 March and provided naval gunfire support to ANZAC during the major Ottoman attack on 19 May.

Length:	131.4 metres
Beam:	22.6 metres
Draught:	7.9 metres
Displacement:	14,500 tons
Main Armament:	Four BL 12-inch Mk VII guns in two twin turrets
Secondary Armament:	Twelve QF 6-inch guns (six on each side); ten 12-pounder guns, six 3-pounder guns; four 18-inch torpedo tubes.

HMS *London.* A subclass of the Formidable class battleships, HMS *London* was the lead ship of the London class pre-dreadnought battleship launched in 1899 and commissioned in 1902. Arriving in theatre after the attempt to force the Dardanelles, she supported the Anzac landings carrying 500 men of the 11th Australian Infantry Battalion from Lemnos as part of the first wave. *London* remained in theatre until late May when she was withdrawn and transferred to the Adriatic Squadron.

Length:	131.6 metres
Beam:	22.9 metres
Draught:	7.9 metres
Displacement:	14,700 tons
Main Armament:	Four BL 12-inch Mk IX guns in two twin turrets

Secondary Armament:	Twelve BL 6-inch Mk VII guns (six on each side); sixteen 12-pounder guns, six 3-pounder guns; four 18-inch torpedo tubes.

HMS *Majestic*. The first of her class, HMS *Majestic* was a Majestic class pre-dreadnought battleship launched in January 1895 and commissioned at the end of that year. She arrived in theatre on 24 February, taking part in the bombardment of the Ottoman forts and the attempt to force the Straits on 18 March. For the landing at Anzac she was one of the covering vessels, engaging Ottoman troops threatening to attack the left flank of the beachhead on the afternoon of 25 April. She continued to provide fire support in the succeeding weeks. *Majestic* was sunk off Cape Helles by *U-21* on 27 May with the loss of three officers and 70 seamen.

Length:	128 metres
Beam:	23 metres
Draught:	8.2 metres
Displacement:	14,890 tons
Main Armament:	Four 12-inch Mk VIII guns in two twin turrets
Secondary Armament:	Twelve 6-inch guns (six on each side); sixteen 12-pounder guns, twelve 3-pounder guns; five 18-inch torpedo tubes.

HMS *Prince of Wales*. A Queen class pre-dreadnought battleship, HMS *Prince of Wales* was launched in 1902 and commissioned in 1904. Arriving in theatre on 23 March, she did not participate in the attempt to force the Dardanelles. For the landing at Anzac, she carried 500 men of the 10th Australian Infantry Battalion from Lemnos as part of the first wave. *Prince of Wales* remained in theatre until 22 May when she was transferred to the Adriatic Squadron.

Length:	131.6 metres
Beam:	22.9 metres
Draught:	7.72 metres
Displacement:	14,150 tons
Main Armament:	Four 12-inch Mk IX guns in two twin turrets
Secondary Armament:	Twelve 6-inch guns Mk VII guns (six on each side); sixteen 12-pounder guns, six 3-pounder guns; four 18-inch torpedo tubes.

HMS Queen. A subclass of the Formidable class battleships, HMS *Queen* was a Queen class pre-dreadnought battleship launched in 1902 and commissioned in 1904. Arriving in theatre on 23 March, she did not participate in the attempt to force the Dardanelles. For the landing at Anzac, she carried 500 men of the 9th Australian Infantry Battalion from Lemnos as part of the first wave. She remained in theatre until 22 May when she was transferred to the Adriatic Squadron.

Length:	131.6 metres

Beam:	22.9 metres
Draught:	7.72 metres
Displacement:	14,150 tons
Main Armament:	Four 12-inch Mk IX guns in two twin turrets
Secondary Armament:	Twelve 6-inch guns Mk VII guns (six on each side); sixteen 12-pounder guns, six 3-pounder guns; four 18-inch torpedo tubes.

HMS *Queen Elizabeth*. The first of the Queen Elizabeth class battleships, HMS *Queen Elizabeth* was launched in 1913 and commissioned in December 1914. Regarded as a super dreadnought, she was the most modern and powerful of the ships engaged at the Dardanelles, becoming the flagship of the British Mediterranean Squadron. She participated in the initial attempts to reduce the Ottoman forts guarding the Dardanelles and the attempt to force the Narrows on 18 March 1915. *Queen Elizabeth* was withdrawn from the theatre in late May following the submarine threat to the battleships.

Length:	196.8 metres
Beam:	27.6 metres
Draught:	10.1 metres
Displacement:	31,500 tons
Main Armament:	Eight 15-inch Mk I guns in four twin turrets
Secondary Armament:	Sixteen 6-inch Mk XIII guns (eight on each side); two single 3-inch guns; four 21-inch torpedo tubes.

HMS *Triumph.* A Swiftshire class pre-dreadnought battleship, HMS *Triumph* was launched in 1903 and commissioned in 1904. She took part in the opening naval bombardment of the forts at the entrance to the Dardanelles in February 1915, and the attempt to force the Straits on 18 March. For the Anzac landings she was the guide ship with the role of establishing the position offshore for the landing in pitch darkness. Despite popular adherence to the view that the Australians were landed over one mile (1.6 kilometres) north of their intended landing site, this is a myth. Although *Triumph*'s position was further north than intended, the right flank of the Australian landing overlapped the left flank of the intended site by several hundred metres. She supported ANZAC until sunk by *U-21* off Gaba Tepe on 25 May 1915, losing three officers and 75 seamen.

Length:	144.9 metres
Beam:	21.7 metres
Draught:	8.3 metres
Displacement:	11,985 tons
Main Armament:	Four 10-inch Mk VII guns in two twin turrets
Secondary Armament:	Fourteen 7.5-inch Mk IV guns (eight on each side); fourteen 14-pounder guns, four 6-pounder guns;

HMS Vengeance. A Canopus class pre-dreadnought battleship, HMS *Vengeance* was launched in 1899 and commissioned in 1902. Arriving in theatre in January 1915, she participated in the naval operation to reduce the forts guarding the Dardanelles in February and March. *Vengeance* provided naval gunfire support to ANZAC during the major Ottoman attack on 19 May. She returned to Britain in June for a major refit.

Length:	131.4 metres
Beam:	22.6 metres
Draught:	7.9 metres
Displacement:	14,500 tons
Main Armament:	Four BL 12-inch Mk VIII guns in two twin turrets
Secondary Armament:	Twelve QF 6-inch guns (six on each side); ten 12-pounder guns, six 3-pounder guns; four 18-inch torpedo tubes.

Cruisers

HMS Bacchante. A Cressy class armoured cruiser, HMS *Bacchante* was launched in 1901 and commissioned in 1902. Transferred to the Dardanelles in March 1915, she was one of the covering ships for the Anzac landing. Closing to the point where her bow touched the bottom, *Bacchante* engaged the 87mm field gun at Gaba

Tepe on 25 April without suppressing it. She remained with the 2nd and later the 3rd naval squadron for much of the campaign, providing fire support to ANZAC, but was not present for the evacuation in December.

Length:	143.9 metres
Beam:	21.2 metres
Draught:	8.2 metres
Displacement:	12,000 tons
Main Armament:	Two single 9.2-inch Mk X guns.
Secondary Armament:	Twelve 6-inch Mk VII guns (six on each side); twelve 12-pounder guns, three 3-pounder guns; two 18-inch torpedo tubes.

HMS Dartmouth. A Town class light cruiser, HMS *Dartmouth* was launched in 1911 and commissioned later the same year. She was sent to the Dardanelles in February 1915 and took part in the diversion in the Gulf of Saros on 25 April. *Dartmouth* supported the attack on Baby 700 on 2 May, after which she was transferred to the 8th Light Cruiser Squadron in the Adriatic Sea.

Length:	131.1 metres
Beam:	14.5 metres
Draught:	4.72 metres
Displacement:	5,360 tons
Main Armament:	Eight BL 6-inch Mk XI guns;

| Secondary Armament: | Four QF 3-pounder guns; two 21-inch torpedo tubes. |

HMS *Endymion*

An Edgar class protected cruiser, HMS *Endymion* was launched in 1891 and commissioned in 1894. She arrived at the Dardanelles in late July 1915. For the August Offensive she was assigned to the 2nd Naval Squadron to support ANZAC. She continued this support after the offensive, also undertaking other tasks until the end of the campaign.

Length:	118.1 metres
Beam:	18.3 metres
Draught:	7.3 metres
Displacement:	7,350 tons
Main Armament:	Two single 9.2-inch Mk VI guns.
Secondary Armament:	Ten 6-inch Mk I guns (six on each side); twelve 6-pounder guns, four 18-inch torpedo tubes.

HMS *Grafton*

An Edgar class protected cruiser, HMS *Grafton* was launched in 1892 and commissioned in 1894. She arrived at the Dardanelles in late July 1915. For the August Offensive she was assigned to the 3rd Naval Squadron to support IX Corps at Suvla. On 27 August *Grafton* provided fire support for the third attempt to take the crest of Hill 60.

Length:	118.1 metres

Beam:	18.3 metres
Draught:	7.3 metres
Displacement:	7,350 tons
Main Armament:	Two single 9.2-inch Mk VI guns.
Secondary Armament:	Ten 6-inch Mk I guns (six on each side); twelve 6-pounder guns, four 18-inch torpedo tubes.

HMS *Talbot*. An Eclipse class protected cruiser, HMS *Talbot* was launched in 1895 and commissioned in 1896. She arrived at the Dardanelles on 27 March 1915 and was initially assigned to the 1st Naval Squadron where she supported the troops at Cape Helles. For the August Offensive *Talbot* was assigned to the 3rd Naval Squadron to support IX Corps at Suvla, and on 27 August she provided fire support for the third attempt to take the crest of Hill 60.

Length:	106.7 metres
Beam:	16.3 metres
Draught:	6.25 metres
Displacement:	5,690 tons
Main Armament:	Eleven 6-inch guns
Secondary Armament:	Six 4.7-inch Mk I guns (six on each side); six 3-pounder guns, three 18-inch torpedo tubes.

Monitors

HMS *Havelock.* An Abercrombie class monitor, HMS *Havelock* was launched in April 1915, commissioned in May and sailed for the Dardanelles in June. There she was assigned to the 2nd Naval Squadron and supported ANZAC for the remainder of the campaign.

Length:	102 metres
Beam:	27 metres
Draught:	3.1 metres
Displacement:	6,250 tons
Main Armament:	Two 14-inch guns
Secondary Armament:	Two 12-pounders.

HMS *Humber.* First of class, HMS *Humber* was a Humber class monitor launched in 1913 for the Brazilian Navy, but when Brazil could not afford to pay for her, she was commissioned into the Royal Navy in August 1914. Sent to the Dardanelles in July 1915, she was assigned to the 2nd Naval Squadron and supported ANZAC during the August Offensive, and thereafter until the end of the campaign.

Length:	81.3 metres
Beam:	15 metres
Draught:	1.7 metres

Displacement:	1,280 tons
Main Armament:	Two 6-inch guns
Secondary Armament:	Two 4.7-inch Mk I guns, four 3-pounder guns.

M15. First of class (M15), *M15* was ordered in March 1915, launched in April and commissioned in June. Like the rest of her class, *M15*'s biggest drawback was her lively motion at sea which impaired her ability to carry out accurate bombardment. Sent to the Dardanelles, she was armed en route at Malta before joining the 2nd Naval Squadron supporting ANZAC for the August Offensive, and thereafter until the end of the campaign.

Length:	54 metres
Beam:	9.4 metres
Draught:	2 metres
Displacement:	540 tons
Main Armament:	One 9.2-inch Mk X gun
Secondary Armament:	One 12-pounder Mk I gun

M18. An M15 class monitor launched in May 1915 and commissioned in July, *M18* was sent to the Dardanelles and joined the 3rd Naval Squadron in October 1915, remaining in the Mediterranean theatre until October 1918.

Length:	54 metres
Beam:	9.4 metres
Draught:	2 metres
Displacement:	540 tons
Main Armament:	One BL 9.2-inch Mk X gun
Secondary Armament:	One 12-pounder QF Mk I gun; one QF six-pounder Mk I anti-aircraft gun.

M19. An M15 class monitor launched in May 1915 and commissioned in June, *M19* served at the Dardanelles from July to December 1915, when she was badly damaged by a gun explosion.

Length:	54 metres
Beam:	9.4 metres
Draught:	2 metres
Displacement:	540 tons
Main Armament:	One BL 9.2-inch Mk VI gun
Secondary Armament:	One 12-pounder QF Mk I gun; one QF six-pounder Mk I anti-aircraft gun.

M20. An M15 class monitor launched in May 1915 and commissioned in July, *M20* was sent to the Dardanelles, armed en route at Malta, and joined the 2nd Naval Squadron in time to support ANZAC for the August Offensive. Following the offensive, she continued to support ANZAC for the remainder of the campaign.

Length:	54 metres

Beam:	9.4 metres
Draught:	2 metres
Displacement:	540 tons
Main Armament:	One BL 9.2-inch Mk VI gun
Secondary Armament:	One 12-pounder Mk I gun

M33. An M29 class monitor launched in May 1915 and commissioned in June, *M33* joined the 2nd Naval Squadron in time to support ANZAC during the August Offensive. She continued to support ANZAC until the evacuation in December.

Length:	54.3 metres
Beam:	9.4 metres
Draught:	1.8 metres
Displacement:	355 tons
Main Armament:	Two 6-inch Mk XII guns
Secondary Armament:	One 6-pounder Mk I gun

Torpedo Boat Destroyers

HMS Beagle. The first of her class, HMS *Beagle* was a Beagle class torpedo boat destroyer launched in October 1909 and commissioned the following April. She was ordered to join the fleet at the Dardanelles on 26 March where, as part of the 2nd Naval Squadron, on 25 April she pulled the tows carrying portions of the 9th and 12th Australian Infantry battalions of the second wave. In the following days she provided fire support to ANZAC before departing to operate off Cape Helles. During the August Offensive, *Beagle* supported IX Corps at the Suvla landings and then helped cover the evacuation from Anzac Cove in December 1915.

Length:	84 metres
Beam:	8.5 metres
Draught:	2.6 metres
Displacement:	874 tons
Main Armament:	One BL 4-inch Mk VIII gun; three 12-pounder Mk I guns; two 21-inch torpedo tubes.

HMS *Bulldog*. Also a Beagle class torpedo boat destroyer, HMS *Bulldog* was launched in 1909 and commissioned in 1910. She joined the fleet at the Dardanelles in March 1915 and, following the August Offensive, she rotated with other destroyers on a 48-hour watch providing support to ANZAC until the end of the campaign.

Length:	84 metres
Beam:	8.5 metres
Draught:	2.6 metres
Displacement:	874 tons

| Main Armament: | One BL 4-inch Mk VIII gun; three 12-pounder Mk I guns; two 21-inch torpedo tubes. |

HMS *Chelmer.* A Thornycroft type River class torpedo boat destroyer, HMS *Chelmer* was launched in December 1904 and commissioned in June 1905. Assigned to the 5th Destroyer Flotilla, she proceeded to the Dardanelles in November 1914 and took part in the naval campaign to destroy the forts guarding the entrance to the Straits. Joining the 2nd Naval Squadron for the military landings, she landed portions of the 11th and 12th Australian Infantry battalions of the second wave. *Chelmer* provided naval gunfire support to ANZAC for the reminder of the campaign.

Length:	68.8 metres
Beam:	7.3 metres
Draught:	2.4 metres
Displacement:	550 tons
Main Armament:	One 12-pounder 12 cwt Mk I gun; three 12-pounder 8 cwt Mk I guns; two 18-inch torpedo tubes.

HMS *Colne.* A Thornycroft type River class torpedo boat destroyer, HMS *Colne* was launched in May 1905 and commissioned in June of the same year. She was assigned to the 5th Destroyer Flotilla and proceeded to the

Dardanelles in November 1914 and took part in the naval campaign to destroy the forts guarding the entrance to the Straits. Assigned to the 2nd Naval Squadron for the landings, she transported elements of the 9th and 12th Australian Infantry battalions of the second wave. *Colne* provided naval gunfire support to ANZAC for the reminder of the campaign.

Length:	68.8 metres
Beam:	7.3 metres
Draught:	2.4 metres
Displacement:	550 tons
Main Armament:	One 12-pounder 12 cwt Mk I gun ; three 12-pounder 8 cwt Mk I guns; two 18-inch torpedo tubes

HMS *Foxhound.* A Beagle class torpedo boat destroyer, HMS *Foxhound* was launched in December 1909 and commissioned in 1910. She was ordered to join the fleet at the Dardanelles on 26 March where, as part of the 2nd Naval Squadron, on 25 April she landed portions of the 9th and 12th Australian Infantry battalions of the second wave.

Length:	87 metres
Beam:	8.5 metres
Draught:	2.6 metres
Displacement:	874 tons

Main Armament:	One BL 4-inch Mk VIII gun; three 12-pounder Mk I guns; two 21-inch torpedo tubes.

HMS *Mosquito*. Also a Beagle class torpedo boat destroyer, HMS *Mosquito* was launched and commissioned in 1910. She joined the fleet at the Dardanelles in March 1915 and, following the August Offensive, rotated with other destroyers on a 48-hour watch providing support to ANZAC until the end of the campaign.

Length:	87 metres
Beam:	8.5 metres
Draught:	2.6 metres
Displacement:	874 tons
Main Armament:	One BL 4-inch Mk VIII gun; three 12-pounder Mk I guns; two 21-inch torpedo tubes.

HMS *Pincher*. A Beagle class torpedo boat destroyer, HMS *Pincher* was launched in March 1910. She joined the 5th Destroyer Flotilla at the Dardanelles in June 1915 and operated with it in the Mediterranean until December 1917.

Length:	84 metres
Beam:	8.5 metres
Draught:	3 metres
Displacement:	975 tons

| Main Armament: | One BL 4-inch Mk VIII gun; three QF 12-pounder Mk I guns; one 3-pounder anti-aircraft gun; two 21-inch torpedo tubes. |

HMS *Rattlesnake*. A Beagle class torpedo boat destroyer, HMS *Rattlesnake* was launched and commissioned in December 1910. She was with the 2nd Naval Squadron off Anzac providing intermittent naval gunfire and other support to ANZAC until at least the end of July 1915.

Length:	87 metres
Beam:	8.5 metres
Draught:	2.6 metres
Displacement:	874 tons
Main Armament:	One BL 4-inch Mk VIII gun; three 12-pounder Mk I guns; two 21-inch torpedo tubes.

HMS *Ribble*. A Yarrow type River class torpedo boat destroyer, HMS *Ribble* was launched in 1903 and commissioned in 1904. Assigned to the 2nd Naval Squadron for the landings, she transported elements of the 12th Australian Infantry battalion and the 3rd Field Ambulance.

Length:	70.5 metres
Beam:	7.1 metres
Draught:	3 metres
Displacement:	590 tons
Main Armament:	One 12-pounder 12 cwt Mk I gun; five 6-pounder Mk I guns; two 18-inch torpedo tubes

HMS *Scourge*. A Beagle class torpedo boat destroyer, HMS *Scourge* was launched in December 1909 and commissioned in 1910. She was ordered to join the fleet at the Dardanelles on 26 March where, as part of the 2nd Naval Squadron, on 25 April she landed portions of the 10th and 12th Australian Infantry battalions.

Length:	84 metres
Beam:	8.5 metres
Draught:	2.6 metres
Displacement:	874 tons
Main Armament:	One BL 4-inch Mk VIII gun; three 12-pounder Mk I guns; two 21-inch torpedo tubes.

HMS *Usk*. A Yarrow type River class torpedo boat destroyer, HMS *Usk* was launched and commissioned in 1904. Assigned to the 2nd Naval Squadron for the landings, she transported elements of the 11th and 12th Australian Infantry battalions.

Length:	70.5 metres
Beam:	7.1 metres
Draught:	3 metres
Displacement:	590 tons
Main Armament:	One 12-pounder 12 cwt Mk I gun; five 6-pounder Mk I guns; two 18-inch torpedo tubes.

Seaplane Carrier

HMS *Ark Royal.* The first ship in history designed and built as a seaplane carrier, HMS *Ark Royal* was launched in September 1914 and commissioned three months later. On 1 February 1915 she sailed for the Dardanelles where her eight floatplanes provided reconnaissance missions during the naval campaign in February-March 1915, and prior to the landings in April. Assigned to the 2nd Naval Squadron, some of her aircraft provided reconnaissance and observation during the landings and the following days. Due to the submarine threat, *Ark Royal* was withdrawn to Imbros in late May where she became, in effect, a depot ship for all aircraft based there.

Length:	111.6 metres
Beam:	15.5 metres
Draught:	5.7 metres
Displacement:	7190 tons
Main Armament:	Four 12-pounder 12 cwt Mk I guns
Aircraft:	Eight floatplanes

Balloon Ship

HMS *Manica.* A converted cargo steamship, HMS *Manica* was the first kite balloon ship for the Royal Naval Air Service. Acquired in March 1915, she arrived at Lemnos on 14 April 1915. *Manica* was assigned to the 2nd Naval Squadron and supported the ANZAC landing on 25 April, sending up an observation balloon at 5.00am from which the two observers reported on the activities ashore for the next nine hours. She remained on station off Anzac, providing observation for naval gunfire support during the remainder of the campaign for both ANZAC and later IX Corps at Suvla.

Length:	80 metres
Beam:	10 metres
Draught:	7.6 metres
Displacement:	4247 tons
Main Armament:	One 12-pounder 12 cwt Mk I gun
Aircraft:	Balloon

APPENDIX 6

ARTILLERY COMMANDERS' SERVICE AFTER ANZAC

Gallipoli had been a severe training and educational ground for ANZAC's artillery commanders, but it held them in good stead for the even more rigorous conditions of the Western Front, and many went on to command at higher levels.

From November 1915 until the withdrawal from Cape Helles in January 1916, Charles Cunliffe-Owen served as the BGRA of the Dardanelles Army (former MEF), and then as the BGRA of I Anzac Corps in Egypt and France until replaced during the fighting at Pozières in July 1916. He commanded the 119th Infantry Brigade from August to November of that year, and the 54th Infantry Brigade from April to October 1917. Completely exhausted after the fighting at Third Ypres, he returned to England and retired from the Army at the end of the war.

Initially Talbot Hobbs remained CRA 1st Australian Division and was acting BGRA of I ANZAC from October to December 1916.

Promoted major general in January 1917, he assumed command of the 5th Australian Division, leading it until the conclusion of hostilities when he took over the Australian Corps from JoÚ Monash.

George Napier JoÚston became CRA of the newly formed New Zealand Division in early 1916, performing with distinction throughout the war, and acting as divisional commander when the incumbent was away. He was promoted major general in early 1919, assuming command of the New Zealand Division during its occupational duties on the Rhine.

The three Australian field artillery brigade commanders on Gallipoli went on to higher command:

- Evacuated ill in October 1915, Sydney Christian (1st AFA Brigade) was promoted temporary brigadier general in January 1916 and appointed CRA 5th Australian Division with the task of raising and training the divisional artillery. It deployed to France in June, and a month later participated in the Battle of Fromelles. Falling ill in January 1917, Christian was invalided to Australia in April.
- George JoÚston (2nd AFA Brigade) commanded the 3rd Australian Infantry Brigade during October-November 1915. In

January 1916 he was appointed CRA 2nd Australian Division, a position he held until November 1917 when he returned to Australia to attend to urgent business affairs.

- Twice wounded on Gallipoli, Charles Rosenthal (3rd AFA Brigade) was promoted brigadier general and appointed CRA 4th Australian Division in February 1916 before taking command of the 9th Australian Infantry Brigade in July. In May 1918 he was promoted major general and assumed command of the 2nd Australian Division, leading it for the remaining seven months of the war.

The two New Zealanders remained in command of their brigades:

- Frank Symon (1st NZFA Brigade) took his brigade to the Western Front until June 1918 when he assumed command of the New Zealand Field Artillery Reserve Depot in England. Returning to the Western Front in late October 1918, he resumed command of his old brigade.
- Francis Sykes (2nd NZFA Brigade) also took his brigade to the Western Front, where he commanded it until March 1918, when he transferred to the British Army.

Stuart Anderson, Hobbs' BMRA, commanded the 1st AFA Brigade from March to November

1916, when he was appointed Commanding Officer, I ANZAC Artillery School, before being promoted to become CRA 1st Australian Division from October 1917 to November 1918.

Eight of the nine Australian battery commanders achieved higher artillery commands, including three appointed as divisional CRA:

- Reginald Rabett (2nd AFA Battery) led the 12th (Army) AFA Brigade from March 1916 until the end of the war.
- Gifford King (3rd AFA Battery) temporarily commanded the 1st AFA Brigade from October 1915 until February 1916, when he took over the 10th AFA Brigade. In July he was transferred to England in charge of Reserve Brigade, Australian Artillery, and in May 1918 commanded the 8th AFA Brigade until after the armistice.
- Owen Phillips (4th AFA Battery) was promoted lieutenant colonel in March 1916 to command the 14th AFA Brigade, before being promoted temporary brigadier general in October 1917 and appointed CRA 2nd Australian Division, a position he held until the end of the war.
- Hector Caddy (5th AFA Battery) was promoted lieutenant colonel to command the 13th AFA Brigade, which he led throughout the war.

- George Stevenson (6th AFA Battery) went on to command the 12th Howitzer Brigade in March 1916, the 2nd AFA Brigade from January 1917, and the 3rd (Army) AFA Brigade from August 1917 until the conclusion of hostilities.
- Francis Hughes (7th AFA Battery) was promoted lieutenant colonel and took command of the 11th AFA Brigade in March 1916, before being transferred to command the 5th Divisional Ammunition Column from February 1917 until February 1918, when he returned to Australia to attend to his father's estate.
- Alfred Bessell-Browne (8th AFA Battery) took over the 2nd AFA Brigade in October 1915, leading it until January 1917 when he was promoted brigadier general and appointed CRA 5th Australian Division for the remainder of the war.
- William Burgess (9th AFA Battery) was a New Zealand PF officer on exchange in Tasmania when the war broke out. Rather than returning to New Zealand he enlisted in the AIF. With the end of the Gallipoli campaign, he was promoted lieutenant colonel in March 1916 to command the 3rd AFA Brigade, and in 1917 was promoted brigadier general and appointed CRA 4th

Australian Division, a position he held until hostilities concluded. After the war he returned to New Zealand as a PF officer, adopting the surname Sinclair-Burgess, and in 1931 was promoted major general and appointed Commandant and GOC New Zealand Forces.

The remaining two original New Zealand battery commanders went on to command artillery brigades in early 1916, when the New Zealand Division was formed:

- Ivan Standish (3rd NZFA Battery) was promoted lieutenant colonel to command the 3rd NZFA Brigade until June 1917, when he took command of the New Zealand Artillery Reserve Depot in England. Returning to the Western Front in June 1918, he took over the 1st NZFA Brigade from Symon, a command he held until October before returning to New Zealand.
- Norris Falla [4th NZFA (Howitzer) Battery] was promoted lieutenant colonel and appointed to command the 4th NZFA (Howitzer) Brigade until June 1917, when he assumed command of the 3rd NZFA Brigade vice Standish. In March 1918 he took over the 2nd NZFA Brigade when Sykes left to join the British Army, and in late October relinquished this post to

command the New Zealand Artillery Reserve Depot.

APPENDIX 7

ARTILLERY ORDERS OF BATTLE

1st Australian Divisional Artillery (October 1914-April 1915)

Headquarters 1st Australian Divisional Artillery

1st AFA Brigade

    Headquarters
    1st AFA Battery (New South Wales)
    2nd AFA Battery (New South Wales)
    3rd AFA Battery (New South Wales)
    1st AFA Brigade Ammunition Column

2nd AFA Brigade

    Headquarters
    4th AFA Battery (Victoria)
    5th AFA Battery (Victoria)
    6th AFA Battery (Victoria)
    2nd AFA Brigade Ammunition Column

3rd AFA Brigade

Headquarters
7th AFA Battery (Queensland)
8th AFA Battery (Western Australia)
9th AFA Battery (Tasmania)
3rd AFA Brigade Ammunition Column

1st Australian Divisional Ammunition Column

New Zealand Field Artillery Brigade (October 1914-April 1915)

Headquarters
1st NZFA Battery
2nd NZFA Battery
3rd NZFA Battery
4th NZFA (Howitzer) Battery (arrived February 1915)
NZFA Brigade Ammunition Column
Howitzer Battery Ammunition Column

1st Australian Divisional Artillery at Anzac (May-August 1915)

Headquarters 1st Australian Divisional Artillery

2nd AFA Brigade

Headquarters
4th AFA Battery (Victoria)
5th AFA Battery (Victoria)
8th AFA Battery (Western Australia)
2nd AFA Brigade Ammunition Column

3rd AFA Brigade

Headquarters
7th AFA Battery (Queensland)
9th AFA Battery (Tasmania)
3rd AFA Brigade Ammunition Column

Australian Heavy Battery (formed 14 July 1915)

Portion of 1st Australian Divisional Ammunition Column

New Zealand Field Artillery Brigade at Anzac (May-July 1915)

Headquarters
1st NZFA Battery
2nd NZFA Battery
4th NZFA (Howitzer) Battery
1x6-inch Howitzer (arrived 16 May)
NZFA Brigade Ammunition Column
Howitzer Battery Ammunition Column

Australian and New Zealand Artillery Units at Cape Helles (May-September 1915)

1st AFA Brigade

> Headquarters
> 1st AFA Battery (New South Wales)
> 2nd AFA Battery (New South Wales)
> 3rd AFA Battery (New South Wales)
> 1st AFA Brigade Ammunition Column

6th AFA Battery (Victoria) (departed Cape Helles 18 August 1915)

3rd NZFA Battery (departed Cape Helles 17 August 1915)

1st Australian Divisional Artillery at Anzac (October-December 1915)

Headquarters 1st Australian Divisional Artillery

1st AFA Brigade (arrived from Cape Helles on 1 October 1915)

Headquarters
1st AFA Battery (New South Wales)
2nd AFA Battery (New South Wales)
3rd AFA Battery (New South Wales)
1st AFA Brigade Ammunition Column

2nd AFA Brigade

Headquarters
4th AFA Battery (Victoria)
5th AFA Battery (Victoria)
6th AFA Battery (Victoria) (arrived from Cape Helles 19 August 1915)
2nd AFA Brigade Ammunition Column

3rd AFA Brigade

Headquarters
7th AFA Battery (Queensland)
8th AFA Battery (Western Australia)
9th AFA Battery (Tasmania)
3rd AFA Brigade Ammunition Column

Australian Heavy Battery

12-pounder anti-aircraft gun (arrived September)

Portion of 1st Australian Divisional Ammunition Column

Note: The 1st AFA Brigade was in reserve during October and the 2nd AFA Battery was not engaged at all during October-December as there were no gun positions available and the intention was to convert it to a howitzer battery.

New Zealand and Australian Division Artillery at Anzac (August-December 1915)

Headquarters New Zealand and Australian Divisional Artillery

1st NZFA Brigade

>   Headquarters
>   1st NZFA Battery
>   3rd NZFA Battery (arrived from Cape Helles 18 August 1915)
>   6th NZFA (Howitzer) Battery (arrived from Egypt 13 October 1915)
>   1st NZFA Brigade Ammunition Column

2nd NZFA Brigade

>   Headquarters
>   2nd NZFA Battery

5th NZFA Battery (arrived from Egypt 27 August 1915)
4th NZFA (Howitzer) Battery
2nd NZFA Brigade Ammunition Column.

1x6-inch howitzer

Daniell's Battery (August only, formed temporarily using excess 18-pounders)

Daltry's Battery (early August only, formed temporarily using excess 18-pounders)

ANZAC Corps Troops

7th Indian Mountain Artillery Brigade (March-December 1915)

> Headquarters
> 21st (Kohat) Battery
> 26th (Jacob's) Battery
> 7th Indian Mountain Artillery Brigade Ammunition Column

4th (Lowland) Howitzer Brigade RFA 52nd (Lowland) Division

> Headquarters (28 July-21 August 1915)

4th (City of Glasgow) Howitzer Battery (28 July-21 August 1915)
5th (City of Glasgow) Howitzer Battery (24 June-December 1915)
4th (Lowland) Howitzer Brigade Ammunition Column (portion arrived 24 June 1915)

Note: The 5th (City of Glasgow) Howitzer Battery was allotted to the 1st Australian Divisional Artillery from 24 June to 28 July until the 4th (Lowland) Howitzer Brigade headquarters arrived, then joined its parent brigade until allotted back to the 1st Australian Divisional Artillery after the 4th (Lowland) Howitzer Brigade headquarters and 4th (City of Glasgow) Howitzer Battery departed for Suvla on 21 August.

69th Howitzer Brigade RFA, 13th (Western) Division (July-December 1915)

- Headquarters
- A Battery
- B Battery
- C Battery
- D Battery
- 69th Howitzer Brigade Ammunition Column

Note: After the August Offensive, A Battery was allotted to the 1st Australian Divisional

Artillery and B, C and D batteries allotted to the NZ&A Divisional Artillery.

GHQ Troops Artillery

10th Heavy Battery RGA (August-December 1915)

17th Siege Battery RGA (September-December 1915)

4-inch gun battery, 24th Siege Brigade RGA (September-December 1915)

TABLE 1

LANDING OF GUNS AT ANZAC

25 April–7 May 1915

Date	Unit	Guns landed	Remarks
25 April			
10.00 am	26th (Jacob's) Battery	Six 10-pounder mountain guns	In action on 400 Plateau from 12.00 pm but forced out of action at 2.30 pm.
3.30 pm	4th AFA Battery	One 18-pounder field gun	In action at the southern end of MacLagan's Ridge at 6.00 pm engaging the Ottoman 87mm gun at Gaba Tepe.
6.00 pm	21st (Kohat) Battery	Six 10-pounder mountain guns	
Total Ashore			Twelve 10-pounder mountain guns and one 18-pounder field gun.
26 April			
3.00 am	1st AFA Battery	One 18-pounder field gun	Positioned on Shell Green and re-embarked that evening.
6.30 am	4th NZFA (Howitzer) Battery	Two 4.5-inch howitzers	Positioned at Anzac Cove.
am	4th AFA Battery	Three 18-pounder field guns	Two guns positioned on MacLagan's Ridge, one gun positioned on Shell Green until late pm then returned to MacLagan's Ridge. Ultimately formed a three-gun battery on McCay's Hill with one gun on MacLagan's Ridge.

Date	Unit	Guns landed	Remarks
12.00 pm	4th NZFA (Howitzer) Battery	Two 4.5-inch howitzers	Positioned on North Beach.
pm	5th AFA Battery	Two 18-pounder field guns	One gun positioned on MacLagan's Ridge, one gun sent to Shrapnel Gully.
pm	7th AFA Battery	Four 18-pounder field guns	Three guns positioned on Bolton's Ridge, later joined by fourth gun.
2.30 pm	8th AFA Battery	Two 18-pounder field guns	Dragged to a rendezvous and then re-embarked that evening.
pm	8th AFA Battery	One 18-pounder field gun	Landed but re-embarked that evening.
Progressive Total Ashore			Twelve 10-pounder mountain guns, fourteen 18-pounder field guns, and four 4.5-inch howitzers, of which four 18-pounder field guns were re-embarked that evening, leaving ten 18-pounders ashore.
27 April			
very early am	2nd NZFA Battery	Four 18-pounder field guns	One section positioned at Ari Burnu on 28 April, one section positioned on Plugge's Plateau on 30 April, both sections on Plugge's Plateau on 9 May.
Progressive Total Ashore			Twelve 10-pounder mountain guns, fourteen 18-pounder field guns and four 4.5-inch howitzers.
28 April			
pm	5th AFA Battery	Two 18-pounder field guns	Held in reserve until suitable gun position could be found. Initially two guns deployed separately opposite Wire Gully on nights 6/7 and 8/9 May but withdrawn. Battery then emplaced on MacLagan's Ridge. Three guns redeployed to the Razorback 23 May.

Date	Unit	Guns landed	Remarks
Progressive Total Ashore			Twelve 10-pounder mountain guns, sixteen 18-pounder field guns and four 4.5-inch howitzers.
30 April	1st NZFA Battery	Two 18-pounder field guns	Deployed to North Beach but withdrawn into reserve two days later. Battery finally established on Russell's Top on 17 May.
Progressive Total Ashore			Twelve 10-pounder mountain guns, eighteen 18-pounder field guns and four 4.5-inch howitzers.
1 May			
	1st NZFA Battery	Two 18-pounder field guns	Deployed to North Beach but withdrawn into reserve two days later. Battery finally established on Russell's Top on 17 May.
	8th AFA Battery	Four 18-pounder field guns	Battery positioned behind Lone Pine on 4 May.
	3rd AFA Battery	One 18-pounder field gun	Joined 9th AFA Battery.
Progressive Total Ashore			Twelve 10-pounder mountain guns, twenty-five 18-pounder field guns and four 4.5-inch howitzers.
7 May	9th AFA Battery	Three 18-pounder field guns	One emplaced on Brighton Beach on 14 May, and two guns employed as mobile section. By 7 June battery located in two locations: McCay's Hill and the next ridge south.
Total Ashore			Twelve 10-pounder mountain guns, twenty-eight 18-pounder field guns and four 4.5-inch howitzers.

Note: The 1st AFA Brigade (1st, 2nd and 3rd AFA batteries) and the 6th AFA and 3rd NZFA batteries were sent to Cape Helles on the night 3/4 May 1915, where they were incorporated into the British 29th Division until they returned to Anzac after the August Offensive.

TABLE 2

ALLOCATION OF GUNS IN IMMEDIATE AND ADDITIONAL SUPPORT OF THE 1ST AND 2ND AUSTRALIAN DIVISIONS, NOVEMBER 1915

Brigade	Immediate Support	Additional Support
5th and 7th Australian Infantry brigades	1st, 4th, 5th and 6th AFA batteries	A Battery, 69th Howitzer Brigade 17th Siege Battery one gun 26th (Jacob's) Battery
6th Australian Infantry Brigade	1st, 3rd and 7th AFA batteries A Battery, 69th Howitzer Brigade	A Battery, 69th Howitzer Brigade [sic] 17th Siege Battery
3rd Australian Infantry Brigade	7th AFA Battery	5th (City of Glasgow) Howitzer Battery
1st Australian Infantry Brigade	7th AFA Battery [sic]	5th (City of Glasgow) Howitzer Battery one gun 6th AFA Battery
2nd LH Brigade	6th[sic] and 8th AFA batteries 5th (City of Glasgow) Howitzer Battery **Note**: No mention of 9th AFA Battery and nomination of 6th AFA Battery possibly a typo in Table 1A	17th Siege Battery

Source: Table 1A HQ ANZAC General Staff Circular No 2 dated 22 November 1915

TABLE 3

ALLOCATION OF GUNS IN IMMEDIATE AND ADDITIONAL SUPPORT OF THE NZ&A AND 54TH (EAST ANGLIAN) DIVISIONS, NOVEMBER 1915

Source: Table 2 HQ ANZAC General Staff Circular No 2 dated 22 November 1915

Section/Division	Immediate Support	Additional Support
No 4 Section Left Flank (54th Division)	3rd NZFA Battery Section, C Battery, 69th Howitzer Brigade	2nd NZFA Battery 6th NZFA (Howitzer) Battery Section, B Battery, 69th Howitzer Brigade Section, C Battery, 69th Howitzer Brigade Section, D Battery, 69th Howitzer Brigade A and B batteries, 55th Howitzer Brigade (IX Corps) 26th (Jacob's Battery) — 4 guns Section, 17th Siege Battery
No 4 Section Right Flank (54th Division)	2nd NZFA Battery 6th NZFA (Howitzer) Battery Section, 17th Siege Battery Section, D Battery, 69th Howitzer Brigade Section, 4th NZFA (Howitzer) Battery two guns 21st (Kohat) Battery four guns 26th (Jacob's) Battery	3rd NZFA Battery C Battery, 69th Howitzer Brigade
NZMR Brigade Left Flank	Section, C Battery, 69th Howitzer Brigade	3rd NZFA Battery 4th and 6th NZFA (Howitzer) batteries Section, C Battery, 69th Howitzer Brigade Section, D Battery, 69th Howitzer Brigade

		4-inch Gun Battery, 24th Siege Brigade Section, 17th Siege Battery two guns 26th (Jacob's) Battery
NZMR Brigade Right Flank	B Battery, 69th Howitzer Brigade two guns 21st (Kohat) Battery	4th and 6th NZFA (Howitzer) batteries 5th NZFA Battery C and D batteries, 69th Howitzer Brigade Section, 17th Siege Battery two guns 26th (Jacob's) Battery
4th Australian and NZ infantry brigades	Section, 1st NZFA Battery 5th NZFA Battery Section, 4th NZFA (Howitzer) Battery	Section, 4th NZFA (Howitzer) Battery Section, 6th NZFA (Howitzer) Battery B, C and D batteries, 69th Howitzer Brigade 17th Siege Battery 4-inch Gun Battery, 24th Siege Brigade two guns 21st (Kohat) Battery
3rd LH Brigade	Section, D Battery, 69th Howitzer Brigade 4-inch Gun Battery, 24th Siege Brigade	4th NZFA (Howitzer) Battery one gun 21st (Kohat) Battery two guns 26th (Jacob's) Battery
1st LH Brigade	Section, D Battery, 69th Howitzer Brigade	4th NZFA (Howitzer) Battery 4-inch Naval Battery one gun 21st (Kohat) Battery two guns 26th (Jacob's) Battery

Note: In the source the 4-inch Gun Battery, 24th Siege Brigade is referred to as 4-inch Naval Battery.

TABLE 4

GUNS AVAILABLE FOR IMMEDIATE SUPPORT AT NIGHT IN EVENT OF ATTACK BY ENEMY, 1ST AND 2ND AUSTRALIAN DIVISIONS' SECTORS

Source: Table 1B HQ ANZAC General Staff Circular No 2 dated 22 November 1915

Zone	Number of Guns	Parent Battery
The Nek	Two 18-pounders	4th AFA Battery
Pope's Hill	Two 18-pounders	5th AFA Battery
Quinn's	Two 18-pounders	1st AFA Battery
Wire Gully to Owen's Gully	One 18-pounder	1st AFA Battery
	Two 5-inch howitzers	A Battery, 69th Howitzer Brigade
Lone Pine	Two 18-pounders	3rd AFA Battery
	Two 18-pounders	7th AFA Battery
Lone Pine to Ryrie's Post	One 18-pounder	6th AFA Battery
	Two 18-pounders	7th AFA Battery
	Two 5-inch howitzers	5th (City of Glasgow) Battery
Ryrie's Post to the Right of Line	Two 18-pounders	8th AFA Battery
	Two 5-inch howitzers	5th (City of Glasgow) Battery

TABLE 5

EVACUATION OF GUNS FROM 1ST AND 2ND AUSTRALIAN DIVISIONS' SECTORS

Nights 11/12/to 19/20 December 1915

	11/12 Dec	14/15 Dec	15/16 Dec	16/17 Dec	17/18 Dec	18/19 Dec	19/20 Dec	Destroyed	Unaccounted for but evacuated
1st Australian Divisional Artillery									
1st AFA Battery	1*		1		1				
2nd AFA Battery	left 23/11/15								
3rd AFA Battery	3				1#		1#		
4th AFA Battery				2					2
5th AFA Battery	2	1					1		
6th AFA Battery		1		1	1				
7th AFA Battery	1		1	1	1				
8th AFA Battery	2		1					1	
9th AFA Battery	2	1						1	
Australian Heavy Battery	1 x 6-inch howitzer		1 x 6-inch howitzer					1 x 4.7-inch gun	
12-pounder anti-aircraft									
3-pounder Hotchkiss								1	
TOTAL 1st Division	11	3	3	4	5	0	2	7	2
Corps Troops									
10-pounder mountain guns				1					
4th City of Glasgow Battery RFA	3	1						1#	
A Battery 69th Howitzer Brigade RFA	1						1#		
TOTAL Corps Troops	4	1	0	1	0	0	1	1	0
TOTAL	15	4	3	5	5	0	3	8	2

Note: 1* One 1st AFA Battery gun was handed to the 3rd AFA Battery and evacuated on the night 11/12 December; the fourth 1st AFA Battery gun was evacuated with the 2nd AFA Battery guns on 23 November.

1# Two 3rd AFA Battery guns were passed to 1st AFA Battery control on 11 December;

one was evacuated on 17/18 December and one destroyed.

18. There are conflicting reports as to whether one 5-inch howitzer was destroyed or two. The weight of evidence suggests one as the total guns destroyed at Anzac is given as ten, including two from the NZ&A Division, and all other guns destroyed are accounted for.

TABLE 6

EVACUATION OF GUNS FROM NZ&A DIVISION'S SECTOR

Nights 11/12/ to 19/20 December 1915

	11/12 Dec	14/15 Dec	15/16 Dec	16/17 Dec	17/18 Dec	18/19 Dec	19/20 Dec	Destroyed	Unaccounted for but evacuated
NZ&A Divisional Artillery									
18-pounders		1	1		1		1		1
4.5-inch howitzers		1	1	1					
6-inch howitzer	1								
3-pounder Hotchkiss								1	
TOTAL NZ&A Division	1	2	2	1	1		1	2	1
Corps Troops									
5-inch howitzers	6						1	1	
6-inch howitzers	1			2					
10-pounder guns				2		1	4		
4-inch guns	1								
TOTAL Corps Troops	10			4		1	5	1	
TOTAL NZ&A Division's sector	18	2	2	11	1	1	6	3	1
TOTAL 1st and 2nd Australian Divisions' sector	15	1	1	1	4	0	1	9	1
TOTAL ANZAC	33	10	10	12	1	1	12	10	1

Note: Figures derived from NZ&A Division War Diary, December 1915, which records number of guns evacuated each night, although one 18-pounder is unaccounted for but was evacuated.

GLOSSARY OF TERMS

TERM	MEANING
10-pounder	A mountain gun firing a 10-pound (4.54kg) shell. See Appendix 1.
18-pounder	A horse-drawn field gun firing a round weighing 18 pounds (8.39kg) and the standard field gun of the British and Anzac infantry divisions. See Appendix 1.
4.5-inch howitzer	A field howitzer of 4.5-inch (114mm) calibre. See Appendix 1. The standard howitzer of the British and Anzac infantry divisions.
4.7-inch gun	A medium gun of 4.7-inch (119mm) calibre. See Appendix 1.
5-inch howitzer	A field howitzer of 5-inch (127mm) calibre. See Appendix 1.
6-inch howitzer	A medium howitzer of 6-inch (152.4mm) calibre. See Appendix 1.
60-pounder	A heavy gun firing a round weighing 60 pounds (27 kilograms) — the heavy gun of a British infantry division. See Appendix 1.
50% zone	The distance straddling a target into which 50% of the rounds aimed at the target will fall. See also 'zone'.
Arc of fire	The arc in which a gun/howitzer is able to engage targets.
Artillery regiment	An Ottoman artillery unit comprising three battalions each of three batteries and commanded by a major.
Artillery battery	An artillery sub-unit consisting of a headquarters and four or six guns. Equivalent in organisational status to an infantry company. A British and Anzac battery numbered 145 all ranks and was commanded by a major.
Breech loading (BL)	In British service, a gun or howitzer in which the breech is sealed on firing using a breech screw fitted with a compressible obturator pad, and the round and propellant cartridge are loaded separately (see Appendix 2).
Brigade Major Royal Artillery (BMRA)	The principal staff officer at a divisional artillery headquarters, normally at the rank of major.
Brigadier General Royal Artillery (BGRA)	The artillery adviser at a corps headquarters.
Brigadier General General Staff (BGGS)	The Principal Staff Officer and Chief of Staff of a corps.
Calibre	The diameter of the bore of a gun or howitzer.
Close fire support	Artillery fire provided in close proximity to friendly troops.
Commander Royal Artillery	The commander of the divisional artillery. Also known as the divisional artillery commander. Normally a colonel.
Common shell	An explosive projectile filled with gunpowder. See Appendix 3.
Common Lyddite shell	An explosive projectile filled with the explosive Lyddite. See Appendix 3.
Corps	A formation consisting of a headquarters and a number of subordinate divisions as well as other allotted fighting and logistic troops, known as Corps Troops. Commanded by a lieutenant general.

Corps Troops	Units in a corps that are not part of a subordinate division, but under command of the corps, for example, heavy artillery, logistic and additional engineer units.
Counter-attack	An attack made by a defender to regain lost positions.
Counter-battery fire	Fire directed onto enemy artillery.
Covering fire	Artillery fire provided to cover the flanks and front of attacking troops during the assault on, and the consolidation of, the objective.
Covering force	A force that provides a screen to cover the main body. The role of the covering force is to delay and disrupt the enemy and prevent it from interfering with the main body.
Defensive fire	Artillery fire placed to protect a defensive position.
Defilade	A position that is hidden from observation and direct fire by cover or ground.
Demonstration	See 'feint'.
Direct fire	Fire relying on a direct line of sight between the gun and the target, and a calculation of range by eye or instrument.
Divisional Artillery Commander	The commander of the divisional artillery. Also known as the Commander Royal Artillery (CRA) of the division.
Doctrine	A frame of reference as to how military forces contribute to campaigns, battles and engagements. It comprises a guide to action rather than hard and fast rules.
Dreadnought	Ships introduced from 1906 onwards featuring all-big-gun armament schemes of uniform calibre.
Embrasure	An opening in a fortification designed to allow a weapon to fire out while the firers remain under cover.
Enfilade fire	Fire along the longest axis of a target, also known as flanking fire. Enfilade fire maximises the effect of the normal dispersion of artillery rounds along the line of fire of a weapon (see also 'zone').
Feint	An attack or manoeuvre designed to draw the enemy's attention away from the principal operation. Also known as a 'demonstration'.
Field Artillery Brigade	An artillery unit consisting of a headquarters, three batteries of horse-drawn field guns or howitzers, and a brigade ammunition column. Equivalent in organisational status to an infantry battalion and the equivalent of a modern artillery regiment. Numbering 626 all ranks it was commanded by a lieutenant colonel.
Field gun/field howitzer	A gun or howitzer with sufficient mobility to accompany an army in the field and be moved readily about the battlefield in response to changing circumstances. In British service, the calibre was usually below 150mm.
Fire plan	An artillery plan for the ordered engagement of specified targets with prescribed ammunition types at nominated rates of fire in support of an operation.
Fixed ammunition	Ammunition where the cartridge case containing the propellant is fixed to

	the projectile. Used with quick firing (QF) artillery (see Appendix 2).
Formation	A group of units under a controlling headquarters, for example, an infantry brigade, a division or a corps.
Gun	An artillery weapon designed to fire with a high muzzle velocity and a relatively flat trajectory.
Gun/howitzer section	A subordinate grouping within a battery, usually of two guns. Each gun was then known as a sub-section.
Heavy gun/heavy howitzer	Guns and howitzers of large calibre, usually greater than 155mm.
High explosive shell	An explosive shell filled with TNT or a compound of TNT with other material. See Appendix 3.
Hostile battery	An enemy battery.
Howitzer	An artillery weapon designed to fire with a lower muzzle velocity and an arcing trajectory so as to engage targets behind cover.
Indirect fire	Fire in which the target is not visible from the gun, relying on calculation of both an azimuth/bearing and an elevation angle.
Infantry (rifle) company	An infantry sub-unit of 227 all ranks consisting at the time of Gallipoli of a headquarters and four rifle platoons and commanded by a captain or a major.
Infantry battalion	An infantry unit consisting of a headquarters and four subordinate rifle companies and a machine-gun section. It numbered 1100 all ranks and was commanded by a lieutenant colonel.
Infantry brigade	An infantry formation consisting of a headquarters and four infantry battalions. It numbered around 4500 all ranks and was commanded by a brigadier general, although ANZAC infantry brigades were initially commanded by a colonel.
Infantry division	A formation consisting of a headquarters and three infantry brigades as well as integral support arms such as signals, artillery and engineers. A British or ANZAC division numbered around 18,000 all ranks and was commanded by a major general.
Harassing fire	Random, unpredictable and intermittent fire applied over time to inhibit the enemy's fighting ability by denying rest and interfering with resupply.
Heliograph	An instrument using reflected rays from the sun to send morse code as flashes of light
Infantry regiment	An Ottoman formation equivalent to a British infantry brigade and comprising three infantry battalions and an attached machine-gun company. Numbering 3300 all ranks, it was commanded by a lieutenant colonel or a colonel.
Lethal radius	The lethal area around a shell burst.
Light artillery	Guns and howitzers of smaller calibre, usually 105mm and below.
Light horse	The Australian term for mounted rifles. A mounted unit trained in all the cavalry functions except the mounted charge (shock action) and not mounted infantry as often incorrectly termed. See mounted rifles and mounted infantry.

	Organised into regiments each of three squadrons, which in turn are organised into four troops. The regiment was commanded by a lieutenant colonel and the squadron by a captain or major. Three light horse regiments form a light horse brigade. The light horse brigade was initially commanded by a colonel and by mid-1915 by a brigadier general.
Mediterranean Expeditionary Force	The allied ground force assembled under General Sir Ian Hamilton to fight the Gallipoli campaign.
Medium gun/medium howitzer	Guns and howitzers of medium calibre, usually 150 to 155mm.
Mountain artillery brigade	An artillery unit consisting of a headquarters and two or more batteries armed with mountain guns.
Mountain gun	A light gun designed for mountain warfare, capable of being broken into mule loads for carriage.
Mounted infantry	Infantry mounted on horses to provide them mobility. Not to be confused with light horse or mounted rifles.
Mounted rifles	Mounted riflemen trained in all the cavalry functions except the mounted charge (shock action). The New Zealand equivalent of the Australian light horse and organised along the same lines.
Neutralisation	The act of preventing the enemy manning his weapons effectively. Also known as 'suppression'.
Normal concentration	The area covered by the fire of a battery firing with parallel lines of fire.
Preparatory fire/ bombardment	Artillery fire in support of an attack prior to the actual assault.
Protective fire	See 'covering fire'.
Semaphore	The use of hand-held flags to spell out messages.
Semi-fixed ammunition	Ammunition where the propellant charges are contained in a cartridge case which can be separated from the projectile for charge selection and then re-fixed to the projectile for loading. Used with quick-firing (QF) artillery (see Appendix 2).
Separate ammunition	An ammunition system in which the round and propellant cartridge are loaded separately. Used with breech-loading (BL) artillery (see Appendix 2).
Shrapnel shell	A shell designed to burst in the air proximate to the target and expel a shower of lead-antimony balls into the target area. The fuse could be set to a time — to burst the rounds in the air — or to percussion — to burst the rounds on the ground. See also Appendix 3.
Star shell	A shell containing illuminating compounds.
Sub-unit	A subordinate grouping within a unit, for example, an infantry company, an artillery battery and a light horse or mounted rifles squadron.
Suppression	See 'neutralisation'.
Unit	A military organisation, predominately of a single arm or service, with self-contained administrative and command functions. Normally an infantry battalion or organisation of equivalent status.
Zero Hour	The designated time in an attack for the infantry assault to begin.
Zone	The normal dispersion of fire of a weapon when fired at the same bearing and elevation. There are zones for line and range, with the range zone the larger of the two. See also '50% zone'.

BIBLIOGRAPHY

Primary Sources

War Diaries

ANZAC General Staff War Diary 1915

ANZAC Administrative Staff War Diary 1915

Heavy Battery 1st Australian Division War Diary 1915

Mediterranean Expeditionary Force War Diary 1915

New Zealand Field Artillery Brigade War Diary 1915

New Zealand and Australian Division General Staff War Diary 1915

New Zealand and Australian Divisional Artillery War Diary 1915

New Zealand Infantry Brigade War Diary 1915

1st AFA Brigade War Diary 1915

1st AFA Battery War Diary 1915

1st Australian Divisional Artillery War Diary 1915

1st Australian Division General Staff War Diary 1915

1st Australian Division Administrative Staff War Diary 1915

1st Australian Light Horse Brigade War Diary 1915

1st Australian Light Horse Regiment War Diary 1915

2nd AFA Brigade War Diary 1915

2nd AFA Brigade Ammunition Column War Diary 1915

2nd AFA Battery War Diary 1915

2nd Australian Infantry Brigade War Diary 1915

2nd Australian Light Horse Regiment War Diary 1915

3rd AFA Brigade War Diary 1915

3rd AFA Brigade Ammunition Column War Diary 1915

3rd AFA Battery War Diary 1915

3rd Australian Infantry Brigade War Diary 1915

3rd Australian Light Horse Brigade War Diary August 1915

4th AFA Battery War Diary 1915

5th AFA Battery War Diary 1915

6th AFA Battery War Diary 1915

69th (Howitzer) Brigade RFA War Diary August to October 1915

7th AFA Battery War Diary 1915

7th Indian Mountain Artillery Brigade War Diary August 1915

8th AFA Battery War Diary 1915

8th Australian Light Horse Regiment War Diary August 1915

9th AFA Battery War Diary 1915

9th Australian Light Horse Regiment War Diary August 1915

10th Australian Light Horse Regiment War Diary August 1915

21st (Kohat) Mountain Battery War Diary April-May 1915

26th (Jacob's) Battery War Diary May 1915

Auckland Mounted Rifles War Diary August 1915

Wellington Mounted Rifles War Diary 6 August 1915

Otago Mounted Rifles War Diary August 1915

Note: All war diaries, except the 7th Indian Mountain Artillery Brigade and 69th (Howitzer) Brigade RFA, are in the AWM4 series on the Australian War Memorial website. The 7th Indian Mountain Artillery Brigade War Diary is at AWM 6 182 and 183, and the 69th (Howitzer) Brigade RFA War Diary is at the National Archives (UK) WO95/4301.

Personal Diaries, Papers and Evidence

Bean, Charles, Diary No 12 and Diary No 16, AWM 38 3DRL 606 series

Bean, Charles, Letters and Correspondence relating to the writing of the Official History, AWM38 3DRL 7953/27 Part 3

Fuzzard, George. Field Service Notebook (private collection)

Hobbs, Talbot, Diary, AWM PR 82/153 Item 1

JoÚston, Napier, Diary, Transcript provided by Dr Christopher Pugsley ONZM

Personal Papers of Lieutenant General J.J.T. Hobbs, AWM 3DRL/2600 Series 1 and 2

The Dardanelles Commission—Evidence given to the Commission, CAB 19/33 National Archives, Kew

Publications

General Staff, *Field Service Regulations, Part I Operations 1909* (reprint with amendments 1914), War Office. HMSO, London.

General Staff, *Field Artillery Training (Provisional) 1912*, War Office, HMSO, London.

General Staff, *Training and Manoeuvre Regulations, 1913*, War Office, HMSO, London.

General Staff, *Field Artillery Training 1914*, War Office, HMSO, London.

General Staff, *Field Service Pocket Book (1914)*, David and Charles reprints, 1971.

General Staff, *Infantry Training 1914*, War Office, HMSO, London.

General Staff, *Range Tables For The 18 Pounder QF Guns Mk I and II*, War Office, London.

General Staff, *Textbook of Service Ordnance 1923*, HMSO, London.

General Staff, *Textbook of Ammunition 1926*, HMSO, London.

Godley, Major General A.J., *Defence Forces of New Zealand-Report of the General Officer Commanding the Forces for the period from 29th June 1913 to 25th June 1914*, Record Number 39/19/14, Archives New Zealand.

Hamilton, General Sir Ian, *Military Forces of New Zealand-Report by the Inspector of Overseas Forces-1914*, New Zealand Defence Force Library, Wellington.

Handbook for the 18-pounder QF Gun, Land Service, 1915, HMSO, London.

Handbook for the BL 6-inch 30-cwt Howitzer Marks I and I*, 1915, HMSO, London.

Handbook for the 5-inch BL Howitzer, 1909, HMSO, London.

Kirkpatrick, Major General G.M., *Annual Report of Major-General G.M. Kirkpatrick CB Inspector-General of the Military Forces of the Commonwealth of Australia. 30th May 1913*, Record Number 68/87, Archives New Zealand.

Notes on Ammunition for the QF 13-pounder, QF 18-pounder and QF 4.5-inch Howitzer, Ordnance College, HMSO, London, 1915.

Notes on Close Shooting by Guns and Howitzers, Registration of Targets and Calibration (Confidential), WO 33/723, British National Archives (PRO) OLD.

Handbook for the 5-inch BL Howitzer, 1915, HMSO, London.

Range Tables for the 4.5-inch Howitzer, War Office, London.

SS139.4. Artillery Notes No 4, Artillery in the Offensive, February 1917, General Headquarters BEF, 1917 (copy available at AWM358.821ART).

Artillery Notes No 5, Wire Cutting, June 1916, General Headquarters BEF, 1916 (copies available in the Imperial War Museum, London).

Treatise on Ammunition (10th edn), War Office, 1915, reprinted by the Naval and Military Press in association with the Imperial War Museum.

Newspapers

The Argus (Melbourne), 19 October 1915,

The Colac Reformer, 25 September 1915.

Daily News (Perth) 5 February 1916

Evening Post (Wellington), 19 June 1920.

The Gippsland Mercury, 19 October 1915.

The Mornington Standard, 2 October 1915.

The Register, 27 August 1915.

Tatura Guardian, 12 October 1915.

Other

Anon, *9th Battery, Australian Field Artillery*, AWM 224, Manuscript 12.

Bessell-Browne, A.J., *Bessell-Browne on 8th Battery*, AWM 224, Manuscript 11.

Cass, W.E.H., 'Early events of the 2nd Infantry Brigade at Anzac 25.4.15', AWM 3 DRL 8042.

Divisional Artillery Communications, September 1915, AWM G7432. G1.S65, XVII.2.

Secondary Sources

Books

Aspinall-Oglander, Brigadier General C.F., *Military Operations. Gallipoli*, Vol. I, William Heineman Ltd, London, 1929.

_____, *Military Operations. Gallipoli*, Vol. II, Imperial War Museum/Department of Printed Books in association with The Battery Press, 1932.

Australian Dictionary of Biography, Vols 7, 9, and 11, Melbourne University Press, Melbourne, 1979, 1983 and 1988.

Badsey, Stephen, *Doctrine and Reform in the British Cavalry 1880-1918*, Ashgate Publishing, Burlington, 2008.

Batten, Simon, *Futile Exercise? The British Army's Preparations for War 1902-1914*, Helion, Warwick, 2018.

Beachham Kiddle, J., *War Services of Old Melburnians*, Melbourne, December 1915.

Bean, C.E.W., *Official History of Australia in the War 1914-18*, Vol. I, *The Story of Anzac* (3rd edn), Angus & Robertson, Sydney, 1937.

———, *Official History of Australia in the War 1914-18*, Vol. II. *The Story of Anzac*, Angus & Robertson, Sydney, 1924.

———, *Official History of Australia in the War 1914-18*, Vol. VI, *The AIF in France, 1918*, Angus & Robertson, Sydney, 1942.

———, *Gallipoli Mission*, Australian War Memorial, Canberra, 1952.

Bidwell, Shelford and Dominick Graham, *Firepower: British Army Weapons and Theories of War 19041-1945*, George Allen & Unwin, Boston and Sydney, 1982.

Bou, Jean, *Light Horse: A History of Australia's Mounted Arm*, Cambridge University Press, Cambridge, 2010.

Bowen, Timothy and Connolly Mark, *The Edwardian Army: recruiting, training and deploying the British Army, 1902-1914*, Oxford University Press, Oxford, 2012.

Breed, Florence (ed) *Gallipoli With Love 1915, Letters from the Anzacs of Wimmera*, History and Natural History Group of the M.L.A. Society, Inc, Victoria, Publication No 4, November 1993, pp.174-76.

Broadbent, Harvey, *Gallipoli, The Turkish Defence—The Story From Turkish Documents*, The Miegunyah Press, Melbourne, 2015.

Brook, David, (ed) *Roundshot to Rapier: Artillery in South Australia 1840-1984*, Investigator Press, 1986.

Burness, Peter, *The Nek, The Tragic Charge Of the Light Horse At Gallipoli*, Kangaroo Press Pty Ltd, Kenthurst, NSW, 1996.

_____, *The Nek: A Gallipoli Tragedy*, Exisle Publishing, Wollombi, NSW, 2012.

Burton, 2nd Lieutenant O.E., *The Auckland Regiment*, Whitcomb and Tombs, Auckland, 1922.

Bush, Captain Eric, RN, *Gallipoli*, George Allen & Unwin, London, 1975.

Byrne, Lieutenant A.E., *Official History of the Otago Regiment, NZEF in the Great War 1914-1918* (2nd edn), J. Wilkie and Co Ltd, Dunedin, nd.

Byrne, Lieutenant J.R., *New Zealand Artillery In The Field 1914-18*, Whitcombe and Tombs Limited, Auckland, 1922.

Callwell, Major General Sir C.F., *The Dardanelles*, Constable and Company, London, 1919.

Cameron, David W, *Sorry Lads, But The Order Is To Go—The August Offensive, Gallipoli, 1915*, University of New South Wales Press, Sydney, 2009.

———, *Gallipoli: The Final Battles and Evacuation of Anzac*, Big Sky Publishing, Newport, NSW, 2011.

Carlyon, Les, *Gallipoli*, Pan MacMillan Australia, Sydney, 2001.

Chambers, Stephen, *Anzac Sari Bair*, Battleground Gallipoli Series, Pen and Sword, Barnsley, 2014.

Cohen, Elliot A. and JoÚ Gooch, *Military Misfortunes: The Anatomy of failure in War*, The Free Press, New York, 1990.

Cooke, Peter and JoÚ Crawford, *The Territorials: The History of the Territorial Forces of New Zealand*, Random House, Auckland, 2011.

Coombes, David, *The Lionheart. A Life of Lieutenant General Sir Talbot Hobbs*, Australian Military History Publications, Loftus, NSW, 2007.

Corbett, Sir Julian, *Naval Operations*, Vol.2, Naval and Military Press reprint of the 2nd edn (1929).

Crawley, Rhys, *Climax at Gallipoli. The Failure of the August Offensive*, University of Oklahoma Press, 2014.

Crawley, Rhys and Michael Locicero, *Gallipoli: New Perspectives on the Mediterranean Force, 1915-16*, Helion, Warwick, 2018.

Cunningham, W.H., Treadwell, C.A.L. and S.H. Hanna, *The Wellington Regiment (NZEF) 1914-1919*, Ferguson and Osborn Limited, Wellington, 1928.

Dunlop, Colonel JoÚ K., *The Development of the British Army 1899-1914*, Methuen, London, 1938.

East, Ronald (ed), *The Gallipoli Diary of Sergeant Lawrence of the Australian Engineers, 1st A.I.F 1915*, Melbourne University Press, Melbourne, 1981.

Emery, Max, *They Rode into History: The Story of the 8th Light Horse Regiment Australian Imperial Force 1914-1919*, Slouch Hat Productions, McCrae, Vic, 2008.

Erickson, Edward J., *Gallipoli, The Ottoman Campaign*, Pen and Sword Military, Barnsley, South Yorkshire, 2010.

_____, *Gallipoli: Command Under Fire*, Osprey. Oxford and New York. 2015.

Erkal, Sukru, *A Brief History Of The Cannakale Campaign In The First World War (June 1914—January 1916)*, Turkish General Staff Printing House, Ankara, 2004.

Farndale, General Sir Martin, *History Of The Royal Regiment Of Artillery—The Forgotten Fronts And The Home Base 1914-18*, The Royal Artillery Institution, Woolwich, 1988.

Ferguson, Captain David, *The History of the Canterbury Regiment, N.Z.E.F. 1914-1919*, Whitcomb and Tombs Limited, Auckland, 1921.

Frame, T., *The Shores of Gallipoli—Naval Aspects of the Gallipoli Campaign*, Hale and Ironmonger, Alexandria, NSW, 2000.

Gilbert, Adrian, *The Challenge of Battle: The Real Story of the British Army in 1914*, Osprey, Oxford, 2014.

Hart, Peter, *Gallipoli*, Profile Books, London, 2011.

Hamilton, JoÚ, *Goodbye Cobber, God Bless You*, Macmillan, Sydney, 2004.

Henderson, Alan, Green, David and Peter Cooke, *The Gunners, A History Of The New Zealand Artillery*, Penguin Group, New Zealand, 2008.

Hickey, Michael, *Gallipoli*, JoÚ Murray, London, 1995.

Hogg, Ian, *Allied Artillery of World War One*, The Crowood Press Ltd, Marlborough, 1998.

Horner, David, *The Gunners: A History of the Australian Artillery*, Allen and Unwin, St Leonards, 1995.

James, Robert Rhodes, *Gallipoli*, Angus & Robertson, Sydney and Melbourne, 1965.

Jones, Spencer, *From Boer War to World War: Tactical Reform in the British Army, 1902-1914*, University of Oklahoma Press, 2012.

_____(ed), *Courage without Glory: The British Army on the Western Front 1915*, Helion, Solihull, 2015.

Knight, Doug, *Guns of the Regiment*, Service Publications, 2016.

Liman von Sanders, Otto, *Five Years in Turkey*, United States Naval Institute, Annapolis, 1927.

Longmore, Captain C., *The Old Sixteenth Being a Record of the 16th Battalion, AIF During the Great War 1914-1918*, History Committee of the 16th Battalion Association, Perth, WA, 1929.

Marble, Sanders (ed), *The History Of Warfare*, Vol.108, *King of Battle: Artillery In World War I*, Brill, 2016.

McGibbon, Ian, *The Path to Gallipoli: Defending New Zealand 1840-1915*, Department of Internal Affairs, GP Books, Wellington, 1991.

Olden, Lieutenant Colonel A.C.N., *Westralian Cavalry in the War: The Story of the Tenth Light*

Horse Regiment AIF in the Great War, 1914-1918, Alexander McCubbin, nd.

Pedersen, Peter, *Monash as Military Commander*, Melbourne University Press, Carlton, 1985.

_____, *The Anzacs: Gallipoli to the Western Front*, Penguin Viking, Camberwell, Victoria, 2007.

Pugsley, Christopher, *Gallipoli: The New Zealand Story*, Libra International, Auckland, 2014.

Roberts, Chris, *The Landing at Anzac, 1915*, Big Sky Publishing, Newport, NSW, 2013 (2015).

Robertson, JoÚ, *Anzac and Empire*, Hamlyn Australia, Port Melbourne, 1990.

Sefik Aker, *The Dardanelles: The Ari Burnu Battles and the 27th Regiment*, Istanbul, 1936.

Sheffield, Gary and Dan Todman, *Command and Control on the Western Front: The British Army's Experience 1914-18*, Spellmount, Staplehurst, 2004.

Simpson, Andy, *Directing Operations: British Corps Command on the Western Front 1914-18*, Helion & Company, Warwick, 2019.

Simpson, Cameron, *Maygar's Boys-A biographical History of the 8th Light Horse Regiment AIF 1914-19*, Just Soldiers, Military Research & Publications, Moorooduc, Vic, 1998.

Stevenson, Robert, *To Win the Battle: The 1st Australian Division in the Great War, 1914-1918*, Cambridge University Press, Cambridge, 2013.

Strong, P. and Sanders Marble, *Artillery In The Great War*, Pen and Sword Books Limited, Barnsley, South Yorkshire, 2011.

Stowers, Richard, *Bloody Gallipoli: The New Zealanders' Story*, David Bateman Ltd, Auckland, 2005.

Travers, Tim, *Gallipoli 1915*, Tempus, Charleston, 2002.

Trawin, Len, *Early British Quick Firing Artillery: Field and Horse*, Special Interest Model Books, 1998.

Treadwell, C.A.L. and Hanna, S.H., *The Wellington Regiment (NZEF) 1914-1919*, Ferguson and Osborn Limited, Wellington, 1928.

Turkish General Staff Ankara, *A Brief History Of The Cannakale Campaign In The First World War*

(June 1914—January 1916), Turkish General Staff Printing House, Ankara, 2004.

Turkish General Staff, *Birinci Dunya Harbinde Turk Harbi V Nci Cilt Canakkale Cepheisi*, 3 NCI Kitap, Ankara, Gnkur, Basimevi, 1978.

Uyar, Mesut, *The Ottoman Defence Against the ANZAC Landing, 25 April 1915*, Big Sky Publishing, Newport, 2015.

Waite, Major F., *The New Zealanders at Gallipoli*, Whitcombe and Tombs Ltd, Auckland, 1919.

Wilkie, Major A.H., *Official War History of the Wellington Mounted Rifles Regiment 1914-1919*, Whitcomb and Tombs Limited, Wellington, 1924.

Wilson, Graham, *Bully Beef and Balderdash*, Vol. II, Big Sky Publishing, Newport, NSW, 2017.

Book Chapters

Erickson, E.J., 'Ottoman Artillery In The First World War' in Sanders Marble (ed), *History of Warfare*, Vol.108, *King Of Battle: Artillery in World War I*, Brill, 2016.

Howard, Michael, 'Men Against Fire: The Doctrine of the Offensive in 1914' in Peter Paret (ed), *Makers of Modern Strategy from Machiavelli to the Nuclear Age*, Clarendon Press, Oxford, 1986.

Occasional Papers

Pugsley, Christopher, *We Have Been Here Before: the Evolution of the Doctrine of Decentralised Command in The British Army 1905-1989*, Sandhurst Occasional Papers No 9, Central Library, Royal Military Academy, Sandhurst, 2011.

Journal Articles

Brooke, Lieutenant Colonel A.F., 'The Evolution Of Artillery In The Great War', Parts I—VIII, *Journal Of The Royal Artillery*, Vol. LI, Nos 5 and 6, 1924/25; Vol. LII, Nos 1 and 3, 1925/26; Vol. LIII, Nos 1, 2, 3 and 4, 1926/27.

Bou, Jean, 'An Aspirational Army: Australian Planning for a Citizen Forces Divisional Structure before 1920', *Sabretache*, Vol. XLIX, No 1, March 2008.

C.G.A.E., 'Gallipoli Viewed From The Turkish Side', *Royal United Services Institute Journal*, Vol.68, 1923.

Cleverly, Jeff, 'More than a Sideshow? An Analysis of GHQ Decision Making during the Planning for the Landings at Suvla Bay, Gallipoli, August 1915', *War in History*, Vol.24, Issue 1, January 2017.

Cunliffe-Owen, Brigadier General C., 'Artillery At Anzac In The Gallipoli Campaign, April to December 1915', *Journal Of The Royal Artillery*, Vol. XLVI, Number 12, 1919/20.

Harrison, Major W.R.E., 'Gallipoli Revisited', *Journal Of The Royal Artillery*, Vol. LIX, Number 3, 1932/33.

Perry, Major Warren, 'Major General Sir Charles Rosenthal: Soldier, Architect and Musician', *The Victorian Historical Magazine*, Vol.40, Number 3, August 1969.

Roberts, Chris, 'The landing at Anzac: a reassessment', *Journal of the Australian War Memorial*, No 22. April 1993.

Rosenthal, Sir Charles, 'Correspondence Regarding General Cunliffe-Owen's Article On Artillery At Anzac In The Gallipoli Campaign', *Journal Of The Royal Artillery*, Vol. XLVII, Number 8, 1921.

Smith, T.F.A. (trans), 'A German Staff Officer On the Dardanelles Expedition', *Royal United Services Institute Journal*, Vol.62, 1917.

Stevens, Dr David, 'Naval Gunfire Support at Gallipoli', *Cannonball, Journal of the Royal Australian Artillery Historical Company*, Number 90, Spring 2015.

Websites and Website Articles/Books

'The Long Long Trail', The British Army in The Great War, at: http://www.longlongtrail.co.uk

'Statement On Artillery By Brigadier General Sir Hugh Simpson Baike, Ex-Commander Of The British Artillery At Cape Helles and Notes By Lieutenant Colonel Charles Rosenthal Relating To Artillery At Anzac From 25th April to 25th August 1915' in Hamilton, General Sir Ian, *Gallipoli Diary*, at: Gutenberg.org

Marble, Sanders, *The Infantry Cannot Do With A Gun Less; The Place Of Artillery In The BEF 1914-1918,* at: Gutenberg-e.org.

Pelvin, Richard, 'Sea Power at Suvla, August 1915: Naval Aspects of the Suvla Bay Landings and the genesis of Modern Amphibious Warfare' at: https://www.awm.gov.au/events/conference/gallipoli_symposium/pelvin/

Royal Australian Artillery: A Tasmanian Gunners' History at: www.vision.net.au/~pwood/6th-field.htm

Uyar, Mesut, 'The Ottoman Artillery At Anzac During The August Offensive', RAA Historical Company, Lessons from The Great War Seminar Series, Seminar 2, 26 August 2015 at: www.artilleryhistory.org

Unpublished Papers/Mss

Pickerd, Jeff, Chronological History of the 8th Light Horse Regiment 3rd Light Horse Brigade A.I.F. 1914-1919.

Uyar, Mesut, The Ottoman Army and the First World War, ms. (Published by Routledge, 2020.)

ENDNOTES

Chapter One

[1] General Report dated 3 May 1915 in 1st Australian Divisional Artillery War Diary, May 1915, AWM4 13/10/9, Part 1.

[2] Peter Cooke and JoÚ Crawford, *The Territorials: A History of the Territorial and Volunteer Forces of New Zealand*, Random House, Auckland, 2011, pp.135, 142—59.

[3] *Report of an Inspection of the Military Forces of the Commonwealth of Australia by General Sir Ian Hamilton* dated 24 April 1914, para 19, p.12, National Archives of Australia (NAA), Series No A5954, Item 830/1, hereafter *Hamilton Australian Report 1914*; Ian McGibbon, *The Path to Gallipoli: Defending New Zealand 1840-1915*, New Zealand Department of Internal Affairs, GP Books, 1991.

[4] Mounted rifles were trained in all cavalry tecÚiques except the mounted charge. This included screening, reconnaissance, providing vedettes (scouts) and advance, flank and rear guards, and dismounted

action with the rifle and machine-gun. They were not mounted infantry, as they are often mistakenly called. Mounted infantry were just that: infantry mounted on horses to provide mobility. The Australians called their mounted rifle regiments 'light horse'. For a detailed discussion on this topic see Jean Bou, *Light Horse: A History of Australia's Mounted Arm*, Cambridge University Press, Cambridge, 2010, pp.7, 8, 28, 184.

[5] Cooke and Crawford, *The Territorials*, p.159; McGibbon, *The Path to Gallipoli*, pp.195-96, 200.

[6] *Hamilton Australian Report 1914*, para 17, p, 11 and fn; Horner, *The Gunners*, p.69.

[7] *Defence Forces of New Zealand. Report of the General Officer Commanding the Forces for the Period From 7th December 1910, to 27th July 1911*, p.3; McGibbon, *The Path to Gallipoli*, pp.196, 202; Cooke and Crawford, *The Territorials*, p.167.

[8] *Military Forces of the Commonwealth. Report of the Minister for Defence on the Progress of Universal Training to 30 June 1912*, paras 4-5, AWM113 MH1/10A. Hereafter *Defence Minister's Report 1912*.

[9] *Annual Establishments of the Commonwealth Military Forces* for the 1st, 2nd 3rd and

5th Military Districts, AWM27/301/8; David Brook (ed), *Roundshot to Rapier: Artillery in South Australia 1840-1984*, Investigator Press, 1986, pp.44-45; Royal Australian Artillery: A Tasmanian Gunner's History at: www.vision.net.au/~pwood/6th-field.htm

[10] *Defence Minister's Report 1912*, para 86; *Hamilton Australian Report 1914*, Appendix E.

[11] *Defence Minister's Report 1912*, para 86.

[12] McGibbon, *The Path to Gallipoli*, p.195; Cooke and Crawford, *The Territorials*, pp.159, 163 and map p.174; *Hamilton Australian Report 1914*, para 12, p.10.

[13] For example, see Horner, *The Gunners*, pp.69-70.

[14] *Defence Forces of New Zealand. Report of the General Officer Commanding the Forces for the Period 28th June 1912, to 20th June 1913*, p.5, Record Number 39/19/14, Archives New Zealand.

[15] In Australia in February 1914 there were three officers and twenty-two other ranks of the PF available as instructors for the CF field artillery, and eleven other rank PF instructors for the CF garrison artillery. *Hamilton Australian Report 1914*, para 24, p.13.

[16] Ibid., para 155, p.38 and para 159, p.39.
[17] General Staff, *Field Service Pocket Book (1914)*, David and Charles reprints, 1971, Table 5, p.6, Table 12, pp.8—9.
[18] McGibbon, *The Path to Gallipoli*, p.195.
[19] Horner, *The Gunners*, p.70.
[20] Timothy Bowen and Mark Connolly, *The Edwardian Army; recruiting, training, and deploying the British Army 1902-1914*, Oxford University Press, Oxford, 2012, p.77.
[21] For consideration of these reforms see, for example, Spencer Jones, *From Boer War to World War: Tactical Reform in the British Army, 1902-1914*, University of Oklahoma Press, 2012; Stephen Badsey, *Doctrine and Reform in the British Cavalry 1880-1918*, Ashgate Publishing, Burlington, 2008, chapters 4 and 5.
[22] *Infantry Training 1902, Infantry Training 1905, Infantry Training 1911* and *Infantry Training 1914*, General Staff, War Office, HMSO, London; *Field Service Regulations, Part I, Combined Training, 1902*, and *Combined Training 1905*, General Staff, War Office, HMSO, London; *Cavalry Training (Provisional)*

1904, *Cavalry Training 1907*, and *Cavalry Training 1912*, General Staff, War Office, HMSO, London; *Field Artillery Training, 1904, Field Artillery Training (Provisional) 1912*, and *Field Artillery Training 1914*, General Staff, War Office, HMSO, London; *Manual of Military Engineering 1905*, General Staff, War Office, HMSO, London; *Field Service Regulations, Part I, Operations, 1909*, reprinted with amendments 1914, General Staff, War Office, HMSO, London; *Field Service Regulations, Part II, Administration, 1909*, reprinted with amendments 1914, General Staff, War Office, HMSO, London.

[23] Jones, *From Boer War to World War*, pp.150, 158; Horner, *The Gunners*, p.8; Shelford Bidwell and Dominick Graham, *Firepower: British Army Weapons and Theories of War 1904-1945*, George Allen & Unwin, Boston and Sydney, 1982, p.12, pp.19—21; Adrian Gilbert, *The Challenge of Battle: The Real Story of the British Army in 1914*, Osprey, Oxford, 2014, p.48.

[24] Bowen and Connolly, *The Edwardian Army*, p.104.

[25] Ibid., pp.75—76.

[26] Ibid., p.78.

[27] Dr Christopher Pugsley, *We Have Been Here Before: the Evolution of the Doctrine of Decentralised Command in the British Army 1905-1989*, Sandhurst Occasional Papers No 9, Central Library, RMA Sandhurst, 2011, pp.7—11.

[28] Quoted in Andy Simpson, *Directing Operations: British Corps Command on the Western Front 1914-18*, Helion & Company, Warwick, 2019 (2006), p.20.

[29] Bidwell and Graham, *Firepower*, pp.19—20. For a discussion of artillery in the pre-war period see *Firepower*, Chapter 1, 'The Artillery as an Accessory'; Bowen and Connolly, *The Edwardian Army*, pp.72—105.

[30] *Field Artillery Training (Provisional) 1912*, Sect 147, p.223; *Field Artillery Training, 1914*, Sect 146, p.231.

[31] *Field Artillery Training (Provisional) 1912*, Sect 190, p.282; *Field Artillery Training, 1914*, Sect 192, p.296.

[32] Bowen and Connolly, *The Edwardian Army*, pp.79—80.

[33] *Field Artillery Training, 1914*, Sect 146, pp.231—32.

[34] Bidwell and Graham, *Firepower*, p.12. See also Gilbert, *The Challenge of Battle*,

pp.47—48, for a discussion on problems with observing fire.

[35] *Field Artillery Training (Provisional) 1912*, War Office, HMSO, 1912, Sec 147, p.223, Sec 161, p.247; *Field Artillery Training, 1914*, War Office, HMSO, 1914, Sec 146, p.231, Sec 163, p.296; 'Practice Camps, 1912, and the Lessons to be Learnt from Them' and 'Lessons to be Learnt from the 1913 Practice Camps' reproduced in Sanders Marble, *The Infantry Cannot Do With A Gun Less; The Place Of Artillery In The BEF 1914-1918*, at: gutenberg-e.org

[36] *Hamilton Australian Report 1914*, p.23; *Annual Report of Major-General G.M. Kirkpatrick CB Inspector-General of the Military Forces of the Commonwealth of Australia. 30th May 1913*, Record Number 68/87, Archives New Zealand, p.10. Hereafter *Kirkpatrick Report*.

[37] Marble, *The Infantry Cannot Do With A Gun Less*, Chapter 2; *Field Artillery Training (Provisional) 1912*, Sect 151, p.230; *Field Artillery Training 1914*, Sect 153, p.240.

[38] Marble, Chapter 2; Bidwell and Graham, *Firepower*, p.20.

[39] Brevet Lieutenant Colonel A.F. Brooke DSO, 'The Evolution of Artillery in the Great War', Part IV, 'The Evolution of Artillery Organization and Command', *Journal of the Royal Artillery*, Vol. LII, No 3, 1925/6, p.377.

[40] Brevet Lieutenant Colonel A.F. Brooke DSO, 'The Evolution of Artillery in the Great War', Part I, 'The Artillery Situation in 1914', *Journal of the Royal Artillery*, Vol. LI, No 5, 1924/5, p.260.

[41] *Field Artillery Training 1914*, Sect 153, p.241.

[42] *Training and Manoeuvre Regulations, 1913*, General Staff, War Office, HMSO, London, Sect 43, p.77.

[43] Horner, *The Gunners*, p.77; Bidwell and Graham, *Firepower*, p.20; Brooke, 'The Evolution of Artillery in the Great War', Part IV, 'The Evolution of Artillery Organization and Command', p.377.

[44] Colonel JoÚ K. Dunlop, *The Development of the British Army 1899-1914*, Methuen, London, 1938, pp.130-40, 262.

[45] Bidwell and Graham, *Firepower*, p.21; Brooke, 'The Evolution of Artillery in

	the Great War', Part I, 'The Artillery Situation in 1914', p.261.
[46]	*Field Artillery Training 1914*, Sections 155 and 158.
[47]	Brooke, 'The Evolution of Artillery in the Great War', Part I, 'The Artillery Situation in 1914', pp.261-62.
[48]	*Field Artillery Training 1914*, Sec 156.
[49]	Ibid.
[50]	Brooke, 'The Evolution of Artillery in the Great War', Part I, 'The Artillery Situation in 1914', p.262.
[51]	Jean Bou, 'An Aspirational Army: Australian Planning for a Citizen Forces Divisional Structure before 1920', *Sabretache*, Vol. XLIX, No 1, March 2008, p.28.
[52]	Horner, *The Gunners*, p.71.

Chapter Two

[1]   C.E.W. Bean, *Official History of Australia in the War 1914-18*, Vol. I, *The Story of Anzac* (3rd edn), Angus & Robertson, Sydney, 1937, p.58; Horner, *The Gunners*, p.80; 1st AFA Brigade War Diary, August-December 1914—17, 19 and 23 August 1914, AWM4 13/29/1 Part 1; 8th AFA Battery War Diary, 14 August

1914, AWM4 13/70/1; 2nd AFA Battery War Diary, 24 August 1914, AWM 4 13/64/1.

[2] Cooke and Crawford, *The Territorials*, p.196; Lieutenant A.E. Byrne, *Official History of the Otago Regiment, NZEF in the Great War 1914-1918* (2nd edn), J. Wilkie and Co Ltd, Dunedin, NZ, p.5.

[3] 1st AFA Brigade War Diary, August-December 1914; 2nd AFA Brigade War Diary, January 1915, AWM4 13/30/3, and February 1915, AWM4 13/30/4; 3rd AFA Brigade War Diary, August 1914, AWM4 13/31/1, September 1914, AWM4 13/31/2 and October 1914, AWM4 13/31/3; 2nd AFA Battery War Diary, August 1914, AWM4 13/64/1, September 1914, AWM4 13/64/2 and October 1914, AWM4 13/64/3; 3rd AFA Battery War Diary, August 1914, AWM 13/65/1, September 1914, AWM 13/65/2 and October 1914, AWM 13/65/3; 6th AFA Battery War Diary, August-December 1914, AWM 4 13/68/1 and October 1914 to March 1915, AWM4 13/68/2; 7th AFA Battery War Diary, 20 August 1914-31 July 1915, AWM4 13/69/1 Part 1 and 20 August 1914-18 July 1915, AWM4

13/69/1 Part 2; 8th AFA Battery War Diary, August 1914, September 1914, AWM4 13/70/, October 1914, AWM4 13/70/3, November 1914, AWM4 13/70/4 and December 1914, AWM4 13/70/5.

[4] Byrne, *New Zealand Artillery In the Field 1914-18*, p.19; Major F. Waite, *The New Zealanders at Gallipoli*, Whitcombe & Tombs Ltd, Auckland, 1919, p.40.

[5] George Napier JoUston, Wikipedia; 'Unbroken War Record,' *Evening Post*, Wellington, 19 June 1920, p.6.

[6] A.J. Hill, 'Hobbs, Sir Joseph JoÚ Talbot' (1864-1938), *Australian Dictionary of Biography (ADB)*, Vol.9, Melbourne University Press (MUP), Melbourne, 1983.

[7] J. Whitelaw, 'Christian, Sydney Ernest (1868-1931)', *ADB*, Vol.7, MUP, Melbourne, 1979.

[8] Phyllis Ashworth, 'JoUston, George Jameson (1868-1949)', *ADB*, Vol.9, MUP, Melbourne, 1983.

[9] A.J. Hill, 'Rosenthal, Sir Charles (1875-1954)', *ADB*, Vol.11, MUP, Melbourne, 1988. Hill has Rosenthal commanding the 5th Field Artillery Brigade, but only the 1st and 2nd Field

Artillery brigades had been raised, with the 2nd being in Victoria. The 3rd Field Artillery Brigade was raised in Queensland in mid-1914.

[10] *Field Artillery Training 1914*, Chapter 1, Sects 6 and 8; 2nd AFA Battery War Diary, January 1915, AWM4 13/64/6 and February 1915, AWM 13/64/7; 4th AFA Battery War Diary, January 1915, AWM4 13/66/4 and February 1915, AWM4 13/66/5; 8th AFA Battery War Diary, January 1915, AWM4 13/70/6, February 1915, AWM4 13/70/7 and March 1915, AWM4 13/70/8; 9th AFA Battery War Diary, February 1915, AWM4 13/71/1 and March 1915, AWM4 13/71/2; Bean, *Official History*, Vol. I, *The Story of Anzac*, p.125; Byrne, *New Zealand Artillery In the Field 1914-18*, pp.16, 17.

[11] 1st Australian Division General Staff War Diary, October 1914 to February 1915, AWM4 1/42/1, Part 1; Transcript of the diary of Major General W.T. Bridges, 1 January 1915 to 23 April 1915, AWM digitised collection, RCDIG0001020; letters from Fred Leslie Biddle to his mother 1914/15, AWM digitised collection,

RCDIG0000202; letters From Norman Griffiths Ellsworth to his mother 1914/15, AWM digitised collection, RCDIG0000230; Byrne, *New Zealand Artillery In the Field 1914-18*, pp.16, 17; 1st Australian Divisional Artillery War Diary, January 1915, AWM4 13/10/6; 2nd AFA Brigade War Diary, January 1915, AWM4 13/30/3; 3rd AFA Brigade War Diary, January 1915, AWM4 13/31/6; 4th AFA Battery War Diary, 21 January 1915; *Field Artillery Training 1914*, Chapter 1, Sect 11.

[12] Quoted in Robert Stevenson, *To Win the Battle: The 1st Australian Division in the Great War, 1914-1918*, Cambridge University Press, Cambridge, 2013, pp.87-88; Horner, *The Gunners*, p.85.

[13] Brigadier General Charles Cunliffe-Owen, 'Artillery at Anzac In The Gallipoli Campaign', *Journal of the Royal Artillery*, Vol. XLVI, No 12, 1919/20, p.536.

[14] Sir Charles Rosenthal, 'Correspondence Regarding General Cunliffe-Owen's article on Artillery At Anzac In The Gallipoli Campaign', *Journal of the Royal Artillery*, Vol. XLVII, No 8, 1921, p.395.

[15] Cunliffe-Owen, 'Artillery at Anzac In The Gallipoli Campaign', p.537.

[16] Personal papers of Lieutenant General J.T.T. Hobbs, AWM 3DRL2600, Series 1, Wallet 7.

[17] 3rd AFA Brigade Ammunition Column War Diary, 30 December 1914, AWM4 13/85/2; letter dated 1 January 1915, letters from Norman Griffiths Ellsworth to his mother 1914/15; *Field Artillery Training 1914*, Chapter XI, Sect 238.

[18] 2nd AFA Battery War Diary, February 1915; 4th AFA Battery War Diary, February 1915; 6th AFA Battery War Diary, October 1914 to March 1915; 8th AFA Battery War Diary, February 1915; 9th AFA Battery War Diary, February 1915.

[19] Byrne, *New Zealand Artillery In the Field 1914-18*, p.21; Henderson et al., *The Gunners, A History Of The New Zealand Artillery*, p.90.

[20] 2nd AFA Battery War Diary, February 1915; 4th AFA Battery War Diary, February 1915; 6th AFA Battery War Diary, October 1914 to March 1915; 8th AFA Battery War Diary, March

	1915; 9th AFA Battery War Diary, March 1915.
[21]	Letter dated 28 February 1915, letters from Fred Leslie Biddle to his mother 1914/15.
[22]	Transcript of the diary of Major General W.T. Bridges, 1 January 1915 to 23 April 1915; 4th AFA Battery War Diary, 15 and 26 March 1915, AWM 4 13/66/6; 6th AFA Battery War Diary, October 1914 to March 1915; 8th AFA Battery War Diary, March 1915; 9th AFA Battery War Diary, March 1915.
[23]	GHQ Cairo Message No 4032 to General Officer Commanding the Australian and New Zealand Army Corps dated 28 March 1915. ANZAC General Staff War Diary, April 1915, AWM4 1/25/1 Part 1.
[24]	4th AFA Battery War Diaries, January to March 1915; Byrne, *New Zealand Artillery In the Field 1914-18*, p.20; evidence of Brigadier General G.N. JoÚston to the Dardanelles Commission, 2nd May 1917, the National Archives, Kew (TNA), CAB 19/33, p.1402; Napier JoÚston diary, 24 August 1915, refers to the fact that

the first time the 4th (Howitzer) Battery ever fired was in action.

[25] Hobbs' comments in the 1st Australian Divisional Artillery War Diary, 10 December 1914, AWM4 13/10/5. Although recorded at the beginning of the December diary, it is evident that Hobbs' entry was written in late March 1915; Byrne, *New Zealand Artillery In the Field 1914-18*, p.21; transcript of the diary of Major General W.T. Bridges, 1 January 1915 to 23 April 1915.

[26] ANZAC Operation Order No 1 dated 17 April 1915 and GOC ANZAC Instructions to GOC 1st Australian Division in ANZAC General Staff War Diary, April 1915, AWM4 1/25/1 Part 7.

[27] 1st Australian Division Operation Order No 1 dated 18 April 1915 in 1st Australian Division General Staff War Diary, April 1915, AWM4 1/42/3 Part 2; GOC 1st Australian Division Instructions to Officer Commanding Covering Force dated 18th April 1915 in 1st Australian Division General Staff War Diary, April 1915, Part 2; 3rd Infantry Brigade Operation Order No

1 dated 21 April 1915, AWM 25 Item 367/175; 2nd Infantry Brigade Operation Order No 5 dated 21 April 1915 in ANZAC General Staff War Diary, April 1915, Part 7; Bean, *Official History*, Vol. I, *The Story of Anzac*, Map no 7, p.227; Chris Roberts, *The Landing at Anzac, 1915* (2nd edn), Big Sky Publishing, Newport, 2015, pp.75-86.

[28] Sir Julian S. Corbett, *Naval Operations*, Vol. II, Naval & Military Press (reprint), UK, 2003, p.320.

[29] Mesut Uyar, *The Ottoman Defence Against the ANZAC Landing, 25 April 1915*, Big Sky Publishing, Newport, 2015, pp.103-04. The Krupp 87mm *Feldkanone* were known as 'Mantelli' guns because of the mantle around the barrel.

[30] Ibid.

[31] Sefik Aker, *The Dardanelles: The Ari Burnu Battles and the 27th Regiment*, AWM MSS 1886, paras 18, 34—35; Uyar, *The Ottoman Defence*, organisation charts pp.68, 70, 76, and text pp.76, 103—04. On page 76, Uyar writes that the *3/39th Artillery* only had four 75mm Krupp mountain guns, the other four arriving on 28 April. On p.104 he

records that the *6th Mountain Battery* had four 75mm Krupp mountain guns which began firing around 10.30am, and on p.104 that it did not receive its guns until 28 April. This is probably a typographical error. Either way, only one of the batteries had been issued its guns by 25 April, as shown in the organisation chart on p.76.

[32] Directions concerning "Observation Officers" for observing fire of H.M. Ships in combined operations dated 15 April 1915 in ANZAC General Staff War Diary, April 1915, AWM4 1/25/1, Part 5; Orders for observing Officers for Covering ships dated 18 April 1915 in ANZAC General Staff War Diary, April 1915, Part 7; ANZAC General Staff War Diary, 21 April 1915, Part 1; Divisional Artillery Order No 1 dated 19 April 1915 in Army Book 152 in Personal Papers Hobbs, Wallet 4. The line (Gallipoli 1:40,000 map, Sheet 2) ran from 224Q.5 to 215C.6. The observers were Lieutenants Goodwin and Vowles (south) and Lieutenant Clowes (north).

[33] Confidential Memorandum No 49 L (Orders for Combined Operations)

issued by Vice Admiral de Robeck dated 12 April 1915 in ANZAC War Diary General Staff, April 1915, Part 6.

[34] ANZAC War Diary, 21 April 1915, Part 1; NZ&A Division General Staff War Diary, 21 April 1915, AWM4 1/53/1 Part 1; Enclosure No 2 to Naval Memorandum No 49 L dated 12 April 1915 in ANZAC General Staff War Diary, April 1915, Part 6; MEF War Diary, April 1915. WA240 217, Item [240c], Archives New Zealand; 'Directions concerning "Observation Officers" for observing fire of H.M ships in combined operations', Appendix II 'Instructions for Intercommunication', Appendix 1(h) Orders for Observing Officers for Covering Ships' in ANZAC General Staff War Diary, April 1915, Part 7; 3rd Infantry Brigade Operation Order No 1.

[35] 1st Australian Division Operation Order No 1 dated 18 April 1915 in 1st Australian Division General Staff War Diary, April 1915, Part 2; 3rd Infantry Brigade Operation Order No 1.

[36] 'Early events of the 2nd Infantry Brigade at Anzac 25.4.15' by Major Cass, AWM 3 DRL 8042, Item 6; Bean, *Official History*, Vol. I, *The Story of Anzac*, pp.276—77, 364—65; Roberts, *The Landing at Anzac*, pp.115—17; Chris Roberts, 'The landing at Anzac: a reassessment', *Journal of the Australian War Memorial*, No 22, April 1993, pp.29—30; Robert Stevenson, 'Crisis in Command; Senior Leadership in the 1st Australian Division at The Gallipoli Landings' and Chris Roberts, 'Brigade Command: The ANZAC Experience', both in *Gallipoli: New Perspectives on the Mediterranean Force 1915-16*, Helion, Warwick, UK, 2018, chapters 11 and 12 respectively.

[37] Sefik Aker, *The Ari Burnu Battles and the 27th Regiment*, 1935. Translation held in the Rayfield Papers, IWM 69/61/Box 8, paras 66, 77; Uyar, *The Ottoman Defence*, pp.103—04, map p.112. In the text, Uyar writes 9.30am but on the map he shows 10.00am, which accords with other accounts which state that the *57th Infantry Regiment* arrived in the area between 10.00 and 10.30am.

[38] Bean, *Official History*, Vol. I, *The Story of Anzac*, pp.393—95; Brigadier General C.F. Aspinall-Oglander, *Official History of the War, Military Operations, Gallipoli*, Vol. I, *Inception of the Campaign to May 1915*, William Heineman Ltd, London, 1929, p.193.

[39] Roberts, *The Landing at Anzac*, Chapter 10; Uyar, *The Ottoman Defence*, Chapter 3.

[40] Headquarters ANZAC General Staff War Diary, 26 April 1915, Part 1.

[41] Uyar, *The Ottoman Defence*, p.103, 3rd AFA Brigade War Diary, 25 April 1915; Corbett, *Naval Operations*, Vol. II, pp.323, 345.

[42] Bean, *Official History*, Vol. I, *The Story of Anzac*, pp.360—66; Cass, 'Early events of the 2nd Infantry Brigade at Anzac 25.4.15'.

Chapter Three

[1] 1st Australian Division Operation Order No 1 dated 18 April 1915.

[2] 'Artillery Landing Notes' and 'Training Notes Naval and Military Operations' SS *Minnewaska*, 14.4.15, personal papers Hobbs, Wallet 3.

[3] 3rd Infantry Brigade Operation Order No 1.

[4] 1st Australian Division General Staff War Diary, 25 April 1915, Part 1; 21st (Kohat) Battery War Diary, 25 April 1915, AWM4 13/59/1; Bean, *Official History*, Vol. I, *The Story of Anzac*, pp.393—95; Aspinall-Oglander, *History of the Great War, Military Operations Gallipoli*, Vol.1, pp.193—94; General Sir Martin Farndale, *History of the Royal Regiment of Artillery: The Forgotten Fronts and the Home Base, 1914-18*, The Royal Artillery Association, Woolwich, 1988, pp.13—14.

[5] 1st Australian Division Operation Order No 1; GOC 1st Australian Division Disembarkation Orders dated 18 April 1915 in 1st Australian Division General Staff War Diary, April 1915, Part 2; Operation Order No 1 by Major General Sir A.J. Godley dated 19 April 1915 in Headquarters NZ&A Division General Staff War Diary, April 1915, Part 2; Appendix VIII to Memorandum A/32, Naval Orders For Second Squadron dated 18 April 1915 in ANZAC General Staff War Diary, April 1915, Part 6.

[6] 1st Australian Division Operation Order No 1; 2nd AFA Brigade War Diary, 9 April 1915, AWM4 13/30/5; 3rd AFA Brigade War Diary, 5/6 April 1915, AWM4 13/31/9.

[7] 1st AFA Brigade War Diary, 6 April 1915; 2nd AFA Brigade War Diary, 9 April 1915; 9th AFA Battery War Diary, 6 April 1915, AWM4 13/71/3; Operation Order No 1 by Major General Sir A.J. Godley dated 19 April 1915, Appendices V, VI and VII.

[8] GOC 1st Australian Division Disembarkation Orders dated 18 April 1915; 1st Australian Division Administrative Staff War Diary, April 1915, AWM4 1/43/5.

[9] Report on the Operations of Australian Divisional Artillery from 10.00am Sunday 25th April until 8.00pm Monday 3rd May 1915 in 1st Australian Division General Staff War Diary, May 1915, AWM4 1/42/4, Part 3.

[10] 3rd AFA Brigade War Diary, 25 April 1915, AWM4 13/31/9; 3rd AFA Brigade Ammunition Column War Diary, 25 April 1915, AWM4 13/85/5, Part 1; Statement in comments on British Official History in AWM38

3DRL7953/27, Part I; Bean, *Official History*, Vol. I, *The Story of Anzac*, p. xiv; C.E.W. Bean *Official History of Australian in the War, Vol II. The Story of Anzac* Angus and Robertson Ltd, Sydney, 1924, p.63. Roberts, *The Landing at Anzac*, p.158; AspinallOglander, *History of the Great War, Military Operations Gallipoli*, Vol.1, p.194; Major Stuart Anderson, BMRA, War Diary, 25 April 1915. From April 1915 there are two 1st Australian Divisional Artillery war diaries, the second written by Major Anderson, hereafter called Anderson War Diary. From May 1915 Anderson's diary is Part 2 in the AWM4 13/10 series.

[11] Aspinall-Oglander to Bean, 22 May 1928, AWM38 3DRL7953/27, Part 2.

[12] Report on the Operations of Australian Divisional Artillery from 10.00am Sunday 25th April until 8.00pm Monday 3rd May 1915 in 1st Australian Division General Staff War Diary, May 1915, AWM4 1/42/4, Part 3; 1st Australian Division Artillery War Diary, 25 April 1915, AWM4 13/10/8; 2nd AFA Brigade War Diary, 25 April 1915; 4th AFA Battery War Diary, 25

April 1915, AWM4 13/66/7; Bean, *Official History*, Vol. I, *The Story of Anzac*, p.464; Aspinall-Oglander, *History of the Great War, Military Operations Gallipoli*, Vol.1, pp.193-94.

[13] 2nd AFA Brigade Ammunition Column War Diary, 25 April 1915, AWM4 13/84/10; 3rd AFA Brigade Ammunition Column War Diary, 25 April 1915, Part I.

[14] 3rd AFA Brigade War Diary, 25 April 1915; Bean, *Official History*, Vol. I, *The Story of Anzac*, pp.456—61; Roberts, *The Landing at Anzac*, pp.167—68.

[15] Farndale, *History of the Royal Regiment of Artillery*, p.18.

[16] NZ&A Division General Staff War Diary, 26 April 1915, Part I; NZ&A Divisional Artillery War Diary, 26 April 1915; Byrne, *New Zealand Artillery In the Field 1914-18*, p.27.

[17] 2nd AFA Brigade Ammunition Column War Diary, 26 April 1915; 3rd AFA Brigade Ammunition Column War Diary, 26 April 1915, Part I; 21st (Kohat) Battery War Diary, 26 April 1915, AWM4 13/59/1.

[18]   1st AFA Brigade War Diary, 26 April 1915; 3rd AFA Brigade War Diary, 26 April 1915.

[19]   Report on the Operations of Australian Divisional Artillery from 10.00am Sunday 25th April until 8.00pm Monday 3rd May 1915 in 1st Australian Division General Staff War Diary, May 1915, AWM4 1/42/4 Part 3; 2nd AFA Brigade War Diary, 26 April 1915; 3rd AFA Brigade War Diary, 26 April 1915; 2nd AFA Battery War Diary, 26 April 1915; 4th AFA Battery War Diary, 26 April 1915; 5th AFA Battery War Diary, 26 April and 28 April 1915; 6th AFA Battery War Diary, 27 April 1915.

[20]   See also distribution of artillery in NZ&A Division defence sections in NZ&A Division Operation Order No 6 in NZ&A Division General Staff War Diary, April 1915, Part 3; 3rd AFA Brigade War Diary, 26 April 1915; 7th AFA Battery War Diary, 26 April 1915; 8th AFA Battery War Diary, 26 April 1915. The 1st Australian Divisional Artillery war diary, Anderson's war diary and Hobbs' personal diary report that the first

guns landed at about noon and, by that evening, only eight field guns were ashore. However, the brigade and battery diaries support one another and the narrative provided in the text. 1st Australian Divisional Artillery War Diary, 26 April 1915; Anderson War Diary, 26 April 1915; Hobbs Diary, 26 April 1915, AWM PR82/153, Folder 1.

[21] Corbett, *Naval Operations*, Vol. II, p.358.

[22] ANZAC General Staff War Diary, 26 April 1915, Part 1; Hobbs also slightly adjusted the zones, with the boundary along the line 224L.4 to 226O.6 (Gallipoli 1:40,000 map, Sheet 2), and Lieutenant Goodwin observing to the south, Lieutenant Clowes to the north. Army Book 152 in Private Records Lieutenant General J.J.T. Hobbs, Wallet 4.

[23] NZ&A Division General Staff War Diary, 27 and 28 April 1915, Part 1; NZ&A Divisional Artillery War Diary, 27, 29, 30 April 1915; Byrne, *New Zealand Artillery In the Field 1914l8*, pp.28—30; 1st Australian Divisional Artillery War Diary, 27—28 April 1915; Anderson War Diary, 27 April

1915; 7th AFA Battery War Diary, 27 April 1915; 21st (Kohat Battery) War Diary, 27 April 1915; Corbett, *Naval Operations*, Vol. II, p.359. The *Goeben* was one of the Ottoman ships involved in the shelling before being forced to move by fire from HMS *Queen Elizabeth*.

[24] Operation Orders No 1 and 3 by Lieutenant General W.R. Birdwood dated 27/4/15 in ANZAC General Staff War Diary, April 1915, Part 8.

[25] NZ&A Division General Staff War Diary, 28 April 1915, Part 1; Anderson War Diary, 28 April 1915; 6th AFA Battery War Diary, 27 April 1915; 5th AFA Battery War Diary, 28 April 1915; Hobbs Diary, 28 April 1915. The 1st Australian Divisional Artillery war diary, Anderson's war diary, and Hobbs' personal diary state that three guns and six wagons were landed on the 28th, but there is no record of the third gun in the battery or FA brigade war diaries. The guns ashore were from the NZ Howitzer Battery, 2nd NZFA Battery, the 4th, 5th and 7th AFA batteries, and the 7th Indian Mountain Brigade. The units offshore

were the 1st AFA Brigade complete, the 6th, 8th and 9th AFA batteries, and the 1st and 3rd NZFA batteries.

[26] ANZAC Order Number 3 dated 28 April 1915 in ANZAC General Staff War Diary, April 1915, Part 8.

[27] Cunliffe-Owen Paper 'For Artillery Observation Officers For Ships' dated 28 April 1915 in ANZAC General Staff War Diary, Part 8; Hobbs Diary, 28 April 1915.

[28] NZ&A Divisional Artillery War Diary, 29 and 30 April 1915; Napier JoUston, Diary Narrative. Typescript provided by Dr Christopher Pugsley. The diary comprises a narrative covering the campaign, followed by daily entries.

[29] NZ&A Divisional Artillery War Diary, 27 and 30 April 1915, and 1 and 2 May 1915, AWM4 13/15/3; Byrne, *New Zealand Artillery In the Field 1914-18*, pp.30, 31.

[30] ANZAC Order Number 5 dated 30 April 1915. This order called for the capture of the knoll at map reference 224.d.5 (Baby 700) and the area south by west along the western bank of the gully 224.o.s and w. NZ&A Division Operational Order Number 4 dated

	30 April 1915. Both in ANZAC General Staff War Diary, April 1915, Part 8.
[31]	The decision that the 1st Australian Division would hold the line was taken after Brigadier General 'Hooky' Walker successfully persuaded Bridges against attacking given the weakened state of the brigades, the divergence of the attacks, and the ground over which it would take place. Bean, *Official History*, Vol. I, *The Story of Anzac*, p.583.
[32]	Operation Order No 1 by Colonel F.E. JoÚston commanding NZ Infantry Brigade dated 2 May 1915 in New Zealand Infantry Brigade War Diary, May 1915, AWM4 35/17/4.
[33]	Annotated ANZAC Order Number 5 dated 30 April 1915, ANZAC General Staff War Diary, April 1915, Part 8; NZ&A Division Operation Order No 5 dated 2 May 1915, and NZG 96 dated 2 May 1915 in NZ&A Division General Staff War Diary, May 1915, AWM4 1/53/2, Part 2; Memorandum Ga 204 from Commander NZ&A Division to Headquarters ANZAC dated 2 May 1915 in ANZAC General Staff War Diary, May 1915,

AWM1/25/2, Part 2; Operation Order No 1 by Colonel F.E. JoÚston commanding NZ Infantry Brigade dated 2 May 1915 in New Zealand Infantry Brigade War Diary, May 1915; Anderson War Diary, 2 May 1915, AWM4 13/10/9, Part 2. The line denoted by Godley and in the NZ&A Division operation order for preliminary fire was between map reference 224.d.2-8, and the parallelogram in the memorandum was designated as 224.d.2, 224.d.8, 224.f.3 and 224.f.9. Fire was then to lift to the line 224.f.3 [Battleship Hill]—237.Z.9—237.U.9. "The lift in the NZ Brigade operation order was from 224.f.8 [Ince Bair]—237.Z.9-273.U.9 [sic]. The first and undoubtedly the third of these grid references were almost certainly typographical errors (Map of Gallipoli, Sheet 2, 1:40,000).

[34] The ships were the battleships *Triumph, London, Prince of Wales, Queen, Canopus* and *Majestic*, and the cruisers *Bacchante* and *Dartmouth*. Christopher Pugsley, *Gallipoli: The New Zealand Story*, Libro International, Auckland, 2014, p.181;

Bean, *Official History*, Vol. I, *The Story of Anzac*, p.585. *Dartmouth* carried eight 6-inch guns as her main armament with two along the centre line and three along each side of the vessel, allowing her a broadside of five guns.

[35] Messages NZG 70, 71 and 72 dated 1 May 1915, in New Zealand Infantry Brigade War Diary, May 1915, Appendix 9.

[36] NZG 96 dated 2 May 1915 in NZ&A Division General Staff War Diary, May 1915, Part 2; 1st Australian Division General Staff, War Diary, May 1915, AWM4 1/42/4, Part 3.

[37] 21st (Kohat) Battery War Diary, May 1915, AWM4 13/59/2; 26th (Jacob's) Battery War Diary, May 1915, AWM4 13/60/1. The 21st Battery recorded firing on 224.d.5, and the 26th Battery on 224.d.4; Anderson War Diary, 2 May 1915; 2nd AFA Brigade War Diary, 30 April to 4 May 1915, AWM4 13/30/6; 4th AFA Battery War Diary, 2 May 1915, AWM4 13/66/8; 5th AFA Battery War Diary, 2 May 1915, AWM4 13/67/2; 8th AFA Battery War Diary, 2 May 1915; AWM4 13/70/10. Anderson recorded that an 8th Battery

gun fired on (224)d.5, and the 2nd AFA Brigade fired on 237u.9, v.9, 224f.3. Anderson War Diary, 2 May 1915.

[38] Captain C. Longmore, *The Old Sixteenth, Being a Record of the 16th Battalion A.I.F. During the Great War 1914-1918*. History Committee of the 16th Battalion Association, Perth, WA, 1929; New Zealand Infantry Brigade War Diary, May 1915.

[39] Bean, *Official History*, Vol. I, *The Story of Anzac*, pp.582—98; Lieutenant A.E. Byrne, *Official History of the Otago Regiment, NZEF in the Great War 1914-1918* (2nd edn), J. Wilkie and Co Ltd, Dunedin, nd., pp.28—32; Longmore, *The Old Sixteenth*, pp.46—49.

[40] There is an unreferenced note in the corps headquarters war diary advising the navy of the position of own and enemy troops and asking for fire as near as could be safely provided on 224.d.5, 6, 7 and 8. ANZAC General Staff War Diary, May 1915, Part 2.

[41] 1st Australian Divisional Artillery War Diary, 2 May 1915, Part 1; 'Report on the Action on Night 2/3rd May 1915',

Appendix 36, in NZ&A Division General Staff War Diary, May 1915, Part 3; Report on the Operations of Australian Divisional Artillery from 10.00am Sunday 25th April until 8.00pm Monday 3rd May 1915 in 1st Australian Division General Staff War Diary, May 1915, AWM4 1/42/4, Part 3; Bean, *Official History*, Vol. I, *The Story of Anzac*, p.594, states that the fire came from a field battery. Major General C.E. Callwell, *The Dardanelles*, Constable, London, 1919, p.171, expresses that it came from the destroyers offshore.

[42] 1st AFA Brigade War Diary, 1 May 1915, AWM 13/29/6; 8th AFA Battery War Diary, 1 May 1915; 9th AFA Battery War Diary, 5 May 1915, AWM4 13/71/4.

[43] 9th AFA Battery War Diary, 7 May 1915; 2nd AFA Brigade Ammunition Column War Diary, April 1915 and May 1915, AWM4 13/84/11; 3rd AFA Brigade Ammunition Column War Diary, April 1915 and May 1915, AWM4 13/85/6.

[44] General Headquarters MEF GSR129, Instructions for GOC A&NZ ARMY

CORPS dated 1st May 1915 in ANZAC General Staff War Diary, May 1915, Part 2; ANZAC General Staff War Diary, 3 May 1915, Part 1.

Chapter Four

[1] General Report dated 3 May 1915 in 1st Australian Divisional Artillery War Diary, May 1915, Part 1.

[2] At the end of May, Headquarters MEF issued Ottoman maps of the southern portion of the peninsula at 1:10,000 scale, but there is no evidence that these were used at Anzac. MEF Force Order Number 18 dated 30 May 1915 in ANZAC General Staff War Diary, May 1915, Part 5 covered the issue of Ottoman maps at 1:10,000 scale; MEF Force Order Number 21 dated 27 July 1915 in MEF General Staff War Diary, July 1915, AWM4 1/4/4, Part 1 covers the issue of the 1:20,000 series.

[3] 1st Divisional Artillery War Diary, April to November 1915, AWM4 13/10/5-12.

[4] 1st Australian Divisional Artillery War Diary, May 1915, AWM4 13/10/9, Part 2 and June 1915, AWM4 13/10/10, Part 7. Hobbs Diary 16 September 1915. He

also records a discussion on 'prematures' on 2 July. For the fuse issue see MEF General Staff War Diary, September 1915, AWM4 1/4/6, Part 2.

[5] ANZAC General Staff War Diary, May 1915, Part 3. Strangely enough, the solution adopted to stop the shrapnel clumping was to boil the rounds.

[6] 1st Australian Divisional Artillery War Diary, April and May 1915; NZ&A Divisional Artillery War Diary, April 1915.

[7] MEF Force Order No 11 dated 13 May 1915 in ANZAC General Staff War Diary, May 1915, Part 3. Also in MEF General Staff War Diary, May 1915, AWM4 1/4/2, Part 3.

[8] General Headquarters letter dated 20 May 1915 in MEF General Staff War Diary, May 1915, Part 4.

[9] 'Instructions for getting Artillery fire on objectives quickly' dated 25/5/1915 in 1st Australian Division General Staff War Diary, May 1915, AWM4 1/42/4, Part 8. N.Z.G. 706, NZ&A Division Special Order dated 25 May 1915 in NZ&A Division General Staff War Diary, May 1915, Part 3.

[10] Force Order No 11, Expenditure of Artillery Ammunition dated 13 May 1915, Appendix 29, ANZAC General Staff War Diary, May 1915, Part 3; 1st Australian Divisional Artillery War Diary, May 1915; Bean, *Official History*, Vol. II, *The Story of Anzac*, p.83; Byrne, *New Zealand Artillery In the Field 1914-18*, pp.56, 59; 1st Australian Divisional Artillery War Diary, May 1915. Scarcity prevailed throughout the campaign. Hobbs Diary, 3 July 1915.

[11] *Field Artillery Training 1914*, Sect 158.

[12] Anderson War Diary, 13 May 1915, Part 2; 1st Australian Divisional Artillery War Diary, May 1915, Part 1. In his diary, Hobbs also records that he even took advantage of the truce on 24 May to look for better positions. Hobbs Diary, 24 May 1915.

[13] Byrne, *New Zealand Artillery In the Field 1914-18*, pp.3, 35; Map dated 25/5/15 in 1st Australian Divisional Artillery War Diary, May 1915, Part 1.

[14] 1st Australian Divisional Artillery War Diary, 3 May 1915, Part 2; Bean, *Official History*, Vol. II, *The Story of Anzac*, pp.65—69.

[15] 8th AFA Battery War Diary, 2 to 8 May 1915; Bean, *Official History, Vol II, The Story of Anzac*, pp.68—69.

[16] 2nd AFA Brigade War Diary, 8 May 1915, and sketch map No 5; 8th AFA Battery War Diary, 7—12 May and 15 May 1915, sketch map of May battery position; 3rd AFA Brigade Ammunition Column War Diary, April 1915.

[17] 2nd AFA Brigade War Diary, May 1915, Sketch Maps 2—7.

[18] 2nd AFA Brigade War Diary, 7, 8, 9, 13, 18 May 1915 and sketch maps 2—7; 4th AFA Battery War Diary, 4, 5, 7, 8 May 1915; 5th AFA Battery War Diary, 7, 8, 9, 12, 16, 18, 19 and 21 May 1915. In the final positioning of its guns, the 5th AFA Battery War Diary places D sub-section (Strachan's) on the 'Southern slope of MacLagan's Hill', but subsequent maps show its location on the northern end of the ridge close to the crest of Plugge's Plateau. Furthermore, in referring to the relocation of A and C sub-sections back to MacLagan's Ridge on the night 12/13 May, the 2nd AFA Brigade War Diary refers to them as sited on 'Plugge's Hill', while the 5th AFA

Battery entry for 12 May states that they were 'put back again on MacLagan's Ridge'. Inconsistencies such as these and the sketch maps occur during the early weeks at Anzac as officers refer to locations in general terms or by different names.

[19] 7th AFA Battery War Diary, 26 April 1915, Part 1; Bean, *Official History*, Vol. I, *The Story of Anzac*, p.507; 1st Australian Divisional Artillery War Diary, 28 April 1915; Anderson War Diary, 29 April 1915; Napier JoÚston Diary, 18 May 1915; Map dated 25/5/15 in 1st Australian Divisional Artillery War Diary, May 1915, Part 1.

[20] 9th AFA Battery War Diary, 30 April—23 May 1915. Burgess' Battery originally contained a gun each from the 4th and 5th AFA batteries, but these were replaced by a 9th Battery gun returned from Cape Helles and another transferred from the 7th AFA Battery.

[21] Map marked XI dated 25 May 1915 in 1st Australian Divisional Artillery War Diary, May 1915, Part 1; 9 AFA Battery War Diary, 7 June 1915,

AWM4 13/7/5; map dated 26.6.15 in 1st Australian Division General Staff War Diary, June 1915, AWM4 1/42/5, Part 9; Sketch map 9th Battery Telephone System in 9th AFA Battery War Diary, June 1915, AWM4 13/71/5.

[22] Operation Memorandum Number 2 dated 24 May 1915 in 1st Australian Division General Staff War Diary, May 1915, Part 11.

[23] Bean, *Official History*, Vol. II, *The Story of Anzac*, p.73.

[24] *Field Artillery Training, 1914*, Sect 153.

[25] Horner, *The Gunners*, p.97. Napier JoÚston, evidence to the Dardanelles Commission, CAB 19/33, p.1400.

[26] Letter Hobbs to Cunliffe-Owen in Army Book 152 in Personal Papers Hobbs, AWM 3DRL/2600, Wallet 4; NZ&A Divisional Artillery War Diary, 25 and 27 May 1915.

[27] Anderson War Diary, 3 May 1915.

[28] 2nd AFA Brigade War Diary, 7 May 1915. See also Force Order No 8 dated 11 May 1915, para 7, Appendix 29 in ANZAC General Staff War Diary, May 1915, Part 3; Byrne, *New Zealand Artillery In the Field 1914-18*, p.36.

[29] Headquarters 1st Australian Division G844 dated 5 May 1915 in 1st Australian Division General Staff War Diary, May 1915, Part 3.

[30] *Field Artillery Training 1914*, Sect 153, p.241.

[31] Note from Major General Godley dated 7 May, 1st Australian Division General Staff War Diary, May 1915, Part 3.

[32] 1st Australian Divisional Artillery Headquarters 'Co-operation between Artillery and Infantry During the Present Phase of Operations at Anzac' dated 9.9 15 in Personal Papers Hobbs, AWM2018.19.86.

[33] MEF Force Order No 8 dated 11 May 1915 in MEF General Staff War Diary, May 1915, Part 3.

[34] Anderson War Diary, 11 and 14 May 1915; NZ&A Divisional Artillery War Diary, 11 and 14-16 May 1915.

[35] DA C1 of 15 May 1815 in Army Book 152 in Personal Papers Hobbs, AWM3DRL/2600, Wallet 4.

[36] Anderson War Diary, 15 and 16 May 1915; NZ&A Divisional Artillery War Diary, 17 May 1915.

[37] Anderson War Diary, 19 May 1915.

[38] Hobbs Diary, 20 May 1915.
[39] NZ&A Divisional Artillery War Diary, 19 May 1915.
[40] NZ&A Division Report on Action of 18/19 May 1915 in ANZAC General Staff War Diary, May 1915, Part 5.
[41] Narrative operations (Artillery) 9-5-15 in Personal Papers Hobbs; 1st Australian Divisional Artillery War Diary, 19 and 20 May 1915, Part 1; Hobbs Diary, 20 May 1915.
[42] NZ&A Divisional Artillery War Diary, 20 May 1915.
[43] Copy of note from CRA ANZAC dated 19 May 1915 in 1st Australian Division General Staff War Diary, May 1915, Part 6.
[44] NZ&A Divisional Artillery War Diary, 21 and 22 May 1915.
[45] Cunliffe-Owen's 'Instructions for Getting Artillery Fire on Objectives Quickly' in 1st Australian Division General Staff War Diary, May 1915, Part 8.
[46] In the 1st Australian Divisional Artillery War Diary, May 1915, Part 1, Hobbs records issuing special instructions to his subordinate commanders regarding the extraordinary conditions under

which the field artillery was working on 15 May. A copy of this order, DA C1, can be found in an Army notebook annotated 'No 14, Orders and Instructions' in his personal papers, AWM3DRL/2600, Series 2, Wallet 4. Ten days later he issued 'Notes for Reference and Guidance of all Artillery Officers, Australian Divisional Artillery, with Special Application to the Recent Phase of Operations at Anzac Cove'. A copy can also be found in Wallet 4, and a further copy is in the 1st Australian Divisional Artillery War Diary, September 1915, AWM4 13/10/13, Part 2.

[47] Hobbs' headquarters was co-located with Divisional Headquarters, but not integrated until 21 May when General Walker acceded to what Bridges had refused. Hobbs Diary, 21 May 1915. Examples of gun registration records can be found in the 4th AFA Battery War Diary, May 1915 and June 1915, AWM 4 13/66/9 and in the 9th AFA Battery War Diary, June 1915.

[48] Artillery communications diagram 16/5/15 to 3/6/16 in 1st Australian

	Divisional Artillery War Diary, June 1915, AWM 13/10/10, Part 1.
[49]	Bean, *Official History*, Vol. II, *The Story of Anzac*, p.73.
[50]	Ibid., p.73; NZ&A Division Report on the Action of 29th May 1915 at Quinn's Post, OC Lieut Col G.J. Burnage VD, 13th Battalion, in ANZAC General Staff War Diary, May 1915, Part 5.
[51]	Cunliffe-Owen, 'Artillery at Anzac', pp.539, 542; T Frame, *The Shores of Gallipoli—Naval Aspects of the Gallipoli Campaign*, Hale & Ironmonger, Alexandria, NSW, 2000, p.206; Richard Pelvin, 'Sea Power at Suvla, August 1915: Naval Aspects of the Suvla Bay Landings and the genesis of Modern Amphibious Warfare', symposium paper, Australian War Memorial, August 2000; Anderson War Diary, 8 May 1915.
[52]	Headquarters ANZAC Ga 432 of 8 May 1915; 2nd Naval Squadron A/47 of 8 May 1915. Both in ANZAC General Staff War Diary, May 1915, Part 3.

[53] Memorandum dated 9 May 1915, 1st Australian Division General Staff War Diary, May 1915, Part 4.

[54] Ibid.

[55] Sir Julian S. Corbett, *Naval Operations*, Vol. III, Naval & Military Press reprint, Uckfield, nd, pp.24—31.

[56] Cunliffe-Owen issued instructions on this system on 28 April and 9 May. Appendix 6(b) in ANZAC General Staff War Diary, 28 April 1915, Part 8; memorandum dated 9 May 1915 in ANZAC General Staff War Diary, May 1915, Part 3; Anderson War Diary, 23 May 1915.

[57] Napier JoÚston Diary, 28 April and 16 May 1915. In evidence before the Dardanelles Commission, Napier JoÚston was highly critical of the lack of howitzers, sheeting home the blame for this to Hamilton and his artillery adviser. Napier JoÚston evidence to Dardanelles Commission, p.1400.

[58] Hobbs Diary, 13 May 1915. See also 1st Australian Divisional Artillery War Diary, 10, 14 May 1915, Part 1.

[59] Appendix IV dated 29 May 1915 in 1st Australian Division General Staff War Diary, May 1915, Part 9.

[60] Headquarters ANZAC Ga 447 dated 8 May 1915 in ANZAC General Staff War Diary, May 1915, Part 3.

[61] Anderson Diary, 16 May 1915; Napier JoÚston Diary, 17 May 1915; NZ&A Divisional Artillery War Diary, 16 May 1915.

[62] Headquarters ANZAC Ga 659 dated 16 May 1915, HQ MEF Memo to GOC ANZAC re request for 4.5-inch howitzer battery, and signal GHQ to ANZAC date 20 May 1915, all in ANZAC General Staff War Diary, May 1915, Part 4.

[63] Remarks and References Column in 1st Australian Divisional Artillery War Diary, 28 and 29 May 1915, Part 1.

[64] Narrative of the campaign in 1st NZFA Brigade War Diary, Archives New Zealand WA 51/1 (this was written by Napier JoÚston); note by C.B.B. White on back of Appendix IV dated 29 May 1915 in 1st Australian Division General Staff War Diary, May 1915, Part 9; See also Bean, *Official History*, Vol. II, *The Story of Anzac*, p.80.

[65] ANZAC General Staff War Diary, 20 May 1915, Part 1; HQ ANZAC Ga 93 of 20 May in 1st Australian Division

General Staff War Diary, May 1915, Part 6; sketch map of 8th Battalion position in 1st Australian Division General Staff War Diary, June 1915, Part 10; NZ&A Division General Staff War Diary, 23 May 1915, Part 1.

[66] 1st Infantry Brigade report on Garland mortar in 1st Australian Division General Staff War Diary, June 1915, Part 4.

[67] Anderson War Diary, 10, 14, 15, 20 and 24 May 1915.

[68] Sketch of gun position, Appendix 17 in 4th AFA Battery War Diary, June 1915; 8th AFA Battery War Diary, May 1915; sketches of gun pits in 9th AFA Battery War Diary, June 1915;Byrne, *New Zealand Artillery In the Field 1914-18*, p.32; Anderson War Diary, 14 May 1915.

[69] *Field Artillery Training, 1914*, Sect 117, p.175; daily reports 7th IMA Brigade in 1st Division General Staff War Diary, June 1915 and July 1915, AWM4 1/42/6.

[70] MEF Memo to Vice Admiral Commanding East Mediterranean Fleet dated 20 May 1915 in MEF General Staff War Diary, May 1915, Part 4.

[71] 'Report On A Sortie From Quinn's Post Night 9/10 May 1915', and 'Report On A Sortie Made From Quinn's Post, Number 3 Section Of Defence By One Squadron, 2nd Australian Light Horse, On The Night of 14/15 May 1915' in ANZAC General Staff War Diary, May 1915, Part 4. Daily Artillery Reports for 12 and 15 May in 1st Australian Division General Staff War Diary, May 1915, Part 5; NZ&A Divisional Artillery War Diary, 10, 12 and 14 May 1915.

[72] ANZAC Summary of Events from Midnight 18/19th to 6a.m. 20th May 1915 in ANZAC General Staff War Diary, May 1915, Part 4; 1st Australian Division Summary from 18/5/15 to 19/5/15, and from 19/5/15 to 20/5/15 in 1st Australian Division General Staff War Diary, May 1915, Part 6; Report on Action 18/19 May in NZ&A Division General Staff War Diary, June 1915, AWM4 1/53/3, Part 2; Reports from Brigadier General Cunliffe-Owen on the artillery action of the Indian Mountain Brigade and the Australian Artillery on 19 May 1915 in 1st Australian Division General Staff War

Diary, May 1915, Part 7; NZ&A Divisional Artillery War Diary, 19 and 20 May 1915.

[73] Ibid.

[74] Lieutenant Colonel G.J. Burnage, 13th Battalion, 'Report On Action 29 May 1915 at Quinn's Post' and 'Report On Actions At Quinn's Post 30 May—1 June' in NZ&A Division General Staff War Diary, June 1915, Parts 2 and 3 respectively.

[75] Corps Order No 12 dated 4 June 1915, and NZ&A Division Operation Order dated 4 June 1915 in NZ&A Division General Staff War Diary, June 1915, Part 2; 1st Australian Division Operation Order Number 6 dated 4 June 1915, and Artillery Daily Report dated 5/6/15 in 1st Australian Division General Staff War Diary, June 1915, Part 2.

[76] NZ&A Division Summary of Events in NZ&A Division General Staff War Diary, June 1915, Part 2; Artillery Daily Report dated 5/6/15 in 1st Australian Division General Staff War Diary, June 1915, Part 2.

Chapter Five

[1] 1st Australian Divisional Engineers War Diary, 4 and 7 June 1915, AWM4 14/7/1, Part 1; 3rd Australian Infantry Brigade War Diary, 7 and 8 June 1915, AWM4 23/3/1, Part 1; notes by Lieutenant Colonel Mather DSO dated 20 September, 1918 [sic] in 1st Australian Divisional Engineers War Diary, March-June 1915, AWM4 14/7/1, Part 2; Bean, *Official History*, Vol. II, *The Story of Anzac*, p.264, Map No 10 opposite p.283, Map No 12 opposite p.472. The sign on Brighton Beach today, inferring that the current road running up Victoria Gully to Lone Pine is Artillery Road, is incorrect. Traces of Artillery Road barely exist today.

[2] Headquarters 1st Divisional Artillery Memo dated 20 June 1915, Headquarters ANZAC Ga 258 dated 21 June, and General Headquarters MEF memo to Headquarters ANZAC dated 24 June, all in ANZAC General Staff War Diary, June 1915, AWM4 1/25/3, Part 4. At about this time, Hobbs also issued 'Additions, Alterations and Amendments to Notes For Reference and Guidance

of All Artillery Officers', stamped page 41 in 1st Australian Divisional Artillery War Diary, September 1915, Part 2. This document shows the 6th Battery providing the mobile section, although it did not arrive for another six weeks.

[3] Artillery Daily Report 17/6/15 in 1st Australian Division General Staff War Diary, June 1915, Part 7.

[4] Daily Operations Report 7th IMA Brigade dated 16 June 1915 in 1st Australian Division General Staff War Diary, June 1915, Part 7.

[5] Byrne, *Official History of the Otago Regiment*, p.50; ANZAC General Staff War Diary, 18 May 1915, Part 1, and 27 June 1915, Part 1.

[6] Sketch map showing hostile guns in 1st Australian Divisional Artillery War Diary, June 1915, Part 1.

[7] Organisation Chart Kuzey Grubunun Kurulusu (19 Haziran [June] 1915) in *Birinci Dunya Harbinde Turk Harbi V Nci Cilt Canakkale Cepheisi*, 3 NCI Kitap, Ankara, Gnkur. Basimevi, 1978; e-mail Mesut Uyar to Roberts, 2 March 2018.

[8] Ibid.

[9] E.J. Erickson, 'Ottoman Artillery in The First World War' in Sanders Marble

(ed), *History of Warfare*, Vol.108, *King of Battle: Artillery in World War I*, Brill, Boston, 2016, p.177. Brigadier General C.F. Aspinall-Oglander, *Military Operations. Gallipoli*, Vol. II, Naval & Military Press/Imperial War Museum (reprint of 1932 edn), nd (1932), p.116; see also Otto Liman von Sanders, *Five Years in Turkey*, United States Naval Institute, Annapolis, 1927, p.75.

[10] Priority message B.98. from GHQ to ANZAC, and Message G.A.275. from ANZAC to GHQ both dated 23 June 1915 in MEF General Staff War Diary, June 1915, AWM4 1/4/3, Part 3; 3rd AFA Brigade Ammunition Column War Diaries, April to July 1915, AWM4 13/85/5, 13/85/6, 13/85/7 and 13/85/8.

[11] 1st Australian Divisional Artillery Memorandum dated 9 May 1915 in Hobbs Papers, Part 3; 1st Australian Divisional Artillery War Diary, 11 May 1915, Part 1; Anderson War Diary, 11 May 1915; Bean, *Official History*, Vol. II, *The Story of Anzac*, p.83; Horner, *The Gunners*, p.97. For an example of the use of crossfire, see the 1st Australian Divisional Artillery War Diary, 15 June 1915, Part 1.

[12] 3rd Infantry Brigade Operation Order No 6 dated 28 June 1915, 3rd Infantry Brigade KC595 dated 28.6.15—Report On Demonstration 28 June 1915, Report to Headquarters 1st Division from 2nd Light Horse Brigade dated 28 June 1915, Operational Memorandum No 1 by Commander 2nd Light Horse Brigade, and Artillery Daily Report for 29 June 1915, all in 1st Australian Division General Staff War Diary, June 1915, Part 10.

[13] Ibid. Headquarters ANZAC Ga 44 of 28 June 1915 in 1st Australian Division General Staff War Diary, June 1915, Part 10.

[14] NZ&A Division Report On The Action Of Night 29th/30th June 1915 dated 2 July 1915 in ANZAC General Staff War Diary, June 1915, Part 4.

[15] 7th AFA Battery War Diary, 9 and 10 July 1915, AWM4 13/69/1, Part 1.

[16] Australian Divisional Artillery Daily Reports for 9/10 and 10/11 July, and NZ&A Division Summaries of Events for 9/10 and 10/11 July in 1st Australian Division General Staff War Diary, July 1915, Part 5.

[17]	Cunliffe-Owen, 'Artillery at Anzac', p.541. Napier JoÚston, evidence to the Dardanelles Commission, p.1396. Australian Divisional Artillery Daily Reports in 1st Australian Division General Staff War Diary, July 1915, Parts 2—10.
[18]	Bean, *Official History*, Vol. II, *The Story of Anzac*, p.84.
[19]	1st Australian Division General Staff War Diary, July 1915, Part 6.
[20]	Australian Divisional Artillery Daily Reports for the period 13/14 to 20/21 July in 1st Australian Division General Staff War Diary, July 1915, Parts 6 to 8.
[21]	Headquarters ANZAC Ga 238 of 11 July 1915, 1st Australian Division Operation Order Number 7 dated 11 July 1915, and Headquarters ANZAC Ga 256 of 12 July 1915, all in 1st Australian Division General Staff War Diary, July 1915, Part 5.
[22]	Headquarters ANZAC Memorandum No Ga 359 of 19 July 1915, ANZAC message Ga 359 of 20 July 1915, ANZAC message Ga 367 of 20 July 1915 and ANZAC message Ga 382 of 21 July 1915, and Appendix 417a, all

in 1st Australian Division General Staff War Diary, July 1915, Part 8. ANZAC note Ga 388 and ANZAC message Ga 399 of 22 July 1915 and Artillery Daily Reports 22 to 26 July 1915 all in 1st Australian Division General Staff War Diary, July 1915, Part 9.

[23] Anderson War Diary, 11 and 18 July 1915, AWM4 13/10/11, Part 2; Heavy Battery 1st Australian Division War Diary, 14 July 1915, AWM4 13/63/1; Artillery Daily Report dated 19.7.15. in 1st Australian Division General Staff War Diary, July 1915, Part 7.

[24] Anderson Diary, 15 and 21 July 1915; 1st Australian Division Summary 6am 15 July to 6am 16th July G879 dated 17/7/15 and Artillery Daily Report dated 16.7.15 in 1st Australian Division General Staff War Diary, July 1915, Part 6.

[25] ANZAC note Ga 364 of 20 July 1915 in 1st Australian Division General Staff War Diary, July 1915, AWM4 1/42/6, Part 8.

[26] Artillery Daily Reports for 29 and 30 July 1915 in 1st Australian Division General Staff War Diary, July 1915, Part 10.

[27] 1st NZFA Brigade War Diary, 26 August 1915, AWM4 35/7/1; Byrne, *New Zealand Artillery In the Field 1914-18*, p.60.

[28] 3rd Infantry Brigade KC 525, 'Report On The Attack On Turkish Work "Norten [sic] Despair" 31st July/1st August 1915', dated 2 August 1915 in 1st Australian Division General Staff War Diary, August 1915, AWM4 1/42/7, Part 2.

[29] Ibid.

[30] Ibid.; Anderson War Diary, 31 July/1 August 1915.

Chapter Six

[1] The initial proposal was presented in a letter from Sir William Birdwood to Sir Ian Hamilton dated 13 May 1915, AWM 3DRL/3376 11/5c, Part 1. For a succinct outline of the chronology of the planning for the offensive see Rhys Crawley, *Climax at Gallipoli: The Failure of the August Offensive*, University of Oklahoma Press, 2014, pp.25—33.

[2] 'Instructions For GOC Australian Division' and 'Instructions For Major General Sir Alex. Godley Commanding

NZ & Aust. Division' in 1st Australian Division General Staff War Diary, August 1915, Part 6; New Zealand and Australian Division Memorandum To: Brigadier-Generals Chauvel and Hughes 'Supplementary Instructions in continuation of Appendix B of this date' dated 5th Aug 1915 in 3rd LH Brigade War Diary, August 1915, AWM4 10/3/7.

[3] Ibid.; New Zealand and Australian Division Instructions issued to Commanders in accordance with Divisional Order No 11, dated 3th [sic] August 1915 in NZ&A Division War Diary, August 1915, AWM4 1/53/5, Part 2; New Zealand and Australian Division Divisional Order No 11 dated 5 August 1915 in NZ&A Division War Diary, August 1915, Part 2; NZG/882, New Zealand and Australian Division Memorandum dated 5 August 1915 in NZ&A Division War Diary, August 1915, Part 2; Operation Order No 1 by Brigadier General F.G. Hughes dated 5 August 1915 in 3rd LH Brigade War Diary, August 1915; Operation Order No 1 by Brigadier General H.G. Chauvel CMG Commanding No 3 Section, ANZAC dated 6/8/1915 in 1st LH

Brigade War Diary, August 1915, AWM4 10/1/13, Part 1.

[4] Hamilton's intentions are argued in Jeff Cleverly, 'More than a Sideshow? An Analysis of GHQ Decision Making during the Planning for the Landings at Suvla Bay, Gallipoli, August 1915', *War in History*, Vol.24, Issue 1, January 2017; and Jeff Cleverly, 'A Failure Inevitable? Command and Staff Work in Planning for the August Offensive and the Landing of IX Corps at Suvla Bay', in Rhys Crawley and Michael Locicero (eds), *Gallipoli: New Perspectives on the Mediterranean Expeditionary Force*, Chapter 4.

[5] 'Instructions For GOC Australian Division' and 'Instructions For Major General Sir Alex. Godley Commanding NZ & Aust. Division' in 1st Australian Division General Staff War Diary, August 1915, Part 6.

[6] Aspinall-Oglander, *Military Operations. Gallipoli*, Vol. II, pp.76, 136.

[7] Table A and Note B to Table A in GSR.Z.18/1 dated 18 July 1915 in MEF General Staff War Diary, July 1915, Part 2. See also ANZAC General Staff War Diary, July 1915, AWM4 1/25/4, Part 3.

[8] 3rd AFA Brigade Ammunition Column War Diary, July 1915, AWM4 13/85/8, Part 1.

[9] NZ&A Division General Staff War Diary, 22 July 1915, AWM4 1/53/4.

[10] Headquarters 1st Australian Division GS 4 dated 29 July 1915 in 1st Australian Division General Staff War Diary, August 1915, Part 6; Army Corps Order No 16 dated 3rd August 1915 including Appendix A-Action of Artillery in Support of Forthcoming Operation and Naval Arrangements for Support of Operations in ANZAC General Staff War Diary, August 1915, AWM4 1/25/5, Part 3; 1st Australian Division Operation Order No 9 dated 4th August 1915 in 1st Australian Division General Staff, War Diary, August 1915, Part 7; 1st Australian Divisional Artillery Operation Order No 1 dated 3-8-15 in 1st Australian Divisional Artillery War Diary, August 1915, AWM4 13/10/12, Part 1; NZ&A Division Order No 11 dated 5th August 1915.

[11] Crawley, *Climax at Gallipoli*, p.76. There is no mention of the conference on 2 August in any of the Anzac war

diaries. Crawley's source for the conference is Cunliffe-Owen's private diary held in the National Archives, United Kingdom, CAB45/246.

[12] Napier JoUston, evidence to the Dardanelles Commission, p.1397; Napier JoUston, War Diary, 3 August 1915; NZ&A Division Order No 11 dated 5 August 1915.

[13] Headquarters 1st Australian Division GS 6 dated 29 July 1915 in 1st Australian Division General Staff War Diary, August 1915, AWM4 1/42/7, Part 6.

[14] 1st Australian Divisional Artillery War Diary, 3 August 1915, Part 1; Hobbs Diary, 4 August 1915; 1st Australian Division Operation Order No 9 dated 4 August 1915 in 1st Australian Division General Staff War Diary, August 1915, Part 7; 1st Australian Divisional Artillery Operation Order No 1 dated 3-8-15 in 1st Australian Divisional Artillery War Diary, August 1915, Part 1.

[15] 5th AFA Battery War Diary, 6-9 August 1915, AWM4 13/67/5; 8th AFA Battery War Diary, 6-10 August 1915, AWM 4 13/70/13; 9th AFA Battery

War Diary, 6-10 August 1915, AWM4 13/71/7; 3rd AFA Brigade Ammunition Column War Diary, 6 August 1915, AWM4 13/85/9, Part 1; 1st NZFA Brigade War Diary, 10 August 1915, AWM4 35/7/2.

[16] 'Instructions For G.O.C. A & NZ Army Corps dated 30 July 1915', MEF General Staff War Diary, July 1915, Part 2; Corbett, *Naval Operations*, Vol. III, p.89.

[17] For *Bacchante, Edgar, Endymion, Talbot, Colne* and *Chelmer*, see *The Naval Annual 1913*, J. Griffin and Co, Portsmouth, 1913, reprinted 1970 by Clarke Doble and Brendon Ltd, Portsmouth. For *Havelock, Humber, M20* and *M33*, see E.H.H. Archibald, *The Fighting Ships of the Royal Navy*, The Blandford Press, 1968—1972, revised and reprinted by the Military Press, UK, 1987.

[18] Corbett, *Naval Operations*, Vol. III, p.89.
[19] Army Corps Order No 16 in ANZAC General Staff War Diary, August 1915, Part 3.
[20] Ibid.
[21] Ibid.

[22]	1st NZFA Brigade War Diary, 3—6 August 1915.
[23]	Byrne, *New Zealand Artillery In the Field 1914-18*, p.72; Napier JoUston Diary, 3 August 1915.
[24]	General Staff at General Headquarters, *Artillery Notes No 5, Wire Cutting*, June 1916.
[25]	Appendix A to Army Corps Order No 16 dated 3 August 1915 in ANZAC General Staff War Diary, August 1915, Part 3; 1 NZFA Brigade War Diary, August 1915; 1st Australian Divisional Artillery War Diary, August 1915; 2 AFA Brigade War Diary, August 1915, AWM4 13/30/9; 5 AFA Battery War Diary, August 1915. Observation of the fire of the batteries directed on JoUston's Jolly and Lone Pine was placed in the hands of the Commander, 2nd AFA Brigade.
[26]	Appendix A to Army Corps Order No 16 dated 3 August 1915 in ANZAC General Staff War Diary, August 1915, Part 3.
[27]	The other sections of the batteries involved were tasked to engage the Tabletop at 9.00pm and perhaps this, in conjunction with the limited

ammunition available, may be the reason they were withdrawn from supporting Lone Pine.

[28] Bean, *Official History*, Vol. II, *The Story of Anzac*, pp.499—500; 1st Divisional Artillery Operation Order No 1 dated 3-8-15 in 1st Australian Divisional Artillery War Diary, August 1915, Part 1.

[29] 1st Australian Division Operation Order No 9 dated 4 August 1915 in 1st Australian Division General Staff War Diary, August 1915, Part 7.

[30] Ibid. The mobile section was formed from guns of the 4th and 5th AFA batteries. Firing from a temporary position near Brown's Dip, it put around 60 rounds into Lone Pine and JoÚston's Jolly before being put out of action by Ottoman counter-fire. The howitzer and field batteries designated to provide counter-battery fire were A and C batteries, 69th Howitzer Brigade, 4th (City of Glasgow) Battery, 5th (City of Glasgow) Battery, 4th NZFA Battery, and the 5th, 7th, 8th and 9th AFA batteries.

[31] Corbett, *Naval Operations*, Vol. III, p.91.

[32]	See also Crawley, *Climax at Gallipoli*, p.71.
[33]	'Times and Messages for the Attack on Lone Pine' in 1st Australian Division General Staff War Diary, August 1915, Part 7.
[34]	The only indication of the number of rounds fired by the howitzer batteries between 4.30 and 5.30 comes from orders to the 4th (City of Glasgow) Battery, which limited expenditure to 100 rounds. Using this as a reference, it might be reasonably assumed that the two sections firing onto Lone Pine expended no more than 200 rounds. Manuscript Orders from Commander 4th Howitzer Lowland Brigade to OC 4th Battery dated 1300hrs 6 August. A copy of these orders was captured by the Ottomans and provided to the authors by Associate Professor Mesut Uyar.
[35]	*Field Artillery Training 1914*, Sect 156.
[36]	1st Australian Divisional Artillery War Diary, 6 August 1915, Part 2.
[37]	'Times and Messages for the Attack on Lone Pine' in 1st Australian Division General Staff War Diary, August 1915, Part 7.

[38] Headquarters 1st Australian Division Dispatch No 15 dated 14 August 1915, in ANZAC General Staff War Diary, August 1916, Part 5; 2nd Australian Infantry Brigade War Diary, 6/7 August 1915, AWM4 23/2/6; 6th Australian Battalion War Diary, 6/7 August 1915, AWM4 23/23/4; Bean, *Official History*, Vol. II, *The Story of Anzac*, pp.600—01; manuscript orders from Commander 4th Lowland Howitzer Brigade to OC 4th Battery.

[39] 1st NZFA Brigade War Diary, 6—9 August 1915, Napier JoÚston Narrative; Hobbs Diary, 7 August; 7th IMA Brigade War Diary, August 1915, AWM6 183.

[40] Headquarters 1st Australian Division Dispatch No 15, dated 16 August 1915 in 1st Australian Division General Staff War Diary, August 1915, Part 7.

[41] Charles Bean Diary No 11, AWM 3DRL 606/11/1.

[42] New Zealand and Australian Division Divisional Order No 11 dated 5 August 1915; NZG/882, New Zealand and Australian Division Memorandum dated 5 August 1915; 3 LH Brigade Operation Order No 1 by Brigadier

General F.G. Hughes VD dated 5 August 1915; all in 3rd LH Brigade War Dairy, August 1915, AWM 4 10/3/7; 1 LH Brigade Operation Order No 1 by Brigadier General H.G. Chauvel CMG Commanding No 3 Section, ANZAC dated 6/8/1915 in 1st LH Brigade War Diary, August 1915, AWM4 10/1/13, Part1.

[43] 1st LH Brigade War Diary, 7 August 1915, Part 1; 3rd LH Brigade War Diary, 7 August 1915; 1st LH Regiment War Diary, 7 August 1915, AWM4 10/6/4; 2nd LH Regiment War Diary, 7 August 1915, AWM 10/7/6; 8th LH Regiment War Diary, 7 August 1915, AWM4 10/13/4; 10th LH Regiment War Diary, 7 August 1915, AWM4 10/15/4; Bean, *Official History*, Vol. II, *The Story of Anzac*, pp.612—31.

[44] Bean, *Official History Vol II, The Story of Anzac*. pp.611—13.

[45] Graham Wilson, *Bully Beef and Balderdash*, Vol. II, *More myths of the AIF examined and debunked*, Big Sky Publishing, Newport, 2017, Chapter 8, 'The Silent Seven Minutes: the myth of the seven-minute time delay at The Nek'. Graham kindly sent the authors

the manuscript before his book was published posthumously. His work was somewhat polemic and, other than Robinson's account, there was no evidence from 8 LH participants in the charge. In undertaking their own investigation, the authors are indebted to Jeff Pickerd for the wealth of sources he gave us, including accounts of 8 LH survivors, some of which the authors passed to Wilson before the publication of his book.

[46] Jeff Pickerd, unpublished manuscript sent to authors; letter Robinson to Bean dated 3.4.24, letter Robinson to Bean dated 9/5/24, letter Robinson to Bean dated 16/5/24, letter Brazier to Bean dated 7.3.24, all in AWM38 3DRL 8042, Item 25; Lyon quoted in Cameron Simpson, *Maygar's Boys—A biographical History of the 8th Light Horse Regiment AIF 1914-19*, Just Soldiers, Military Research & Publications, Moorooduc, Vic, 1998, p.280.

[47] *The Argus* (Melbourne), 19 October 1915, p.5.

[48] Letter Kent Hughes to Bean dated 29.2.24, AWM 3DRL 6673/196; letter

Boyle dated 8 September 1915 in *The Gippsland Mercury*, 19 October 1915.

[49] Ronald East (ed), *The Gallipoli Diary of Sergeant Lawrence of the Australian Engineers, 1st A.I.F 1915*, MUP, Melbourne, 1981, diary entry 7 August 1915, pp.62—64; Faulkner letter in 'Sanguinary August', article in Florence Breed (ed), *Gallipoli With Love 1915, Letters from the Anzacs of the Wimmera*, History and Natural History Group of the M.L.A. Society, Inc., Donald, Victoria, Publication No.40, November 1993, pp.174—76.

[50] Bean Diary No 12, AWM 606/12/1; 'Light Horse Charge. Self Sacrifice and Heroism', *The Register*, 27 August 1915, p.8; Historical Note in AWM38 3 DRL8042 Item 25; Charles Bean, Diary No 16, AWM 606/16/1; Tim Travers, *Gallipoli 1915*, Tempus, Stroud, US, 2002, p.120.

[51] 1st LH Brigade War Diary, 7 August 1915, AWM 4 10/6/4, Part 1; 3rd LH Brigade War Diary, 7 August 1915; 1st LH Regiment War Diary, 7 August 1915; 2nd LH Regiment War Diary, 7 August 1915 AWM4 10/7/6; 8th LH Regiment War Diary, 7 August 1915

AWM4 10/13/4; 9th LH Regiment War Diary, 7 August 1915 AWM4 10/14/8;', 10th LH Regiment War Diary, 7 August 1915 AWM4 10/15/4; HMS *Endymion* log in Travers, *Gallipoli 1915*, pp.118—22.

[52] Report written by Major Deeble, A/CO 8th Light Horse Regiment, dated 7 August 1915 in 3rd LH Brigade War Diary, August 1915.

[53] 3rd LH Brigade S.C. 329 dated 7 August 1915—Dispatch on Operations 6/7 August 1915—No 4 Section Russell's Top in AWM25/367/30, Part 4.

[54] 'Report on operations of 10th L.H. Regt on Russell's Top on morning of 7/8/15 by LTCOL Brazier CO 10 L.H.' and '9th Light Horse Regt Results of Operations 7-8-15 for Brigade Headquarters submitted by Major Reynell' both in 3rd LH Brigade War Diary, August 1915; Noel Brazier Diary, 7 August 1915, AWM DRL 147; 'Report of Operations against the Sari Bair Position 6th-10th August 1915 of the Force under the Command of Major-General Sir A.J. Godley K.C.M.G. Commanding New Zealand and

Australian Division dated 16th August 1915' in NZ&A Division General Staff War Diary, August 1915, Part 2.

[55] Letter Brazier to Bean, 13 April 1931, AWM38 3DRL 7953, Part 3; Bean, *Official History*, Vol. II, *The Story of Anzac*, p.613.

[56] 3rd LH Brigade Operation Order No 1; Map Nek Forming Up Plan, AWM G7432. G1.S65XI.12; Ashburner in Charles Bean Diary No 32, AWM38 3DRL 606/32/1.

[57] McGarvie letter published in *The Colac Reformer*, 25 September 1915; Pickerd unpublished ms; Merrit quote in Max Emery, *They Rode into History: The Story of the 8th Light Horse Regiment Australian Imperial Force 1914-1919*, Slouch Hat Publications, McCrae, Vic, 2008, p.4; Crawford letter published in *Tatura Guardian*, 12 October 1915; Letter St Pinnock to his father dated 15 August 1915, AWM 1DRL 574.

[58] Fuzzard Field Service Notebook held by Jeff Pickerd; Meldrum letter in *The Mornington Standard*, 2 October 1915; 'With the 10th A.L.H on the Field of Glory. From W.A to Gallipoli. Notes

from an Officer's Diary. No V.', *The Daily News* (Perth), 5 February 1916.

[59]   Major Redford Diary, 7 August 1915, AWM PR85/064; Mack letter dated 12 September 1915 quoted in JoÚ Hamilton, *Goodbye Cobber, God Bless You*, Macmillan, Sydney, 2004, pp.280—81; Private Jack Dale, letter dated 16 August 1915, in 'Letters from Old Melburnians' in Kiddle J. Beachham, *War Services of Old Melburnians*, p.138; William Cameron Diary, 17 August 1915, AWM 1DRL/0185; Map Nek Forming up Plan.

[60]   Letter Kent Hughes to Bean dated 29.2.24.

[61]   Appendix A to Army Corps Order No 16 dated 3 August 1915 in ANZAC General Staff War Diary, August 1915, AWM 4 1/25/5, Part 3.

[62]   Ibid.

[63]   1st Australian Divisional Artillery Operation Order No 1, in 1st Australian Divisional Artillery War Diary, August 1915, Part 2; NZ&A Division Order No 11 dated 5 August 1915.

[64]   Ibid.

[65]   Ibid.

[66] Ibid.

[67] For example, 'sweeping and searching', a tecÚique whereby the line of fire (sweeping) and the range (searching) was altered between rounds or bursts of fire by using designated turns of the elevation and traverse hand-wheels.

[68] 8th LH Regiment War Diary, 6 August 1915.

[69] The New Zealand howitzer battery was directed onto an area approximately 37x55 metres, well within its normal coverage. However, artillery rounds fired at the same bearing and elevation and using the same propellant charge do not fall on a single point, but in a zone along the line of fire. At the firing range involved, the 100% zone was 92 yards (84.1246 metres). See AWM 038339.5, Call No 623.42021 R196, *Range Tables For The 4.5inch Howitzer*, War Office, London. To this must be added a safety factor to account for the lethal radius of a shell bursting at the extremity of the zone. See also NZ&A Division General Staff War Diary, 14 July 1915.

[70] 3rd LH Brigade Operation Order Number 1.
[71] Letter Brazier to Bean, 13 April 1931.
[72] Harvey Broadbent, *Gallipoli, The Turkish Defence—The Story From Turkish Documents*, The Miegunyah Press, Melbourne, 2015, pp.271—72; Charles Bean Diary No 16; ANZAC Trench Diagram No III Corrected to 20th July 1915, AWM G7432.G1S65X-4a.
[73] Sukru Erkal, *A Brief History Of The Cannakkale Campaign In The First World War (June 1914—January 1916)*, Turkish General Staff Printing House, Ankara, 2004, Plate 50; ANZAC Trench Diagram No III Corrected to 20th July 1915; 'Consideration of an Attack on Baby 700' in 3rd LH Brigade War Diary, August 1915.
[74] NZ&A Division amendments and additions to Operation Order No 11 dated 5 August in 3rd LH Brigade War Diary, August 1915. See also 'Report of Operations against the Sari Bair position 6th-10th August 1915 of the Force under the Command of Major-General Sir A.J. Godley K.C.M.G. Commanding New Zealand and

	Australian Division dated 16th August 1915.'
[75]	Hobbs Diary, 24 August 1915. The 4th AFA Battery's war diary for August 1915 is missing, but the 5th's records firing according to the plan, and the 8th's, although not specific, indicates it also fired. 5th AFA Battery War Diary, 7 August 1915; 8th AFA Battery War Diary, 6—7 August 1915. See also Travers, *Gallipoli 1915*, p.121.
[76]	Confidential Report, Headquarters 1st Australian Division, dated 26 August 1915, AWM 3DRL/2600, Part 3; Artillery Timetable for night of 6/7 August and morning of 7th August 1915, Appendix A to NZ&A, also in Confidential Report, Headquarters 1st Australian Division, dated 26 August 1915, AWM 3DRL/2600, Part 3.
[77]	Letter Brazier to Bean, 13 April 1931.

Chapter Seven

[1]	NZ&A Division Order No 11 dated 5 August 1915; New Zealand and Australian Division Instructions Issued to Commanders in accordance with Divisional Order No 11, dated 5 August

1915, NZ&A Division War Diary, August 1915, AWM 1/53/5 Part 2; Pugsley, *Gallipoli*, p.272; Bean, *Official History*, Vol. II, *The Story of Anzac*, p.567; Aspinall-Oglander, *Military Operations. Gallipoli*, Vol. II, p.185.

[2] Ibid.

[3] Manuscript for The Ottoman Army in the First World War provided by Associate Professor Mesut Uyar. Broadbent, *Gallipoli, The Turkish Defence*, pp.277—80. Broadbent has the *2/14th* and the *3/14th* deployed between Sari Bair and the Anafarta Valley, whereas Uyar relates that it was only the *2/14th*. Uyar has the advantage over many historians of being able to read the Ottoman script rather than relying on translations. Broadbent's book is littered with mistakes, for example confusing artillery batteries with battalions and infantry platoons with companies, while his nomenclature of unit titles is often incorrect. He should be consulted with care.

[4] NZ&A Division Order No 11 dated 5 August 1915, and Appendix A; NZ&A Division 'Report on Operations against the Sari Bair Position 6th-10th August

1915' dated 16 August 1915; NZMR Brigade War Diary, 6 August 1915, AWM4 35/1/4, Part 1; Auckland Mounted Rifles War Diary, 6 August 1915, AWM4 35/2/5; Wellington Mounted Rifles War Diary, 6 August 1915, AWM4 35/5/14; Otago Mounted Rifles War Diary, 6 August 1915, AWM4 35/4/6; Bean, *Official History*, Vol. II, *The Story of Anzac*, p.458fn, pp.568—71; Pugsley, *Gallipoli*, pp.272—75; Richard Stowers, *Bloody Gallipoli*, David Bateman, Auckland, 2005, pp.146—50; Aspinall-Oglander, *Military Operations. Gallipoli*, Vol. II, pp.187—88; Stephen Chambers, *Anzac Sari Bair*, Battleground Gallipoli Series, Pen & Sword, Barnsley, UK, 2014, pp.65—68; Robert Rhodes James, *Gallipoli*, Angus & Robertson, Sydney and Melbourne, 1965, pp.267—69.

[5] Pugsley and Stowers write that Bauchop's Hill was not taken until 1.10pm, but the NZMR Brigade War Diary recorded its operation as successfully carried out by midnight (one hour behind schedule). However, reading the NZ&A Division War Diary for 6 August and report on the operation, it

is apparent that this time refers to the British 40th Brigade taking Damakjelik Bair. NZ&A Division 'Report on Operations against the Sari Bair Position 6th-10th August 1915 dated 16 August 1915 in NZMR Brigade War Diary, 6 August 1915; NZ&A Division General Staff War Diary, 6 August 1915; Otago Mounted Rifles War Diary, 6 August 1915 AWM4 35/4/6; Canterbury Mounted Rifles War Diary, August 1915, AWM4 35/3/4; Pugsley, *Gallipoli*, p.275; Stowers, *Bloody Gallipoli*, p.150.

[6] Uyar manuscript, The Ottoman Army in the First World War.

[7] Edward J. Erickson, *Gallipoli: Command Under Fire*, Osprey, Oxford, 2015, p.195.; E.J. Erickson, *Gallipoli: The Ottoman Campaign*, Pen & Sword, Barnsley, 2010, p.191; Broadbent, *Gallipoli, The Turkish Defence*, pp.277—80; Uyar manuscript for The Ottoman Army in the First World War.

[8] Byrne, *New Zealand Artillery In the Field 1914-18*, pp.77, 81; 1st NZFA Brigade War Diary, August 1915; Appendix A-Action of Artillery in Support of Forthcoming Operations-III Second Phase-Attack on Baby 700 and Chunuk

Bair, and Force Order No 16 dated 11 August 1915, both in NZ&A Division General Staff War Diary, August 1915, Part 3. Byrne maintains that the 1st NZFA Battery could provide the fire of a section, but the New Zealand war diaries show that the first gun of this section was not positioned to fire towards Chunuk Bair until the next day (8 August), and the second was not so positioned until 10 August. Byrne also suggests that some fire could be provided by the 2nd NZFA Battery. Three days later one of its sections could definitely fire up onto the heights, but the war diaries are silent on whether this capability existed on 7 August. Byrne and other records show that two scratch batteries were formed, Daniell's and Daltry's. Byrne indicates that Daniell's four-gun battery supported the attacks on Sari Bair, but Daltry's was quickly disbanded. However, NZ&A Division (Forces Attacking Sari Bair) Force Order 16 of 11th August indicates it was in existence at that time, so it too may have supported the assaults.

[9] 7th IMA Brigade War Diary, 7 August 1915, AWM6 183.

[10] Corbett, *Naval Operations,* Vol. III, p.97.

[11] 5th AFA Battery War Diary, 7 August 1915; 8th AFA Battery War Diary, 7 August 1915.

[12] Bean, *Official History,* Vol. II, *The Story of Anzac,* pp.641-42; Aspinall-Oglander, *Military Operations. Gallipoli,* Vol. II, pp.206—07; Pugsley, *Gallipoli,* p.283—86; Stowers, *Bloody Gallipoli,* pp.158—60. Although Aspinall-Oglander mentions that British field and naval artillery fired on Chunuk Bair from 10.15am, this is highly unlikely. There is no mention of it in the NZ&A Divisional Artillery or 1st NZFA Brigade war diaries nor by Bean, Pugsley or Stowers.

[13] 1st NZFA Brigade War Diary, August 1915, Appendix II; Napier JoÚston Diary, 7 August 1915.

[14] NZ&A Division Order No 12 dated 7 August 1915 in NZ&A Division General Staff War Diary, August 1915, Part 2.

[15] Napier JoÚston Diary, narrative section; 7th IMA Brigade War Diary, 8 August 1915; DA 903 dated 7/8/15 in Headquarters 1st Australian Division

	General Staff War Diary, August 1915, Part 1.
[16]	1st Australian Division General Staff War Diary, August 1915, Part 2.
[17]	5th AFA Battery War Diary, 7—8 August 1915; 8th AFA Battery War Diary, 7—8 August 1915; Heavy Battery War Diary, 7—8 August 1915, AWM4 13/63/2.
[18]	NZ&A Division Order No 12 dated 7 August 1915. In his report on the attacks on Sari Bair, the GOC NZ&A Division recorded that the bombardment on the morning of 8 August began at 4.15am. In view of the orders issued, this appears to be a mistake. NZ&A Division War Diary, August 1915, Part 2.
[19]	2nd AFA Brigade War Diary, 8 August 1915; 5th AFA Battery War Diary, 8 August 1915; 8th AFA Battery War Diary, 8 August 1915; Heavy Battery War Diary, 7—8 August 1915.
[20]	Bean, *Official History*, Vol. II, *The Story of Anzac*, pp.656—58; 7th IMA Brigade War Diary, 8 August 1915.
[21]	Napier JoÚston Diary, 8 August 1915; Wellington Battalion War Diary, 8 August 1915, AWM4 35/20/5;

Broadbent, *Gallipoli, The Turkish Defence*, p.290; W.H. Cunningham, C.A.L. Treadwell and S.H. Hanna, *The Wellington Regiment (NZEF) 1914-1919*, Ferguson and Osborn Limited, Wellington, 1928, pp.68—70; James, *Gallipoli*, pp.284—85; Bean, ibid., p.668; Pugsley, *Gallipoli*, pp.287—94; Stowers, *Bloody Gallipoli*, pp.166—68. Bean makes no mention of the bombardment while, oddly, Stowers says the bombardment proved 'totally ineffectual, possibly not causing a single casualty amongst the Turks.' (p.167)

[22] 8th AFA Battery War Diary, 8 August 1915.

[23] 5th AFA Battery War Diary, 8 August 1915.

[24] Uyar manuscript, The Ottoman Army in the First World War; Erickson, *Gallipoli: The Ottoman Campaign*, pp.154—55.

[25] Heavy Battery War Diary, 8 August 1915; 5th AFA Battery War Diary, 8 August 1915.

[26] 7th IMA Brigade War Diary, 8 August 1915.

[27] NZ&A Division Order No 13 dated 8 August 1915 in NZ&A Division

General Staff War Diary, August 1915, Part 3, 'Report of the Operations against the SARI BAIR position 6th-10th August of the Force under the Command of Major-General Sir A.J. Godly KCMG, CB Commanding New Zealand and Australian Division', dated 16 August 1915.

[28] Ibid.
[29] Ibid.
[30] NZ&A Division Order No 13 dated 8 August 1915.
[31] Ibid.; Napier JoUston Diary, 9 August 1915.
[32] Aspinall-Oglander, *Military Operations. Gallipoli*, Vol. II, p.218; Bean, *Official History*, Vol. II, *The Story of Anzac*, p.691; Stowers, *Bloody Gallipoli*, p.184; 5th AFA Battery War Diary, 8 and 9 August 1915; 8th AFA Battery War Diary, 8 and 9 August 1915; Heavy Battery War Diary, 9 August 1915.
[33] Bean, *Official History, Vol II The Story of Anzac*, p.692; Major A.H. Wilkie, *Official War History of the Wellington Mounted Rifles Regiment 1914-1919*, Whitcomb and Tombs Limited, Wellington, 1924, p.55; Pugsley, *Gallipoli*, p.310; Stowers,

Bloody Gallipoli, p.188; 2nd AFA Brigade War Diary, 9 August 1915.

[34] Napier JoÚston Diary, 9 August 1915; letter Lieutenant General Sir William Birdwood to Lady Birdwood dated 9 August 1915, AWM 3DRL/337; report from Lieutenant General Birdwood to Sir Ian Hamilton dated 10 August 1915, p.22 in ANZAC General Staff War Diary, August 1915, Part 5; Pugsley, *Gallipoli*, p.310; Bean, *Official History, Vol II, The Story of Anzac*, p.695; James, *Gallipoli*, p.290; Chambers, *Anzac Sari Bair*, p.129. Pugsley writes that they were artillery shells, and Bean, James and Chambers argue that the shells came from the howitzers.

[35] Aspinall-Oglander, *Military Operations. Gallipoli*, Vol. II, pp.218—20; 2nd AFA Brigade War Diary, 9 August 1915; 5th AFA Battery War Diary, 9 August 1915; 8th AFA Battery War Diary, 9 August 1915.

[36] Erickson, *Command at Gallipoli*, p.208, and *Gallipoli: The Ottoman Campaign*, pp.164—66; Broadbent, *Gallipoli, The Turkish Defence*, pp.307—10; 2nd Lieutenant O.E. Burton, *The Auckland Regiment*, Whitcomb and Tombs,

Auckland, 1922, p.63; Major F. Waite, *The New Zealanders at Gallipoli*, Whitcombe and Tombs Ltd, Auckland, 1919, pp.226—28; Byrne, *Official History of the Otago Regiment*, p.62; 7th IMA Brigade War Diary, 10 August 1915; 5th AFA Battery War Diary, 10 August 1915.

[37] Napier JoÚston, Evidence to Dardanelles Commission, p.1395.

[38] Napier JoÚston Diary, Narrative.

[39] Report On Operations Against The Sari Bair Position 6th-10th August 1915 dated 16th August 1916.

[40] 'Extracts from Memo to Troops by Lieutenant General Commanding', Hobbs Papers, AWM3DRL/2600, Wallet 2.

[41] ANZAC General Staff War Diary, August 1915, Part 1; 2nd AFA Brigade War Diary, 7August 1915; 1st NZFA Brigade War Diary, 6 August 1915; Napier JoÚston Diary, 6 August 1915; 7th AFA Battery War Diary, 6-10 August 1915, AWM4 13/69/2; 8th AFA Battery War Diary, 8 and 9 August 1915; Crawley, *Climax at Gallipoli*, p.84.

Chapter Eight

[1] Napier JoUston Diary, Narrative; 6th AFA Battery War Diary, 18,19, 20 August 1915, AWM4 13/68/7; Report On Operations 11th-31st August 1915 in NZ&A Division General Staff War Diary, August 1915, Part 3; 2nd AFA Brigade War Diary, 20 August 1915; 2nd AFA Brigade War Diary, 20 September 1915, AWM4 13/30/10. Major Stevenson replaced Mills, the original commander of the 6th Battery, who died at Helles.

[2] Force Order No 19 dated 20 August 1915, and 'Report on Operations 11-31 August 1915 from the Force Under Command of Major General Godley dated 3 September 1915' in NZ&A Division General Staff War Diary, August 1915, Part 3.

[3] Force Order No 19 dated 20th August 1915 in NZ&A Division General Staff War Diary, August 1915, Part 3; Operation Order No 1—Reference Force Order No 19—by Major General H.V. Cox dated 20 August 1915 in 5th Australian Infantry Brigade War Diary, August 1915, AWM4 23/5/2.

[4] NZ&A Divisional Artillery Report on 21st and 22nd August dated 23 August 1915 in the NZ&A Divisional Artillery War Diary, August 1915, AWM4 13/15/4.

[5] NZ&A Divisional Artillery Report for 20 August 1915 in NZ&A Divisional Artillery War Diary, August 1915; Operation Order No 1—Reference Force Order No 19—by Major General H.V. Cox dated 20 August 1915.

[6] Aspinall-Oglander, *Military Operations. Gallipoli*, Vol. II, p.357.

[7] Bean, *Official History*, Vol. II, *The Story of Anzac*, pp.730—35.

[8] NZ&A Divisional Artillery Report on 21st and 22nd August dated 23 August 1915.

[9] Ibid.

[10] Ibid.; 7th IMA Brigade War Diary, 21 August 1915.

[11] NZ&A Divisional Artillery Report on 21st and 22nd August dated 23 August 1915; Appendix II to NZ&A Divisional Artillery Report dated 21st August 1915 in the NZ&A Divisional Artillery War Diary, August 1915.

[12] Pugsley, *Gallipoli*, p.321; 'Report on Operations 21/8/15' in NZMR Brigade War Diary, August 1915, Part 2.

[13] NZ&A Division Artillery Report 21st and 22nd dated 23 August 1915.

[14] Appendix 1 to NZ&A Divisional Artillery Report on 21st and 22nd August dated 23 August 1915. On the 1/20,000 map in use, Hill 60 is between grid reference 92J4 and 92J7. The battery commander reported firing on the line 92I3 and 92J8, which runs across or just behind the crest on the map. In practice it is likely that he would have registered the crest.

[15] The Otago Battalion faced a similar problem with the length of the assault on 2 May, as did some attacking forces in the attacks on Sari Bair. It was not a problem encountered at Lone Pine and the Nek because the jumping-off trenches were much closer to the initial objective. As an indication of the time for which troops might be exposed, later in the war, rates of advance in the assault for a creeping barrage of 100 yards in four minutes were common.

[16]	Appendix I to NZ&A Divisional Artillery Report on 21st and 22nd August dated 23 August 1915.
[17]	Ibid.
[18]	Appendix II to NZ&A Divisional Artillery Report on 21st and 22nd August dated 23 August 1915.
[19]	Extract from diary of Captain S.P. Goodall Commanding C Company, 18th Battalion, AIF, 21st August 1915 in 5th Australian Infantry Brigade War Diary, August 1915; Bean, *Official History*, Vol. II, *The Story of Anzac*, pp.740—44.
[20]	Operation Order No I by Major General H.V. Cox CB, CSI Commanding No 6 Section Sari Bair Assaulting Force dated 26th August 1915, and 'The Attack on Kaiajik Aghala and Hill 60 Artillery Timetable' dated 27th August 1915 both in NZ&A Divisional Artillery War Diary, August 1915.
[21]	Quoted in Aspinall-Oglander, *Military Operations. Gallipoli*, Vol. II, p.361.
[22]	Operation Order No I by Major General H.V. Cox CB, CSI Commanding No 6 Section Sari Bair Assaulting Force dated 26 August 1915.

[23] Ibid.

[24] The Attack on Kaiajik Aghala and Hill 60 Artillery Timetable dated 27 August 1915.

[25] NZ&A Divisional Artillery Report dated 28 August 1915 in NZ&A Divisional Artillery War Diary, August 1915.

[26] 'NZMR Report 27/8/15' in NZMR Brigade War Diary, August 1915, Part 2.

[27] ANZAC General Staff War Diary, 27th August 1915, Part 1.

[28] Bean, *Official History*, Vol. II, *The Story of Anzac*, p.749; Pugsley, *Gallipoli*, p.328.

[29] 'Report on Operations 11-31 August 1915 from the Force Under Command of Major General Godley dated 3 September 1915'; Bean, *Official History*, Vol. II, *The Story of Anzac*, pp.747-56.

[30] The Attack on Kaiajik Aghala and Hill 60 Artillery Timetable dated 27 August 1915.

[31] 7th IMB War Diary, 27 August 1915.

[32] Appendix III, Reports from 1st and 2nd NZFA Brigade to CRA NZ&A Division, FZB 680 and ZF 256, dated 28 August 1915 both in NZ&A Divisional Artillery War Diary.

[33] Ibid.; see also Appendix I, Report from 69th Brigade RFA to CRA NZ&A Division dated 29 August 1915 in NZ&A Divisional Artillery War Diary, August 1915.

[34] The Attack on Kaiajik Aghala and Hill 60 Artillery Timetable dated 27 August 1915.

[35] Appendix III Reports from 1st and 2nd NZFA Brigade to CRA NZ&A Division, FZB 680 and ZF 256, dated 28 August 1915.

[36] AWM 358.821ART; General Headquarters, BEF, *SS139.4, Artillery Notes No 4, Artillery In The Offensive, February 1917, Appendix 4,* 1917.

[37] ANZAC No. R.A. 896 dated 28 August 1915, 1st Australian Division General Staff War Diary, August 1915, Part 9.

[38] For examples of how the British on the Western Front sought to learn lessons from each attack, and especially how to better employ the artillery during 1915 see Spencer Jones (ed), *Courage without Glory: The British Army on the Western Front 1915*, Helion, Solihull, 2015. *passim*

[39] Marble, *History of Warfare*, Vol.108, Chapter 3.

Chapter Nine

[1] The 54th Division entered the line on 1 September and the 2nd Division on 8 September.

[2] The Long, Long Trail, Order of Battle of Divisions, 54th (East Anglian) Division at: http://www.longlongtrail.co.uk/army/order-of-battle-of-divisions/54th-east-anglian-division/; 2nd Australian Division War Diary, June—August 1915, AWM4 1/44/1, Part 2.

[3] Army Corps Order Number 18 dated 19 September 1915 in ANZAC General Staff War Diary, September 1915, AWM4 1/25/6, Part 3.

[4] 1st Divisional Artillery War Diary, August 1915, Part 1; NZ&A Divisional Artillery War Diary, August 1915. For the departure of the 4th (City of Glasgow) Battery see Anzac General Staff War Diary, 19 August 1915, Part 1.

[5] 17th Siege Battery War Diary, 15-16 September 1915 in Ancestry.com; Appendix III to the Artillery Report for

24 September in NZ&A Divisional Artillery War Diary September 1915, AWM 4 13/15/5; 1st Australian Divisional Artillery War Diary 3/10/15 and 13/10/15, AWM4 13/10/14 Part 1; Artillery Report dated 14/10/15 in 1st Australian Division General Staff War Diary September 1915, AWM4 1/42/9, Part 4; 1st AFA Brigade War Diary, 1-3 October 1915, AWM4 13/29/11; NZ&A Division Artillery Reports dated 13 October and 17 October 1915 in NZ&A Divisional Artillery War Diary October 1915, AWM4 13/15/6; BM 490A, Memorandum Re Artillery And Its Support of Infantry etc Brigades dated 18 November 1915 in NZ&A Division War Diary, November 1915, AWM4 1/53/8, Part 2.

[6] MEF GSR 184 and MEF GSRZ 31 to the Vice Admiral Commanding East Mediterranean Squadron, both dated 3 September 1915 in MEF General Staff War Diary, September 1915, AWM4 1/4/6, Part 2.

[7] Byrne, *New Zealand Artillery In the Field 1914-18*, p.94. Byrne doesn't indicate which feature the tunnel was driven

through, but presumably it was Damakjelik Bair.

[8] Byrne, ibid., p.91; Daily Artillery Reports in the NZ&A Divisional Artillery War Diaries, September to December 1915, AWM4 13/15/5—AWM4 3/15/8.

[9] Artillery Reports in 1st Australian Divisional Artillery War Diaries August to November 1915, AWM4 13/10/12-AWM4 13/10/15.

[10] For reference to the issue of notes on guidance for artillery officers and infantry-artillery cooperation see 1st Divisional Artillery War Diary, 9 and 30 September 1915, Part 1. The notes themselves can be found in the September diary, Part 2.

[11] Situation maps in ANZAC General Staff War Diary, September 1915, AWM4 1/25/6, Part 3; Anderson War Diary, 17 and 20 September 1915, AWM4 13/10/13, Part 3; 7th AFA Battery War Diary 8 October 1915, AWM4 13/69/4.

[12] Artillery Headquarters Report dated 10-9-15 in 1st Australian Divisional Artillery War Diary, September 1915, AWM4 13/10/13, Part 2; ANZAC Ga 310 dated 16 September 1915 in

	ANZAC General Staff War Diary, September 1915, Part 3.
[13]	1st Divisional Artillery War Diary, 10 and 25 September 1915.
[14]	Hobbs Diary, 28 August 1915.
[15]	MEF memo to GOC IX Corps dated 8 September 1915 in MEF General Staff War Diary, September 1915, Part 2.
[16]	HQ MEF GSR135/1 dated 9 September 1915 in MEF General Staff War Diary, September 1915, Part 2.
[17]	3rd AFA Brigade Ammunition Column War Diary, 24 September 1915, AWM4 13/85/10.
[18]	MEF 668 dated 25 September 1915 in MEF General Staff War Diary, September 1915, Part 3.
[19]	On 3 July, Headquarters 1st Division Artillery issued amendments to the May 1915 instruction 'Notes For The Reference and Guidance Of All Artillery Officers'. In early August it issued a revised version and, on 9 September, issued instructions on 'Cooperation Between Artillery and Infantry During The Present Phase Of Operations At Anzac'. See 1st Australian Division Artillery War Diary,

September 1915, Part 2. These documents contained the basic allotment of artillery to defensive sections.

[20] ANZAC Ga/96 dated 5 September 1915 in ANZAC General Staff War Diary, September 1915, Part 3; typed sheet dated 6.9.15 in 2nd Australian Division General Staff War Diary, September 1915, AWM4 1/44/2, Part 1. The other guns and howitzers available to assist were A Battery, 69th RFA Brigade, 4th, 5th (less two guns in his section) AFA batteries, and one gun each of the 8th AFA, 21st (Kohat) batteries, and one 6-inch howitzer—all controlled by the 1st Australian Division—and two guns of 4th NZFA (Howitzer) Battery controlled by the NZ&A Division.

[21] 1st Australian Divisional Artillery Order No 67a dated 7 November 1915 in 1st Australian Divisional Artillery War Diary, November 1915, AWM4 13/10/15.

[22] 1st AFA Brigade War Diary, August-November 1915, AWM4 13/29/2, Part 2; 1st AFA Brigade War Diary, November-December 1915,

AWM4 13/29/2, Part 3. These are additional to the monthly war diaries kept by the brigade.

[23] 1st Australian Divisional Artillery Order No 67a dated 7 November 1915 in 1st Australian Divisional Artillery War Diary, November 1915; 1st AFA Brigade War Diaries, August-November 1915 and November-December 1915, AWM 4 13/29/2 Part 2 and Part 3; 5th AFA Battery War Diary, 9 November 1915, AWM4 13/67/8; 6th AFA Battery War Diary, 1-7 November 1915, AWM4 13/68/9; 8th AFA Battery War Diary, 9 November 1915, AWM4 13/70/16; 9th AFA Battery War Diary, 9 November 1915, AWM4 13/71/10. See also Map of the Situation 1st Aust Division dated 8.11.15 in 1st Australian Division General Staff War Diary, November 1915, AWM4 1/42/10, Part 4; and Map of the Situation dated 15.11.8 in 1st Australian Division General Staff War Diary, November 1915, Part 5.

[24] 1st AFA Brigade War Diary, 30 September 1915, AWM4 13/29/10; also handwritten notebook diary, 1st AFA

Brigade War Diary, August-November 1915, Part 2.

[25] 1st Australian Divisional Artillery Order No 67a dated 7 November 1915 in 1st Australian Divisional Artillery War Diary, November 1915; 1st AFA Brigade War Diary, 24 November 1915, AWM4 13/29/12 and 1st AFA Brigade War Diary, November-December.

[26] BM 490A, Memorandum Re Artillery And Its Support Of Infantry etc Brigades dated 18 November 1915 in NZ&A Division War Diary, November 1915, AWM4 1/53/8, Part 2.

[27] Australian and New Zealand Army Corps Headquarters General Staff Circular No 2 dated 22nd November 1918, and the accompanying Tables 1A, 1B, and 2 in ANZAC General Staff War Diary, December 1915, AWM4 1/25/9, Part 4.

[28] Ibid.
[29] Ibid.
[30] Ibid.
[31] HMS *Bacchante* 20th September 1915 Memorandum No 1./S.3. of 13th August (revised to date); HMS *Triad* 4th November 1915 No C.33

Memorandum 'Communication with local shore stations'; Australian and New Zealand Army Corps No Ga 47 dated 7th November 1915; Memorandum re Vice Admiral's Memorandum of 12th August and 5th November; and HMS *Endymion* Memorandum S.3/3 dated 24th November 'Arrangements for the Gun Support of 3rd Detached Squadron to the Army at Anzac', all in ANZAC General Staff War Diary, December 1915, Part 4.

[32] ANZAC General Staff War Diary, September 1915, Part 1.

[33] Commodore Roger Keyes, *Naval Memoirs 1919-1915*, quoted in Dr David Stevens, 'Naval Gunfire Support at Gallipoli', *Cannonball, Journal of the Royal Australian Artillery Historical Company*, Number 90, Spring 2015.

[34] HMS *Endymion* Memorandum No S 3/3 dated 24 November 1915 in ANZAC General Staff War Diary, December 1915, Part 4.

[35] GHQ MEF G.s.R.Z. 46 dated 29 October, 1915; 'Report of a conference held at H.Q 9th Corps, Suvla, on Wednesday 3rd November,

1915, in accordance with instructions contained in G.H.Q letter G.S.R.Z.46 of 29th October, 1915'; Army Corps Headquarters General Staff Circular No 5 dated 6 November 1915; IX Corps GR 786 dated 16 November; ANZAC NA 500 dated 16 November 1915; NZ&A Division unreferenced message dated 16/11; ANZAC Ga 201 dated 16 November; ANZAC Ga 202 dated 16 November; ANZAC Ga 211 dated 17 November 1915. See also IX Corps G.S. 517/1 dated 11.11.15 and table attached, and table—Artillery Support Left Flank ANZAC dated 13/11/15. All in ANZAC General Staff War Diary, December 1915, Part 4.

[36] Artillery Reports 12-22 September 1915 in NZ&A Divisional Artillery War Diary, September 1915.

[37] New Zealand and Australian Division Artillery Report dated 3 October 1915 in NZ&A Divisional Artillery War Diary, October 1915.

[38] 9th AFA Battery War Diary, 15 October 1915, AWM4 13/71/9.

[39] The war diary records that, by this stage, the 4th Battery gun had been knocked out four or five times and all

that was left of the original gun was the trail, breech block and dial sight carrier. 1st Australian Divisional Artillery War Diaries, September 1915, Parts 1 and 2, and October 1915; Daily Artillery Report 20 November in NZ&A Divisional Artillery War Diary, November 1915, AWM4 13/15/7; Byrne, *New Zealand Artillery In the Field 1914-18*, p.91.

[40] NZ&A Divisional Artillery War Diaries, August to November 1915; 1st Divisional Artillery War Diaries, August to November 1915.

[41] NZ&A Divisional Artillery War Diaries, August to November 1915; 2nd AFA Brigade War Diaries, August to November 1915, AWM4 13/30/9 to AWM4 13/30/12; 3rd AFA Brigade War Diaries, August to November 1915, AWM4 13/31/13 to AWM4 13/31/15;Byrne, *New Zealand Artillery In the Field 1914-18*, pp.92, 93.

[42] 1st Australian Divisional Artillery ERT/KW dated 30 September 1915 in ANZAC General Staff War Diary, September 1915, Part 9; NZ&A Divisional Artillery War Diary, August to November 1915; Daily Artillery

Report for 12 September in NZ&A Divisional Artillery War Diary, September 1915.

[43] Heavy Battery 1st Australian Division War Diaries, July to December 1915, AWM4 13/63/1 to AWM4 13/63/6.

[44] 1st Australian Division Artillery War Diary, 19 August 1915, Part 1; Cunliffe-Owen, 'Artillery at Anzac', p.541; C.E.W. Bean, *Gallipoli Mission*, Australian War Memorial, Canberra, 1952, p.257fn.

[45] 1st Australian Division No G 619 dated 14 October 1915, in 1st Australian Division War Diary, October 1915, AWM4 1/42/9 Part 2; 1st Australian Divisional Artillery Operation Order No 12 dated 15 October 1915, in 1st Australian Divisional Artillery War Diary, October 1915, Part 1; Artillery Report dated 16 October 1915 in NZ&A Divisional Artillery War Diary, October 1915.

[46] 1st Australian Divisional Artillery War Diary, 16 October 1915, Part 1; Artillery Report dated 16 October 1915 in NZ&A Divisional Artillery War Diary, October 1915; NZ&A Division

	War Diary, 16 October 1915, AWM4 1/53/7.
[47]	1st Australian Divisional Artillery War Diary, 16 October 1915, Part 1; 1st Australian Division War Diary, 16 October 1915, Part 1; Artillery Report dated 16 October 1915 in NZ&A Divisional Artillery War Diary, October 1915; NZ&A Division War Diary, 16 October 1915, AWM4 1/53/7.
[48]	2nd Australian Division General Staff War Diary, 1 and 22 October 1915, AWM4 1/44/3, Part 1; G578, Report On Operations 1st September—31st October 1915 in NZ&A Division General Staff War Diary, November 1915, Part 1.
[49]	1st Divisional Artillery War Diary, 12 and 13 November 1915.
[50]	Notes On Trench Mortars in 1st Australian Division General Staff War Diary, November 1915, Part 1; G84, Memo To OC Infantry Brigades On Trench Mortars in 2nd Australian Division General Staff War Diary, September 1915, AWM4 1/44/2, Part 2; 2nd Australian Division General Staff War Diary, 18 November 1915, AWM4 1/44/4 Part 1; NZ&A Divisional

Artillery War Diary, 12 October 1915; G620, Memo To Brigades On Catapults in NZ&A Division General Staff War Diary, November 1915, Part 1.

[51] 54th Division G1280 Proposal for the Assault and Capture of the Crest of Hill 60 dated 23 September 1915 and NZ& A Divisional Artillery BM (105), Assault On Hill 60 (92J4-8), Instructions For The Artillery By The CRA NZ&A Division both in ANZAC General Staff War Diary, November 1915, AWM4 1/25/8, Part 3; NZ&A Divisional Artillery War Diary, September 1915.

[52] 54th Divisional Order No 2 dated 4-10-15, BM 350 Operations on Hill 60, Instructions for the Artillery by CRA NZ&A Division, dated 2 November 1915; ANZAC Ga 992 of 5 November 1915; 54th Divisional Operation Order No 3 dated 5-11-15; letter Birdwood to White dated 9 November 1915; message Ga 43 dated 1311-15 from De Costa (GSO1 54th Division) and Australian and New Zealand Army Corps General Headquarters No Ga 215 dated 17th

November 1915 all in ANZAC General Staff War Diary, November 1915, Part 3; NZ&A Divisional Artillery Daily Artillery Report for 16 November 1915 in NZ&A Divisional Artillery War Diary, November 1915.

[53] BM (105) Assault on Hill 60 (92 J 4/8) Instructions For The Artillery By The CRA NZ&A Division, BM 350 Operations on Hill 60 Instructions for the Artillery by CRA NZ&A Division dated 2 November 1915, and Plan of Trenches on Hill 60 all in ANZAC General Staff War Diary, November 1915, Part 3.

[54] BM 350 dated 2 November 1915; memorandum from Birdwood to White dated 9 November 1915; letter Godley to White dated 14/11/15 all in ANZAC General Staff War Diary, November 1915, Part 3.

[55] The daily scales listed were: 18-pounder, 35 (19 after 15 December); 4.5-inch howitzer, 5; 5-inch howitzer, 6; 6-inch howitzer, 7; 10-pounder, 19. HQ MEF GSR 135/1 of 20 November 1915 in MEF General Staff War Diary, November 1915, AWM4 1/4/8, Part 1.

Chapter Ten

[1] Signal from *Lord Nelson* to ANZAC No 211 dated 22 November in ANZAC General Staff War Diary, December 1915, Part 6.

[2] Lord Hankey, *The Supreme Command 1914-1918*, Vol. I, George Allen and Unwin Limited, London, 1961, p.429; Aspinall-Oglander, *Military Operations. Gallipoli*, Vol. II, p.382.

[3] Aspinall-Oglander, ibid., p.399. The instructions are at Appendix 17 in the separate volume of maps and appendices.

[4] Ibid., pp.402—04.

[5] Special ANZAC Corps Order dated 23 October 1915 in NZ&A Division General Staff War Diary, October 1915; 'Recommendation Of The General Staff On The Question Of The Action To Be Taken At Gallipoli' in MEF General Staff War Diary, November 1915, Part 2.

[6] Lord Hankey, *The Supreme Command 1914-1918*, Vol. II, George Allen and Unwin Limited, London, 1961, pp.459—63; Aspinall-Oglander, *Military Operations. Gallipoli*, Vol. II, Chapter XXIX.

[7] Liman von Sanders, *Five Years in Turkey*, p.96; web information citing Peter Jung, 'Der Kaiser und Konig Wustenkrieg—Osterrich-Ungarn in Vorderen Orient 1915-1918', Verlag, Styria, 1992, identifies this battery as the 24cm Motormorser Batterie M98, Number 9.

[8] Liman von Sanders, ibid., p.93; Operations Section, Review of Operations During Periods 4th-18th November and 19th November-4th December in MEF General Staff War Diary, November 1915, Part 2; 2nd Australian Division General Staff War Diary, 29 November 1915, Part 1; 1st Australian Divisional Artillery War Diary, 29 November 1915.

[9] 'Outline Scheme for Evacuation of the Peninsula' dated 16/11/15 in ANZAC General Staff War Diary, December 1915, Part 6.

[10] Secret Memo to GOC ANZAC in MEF General Staff War Diary, November 1915, Part 1.

[11] 'Notes on proposed operation' dated 27/11/15 in ANZAC General Staff War Diary, December 1915, Part 6.

[12] 1st AFA Brigade War Diary, 23 November 1915, AWM4 13/29/13.

[13] 1st Divisional Artillery War Diary, 24 to 27 November 1915; artillery report dated 28 November in NZ&A Divisional War Diary, November 1915.

[14] 'Notes on proposed operation' dated 27/11/15. However, a table of ANZAC guns dated 5/12/15 in ANZAC General Staff War Diary, December 1915, Part 3, lists 101 guns by grid reference and battery. The discrepancy is likely to be the inclusion of four 60-pounders of the 10th Heavy Battery RFA that were not part of ANZAC.

[15] Byrne, *New Zealand Artillery In the Field 1914-18*, p.97.

[16] Dardanelles Army G.S.R Z.48 Instructions to General Officers Commanding 9th Corps and Australian and New Zealand Army Corps dated 10th December 1915-Appendix B in Dardanelles Army General Staff War Diary, November-December 1915, AWM4 1/17/2, Part 2. Also in ANZAC General Staff War Diary, December 1915, Part 7. The list has six 6-inch howitzers on Anzac, but there were seven, two with the Australian Heavy

Battery, one with the NZ&A Divisional Artillery and four with the 17th Siege Battery RGA. The war diaries of the Australian Heavy Battery and the NZ&A Division General Staff show seven 6-inch howitzers being evacuated. In all, it lists 104 guns and howitzers, twenty-seven 18-pounders, seven 6-inch howitzers, the 4.7-inch naval gun, sixteen 5-inch howitzers, eight 4.5-inch howitzers, two 4-inch naval guns, two 3-pounder HotcŠiss guns and the anti-aircraft gun.

[17] ANZAC Memo to NZ&A Division dated 8 December 1915, and ANZAC Memo to 1st Australian Division dated 10/12/15 in ANZAC General Staff War Diary, December 1915, Part 7; Bean, *Official History*, Vol. II, *The Story of Anzac*, pp.864—65. NZ&A Division embarked two 4-inch guns, three 6-inch howitzers, six 5-inch howitzers and seven 18-pounder guns. NZ&A Division General Staff War Diary, 12 December 1915, AWM 4 1/53/9. 1st Australian Division embarked one 6-inch howitzer, four 5-inch howitzers (two from the 5th Lowland Battery and two from A Battery, 69th

Howitzer Brigade), and ten 18-pounders (one each from the 1st and 7th AFA batteries, and two each from the 3rd, 5th, 8th and 9th AFA batteries).

[18] Napier JoUston Diary, 11 December 1915.

[19] ANZAC Memo to 1st Australian Division dated 10/12/15; ANZAC Memo to 1st Australian Division dated 12.12.15; ANZAC Memo Ga 607 to 1st Australian Division dated 15.12.15; ANZAC Memo to NZ&A Division dated 8 December 1915; ANZAC Memo to NZ&A Division dated 13.12.15; and ANZAC Memo Ga606 to NZ&A Division dated 15.12.15 all in ANZAC General Staff War Diary, December 1915, Part 7.

[20] 2nd AFA Brigade War Diary, 11 December 1915, AWM4 13/30/13; 5th AFA Battery War Diary, 10, 12 and 13 December 1915, AWM4 13/67/9; 8th AFA Battery War Diary, 10 and 11 December 1915, AWM4 13/70/17.

[21] NZ&A Division General Staff War Diary, 12 December 1915. The war diaries of the AFA and heavy batteries show the same number of guns

withdrawn as detailed in the ANZAC instruction, together with two howitzers each from the 5th (City of Glasgow) Battery RFA and the 69th Howitzer Battery RFA.

[22] 1st Australian Division Order No 3 dated 12.12.15 in 1st Australian Division General Staff War Diary, December 1915, AWM4 1/42/11, Part 1; Notes on the withdrawal from Anzac, AWM 25/367/11; 7th AFA Battery War Diary, 17 December 1915, AWM4 13/69/6; 8th AFA Battery War Diary, 15 December 1915.

[23] 1st AFA Brigade War Diary, 14-16 December 1915, AWM4 13/29/13; 2nd AFA Brigade War Diary, 11-16 December 1915; 3rd AFA Brigade War Diary, 11-16 December 1915, AWM4 13/31/16.

[24] NZ&A Division General Staff War Diary, 12 to 20 December 1915.

[25] 'Instructions for Rear Guard Commander' dated 18 December 1915 in NZ&A Division General Staff War Diary, December 1915.

[26] Heavy Battery 1st Australian Division War Diary, 10-15 December 1915, AWM4 13/63/6.

[27] For example, the 6-inchers did not fire on 11-13 November and 25-28 November. Heavy Battery War Diary, November 1915, AWM4 13/63/5.

[28] ANZAC Memo to GOC 1st Australian Division dated 12.12.15 in ANZAC General Staff War Diary, December 1915, Part 7; 1st AFA Brigade War Diary, 11-18 December 1915; 5th AFA Battery War Diary, 14-19 December 1915; 6th AFA Battery War Diary, 14-17 December 1915, AWM4 13/68/10; 7th AFA Battery War Diary, 15-17 December 1915; 8th AFA War Diary, 15 December 1915; 9th AFA Battery War Diary, 14 December 1915, AWM4 13/71/11. The 4th AFA Battery's war diary is missing and there is no record of when its guns were removed, other than a mention of members of the 8th AFA Battery assisting with the withdrawal of a 4th Battery gun for embarkation on 16 December. They are not included in the ANZAC memo dated 10 December listing which batteries are to withdraw guns on the night 11/12 December and, according to the AFA battery war diaries, all of the

18-pounders listed were evacuated as instructed.

[29] The 1st AFA Battery's gun on Russell's Top had been taken over from the 3rd AFA Battery on 11 December, hence Table 5 shows the gun destroyed as being from the 3rd AFA Battery.

[30] 2nd AFA Brigade War Diary, 18 December 1915.

[31] 5th AFA Battery War Diary, 19 December 1915; 8th AFA Battery War Diary, 19 December 1915; 9th AFA Battery War Diary, 19 December 1915.

[32] Appendix F to 1st Australian Divisional Order No 4 dated 16.12.15, and 1st Australian Division Operation Order No 6 dated 18.12.15 in 1st Australian Division General Staff War Diary, December 1915, Part 1. See also 1st AFA Brigade War Diary, 19 and 20 December 1915; 2nd AFA Brigade War Diary, 19 December 1915; 5th AFA Battery War Diary, 19 December 1915; 8th AFA Battery War Diary, 19 December 1915; and 9th AFA Battery War Diary, 19 and 20 December 1915. One report states that two 5-inch

howitzers were destroyed in the 1st Divisional Artillery's sector, but several other documents do not reflect this.

[33] 'Report Evacuation from Anzac GOC Australian and New Zealand Army Corps to GOC Dardanelles Army' dated 23 December 1915 in ANZAC General Staff War Diary, December 1915, Part 11; Telephone message from 1st Australian Division 22/12/15, NZQ14 dated 22 December 1915, and ANZAC Ga 694 dated 22 December 1915 in ANZAC General Staff War Diary, December 1915, Part 12.

[34] Liman von Sanders, *Five Years in Turkey*, p.99.

[35] Conversation Roberts and Uyar 8 March 2017; Liman von Sanders, ibid., p.97.

[36] Napier JoÚston Diary, 20 December 1915.

BACK COVER MATERIAL

This meticulously researched book provides the first comprehensive study of the employment of artillery and naval gunfire support at Anzac. Faced with huge difficulties on inferior ground the Australian, New Zealand, Indian, and British gunners quickly adapted to a hostile environment, employing innovative technique to counter superior numbers of Ottoman artillery and provide fire support to their infantry and light horse colleagues. How well they performed is a central theme of The Artillery at Anzac.

Using a host of primary sources including official manuals, war diaries, operation orders, letters, and private papers the authors trace the story of this neglected feature of the Gallipoli campaign. Commencing with an evaluation of the nascent prewar Australian and New Zealand artillery, they take the reader through the testing Introduction to the realities of modem warfare, the trials and difficulties the gunners experienced throughout the campaign, to the phased evacuation in December, without alerting the Ottomans to the reduced number of guns, Along the way, they challenge a long held controversy concerning the light horse charger at the Nek, and evaluate the effectiveness of the fire support provided to the infantry attacks, including that at Lone Pine, the attacks on the Sari Bair Range, and at Hill 60. In doing so, the authors illuminate long-buried information to provide new and penetrating insights into the campaign at Anzac.

The Artillery at Anzac reveals a largely unknown aspect of the campaign, deepening our understanding of it, and providing a new perspective that is of value not only to Gunners past and present, but to historians, and the wider public. Although occurring over a century ago the experience at Anzac offers lessons today's Gunners.

Index

A

400 Plateau, *64, 68, 69, 71, 81, 84, 92, 93, 114, 121, 137, 147, 162, 163, 246, 291, 382*

Abdul Rahman Bair, *291, 345, 347*

Achi Baba Ridge, *57*

adaptation, *135, 201, 246*

Aghyl Dere, *249, 291, 374, 397*

air observation, *226, 229, 404, 414*

aircraft, *74, 215, 229*

Alexandria, *54, 96, 375, 384*

   16-kilogram HE shell, *5*

   18-pounder high explosive (HE), *2, 98, 135, 266*

   375 lead-antimony balls, *2*

accounting methods, *429, 431*

August Offensive, *60, 249, 253, 266, 268, 272, 291*

   expenditure, *135, 137, 387, 389, 409, 412, 422, 425, 429, 431*

   field batteries, carried by, *98*

   high explosive (HE), *2, 5, 137, 266, 291*

   picric acid, *5, 73*

   Hill 60 assault, *354, 357*

   Lyddite shells, *5, 126, 284, 289*

   problems associated with, *135, 202*

   resupply, *41, 135*

   shortages, *135, 137, 170, 174, 181, 215, 217, 354, 357, 365, 367, 387, 389, 429*

   shrapnel,

   see shrapnel star (illumination) shells, *223, 235*

   supply arrangements, *152, 387, 389*

Anafarta Gap, *291*

Anafarta Valley, *63, 211, 214, 215, 291*
Anderson, Major Stuart, *98, 141, 152, 156, 162, 163, 181, 220*
   naval gunfire support, on, *170, 174*
anti-aircraft guns, *195, 197, 382*
   12-pounder (3-inch 77mm), *375*
Antill, Colonel JoÚ, *291*
artillery deployment, *141, 142, 146, 147, 152*
artillery strengthening, *235, 238, 241*
   battlefield topography, *57, 60, 63, 64, 68, 69, 215*
   evacuation, see evacuation from Gallipoli landing, *81, 83, 84, 87, 89, 92, 93, 96, 98, 101, 104, 105, 109, 111, 114, 116, 118, 121*
artillery disembarkation, *93, 96, 98, 101, 104, 105, 109, 111, 114*
   plans for, *69, 71, 93*

Ottoman defence, *71, 73, 81, 83, 84, 87, 92, 105, 111, 114*
   road network, *206, 208*
   static defence, *208, 211*
Anzac Cove, *68, 69, 81, 87, 89, 92, 98, 206, 291*
   Ottoman defences, *71*
Apex, the, *291, 374, 397*
arc of fire, *105, 141, 147, 152, 162, 181, 184, 186, 215, 217, 238, 286, 291, 384, 416*
Ari Burnu, *98, 116, 118, 181*
armistice, *198*
artillery,
   brigades, *29*
   defensive tasks, *141*
   doctrine, *5, 7, 10, 11, 14, 18, 20, 24, 26, 29*
   Gallipoli, problems at, *135, 137, 139*
   infantry support, as, *14, 26, 198, 226, 244, 362, 365, 371*
   arrangements, *389, 392, 394, 395, 397, 401, 409*
   lessons learned, *429*
   primary function, *14*
   support tasks, *409, 412*

training, *5, 7, 10, 11, 14, 18, 20, 24, 26, 29, 384*
Egypt, in, *41, 44, 46, 48, 50, 54, 57, 384, 394*
weapons, *2, 5*
Artillery Road, *206, 208, 414*
Asma Dere, *291*
August Offensive, *60, 249, 253, 266, 268, 272, 291*
ammunition, *253, 266, 268, 272, 291*
   coordination of forces, *291*
   Corps fire plan, *269, 272*
   debate about delay before attack, *291*
   fire support resources, *266, 268, 269*
   Lone Pine, *251, 253, 269, 272, 275, 278, 280, 282, 284, 286, 289, 291*
   naval gun support, *253, 268, 269, 282, 284, 291*
   Nek, the, *269, 275, 291*
   fire plan, *291*
   plan deficiencies, *291*
   Ottoman defence, *286, 289, 291*

planning, *257, 260, 263, 266, 291*
preparations, *251, 253*
Australia,
   Citizen Forces (CF), *2*
   mobilisation, *29, 32*
   training, *5*
   Militia, *2, 29*
   Permanent Force (PF), *29*
Australia Valley, *291*
Australian and New Zealand Army Corps (ANZAC), *32*
artillery commanders, *35, 38, 39, 41, 46*
artillery complement, *35*
   defensive sections, *156, 373, 374*
   Gallipoli landing, plans, *69, 71*
   staff processes (August Offensive), *291*
   training in Egypt, *41, 44, 46, 48, 50, 54, 57*
Australian Army,
   1st Australian Division, *32, 44, 50, 69, 93, 96, 104, 114, 116, 133,*

152, 156, 158, 162, 165, 220, 235, 238, 257, 280, 286, 291, 373, 384, 404, 425
2nd Australian Division, 373, 389, 425
Artillery, 5, 18
1st Australian Divisional Ammunition Column, 32
1st Australian Divisional Artillery, 32, 34, 123, 260, 374, 382, 392
1st Australian Field Artillery Battery (1st AFA Battery), 32, 44, 96, 105, 134, 395, 401
1st Australian Field Artillery Brigade (1st AFA), 29, 32, 39, 105, 111, 134, 375, 382, 384, 389, 392, 431
1st Australian Heavy Battery (1st Heavy Battery), 235, 246, 268, 280, 291, 382, 418
2nd Australian Field Artillery Battery (2nd AFA Battery), 32, 96, 134, 394

2nd Australian Field Artillery Brigade (2nd AFA), 29, 32, 41, 96, 101, 105, 111, 114, 123, 126, 133, 156, 163, 291, 382
2nd Australian Field Artillery Brigade Ammunition Column, 104
3rd Australian Field Artillery Battery (3rd AFA Battery), 32, 48, 93, 96, 105, 133, 134, 395
3rd Australian Field Artillery Brigade (3rd AFA), 29, 32, 41, 48, 81, 93, 96, 98, 101, 105, 111, 133, 156, 382, 392
3rd Australian Field Artillery Brigade Ammunition Column, 217, 253, 268, 387
4th Australian Field Artillery Battery (4th AFA Battery), 32, 44, 48, 96, 101, 104, 105, 111, 126, 133, 142, 147, 152, 156, 181, 183, 184, 195, 198, 201, 208,

232, 275, 280, 291, 392, 395, 401, 414

5th Australian Field Artillery Battery (5th AFA Battery), *32, 96, 105, 111, 116, 126, 133, 142, 147, 152, 156, 163, 169, 195, 198, 208, 232, 266, 275, 280, 291, 389, 392, 395, 401*

6th Australian Field Artillery Battery (6th AFA Battery), *32, 96, 114, 133, 134, 156, 206, 208, 291, 374, 384, 389, 392, 395, 414*

7th Australian Field Artillery Battery (7th AFA Battery), *32, 96, 105, 109, 111, 133, 134, 147, 156, 175, 181, 208, 220, 223, 226, 235, 244, 268, 280, 291, 384, 395*

8th Australian Field Artillery Battery (8th AFA Battery), *29, 32, 96, 111, 123, 126, 133, 142, 146, 147, 156, 181, 186, 198, 220, 226, 244, 268, 280, 291, 384, 392, 395*

9th Australian Field Artillery Battery (9th AFA Battery), *32, 96, 133, 147, 152, 156, 181, 186, 189, 195, 197, 217, 220, 226, 229, 244, 268, 280, 289, 392, 395, 397, 412, 414, 418*

Brighton Battery, *147*
Headquarters (HQ) Divisional Artillery, *32*
Jopp's Battery, *147, 181*
orders of battle,
    1st Australian Infantry Brigade, *32, 114, 251, 282, 291, 395*

2nd Australian Infantry Brigade, *32, 69, 81, 83, 116*
3rd Australian Infantry Brigade, *32, 69, 81, 244, 395*
4th Australian Infantry Brigade, *32, 114, 121, 123, 291, 397*
5th Australian Infantry Brigade, *373, 395*
6th Australian Infantry Battalion, *251, 289*
6th Australian Infantry Brigade, *373, 395*

7th Australian Infantry Brigade, *373, 395*
11th Australian Infantry Battalion, *84, 244*
13th Australian Infantry Battalion, *121, 129*
16th Australian Infantry Battalion, *121, 126, 129, 133*
18th Australian Infantry Battalion, *353, 369*
Light Horse, *291*
1st Australian Light Horse Brigade, *32, 251, 291*
1st Light Horse Regiment, *291*
2nd Australian Light Horse Brigade, *373, 395, 397*
2nd Light Horse Regiment, *291*
3rd Australian Light Horse Brigade, *251, 291*
5th Light Horse Regiment, *403*
8th Light Horse Regiment, *291*
9th Light Horse Regiment, *291*
10th Light Horse Regiment, *291, 367*
manuals, *11*
organisation, *34, 260, 392*
training, *32*
Australian Imperial Force (AIF),
see also Australian and New Zealand Army Corps (ANZAC),
establishment and mobilisation, *29, 32*

B

Baby 700, *64, 68, 69, 84, 87, 92, 105, 114, 142, 147, 189, 223, 291, 403, 406*
attack (30 April–3 May 1915), *121, 123, 126, 129, 133, 284*
August Offensive, *249, 251, 291*
demonstration firing, *232*

Ottoman defence, *291*
Baldwin, Brigadier General Anthony, *291*
Balkan gun pits, *220*
Barber, Gunner Charles, *291*
   training, *41, 44*
Battleship Hill, *64, 68, 84, 123, 126, 147, 291, 404*
   August Offensive, *251, 291*
Bauchop's Hill, *291, 349*
Bean, Charles, *29, 89, 123, 168, 418*
   August Offensive, *291*
Belcher, Gunner Harry, *291*
Bessell-Browne, Lieutenant Colonel Alfred, *111, 133, 142, 186, 226*
   August Offensive, *280, 291*
Bird Trench, *404*
Birdwood, Lieutenant General Sir William, *32, 46, 48, 50, 101, 178, 198, 215*
   ANZAC plans, *69, 73, 114, 116, 156, 201, 249*
   artillery training, *384*
August Offensive, *266, 291*
Baby 700 assault, *121*
evacuation plans, *435*
Hill 60 assaults, *291, 354, 427, 429*
Bloody Angle, *92*
Boghali, *211*
Bolton's Ridge, *64, 68, 81, 92, 101, 105, 109, 114, 116, 134, 147, 206, 220, 232, 244, 291, 392, 395*
   field gun siting, *141*
bombs (grenades), *198*
Boyle, Sergeant Francis, *291*
Brazier, Lieutenant Colonel Noel, *291*
breech loading (BL) weapons, *73*
Bridges, Major General William Throsby, *32, 44, 69, 162*
   artillery at Gallipoli, *142, 146*
   Gallipoli landing, *69, 96, 101, 105*
Brigade Major Royal Artillery (BMRA), *24*

Brighton Battery, *147*
Brighton Beach, *64, 68, 69, 147, 206*
British Army,
  Artillery, *375*
  4-inch Battery 24th Siege Brigade RGA, *375, 380*
  4th (City of Glasgow) Howitzer Battery RFA, *217, 238, 253, 275, 280, 382*
  4th (Lowland) Howitzer Brigade RFA, *217, 238, 244, 253, 289, 291*
  5th (City of Glasgow) Howitzer Battery RFA, *223, 241, 291, 395*
  10th Heavy Battery RGA, *354, 360, 375, 377, 380, 414*
  17th Siege Battery RGA, *375, 380, 382, 395, 397, 422*
  55th Howitzer Brigade RFA, *409*
  69th Howitzer Brigade RFA, *238, 244, 253, 275, 280, 291, 347, 353, 354, 360, 367, 380, 382, 395, 397, 412, 422*
  Divisional Artillery organisation, *260*
  Corps, *24*
  Australian and New Zealand Army Corps see Australian and New Zealand Army Corps (ANZAC) I Corps, *24*
  VIII Corps, *251*
  IX Corps, *249, 251, 291, 345, 354, 374, 387, 401, 409, 433*
  Divisions,
    11th (Northern) Division, *375*
    13th (Western) Division, *238, 249, 253, 291*
    29th Division, *57, 101, 134*
    54th (East Anglian) Division, *373, 380, 397, 427, 429*
  Infantry,

5th Battalion, the Connaught Rangers, *291*
5th Battalion, the Wiltshire Regiment, *291*
6th Battalion, the Loyal North Lancashire Regiment, *291*
6th Battalion, the South Lancashire Regiment, *291*
7th Battalion, the Gloucestershire Regiment - Glosters, *291*
8th Battalion, the Cheshire Regiment, *291*
8th Battalion, the Royal Welsh Fusiliers, *291*
8th Battalion, the Welsh Regiment/8th Welsh, *291*
9th Battalion, the Royal Warwickshire Regiment, *291*
10th Battalion, the Hampshire Regiment/10th Hants, *291*
39th Infantry Brigade, *291*
40th Infantry Brigade, *291*
organisation, *24, 375*
tactics, *5*
training manuals, *10, 11, 14, 18*
British Expeditionary Force (BEF), *24*
    Aldershot Command, *24*
    'Notes On Artillery In The Present War', *48*
Brooke, Lieutenant Colonel Alan British military doctrine, on, *20, 24, 26*
Brown's Dip, *142, 206, 373*
Burgess, Major William, *133, 147, 186, 226, 244, 395, 412*
August Offensive, *280*

Byrne, Lieutenant J.R., *44, 48, 57, 137, 291*
bombardment, *74, 83, 111*

C

Caddy, Major Hector, *105, 111, 133, 147, 169*
    August Offensive, *251, 280, 291*
    Cam Tepe, *71*
    Camel's Hump, *374*
    Cameron, Sergeant William, *291*
camouflage, *109, 126, 142, 184, 289*
    painting, *50*
Cape Helles, *57, 101, 134, 156, 206, 208, 232, 249*
    August Offensive, *251, 280, 291*
    June assaults, *220*
    troops returning from, *206, 241, 291, 374, 392, 431*
casualties, *121, 146, 175, 220, 384*
    August Offensive, *282, 291*
    friendly fire, *291*
    Hill, *101*
    assault, *291*
    Ottoman, *198, 284*
'Cement Emplacement', *223*
Chailak Dere, *249, 291*
Chakajak Kuyu, *412*
Chatham's Post, *206*
Cheshire Ridge, *291, 374, 397*
Chessboard, *121, 129, 147, 223, 232*
    August Offensive, *275, 280, 282, 284, 286, 289, 291*
Christian, Lieutenant Colonel Sydney, *39, 134*
Chunuk Bair, *63, 64, 69, 123, 226, 291, 380, 406, 412*
    August Offensive, *251, 291*
    Ottoman defence, *83, 84, 291*
close fire support, *291*
Colenso, *5*
command and control, *14, 152, 156, 158, 162, 163, 165, 168, 169, 201*
    divisional artillery commander (CRA),

18, 20, 24, 152, 162, 241, 291, 394
  doctrinal debate, *18, 20, 24*
communications, *24*
  artillery, *374, 409*
  August Offensive, during, *291*
  diagrams, *152, 168, 169, 374*
  flags, *77*
  offshore, *403*
  problems, *18, 89, 152, 168, 169, 291*
  radio stations, *77, 89, 114, 374*
  rapid, *14*
  requests for artillery support, *389, 392*
  signal stations, *389, 403, 406*
concealment, *14, 18, 26*
counter-battery work, *92, 211, 217, 220, 223, 226, 229, 232, 380, 382, 412, 414, 416, 418, 422, 429*
  August Offensive, *269, 278, 286, 291*

Hill 60 assault, *291, 354, 360*
  Ottoman, *135, 211, 412, 414, 416*
  retaliation, *414, 416, 422*
counter-mines, *198, 427*
Courtney's Post, *114, 142, 156, 163, 232, 238*
covered positions, *14, 18, 418*
covering fire, *201, 345, 347, 429*
  August Offensive, *278, 280, 289, 291*
  Hill 60 assault, *351, 369*
covering force, *64, 69, 73, 81, 93, 291*
Cox, Major General Herbert, *291*
  Hill 60 assault, *291, 345, 347, 354, 357, 362*
Crawford, Lieutenant Andrew, *291*
creeping barrages, *371*
crossfire, *220, 229*
Cunliffe-Owen, Brigadier General Charles, *44, 46, 48, 137, 152, 226, 365, 418, 429*

artillery support coordination, *395*
August Offensive, *257, 263, 291*
command and control at Anzac, *162, 163, 165*
naval gunfire support, *73, 74, 77, 152, 174, 403*

D

Dale, Private Jack, *291*
Daltry, Captain H.J., *291*
Damakjelik Bair, *291, 345, 351, 374, 397*
August Offensive, *291*
Daniell, Captain Groves, *291*
Dardanelles, *57, 60, 63, 71*
Dardanelles Commission, *152, 257, 291*
Dawkin's Point, *206*
de Robeck, Admiral, *404*
Dead Man's Ridge, *92, 133, 291*
Deeble, Major Arthur, *291*
defensive fire, *401, 431*
defilade, *92, 170, 214, 246, 291*
position, *181, 186, 198*
demonstrations, *232, 235, 422, 425*
August Offensive, *251*
deployment at Anzac, *141, 142, 146, 147, 152*
Dervish Ali Kuyu, *291, 351*
Destroyer Hill, *291*
Diamond Hill, *5*
direct fire, *7, 14, 18*
divisional artillery commander (CRA), *18, 20, 24, 152, 162, 241, 291, 394*
headquarters, *24*
operational planning, and, *24, 26*
dry firing, *41*
dugouts, *165*

E

Echelon Trench, *220*
war as educational process,
Elandslaagte, *5*
elevation, *291*
Ellsworth, Sergeant, *48*
enfilade fire, *129, 214, 291, 349*
entrenching, *206*

equitation, *41*
  plans, *394, 435*
Ewing, Gunner Thomas, *291*

F

field gun siting, *141, 152*
Falla, Major Norris, *104, 133, 291, 351*
Farm, the, *291*
Faulkner, Trooper JoÚ, *291*
field guns, *111, 133, 135*
  3-pounder (2-inch 47mm) HotcŠiss, *375*
  15-pounder BL, *2, 7, 14*
  18-pounder, *2, 5, 7, 32, 34, 35, 44, 92, 101, 104, 109, 123, 126, 195, 202, 208, 212, 241, 275, 291, 367, 377, 389, 397, 401*
  ammunition, *135, 152, 387, 389, 409*
  August Offensive, *266, 286*
  Mark I, *2*
  Mark II, *2*
  problems at Anzac, *174, 175*
  command and control structures, *152*
  heavy,
    see heavy field guns,
  Hill 60 assault, *291, 354, 362*
  indicative coverage, *291*
  landing at Anzac, *104, 105*
  siting, *141, 142, 146, 147, 181, 183, 184, 186, 189, 191, 195, 197, 201, 202*
  diagrams, *183, 186*
fire discipline, *41*
fire plans, *220*
  August Offensive, *257, 260, 263, 269, 272, 291*
  Nek, the, *291*
  Baby,
    assault, *121, 123, 129, 133*
  Hill 60 assaults, *291, 351, 353, 354, 357, 360, 362, 365, 369, 427, 429*
  Turkish Despair,
    capture of, *244, 246*
First Ridge, *64, 68, 69*
Fisherman's Hut, *69, 71, 104*

Franco-Prussian War (1870-71), *5, 26*
French Army, *24*
   Corps Expeditionnaire D'Orient (CEO), *57*
   manuals, *10*
   fuse setting, *41, 384*
Fuzzard, Sergeant George, *291*

G

Gaba Tepe, *60, 63, 68, 69, 71, 116, 147, 156, 201, 291*
   August Offensive, *253, 269, 282*
   Ottoman artillery, *81, 89, 101, 114, 211, 214, 220*
Gallipoli, *57*
   assault plan, *57, 60*
   departure for, *50, 54*
   naval gunfire support, *73, 74, 253*
German Army, *24*
   manuals, *10*
German Officers' Trench, *181, 201*
   August Offensive, *251, 269, 272, 275, 278, 280, 289, 291*

Godley, Major General Sir Alexander, *32, 158, 163, 435*
   August Offensive, *291*
   Baby 700 assault, *121, 123, 129*
   Hill 60 assaults, *291, 429*
Gravelotte, *5*
Green Patch Farm, *291*
gun drill, *41, 384*
Gun Lane, *206*
gun maintenance, *41*
gun pits, *181, 183, 184, 186, 195, 197, 217, 241, 268, 291, 414*
Gun Ridge,
   see Third Ridge,

H

Hamilton, General Sir Ian, *18, 197, 375, 387*
   August Offensive, *251, 253, 257*
   Gallipoli plans, *57, 101, 134, 249*
harassing fire, *211, 232*
Harris Ridge, *206, 220, 244, 403, 404, 406*

see also naval guns
60-pounder
(5-inch/127mm), *5, 34, 35, 375, 377, 414*
heliograph, *24*
Hell Spit, *68, 101*
   field gun siting, *141*
Henderson, Alan, *48*
Hill 60 (Kaiajik Aghala), *291, 345, 374, 377, 397*
   assault on, *291, 345, 347, 349, 351, 353, 354, 357, 360, 362, 365, 367, 369, 371*
   44429, *291, 345, 347, 349, 351, 353*
   44430, *353*
   44435, *354, 357, 360, 362, 365, 367*
   fire plans, *351, 353, 354, 357, 360, 362, 369, 371*
   naval gun support, *291, 354*
   plans for future assault, *427, 429, 431*
Hill 100, *291, 345, 347, 349, 357, 362, 416, 427*
Hill 971, *60, 63, 69, 175, 291, 406*

August Offensive, *249, 251, 266, 291*
   Ottoman defence, *291*
Hill Q, *63, 69, 291, 345*
   August Offensive, *251, 291*
Hobbs, Colonel JoÚ Joseph Talbot, *38, 39, 74, 81, 93, 152, 226, 229, 387*
   artillery at Anzac, *135, 137, 141, 142, 158, 162, 163, 165, 175, 178, 186, 206, 208, 229, 235, 238, 241, 246, 365, 374, 389, 392, 394, 414, 416, 422, 431*
   artillery support coordination, *395*
   artillery training, *48, 57, 384*
   August Offensive, *257, 263, 266, 278, 280, 286, 291*
   landing at Anzac, *98, 101, 105, 111, 116*
Holly Ridge, *64, 206, 220, 392, 395*
Hore, Captain Leslie, *291*
howitzers, *18, 34, 54, 111, 123, 133, 163, 175, 178, 181, 195, 198, 380, 382, 425, 431*

4.5-inch (114mm), *2, 5, 34, 35, 104, 116, 135, 156, 178, 212, 241, 266, 280, 291, 347, 349, 351, 353, 354, 362, 365, 389, 416*

5-inch (127mm), *2, 5, 178, 215, 220, 238, 241, 253, 266, 275, 278, 291, 347, 349, 354, 360, 362, 365, 367, 394, 397, 418*

6-inch (152mm), *24, 74, 123, 178, 201, 211, 212, 215, 217, 220, 235, 266, 268, 269, 278, 280, 291, 354, 360, 375, 389*

'the Kanga', *286, 418*

9.2-inch (234mm), *375*

15-inch (381mm), *375*

August Offensive, *251, 253, 266, 275, 278, 280, 282, 284, 286, 291*

command and control structures, *152, 165*

Hill 60 assault, *291, 345, 347, 349, 351, 353, 354, 357, 360, 362, 365*

  Krupp 150mm, *114, 215* schwere Feldhaubitze 1893, *73*

siting, *141, 142, 178, 181*

Hughes, Brigadier General Frederic, *291*

Hughes, Major Francis, *105, 109, 133, 147, 156, 226*

  August Offensive, *280, 291*

I

Imbros Island, *401*

Indian Army Artillery, 7th Indian Mountain Artillery (IMA) Brigade, *54, 81, 93, 111, 116, 135, 269, 291, 345, 362*

  21st (Kohat) Battery, *54, 93, 105, 114, 137, 201, 211, 291, 345, 397*

  26th (Jacob's) Battery, *54, 84, 87, 93, 104, 116, 121, 147, 162, 280, 291, 345, 397*

Infantry, 29th Indian Infantry Brigade, *291, 412*

  Mountain Artillery, *54, 87*

indirect fire, *7, 14, 18, 365*

  practice, *48, 50*

  tecÚiques, *195, 404*

infantry,
　artillery support, *14, 26, 198, 226, 244, 362, 365, 371*
　arrangements, *389, 392, 394, 395, 397, 401, 409*
　lessons learned, *429*
innovation, *246*
Ismail Oglu Tepe, *291*

J

JoÚston, Colonel Earl, *291*
JoÚston, Lieutenant Colonel George, *39, 41, 101, 133, 156, 291*
JoÚston's Jolly, *64, 69, 92, 93, 162, 163, 181, 198, 201, 206, 211, 223, 226*
　August Offensive, *272, 275, 278, 280, 282, 291*
　demonstration firing, *232, 422*
　field gun siting, *141, 384*
Jopp, Lieutenant Arthur, *147, 181*

K

Kabak Kuyu, *291*

Kaiajik Dere, *291, 345, 347, 357, 374*
Kemal, Mustafa, *223, 291*
Kent Hughes, Wilfred, *291*
Kephalo Bay, *401, 403*
Keyes, Commodore Roger, *404*
Kiggell, Brigadier General Lancelot, *11*
Kilid Bahr Plateau, *57, 60, 63, 71, 251, 412*
King, Major Gifford, *105*
Kirkpatrick, Major General, *18*
Kitchener, Lord, *435*
Knife Edge, *220*

L

lamps, communication, *24*
Lawrence, Lance Corporal Cyril, *291*
Laying, *41*
Legge, Major General James, *373, 384, 389*
Legge Valley, *68, 69, 226, 384, 406*
Lemnos, *54, 178*

troops sent for rest, *384*
Liman von Sanders, General Otto, *71*
Lone Pine, *64, 81, 84, 87, 92, 93, 114, 156, 162, 198, 206, 238, 244, 357, 373, 384, 392, 395*
   August Offensive, *251, 253, 269, 272, 275, 278, 280, 282, 284, 286, 289, 291*
   demonstration firing, *232*
   field gun siting, *141*
   Ottoman defences, *114, 178, 422*
Loos, Battle of, *369*
Love, Major Alan, *291*
Lyon, Sergeant Charles, *291*

M

McCay's Hill, *64, 69, 81, 137, 147, 181, 184, 206, 289, 392*
McCay's Ridge, *246*
McGarvie, Private David, *291*
McGrath, Major William, *291*
machine-guns, *10, 232, 422*
   August Offensive, *291*
   Hill 60 assault, *291, 353, 360*
   position, *291*
Mack, Lance Corporal Ernie, *291*
MacLagan's Ridge, *68, 98, 101, 105, 147, 206, 392*
MacLaurin, Colonel Henry, *121*
Magersfontein, *5*
Maidos (Eceabat), *60, 63, 64, 71, 83*
Mal Tepe, *63*
Mal Tepe Ridge, *63, 64, 69*
manuals, *10, 11, 14, 18*
   Cavalry Training (Provisional) 1904, *10*
   Field Artillery Training 1904, *10, 14*
   Field Artillery Training (Provisional) 1912, *11, 18, 20, 26, 41, 54, 141, 152, 156, 195, 284*
   Field Service Regulations, *14*
   Part 1, Combined Training 1902, *10*

Part I, Operations 1909, *10*
Part II, Administration 1909, *10*
Infantry Training 1902, *10*
Manual of Military Engineering 1905, *10*
   Training and Manoeuvre Regulations 1913, *20*
maps, *135, 147, 163*
Mars-le-Tour, *5*
Meldrum, Colonel William, *291*
Meldrum, Private Alex, *291*
Merrit, Private Frank, *291*
Mills, Major JoÚ, *134*
mines, *244, 427*
mining, *198, 206, 429*
mobile batteries, *195, 197, 206, 208*
mobile warfare, *5, 7, 14, 18, 26*
Monash Valley, *68, 87, 92, 105, 121, 126, 129*
   August Offensive, *291*

Monro, General Sir Charles, *435*
Mortar Ridge, *68, 121, 123*
mortars, *178, 181*
   2.5-inch (63.5mm) Garland, *181*
   3-inch (77mm) Japanese, *178, 181*
   3.7-inch (95mm) *122*
   demonstrations, *232*
   Ottoman, *214, 425*
mountain guns, *84, 111, 114, 123, 133, 156, 174, 198*
   10-pounder BL (2.75-inch 70mm), *54, 87, 135, 212, 266, 389*
   12-pounder, *135*
   ammunition issues, *135*
   command and control structures, *152, 165*
   Hill 60 assault, *291, 354, 357*
   siting, *181*
Mudros, *54, 57, 93, 401*
Mukden, *7*
Mule Valley, *223*
musketry, *41*

N

Napier Joúston, Lieutenant Colonel George, *35, 38, 81, 152, 178, 226, 241, 422*
  artillery at Anzac, *141, 162, 163, 175, 201, 246, 291, 367, 373, 374, 394, 409, 431*
  artillery support coordination, *394, 395, 401, 409*
  artillery training, *48, 57*
  August Offensive, *257, 263, 266, 272, 291*
  Baby 700 assault, *123*
  Hill 60 assaults, *291, 354, 369, 427*
  landing at Anzac, *98, 121*

naval guns, *404, 406*
  see also Royal Navy
  4-inch, *397*
  4.7-inch (120mm), *5, 235, 238, 266, 269, 280*
  6-pounder (57mm), *269*
  7.5-inch, *123*
  9.2-inch (233.68mm), *268, 291, 375*
  9.5-inch, *123*
  10-inch, *123*
  12-inch, *74, 114, 123*
  12-pounder (76mm), *268, 269*
  14-inch (355.6mm), *269*
  15-inch, *114*
  ANZAC landing, support for, *87, 89, 116*
  August Offensive, *251, 253, 268, 269, 282, 284, 291*
  Baby 700 assault, support for, *123, 129, 133*
  bombardment targets, *74, 77*
  coordination, *152, 170, 174, 401, 403, 404, 406, 431*
  demonstrations, *232*
  fire support request arrangements, *389, 392*
  Hill 60 assault, *291, 354*

Nek, *68, 87, 92, 129, 147, 223, 226, 232, 403, 404, 406*
  August Offensive, *269, 275, 291*
  debate about delay before attack, *291*

fire plan, *291*
plan deficiencies, *291*
Permanent Force (PF), *29*
Territorial Force (TF), *7*
mobilisation, *29, 32*
training, *5*
New Zealand Army Artillery, *5, 18*
  1st New Zealand Field Artillery Battery (1st NZFA Battery), *34, 96, 118, 121, 133, 142, 156, 162, 178, 198, 223, 226, 232, 241, 272, 278, 280, 291, 354, 377, 389*
  1st New Zealand Field Artillery Brigade (NZFA Brigade), *34, 38, 241, 257, 268, 286*
  2nd New Zealand Field Artillery Battery (2nd NZFA Battery), *34, 96, 116, 118, 133, 142, 156, 169, 186, 198, 201, 241, 280, 291, 354, 357, 362, 409, 412*
  2nd New Zealand Field Artillery Brigade, *114, 241*
  3rd New Zealand Field Artillery Battery (3rd NZFA Battery), *96, 134, 241, 291, 354, 357, 362, 374, 409, 412*
  4th New Zealand Field Artillery (Howitzer) Battery (4th NZFA (Howitzer) Battery), *34, 96, 104, 111, 116, 133, 142, 181, 183, 184, 198, 223, 226, 241, 275, 291, 347, 349, 416, 422*
  5.th New Zealand Field Artillery Battery (5th NZFA Battery), *241, 354, 360, 374*
  6th New Zealand Field Artillery (Howitzer) Battery (6th NZFA (Howitzer) Battery), *241, 375, 409*
  Brigade Ammunition Column, *34*
  Daniell's Battery, *291*
  orders of battle,

Infantry
  Auckland Battalion (Aucklanders), *291*
  Canterbury Battalion (Cantabrians), *291*
New Zealand Infantry Brigade, *114, 121, 123, 126, 251, 291*
  Otago Battalion (Otagos), *121, 129, 291*
  Wellington Battalion (Wellingtons), *291*
manuals, *11*
Mounted Rifles
  Auckland Mounted Rifles, *291*
  Canterbury Mounted Rifles, *291*
New Zealand Mounted Rifles Brigade (NZMR Brigade), *32, 291, 369, 397*
  Otago Mounted Rifles, *291*
  Wellington Mounted Rifles, *291*
New Zealand and Australian Division (NZ&A Division), *32, 34, 50, 373, 380, 414, 416*

Anzac, at, *96, 104, 114, 135, 137, 156, 158, 181, 198, 238, 241, 394*
area of control post-August Offensive, *291*
August Offensive, *249, 257, 291*
Baby 700 assault, *121, 123, 126, 129, 133, 134*
Divisional Artillery organisation, *260, 382*
organisation, *35*
New Zealand Expeditionary Force (NZEF),
  see also Australian and New Zealand Army Corps, (ANZAC)
  establishment and mobilisation, *29, 32, 35*
Nibrunesi Point, *401*
No 1 Outpost, *291, 373*
No 2 Outpost, *291*
No 3 Outpost, *291*
North Beach, *68, 104, 118, 241, 291*
naval guns, *404, 406*

see naval guns,
Russell, Major General Andrew, *351, 353, 367, 369*
Russell's Top, *64, 68, 92, 114, 133, 142, 152, 156, 162, 178, 181, 211, 223, 238, 246, 291, 373, 377, 382, 392, 401*
August Offensive, *251, 253, 268, 269, 282, 284, 291*

O

observation, *14, 215, 291*
   aerial, *226, 229, 404, 414*
   fire, of, *50, 116, 135*
   posts, *186, 211, 223, 380*
   sketches, *189, 191*
   observers, *109, 158, 165*
   naval gunfire, *174*
Old No 3 Outpost, *253, 269, 291*
Olive Grove,
open positions, *14*
opportunity targets, *291, 345, 380*
orders of battle,
Ottoman Army, *60*
   Artillery, *198, 211, 212, 214, 215, 217, 220, 226, 229, 232, 246*
   2nd Artillery Regiment, *214*
   5th Artillery Regiment, *214*
   6th Mountain Battery, *73, 83, 84*
   7th Field Artillery Regiment, *114*
   7th Mountain Battery, *71, 81, 83, 84*
   8th Mountain Battery, *71, 83, 84*
   9th Field Artillery Regiment, *71*
   11th Artillery Regiment, *214*
   16th Artillery Regiment, *214*
   39th Field Artillery Regiment (39th Artillery), *71, 111, 214*
   Anafarta Group, *214*
   Olive Grove Battery, *412, 414, 422*
      Fifth Army, *71*
      Infantry,

5th Infantry Division, *214*
7th Infantry Division, *114, 291*
8th Infantry Division, *291*
9th Infantry Division, *71, 214, 291*
12th Infantry Division, *291*
14th Infantry Regiment, *291*
16th Infantry Division, *214*
18th Infantry Regiment, *223, 291*
19th Infantry Division, *71, 83, 214, 223, 291*
25th Infantry Regiment, *291*
27th Infantry Regiment, *71*
32nd Infantry Regiment, *291*
33rd Infantry Regiment, *291*
57th Infantry Regiment, *83, 84*
64th Infantry Regiment, *114, 291*
72nd Infantry Regiment, *291*
machine gun companies 27th Machine Gun Company, *71, 83*
Ottoman Navy, *83, 89, 111, 174*
Owen's Gully, *291*
Ottoman defence, *87, 114, 129, 291*
    Russian 107mm K77 guns, *214, 215*
Russo-Japanese War (1904-05), *5, 7, 10, 11, 24*
Ryrie's Post, *206, 232*

P

Palamutluk Sirti (Olive Grove), *71, 111, 189, 211, 215, 220, 226, 382, 406*
    August Offensive, *280, 282*
Phillips, Major Owen, *101, 105, 133, 147, 181*
    August Offensive, *280, 291*

Pimple, the, *146, 206, 291*
  gun emplacements, *146, 147, 186, 384*
Pine Ridge, *64, 68, 69, 121, 147, 220, 384*
  August Offensive, *280*
Pinnacle, the, *291*
Plugge's Plateau, *68, 104, 118, 121, 142, 291, 382, 392, 414*
  field gun siting, *141, 186, 384*
Pope's Hill, *92, 121, 156, 198, 401*
  August Offensive, *251, 269, 291*
Poppy Valley, *206, 244*
Port Arthur siege, *7*

Q
quick firing (QF) weapons, *10*
Quinn's Post, *92, 114, 121, 163, 169, 198, 220, 232, 238*
  August Offensive, *251, 269, 280, 291*

R
Rabett, Major Reginald, *105*
range finding, *41, 48, 50, 109*
  see also registration, board, *197*
  problems, *135*
Razor Edge, *68*
Razor Ridge, *133*
Razorback, *64, 147*
  gun emplacement, *189*
recoil and traverse mechanisms, *178*
  on-carriage, *54, 73, 178, 235*
reconnaissance, *41*
Reconnaissance Officer, *24*
Redford, Major Thomas, *291*
registration, *135, 429*
  cards/lists, *186, 195*
  orders (August Offensive), *291*
retaliatory fire, *229*
Rhododendron Ridge, *291, 374, 397, 422*
rifles magazine-fed breech-loading, *10*
road construction, *206*
Robinson, Lieutenant Wilfred, *291*

Rosenthal, Lieutenant Colonel Charles, *41, 46, 109, 156*
    landing at Anzac, *101, 105, 111, 133*
route marching, *41, 44*
Royal Field Artillery (RFA), *18*
    practice camps, *18*
Royal Garrison Artillery (RGA), *24*
    2nd Naval Squadron, *69, 170, 268, 282*
    3rd Naval Squadron, *401*
    August Offensive, role in, *253*
    Gallipoli, support at, *69, 71*
    HMS Ark Royal, *74*
    HMS Bacchante, *73, 83, 89, 268, 269, 282, 291, 401*
    HMS Bulldog, *401, 403*
    HMS Canopus, *174*
    HMS Chelmer, *223, 268, 269, 291, 401, 403, 404*
    HMS Colne, *223, 268, 269, 291, 401, 403, 404*
    HMS Endymion, *268, 269, 291, 401, 403, 404*
    HMS Grafton, *291, 354, 401*
    HMS Havelock, *268, 269, 282, 284*
    HMS Humber, *268, 269, 282, 401, 403*
    HMS Implacable, *174*
    HMS London, *73, 174*
    HMS Majestic, *73, 74, 89, 174*
    HMS Manica, *77*
    HMS Mosquito, *401*
    HMS Pincher, *401*
    HMS Prince of Wales, *73, 174*
    HMS Queen, *73, 114, 116, 174*
    HMS Queen Elizabeth, *114, 174*
    HMS Talbot, *354*
    HMS Triumph, *73, 74, 89, 170, 174*
    M15, *268, 269*
    M18, *401*
    M19, *401*
    M20, *268, 269, 401*
    M28, *401*

M33, *268, 269, 401*

S

Sari Bair,
 see Sari Bair,
Sadik, Captain, *81, 83*
St Pinnock, Private Clifford, *291*
Sandpit, the, *189, 286*
saps, *198*
Sari Bair Range, *60, 63, 71, 84, 249, 345, 380, 406*
 August Offensive, *269, 291*
 7 August, *291*
 8 August, *291*
 9 August, *291*
 10 August, *291*
 breakout plan, *291*
 commencement of assault, *291*
 navigation of terrain, *291*
 Ottoman defence, *291*
 overview, *291*
 terrain, *291*
Sazli Beit Dere, *249, 291*
Scrubby Knoll, *142, 189, 286, 406*

Second Ridge, *64, 68, 69, 81, 84, 87, 92, 93, 98, 114, 121, 133, 142, 291*
 August Offensive, *251, 291*
 field gun siting, *141*
 section shooting, *48*
Sedan, *5*
semaphore, *24*
Semerly Tepe, *71*
semi-covered positions, *14*
Shell Green, *101, 105, 206, 217*
 field gun siting, *141*
shrapnel, *54, 74, 137, 202, 220, 244*
 August Offensive, *272, 275, 284, 291*
 Hill 60 assault, *291*
shells, *2, 5, 73, 137*
 wire cutting with, *272, 275, 284*
Shrapnel Gully, *64, 68, 105, 147, 206, 392*
Signal Station W, *389, 403, 406*
Signal Station W, *389, 403, 406*

signalling, *41*
Silt Spur, *64*
Sinclair-MacLagan, Colonel Ewan, *81*
Skeen, Lieutenant Colonel Andrew, *291*
snipers, *198*
Sniper's Ridge, *64, 220, 223, 244*
South African War (1899-02), *5, 10, 11*
Sphinx, The, *68*
Spicheren, *5*
Standish, Major Ivan, *134*
Steele's Post, *181, 289*
Stevenson, Major George, *291*
Stormberg, *5*
suppression fire, *133, 174, 226, 284, 369, 371, 414*
Susak Kuyu, *291, 354, 397*
Suvla, *249, 251, 291, 401*
Sweetland, Major Henry, *105*
Sykes, Major Francis, *114, 133, 169, 186*
Symon, Major Frank, *118, 121, 133, 142, 163, 241*

August Offensive, *272, 278*

T

Tabletop, *226, 253, 269, 291*
targets, designation of, *186, 189*
Tasmania Post, *206, 232, 244*
Taylor's Gap, *291*
Taylor's Hollow, *291, 349, 416*
telephone communications, *24, 135, 147, 168, 169, 202, 246, 291*
    diagrams, *152, 168, 169, 374*
Third Ridge, *63, 64, 68, 69, 81, 93, 142, 189, 211, 215, 422*
    August Offensive, *253, 291*
    Ottoman defence, *83, 84, 92, 214, 226*
Thursby, Admiral Sir Cecil, *69, 170*
transport ships,
    Armadale, *96*
    Atlantian, *96*
    Australind, *96*

Californian, *96*
Cardiganshire, *96, 105, 111*
Hessen, *93*
Indian, *96*
Itria, *96*
Karoo, *96, 105, 111*
Katuna, *96*
Minnewaska, *74*
Pera, *93*
Surada, *96*
traverse and recoil mechanisms, see recoil and traverse mechanisms,
trench warfare, *246, 409*
    lessons learned, *369, 371*
    static, *134, 431*
troop movement, *232*
Turkish Despair, *244, 246*
Turk's Hump, *191, 226, 286, 291*
Twin Trenches, *244, 406*

V

Valley of Despair, *244*
Victoria Gully, *147, 206, 235*

W

W beach, *101*
W Hills, *291*
Walden Point, *291*
Walker, Brigadier General Harold 'Hooky', *121, 162, 163, 291, 384*
Walker's Ridge, *68, 89, 104, 114, 118, 121, 142, 156, 291, 373, 382, 395, 397*
Waterfall Gully, *92, 291*
Weir Ridge, *64*
Western Front, *369, 371*
Wheatfield, the, *105, 147, 211*
White, Brigadier General Cyril Brudenell, *101, 291*
    ANZAC/IX Corps cooperation arrangements, *409*
    evacuation plans, *435*
White Valley, *268*
Wineglass Hill, *211, 215, 280*
wire, destruction of, *272, 275, 284, 371, 427, 429*
Wire Gully, *147, 395*
Wissembourg, *5*

Worth, *5*

X
X beach, *101*

Y
Yauan Tepe, *291, 345, 347, 357, 362, 427, 429*

www.ingramcontent.com/pod-product-compliance
Lightning Source LLC
Chambersburg PA
CBHW012107010526
44111CB00043B/2931